leadership blueprints
adopt, adapt, adjust

Sadhana Warty Hall
Deputy Director
The Nelson A. Rockefeller Center for Public Policy and the Social Sciences
Dartmouth College, USA

Book Cover Design: Catherine Zhao, Dartmouth class of 2020

As the book cover adapted over time, to the one in your hands now, my perceptions of leadership and the way I fit into leadership have shifted as well. Through this process of creating Leadership Blueprints, *I have learned to intentionally carry the fact that I am always a leader in any situation I am in.*
—Catherine Zhao

TEACHING LEADERSHIP COOPERATIVE

Teaching Leadership Cooperative
teachingleadershipcooperative.com

And

R

The Nelson A. Rockefeller Center
for Public Policy and the Social Sciences
Dartmouth College
6082 Rockefeller Hall, Hanover, NH, 03755, USA
https://rockefeller.dartmouth.edu/

Published by

TEACHING LEADERSHIP COOPERATIVE

Teaching Leadership Cooperative
teachingleadershipcooperative.com

And

The Nelson A. Rockefeller Center
for Public Policy and the Social Sciences
Dartmouth College
6082 Rockefeller Hall, Hanover, NH, 03755, USA
https://rockefeller.dartmouth.edu/

Library of Congress Control Number: 2021902345

ISBN: 978-1-7366054-0-0 (Kindle)
ISBN: 978-1-7366054-1-7 (Amazon Pbk)
ISBN: 978-1-7366054-2-4 (ePub)
ISBN: 978-1-7366054-3-1 (ePDF)
ISBN: 978-1-7366054-4-8 (Hardcover)
ISBNL 978-1-7366054-5-5 (Paperback)

eBookBurner Technologies Private Limited
Chennai 600 026, India
Email: satya@ebookburner.com

Reflections About This Book

Many academics, scholars, and practitioners from within and outside Dartmouth College generously gave time to review the contents of the book. Special thanks to all of you who provided me with "quotable quotes," which are included here:

This book offers equal parts valuable knowledge and practical tools to ways that we may ensure our learning programs are engaging, transformative and continue to teach students long after they have graduated.

> —Jacinta Bailey, Tranby National Indigenous Education and Training, Australia

A valuable "how to" guide for anyone interested in emulating the success of the leadership programs at the Nelson A. Rockefeller Center for Public Policy and the Social Sciences.

> —Jason Barabas, Director, The Nelson A. Rockefeller Center for Public Policy and the Social Sciences, Dartmouth College, Hanover, NH, USA

Leadership Blueprints *demonstrates how a diverse and devoted community of students, educators, and field experts can improve institutional practices by creating space for meaningful reflection on management and leadership development, locally and globally, to help leave the world better than we found it.*

> —Ariel Murphy Bedford, AMB National Consulting LLC and FYF, MLDP and RLF alumna, Baton Rouge, USA

As the title suggests, Sadhana Hall shares the blueprint for effectively teaching and learning leadership. It is a reminder that even when the stakes are highest and the need for leadership is most urgent, we are each empowered to develop ourselves into better leaders.

> —Julius Bedford, Bernhard Capital Partners, Baton Rouge, Louisiana, USA

Sadhana's prose is equal parts accessible and authoritative, inviting readers to see themselves in the book's lessons and giving them confidence that they can effectively apply those lessons to their own organizations.

> —Christopher Bordeau, Undergraduate Admissions, Hanover, NH, Dartmouth College, USA

We live in an age where ubiquitous technology gives us global access while leaving us more siloed than ever. The author offers an antidote in Leadership Blueprints, *providing the framework and tools required to teach leadership in a functional, human, and connected way.*

> —Shala Burroughs, Founder, Wild Turn LLC and RLF alumna, CO, USA

A must-read for anyone who works in leadership development from university faculty to practitioner. You will learn a great deal both theoretically, with the research base included, and practically, with the activity examples and tools provided.

> —Francis Eberle, Price Associates, ME, USA

This book will guide the reader through the process of adjusting your leadership, teaching and coaching practices to meet the rapidly changing and growing demands of the world, how to adjust your program offerings to engage your students and prepare them for a highly virtual environment while keeping the connection with the self, creating their online leadership presence, and finding a sense of community. It's a must-read!

> —Tatyana Gao, Harvard Kennedy School, Cambridge MA, USA

Leadership Blueprints *is a much-needed reference and guide for anyone teaching, facilitating, or learning in the space of leadership. Sadhana Hall and her colleagues have created a paradigm-shifting resource that does not just describe leadership but demonstrates it and teaches it in a way to make meaningful and lasting change in any context.*

> —Stephen Gonzalez, Athletics Department, Dartmouth College, Hanover, NH, USA

This is a practical, accessible, and easy-to-adapt guide to creating group programming that supports mission. While specifically focused on leadership, I found the impact of the teachings as much in the process of running the program than in the content, and in fact you could adopt the lessons from this book for any material and model leadership development in the implementation.

> —Christianne Hardy, Interim Director, Dickey Center for International Understanding, Dartmouth College, Hanover, NH, USA

Leadership must not only be about transmitting what you know—it must also be about admitting what you do not.

> —Antonia Hoidal, pre-medical student, MLDP and RGLP alumna

An incredible synthesis of work. Great examples and session descriptions! Sadhana's writing voice makes me feel as if she is right there conversing with me about leadership!

> —Sophia Koustas, Business Administration and Management, Southern New Hampshire University, NH, USA

This is a very comprehensive look at teaching leadership that adeptly weaves together personal stories and theoretically sound strategies. It is a very well written and helpful guide for teaching leadership.

> —Shawn Martin, Head of Scholarly Communication, Copyright, and Publishing at Dartmouth Library, Dartmouth College, Hanover, NH USA

Leadership Blueprints *fills the gap in leadership curriculum and provides an outlined method to create valuable leadership content designed in a tangible experiential format. The leadership curriculum within* Leadership Blueprints *is fundamental and should be adopted beyond higher education. Educators in middle and high school, community college, and technology and trade schools would benefit using the curriculum. Human resource training in all industries in the not-for-profit, for-profit, in higher education, and in local and national government should implement the leadership guidelines described in this book.*

> —Sarah I. Morgan, Program Manager, Experiential Learning, The Magnuson Center for Entrepreneurship, Hanover, NH, Dartmouth College USA

In this thorough and comprehensive work by an expert in the teaching of leadership, Sadhana Hall generously shares lessons learned and sketches blueprints for success—all with her own warmth, empathy, and clarity.

—John Mott, Judge, DC Superior Court and FYF Mentor, Washington, DC, USA

A comprehensive example of how to scaffold leadership education programs to meet students' needs throughout their college experience and a useful "blueprint" to intentionally create meaningful learning opportunities. In addition, Hall generously shares the Rockefeller Center's curricula, lessons learned, and insights on steps to take when adapting and adjusting to remote learning. This is an accessible and valuable resource for anyone who is interested in strengthening their leadership programs.

—Christie Navarro, Director, Center for Leadership Learning, Office of Undergraduate Education, University of California, Davis, CA, USA

In the chaos of navigating a "new normal," Leadership Blueprints masterfully charts a way to pivot program design with best practices and important considerations. An expert in her field, Sadhana Hall humbly charts her journey to creating excellent and effective programs for the Rockefeller Center. Her tangible passion is infused in the stories she tells, and it left me feeling inspired and in awe. I will certainly be utilizing this book as a guide for the programs I develop in my organization.

—Cameron Outlaw, Global Impact Director, P4H Global, Florida, USA

Sadhana Hall has worked for over 15 years at the Rockefeller Center to envision, design, implement, and evaluate a suite of undergraduate leadership programs that are second to none. In Leadership Blueprints, *she patiently and thoughtfully guides the reader through her creative and analytical processes and shares the lessons and successes she has had. This book is key to unlocking a program of leadership development for young adults at a time when the need for better leadership has never been more pressing.*

—Andrew Samwick, Former Director, the Nelson A. Rockefeller Center for Public Policy and the Social Sciences, Dartmouth College, Hanover, NH, USA

This is an accessible, practical, and engaging guidebook for those seeking impactful leadership insights, based on the wisdom of a seasoned practitioner directing one of the most significant and pioneering leadership programs.

—Devin Singh, Associate Professor of Religion, Hanover, NH, Dartmouth College, USA

This is a hands-on book that takes you on a journey of discovery on how to create an environment for learning, teaching, and realizing "leadership." It is a good source of inspiration for institutions across the world to rethink their work and contribution in these changing times.

—Tara Rao, Founder, ourGroundworks, Bangalore, India

This is truly a "blueprint" for how to approach, design, and evaluate an experiential leadership training program. The concept of leadership is grounded in theory and values. Models for conceptualizing programs, developing and improving programs, and engaging stakeholders are shared, as are specific examples of how these concepts, models, and values are used to develop each program and each class. Course outlines are provided to readers for their use, as well as a platform to stimulate their own creativity. Not only is this a useful book, but it is also an inspiring one. I highly recommend it to anyone charged with the responsibility of training others to be skilled leaders.

—Pamela Skyrme, President, Skyrme and Associates, Dunedin, FL, USA

At a time when the world is screaming out for new, better, and more diverse leadership, this is a book that can help educators prepare students to assume that role.

> —Charlie Wheelan, Senior Lecturer and Policy Fellow, Rockefeller Center, Hanover, NH, Dartmouth College, USA

Table of Contents

List of Tables, Figures, and Handouts

Tables

Figures

Handouts

Foreword

By Gama Perruci

Since the 1980s, we have seen a dramatic increase in the number of leadership programs at the undergraduate, graduate, nonprofit, and for-profit levels. These programs offer a wide variety of approaches. They also reflect our increasing preoccupation with the development of thoughtful leaders who will have an impact at all levels of organizations, society, and the world. We know the *why* of leadership programming—we need more thoughtful leaders—but we also need more examples of the *how*—how to build an intentional and rigorous program that becomes effective in the fulfilment of its mission. *Leadership Blueprints* serves as a powerful "how to."

When developing a leadership program, we are always confronted with the "how to" challenges. Leadership educators, leaders, or managers certainly bring energy and enthusiasm to the creative process, but that is not enough. When taking concrete steps toward the development of a leadership program (e.g., development of resources, attainment of institutional buy-in), we can benefit from others' experiences and insights. While each program is unique in its own institutional context (e.g., small liberal-arts college, large state institution, nonprofit and for-profit organization), there are some common challenges that we all face (e.g., developing a mission statement, grounding the program in a clear theoretical framework).

In our book, *Teaching Leadership: Bridging Theory and Practice* (2018), Sadhana Hall and I introduced our respective programs (Dartmouth College's Rockefeller Center and Marietta College's McDonough Center) to show how the teaching of leadership can bridge theory and practice. In *Leadership Blueprints*, Hall goes a step further and invites her readers backstage. Through this book, we are given access to the tools that have made the Rockefeller Center so successful.

Hall invites her readers to "adopt, adapt, and adjust." This book is not just the recounting of accomplishments; it comes from a position of generosity. It allows the reader to gain insights about the ways in which leadership programs can be thoughtfully constructed. As we develop our own programs, we can use *Leadership Blueprints* as a valuable resource.

The depth and breadth of the Rockefeller Center programs are truly impressive. They range from the individual (First-Year Fellows Program) to the global (Rockefeller Global Leadership Program) levels. Underlying the different levels is the focus on how students can be impactful in their organizations, communities, and beyond. The programs also take into consideration where the students are in their own leadership-development journey. The First-Year Fellows are carefully mentored as they make the transition to college life. In contrast, the Rockefeller Leadership Fellows Program focuses on undergraduate participants who are in their final year of college.

Leadership Blueprints also has an element of self-reflection. The book is an excellent example of how institutions can strive toward continuous quality improvement. Assessment has become a prominent feature in American higher education. This book can be used as a guide to help us think through the key questions that an evaluator would ask when assessing a leadership program. As Hall examines the components of her programs, she is also engaging in a process of self-evaluation. When reading this book, therefore, you need to consider how she is modeling the very mindset that one expects when educators or practitioners seek to improve their own practices.

Developing a rigorous leadership program is not an easy task. It requires careful attention to the quality and quantity of programming and activities. There is no magic bullet. However, we can benefit from the experiences of others. *Leadership Blueprints* will serve as an excellent "how-to" guide to your creative process.

Gama Perruci, Ph.D.
Dean
McDonough Leadership Center
Marietta College
Marietta, Ohio

Acknowledgments

*We must find time to stop and thank the people who
make a difference in our lives.*

—John F. Kennedy

"A good idea becomes a great idea when it has the input of many because it combines many perspectives." Gama Perruci and I said this in our co-authored book, *Teaching Leadership: Bridging Theory and Practice*. This second book, *Leadership Blueprints*, also represents the thoughts and ideas of many program participants, program alumni, speakers, and facilitators, faculty, and staff. There are countless people I would like to recognize and thank for helping me to think about my own contributions to the fields of management and leadership. I am acknowledging a few of you who have helped me to bring this book to fruition.

First and foremost, I acknowledge the former director of the Rockefeller Center, Andrew Samwick. You have supported and encouraged me to achieve so much in over a decade of our work together.

Thank you, too, Jason Barabas. As the incoming director of the Center, you have also provided support and feedback in these past few months. I look forward to working with you to continue all the good work that is done through our leadership programs.

Hannah Andritsakis, Joanne Blais, Robert Coates, Robin Frye, Laura Hemlock, Eric Janisch, Joanne Needham, Lynn Spencer, and Leslie R. Wagner-Ould Ismail: Our thought-provoking conversations about how we can improve our leadership programs at the Center are inspiring! It is such a pleasure to work with all of you. I also acknowledge former colleagues at the Rockefeller Center who have worked with me to develop and implement these programs.

To all the speakers—thank you. Each session description acknowledges you for your hard work. But the conversations with you and your willingness to further strengthen the sessions made me grow intellectually—as a person and as a professional. Your work shines through our programs and creates the basis upon which program participants discover their potential to manage and lead.

Thank you, Gama Perruci, for writing the foreword! It continues to be a pleasure for me to work with you. To all manuscript reviewers and readers: Your experiences range from higher education, government, K-12 education, nonprofit, and for-profit management. Your expertise in areas such as leadership development and education, leadership training, coaching, and entrepreneurship shaped the book in the form it is today. I appreciate your enthusiasm, your input, and your willingness to assess whether this book can be adopted, adapted, or adjusted in your different fields. Without your thoughts, it would have been nothing but a figment of my imagination! So, thank you so much, Milla Anderson, Jacinta Bailey, Jason Barabas, Ariel Murphy Bedford, Julius Bedford, Alicia Betsinger, Christopher Bordeau, John Burroughs, Shala Burroughs, Ben Campbell, Meredith Wilson Chang, Welton Chang, Jay Davis, Francis Eberle, Catherine Etmanski, Tatyana Gao, Stephen Gonzalez, Christianne Hardy, Michael Heslin, Antonia Hoidal, Dan Jenkins, Joshua Kim, Sophia Koustas, Chris Lowell, Shawn Martin, Sarah Morgan, John Mott, Herchel Nachlis, Christie Navarro, Cam Outlaw, David Pack, Gama Perruci, Kerry Priest, Tara Rao, David Rosch, Andrew Samwick, Avneesh Sarwate, Ron Shaiko, Devin Singh, Pamela Skyrme, and Charles Wheelan. Your feedback on the manuscript was most helpful.

I also appreciate the support of the Board members of the Rockefeller Center. Special thanks to Fritz and Glenda Corrigan, Ron Schram, Curt Welling, and Tim Harrison. You have supported leadership programming at the Rockefeller Center, for which I am grateful!

My family members and friends are always by my side when I take on such projects. Rick Hall, you have always pushed me to do my best. Mary Ann Hall, Kathryn Guare, and Corey Seemiller—thank you for giving me advice about how and where to publish this book. Gouri Seth and Daksha Warty, your humor and sisterly candor mean the world to me! Ted and Laurie Bolognani, thank you for your friendship and support. Christine Peterson, as our copyeditor, you not only gave generously of your time, but you shared your wisdom, wit, and skills whenever the situation asked for it. My heartfelt thanks to you.

Satya and the ebookburner team: You are indeed "flawless!" Thank you so much for all the work you put into this project. I just knew it was in the right hands when I first talked to you about the project.

Thank you to my student assistant team: Caitlin Deerin, Dylan Giles, Elizabeth Poselski, and Catherine Zhao, and to those who joined our team later: Madeleine Bernardeau, Gia Kim, and Kristabel Konta. Cat, we love your cover design. Thank you, Rik Abels, and Ezinne Anozie, you were so willing to help with program information. And Nathan Pucci, thank you for your contributions to all the data and other ideas presented in *Leadership Blueprints*!

Finally, Katie Dunn and Chris Burgess, 2020 was a year we will never forget. Katie, you pushed me to write this book by asking me to turn my "talk into action." Sadly, you are no longer with us and I miss our conversations every single day. Wherever you are, please know that you will live in my heart forever.

1 | Introduction

All of us should be concerned with leadership. It is more important than ever that we develop ethical, moral, and principled leaders who can tackle our complex global challenges, as well as those close to home. Current literature on management and leadership suggests that we should not think of leadership as simply positional or even hierarchical. Current literature on management and leadership also suggests that leadership can be taught. When we take the time to develop our competencies as leaders, we benefit not only our own organizations but also our communities and society at large. Leadership can exist anywhere and should exist everywhere, and this book aims to make each one of us a stronger leader no matter what we do or where we are within the hierarchy of organizations. To become good leaders and exercise leadership, we need to reflect deeply on our values and our sense of ethics. As Bennis and Nanus (1985) remind us, we should strive to "do things right and do the right thing."[1] In this effort, we need to lift voices of communities that thus far have been forced into silence through systemic and institutional oppression to a place where they have the agency to make positive changes in their own lives, as well as in the lives of others.

The good news is that there are examples of good leadership all around the world. When you look intentionally, you will find excellent examples of leadership that show up at individual, community, and organizational levels both locally and globally. We only need to become aware of them to begin to make our contribution to the world and feel satisfied that, at the end of our lives, we did our best for the rest. This is not an idealistic concept. This is exactly why we should concern ourselves with the study of leadership. If we require technical preparation for other fields of endeavor, then the study of leadership—a topic that spans *all* fields of endeavors—especially deserves this consideration.

Through my firsthand experiences and deep reflection, thoughtful conversations, and rigorous study, I have observed the external and internal forces that influence the work that leaders and managers do. On the one hand, leaders and managers influence their socio-cultural and political environments through their values, behaviors, and actions. On the other, these values, behaviors, and actions are equally influenced by socio-cultural and political environments. The net result appears in the form of good or bad leadership.

Developing good management and leadership starts with observing and learning from good and bad leaders, their followers, and their environments. In studying these concepts, we should ask ourselves these questions: What are the espoused values of those in leadership positions? How are they present in their attitudes and behaviors? How successful is leadership in the process of inspiring teams and accomplishing a shared vision and goals?

Throughout my professional career, working and collaborating with good leaders has been a great touchstone for my observation of leadership.[2] Good leaders demonstrate their values with their thoughts, words, and actions. Through their support and example, good leaders empower others to discover their purpose and meaning. They are service-oriented and genuinely care for those they are leading. In work environments, they recognize how important it is to have happy and satisfied employees and know that such a work environment leads to productivity and efficiency. As a result, they foster curiosity, lifelong learning, laughter, and fulfilment. They know when to lead and when to follow others to make meaningful progress toward their shared goals.[3] From an organizational perspective, they understand the importance of addressing issues before they become a crisis. They are clear about the organization's mission, goals, and objectives. They take a systems approach to implementation. They are reflective, introspective, and thoughtful about communication with others. They are comfortable with their strengths and weaknesses and can always say, "I don't know, and I will get back to you."

Conversely, I have also had the experience of working with leaders who demonstrate what is—to me—bad leadership. These lessons are equally valuable, and so I have listed Kellerman (2004) and Lipman-Blumen's (2006) books about bad or "toxic" leadership in the reference section for your own study.[4] Bad leaders have taught me to avoid self-interest and self-promotion. My experiences always remind me that people within an organization and the systems that support the achievement of its goals deserve primary consideration. Often, bad leaders are in positions of authority and use that authority and their power to instill fear and uncertainty. They also use language to create divisiveness and misinformation. This results in an unproductive environment—one that is riddled with conflict, miscommunication, and gossip. It also leads to lack of productivity. Being in this kind of an environment requires us to dig deep within ourselves to develop strength and resilience.

In the end, however, I am realistic enough to understand that some situations are and do become unbearable. In those instances, we must always remember that our choices lie with us! It is an act of bravery and courage to walk away from a challenging work environment to keep your dignity and self-worth, especially when there do not seem to be any alternatives or options. At the end of such experiences, we must move on once we feel we have done our best.

My experiences have also led me to conclude that good management and leadership must exist at all levels to achieve positive change and to address the complex issues we face today, some of which are global economic recessions, social injustice, health disparities, and climate change. Working within a political, organizational, or social context, solving such complex problems involves an individual's capacity as a leader or a follower to develop several competencies. Leaders need to be skilled at analytical and critical thinking. They need to use their creativity to solve problems and learn to deal with uncertainty and ambiguity. When they work with groups and teams, they need to demonstrate empathy, compassion, and emotional intelligence. Before they can do all these things, leaders need to develop self-awareness of their strengths, weaknesses, and preferences.[5] At the intersection of all these competencies, true understanding, cooperation, and collaboration are born.

The opportunities for higher education and other technical and vocational institutions of learning to prepare ambitious and intellectual individuals to "give the work back" meaningfully to society are great, as are the opportunities for institutions and organizations in the for-profit and nonprofit sectors.[6] The more effort we put into preparing leaders and managers at all levels, the better off we will be as a global society. Another observation: Informal leadership is just as great a force for good as formal leadership can be and we should do everything we can to support and nurture it.

Our work at the Nelson A. Rockefeller Center for Public Policy and the Social Sciences (the Rockefeller Center or the Center) at Dartmouth College is what I offer to the pursuit of teaching and learning about leadership and management for societal good. All that I have just shared with you is intentionally crafted into the co-curricular leadership programs of the Rockefeller Center. From the founding of our first program in 2001 to the rapid adjustments we have made to continue our work virtually during the COVID-19 pandemic, this book presents our collective experiences in teaching and learning about leadership and the insights gained through the development of our continuum of leadership programs.

I invite you to explore how you might adopt, adapt, and adjust the content from this book in your own field of endeavor. But before we delve into the details of these programs, let us look at the context within which these programs are offered.

Theoretical Context

As we know, there are many definitions for leadership, as well as models of leadership theories. I define leadership as the process that influences people to mobilize resources to address an identified problem and come up with innovative solutions toward accomplishing an identified goal. It is about developing relationships between leaders and followers to engage groups of people to become larger than the sum of their parts. Based upon the core values of integrity, authenticity, ethical and appropriate behavior, and responsibility to community, leaders create the conditions to empower others to make lasting impact. Based on this definition, the Center focuses on individual growth and self-awareness through reflective practices and relational processes that create common understanding between participants and stakeholders committed to addressing a problem they collectively identify.

The Center also offers ideas on management. Again, there are many definitions, but the one that resonates with me is, "Management is the coordination and administration of tasks to achieve a goal. Such administration activities include setting the organization's strategy and coordinating the efforts of staff to accomplish these objectives through the application of available resources. Management can also refer to the seniority structure of staff members within an organization."[7] At the Center, we view management and leadership along a continuum. Further, although we refer to our five programs as leadership programs, there are many discussions on the management aspects of leadership that make individuals and organizations thrive.

Many models of leadership drive the Center's programming. The framework that supports our implementation of programs is based upon Kolb's Cycle of Experiential Learning, the Learning Zone Model, and the Leadership Identity Development Model. Most recently, as a result of COVID-19, we have added the Community of Inquiry (CoI) Model as a basis for offering virtual co-curricular programming. All these are discussed in more detail in Chapter 2 under the Eight Pillars of Program Design. As you will observe, speakers base their sessions on these theoretical frameworks. For instance, every single session contains all the elements from the Kolb Cycle of Experiential Learning. As another example, every speaker aims to deliver information to put participants in the learning zone, rather than the comfort zone or panic zone as described by Tom Senninger's Learning Zone Model.

With this common framework in mind, program officers, guest facilitators, and student participants can collaborate creatively and successfully. Another equally important step is to capture leadership competencies we expect learners to gain. The Center's working definitions for the competencies are provided in Handout 1.1. As individuals understand and absorb each element of the program, they try to foster collective learning within the community of each co-curricular program. This is the mental space that the Rockefeller Center strives to create and maintain in order to meet its mission statement. What follows is more about the Center itself.

About the Rockefeller Center

Established in 1983, the Center's mission is to "educate, train, and inspire the next generation of public policy leaders in all fields of endeavor, through multidisciplinary education, public policy-oriented research across the social sciences, leadership training, and public lectures by visiting scholars and dignitaries."[8] This mission is rooted in the interdisciplinary approach the Center takes to support faculty and student offerings. As an academic center reporting to the dean of faculty, learning about public policy and leadership are at the center of its operations. Students receive academic credit for public policy courses offered through its curricular side. These courses may have a focus on leadership, but leadership programming is offered primarily through the co-curricular offerings of the Center. Although the Center does not have dedicated tenure-line faculty, it is well resourced with dedicated gifts to endow several of its programs.

Figure 1.1 (see the end of this chapter) illustrates the range of courses and programs offered through the Center. The Center works intentionally to link the curricular to the co-curricular and vice versa where possible. *Leadership Blueprints*, however, focuses exclusively on the Center's five key co-curricular leadership programs. I will now share how the five co-curricular programs evolved and explain what they are.

Evolution of the Continuum of Leadership Offerings

Currently, the Center offers five major programs as part of its leadership offerings. This is the story of the context and history behind their evolution. The Rockefeller Center's commitment to leadership began in 1999 with a two-day leadership conference. Former director of the Center, Professor Linda Fowler, recalls the event was organized for and by women faculty, staff, and students who were active at the Center during that time:[9]

> Back then, the percentage of female students was about 38%, and women were saying to me, "Dartmouth says we are here to be leaders, but wherever we look we see only men." They were taking issue with the assumption that because Dartmouth had admitted them, they would inevitably become leaders. I was, at the time, one of the most visible females on campus as director of Rocky [the Rockefeller Center], and as a graduate of a women's college, I was quite aware of the different challenges women face. We did the women's conferences for several years, but then [in 2001] the men said that they felt the need of coaching, too. That was when the Thursday night Rockefeller Leadership Group started. At the time, I ran each session. Many of the guests were board members or people I knew.[10]

The program continued to be offered after Professor Andrew Samwick was appointed director in 2004, and by 2007 it was firmly established as a year-long program for seniors. Popularly known as "RLF" (Rockefeller Leadership Fellows Program), the program attracted senior students from different departments and majors throughout the college and had evolved to include a fall and a winter retreat; weekly leadership sessions offered by faculty, staff, and practitioners during the fall and winter terms; and peer teaching through student-directed sessions. As a key feature of the program, each cohort of fellows practiced their learned management and leadership skills by selecting their successors. Demand grew as the program gained visibility and popularity. Eventually, for every 25 final-year students accommodated in the program, the Center was turning away more than 50 applicants.

Although there were some discussions about program RLF expansion, the Center's administrators believed a larger program would change the group dynamics and adversely impact the deep learning taking place within each cohort. They also feared it would dilute the sense of camaraderie created among the diverse group of participants the program attracted and the strong support network that continued after its completion. Further, an expanded number of participants would also change the perception of the program as a year-long fellowship program that required a high level of commitment.

Meanwhile, a parallel development was taking place on the curricular side of the Rockefeller Center in 2007, which included the redesign of the public policy minor and the development of the Policy Research Shop on the curricular side. Through its co-curricular offerings, the Center had been implementing a popular program called the Civic Skills Training Program (CST). This program was offered three times a year in Washington, D.C. for students from all class years with approved internships in that city. The program's purpose was to help students become successful in their internship responsibilities and learn about managing themselves and applying leadership concepts. CST, however, was resource intensive, and it led the Center's administrators to begin thinking about how a similar program could be offered on campus to benefit a larger number of students. This observation resulted in delinking CST with internships. As a result of this change, on-campus orientations and debriefs specifically related to the internships were introduced.

Civic Skills Training has evolved now to become available only to participants in the First-Year Fellows Program established shortly after all the changes to it were implemented. Eventually, further development of the First-Year Fellows Program created a robust experience in and out of the classroom, on and off-campus, for up to 25 students through the inclusion of both curricular courses (Introduction to Public Policy and a statistical methods course) and co-curricular programs (Civic Skills Training and fellowship placements). It also helped students cultivate an interest in the public policy minor and other co-curricular programs. The First-Year Fellows Program (FYF) and the Rockefeller Leadership Fellows Program (RLF) now formed the "bookends" for a student's four-year experience but left a gaping hole in the middle for the Center to address.

Now that the Civic Skills Training Program had become part of First-Year Fellows Program, students needed a program on campus that fulfilled their need to develop their management and leadership competencies through a program like Civic Skills Training. Committed to addressing this unmet need for a larger cohort of students, the Center's director approved the development of a new program that would be based on open enrollment, capped at 95 students per term, and open to all class years. With a donor generously supporting its development and implementation, a pilot offering of the Management and Leadership Development Program (MLDP) was offered in the fall term of 2009 and made its debut as a full-fledged program in the winter term of 2010. Through its evolution and intentional outreach, the Center has observed that it engages many students who would not otherwise have come to the Center.

At this point, the Center was able to offer the First-Year Fellows Program, the Management and Leadership Development Program, and the Rockefeller Leadership Fellows Program for participants ranging in age, development, and maturity. Thus, the Center had moved toward the establishment of a continuum of co-curricular leadership programs for the undergraduate experience on campus. But we could not rest. We recognized that leaders today face additional challenges when operating in unfamiliar environments and cultures, and they often find themselves managing multi-national team members with expectations and attitudes different from their own. We also observed that that the Center did not yet offer a program with an in-depth look at the concepts and capacities required for leadership in a global context. Given the College's mission to prepare global leaders and given the participants' interest, the Rockefeller Global Leadership Program (RGLP) was born out of this identified gap, and its pilot offering took place in the spring term of 2012.

As programs continued to develop and mature, the administrators and educators at the Center monitored and evaluated curricular and co-curricular offerings based on the perceived need for programs and budget availability. The criteria for program evaluation included student learning outcomes, participation, and effectiveness and efficiency; programs were added and revised, and specific sessions or program components were dropped according to the results of these reviews.[11]

Rounding out the Center's continuum of leadership offerings was the Dartmouth Leadership Attitudes and Behaviors Program (D-LAB), which was added in 2014. This program was included to enable first-year students to examine their personal values, the relationship of behaviors to the values they identified, and the impact of individual and group behavior on community. The Rockefeller Center faculty and staff believed it appropriate to introduce this program in the first year of student life on campus because of the high level of professionalism they sought from students engaged in the First-Year Fellows Program and because of the competitive work environment in which they are placed for their fellowships. This level of professionalism had its roots embedded in helping students to examine their values and to align them with their behaviors. Other considerations included the need for introducing civility and respect in dialogue, as well as the need for these topics to be introduced early in the Rockefeller Center leadership development experience. As a result, Dartmouth Leadership Attitudes and Behaviors Program became one of the three prerequisites for students to participate in the First-Year Fellows Program. With the benefit of broadening the reach of the program, it is currently offered in collaboration with Dartmouth's Office of Student Life and the Office of Residential Life. Recently, it was expanded again through Dartmouth's newly established house system to make it a campus-wide offering.[12]

Figure 1.2

Continuum of Co-Curricular Leadership Programs 2001–Present

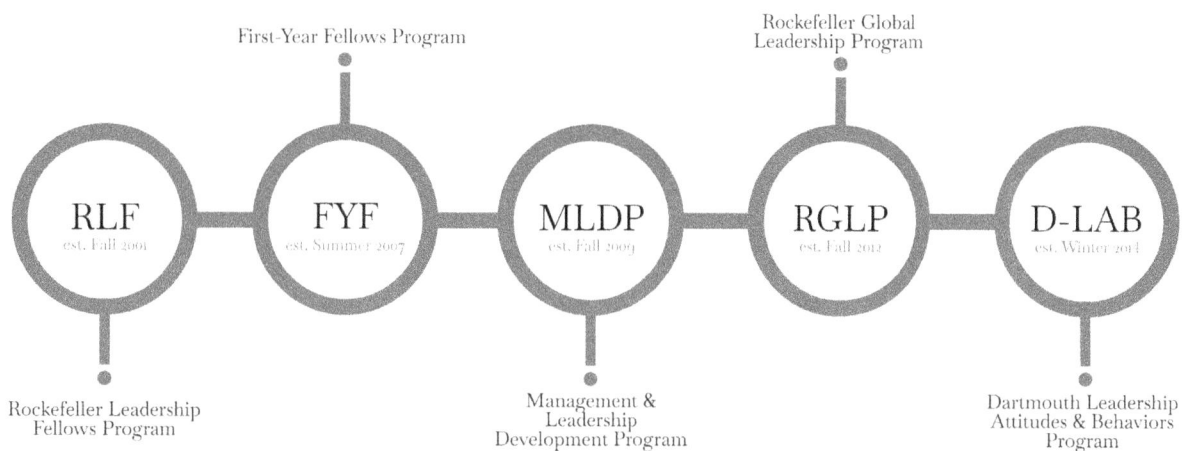

The development of the continuum of leadership and management programs—now complete as shown in Figure 1.2—was based on identified needs and our growing understanding of how to prepare students for success in the workplace and as leaders. Of the programs offered in this continuum, only two (FYF and RLF) are selective and competitive, whereas the other three are open to all students on campus as their schedules and unique Dartmouth D-Plan allow.[13] One also must consider budget constraints and available resources; unfortunately, these can result in a first-come-first-served approach to accepting applications, as is the case with the RGLP program.

Although the set of leadership programs was put together block-by-block, they have emerged as a menu of programs that provide the opportunity for students and practitioners to adapt, adopt, and adjust it to their needs and aspirations.

Creative minds, working together, create extraordinary programs. Co-curricular programs at the Rockefeller Center have flourished because of the combined effort, creativity, and imagination of colleagues, student program assistants, speakers, students, and alumni. In addition to extraordinary minds, extraordinary results require institutional will and the support of senior leadership. These factors have allowed these programs to emerge and mature. Without this context, our programs would not have served and inspired our participants so thoroughly throughout the years.

Overall Participation in Rockefeller Center Programs

Table 1.1 summarizes student participation in Rockefeller Center co-curricular programs beginning with the class of 2015. As is evident in the table, participation as a percentage of students in each class has increased significantly in the past five years, from 14% of the class of 2015 to 25% of the classes of 2019 and 2020. The jump in participation in the class of 2017 was, in part, due to the growth of D-LAB. In 2019–2020, an analysis of Rockefeller Center records indicated that, in the two most recent graduating classes in 2019 and 2020, at least a quarter of the Dartmouth student body had participated in at least one major co-curricular program at the Center during their time at Dartmouth.

Table 1.1

Rockefeller Center Co-Curricular Participation in at Least One Program as a Percentage of Graduating Class

Class Year	Number of Student Participants	Number of Graduates	Percentage of Graduating Class
2015	150	1087	14%
2016	165	1075	15%
2017	228	1073	21%
2018	225	1105	20%
2019	259	1036	25%
2020	239	945*	25%

Note: *The graduation number is low because students decided to complete coursework in a later term or decided to take a gap year because of COVID-19.

The Rockefeller Center is committed to diversity, equity, and inclusion. Our records indicate that the Center's programs are successful in their efforts to attract diverse individuals from diverse backgrounds. Here is the evidence to support that this is not merely an empty promise.

As stated earlier, it is important to prepare leaders to address the complex challenges we face today. Just looking at the U.S. alone, despite outnumbering men on college campuses, women overwhelmingly still do not occupy positions of power; are often not in top leadership positions where they should be; get paid less than men for the same job; and represent only 24% of the members of Congress.[14] It is important for higher education and other teaching institutions to place an emphasis on addressing this inequity and prepare women for leadership positions. Rockefeller Center records indicate that its programs attract more female participants than male participants. Since the fall of 2014, 56% of students completing the five leadership programs described in this book were female. This roughly corresponds to the ratio of female to male students admitted on campus each year. The Center began collecting data on transgender and nonbinary students more recently, and it is too early to report information at this time.

The Rockefeller leadership programs attract a variety of students with different academic and extracurricular interests. Overall, we have served participants representing at least 42 distinct majors out of the over 60 majors offered to undergraduates at Dartmouth. In addition, many of these unique majors are modified with some other field of endeavor, as shown in the word cloud in Figure 1.3. The size of each major in this word cloud figure is reflective of its popularity among Rockefeller Center leadership program participants. We attract most participants from the two majors offered by the Government and Economics departments. While these are also two of the most popular majors on campus, the Center's programs have also served a significant number of STEM students. That we attract many economics and government majors is not surprising, given that 18% and 15% of Dartmouth students have pursued degrees in these departments, respectively, on average in each of the past five years (classes of 2016–2020).

Figure 1.3

Word Cloud of Rockefeller Center Participants' Majors

The Rockefeller Center Leadership programs draw students of all backgrounds, and we have served a significant number of international students from all over the world. These students are essential to our programming. Not only do they add a unique perspective to discussions on leadership and civic responsibility, but they also gain knowledge and can put into practice cultural and workforce expectations in the U.S. International students in MLDP, RGLP, and RLF constitute, on average, 12.8% of each cohort. For reference, 10% of Dartmouth's student body is made up of international students.[15] FYF is not included in this analysis due to the difficulties of ensuring summertime employment for international students as a result of visa and regulatory barriers.

The impact our programs have on international students—and vice versa—continues to grow. They not only make personal growth improvements but also add tremendously to our weekly conversations. In RGLP, for example, international students bring their unique cultural experiences to discussions about global leadership and often shed light on cultural similarities and differences. In MLDP, international students gain from learning about workplace expectations in the U.S. and often share the different expectations in their home countries.

The Center is also concerned with the socioeconomic diversity of our participants. An analysis of Rockefeller Center records, in conjunction with data provided by the Office of Institutional Research, indicates that since 2014, 16% of Rocky program participants were Pell Grant recipients.[16] Over the same time span, 15.3% of total Dartmouth students were Pell Grant recipients. The Center is attracting a significant number of low-income students, which suggests that our programs are inclusive and welcoming to students of all socioeconomic backgrounds.

Table 1.2 and Figure 1.4 show diversity by race of participants in the co-curricular programs at Dartmouth. The Center makes significant outreach efforts to all parts of campus and, as a result, participants in our programs approximately match the racial distribution of campus. Analyzing participation in each program by race would give program officers a sense of where they need to direct their outreach efforts to broaden the diversity of cohorts.

Table 1.2

Dartmouth College Undergraduates and Rockefeller Center Participants by Race 2014–2020

Race	Dartmouth College Undergraduates (Fall 2014 – Fall 2020)	Rockefeller Center Participants (Fall 2014 – Spring 2020)
American Indian or Alaskan Native	2%	2%
Asian or Pacific Islander	19%	25%
Black Non-Hispanic	8%	15%
Hispanic	11%	9%
Other	8%	5%
White Non-Hispanic	52%	44%

Note. Data and categories provided by the Office of Institutional Research, Dartmouth College.[1]

---

[1] Office of Institutional Research at Dartmouth College. (2020). *Trends: Enrollment Characteristics (2016–2020).* Student Enrollment Interactive Factbook. https://www.dartmouth.edu/oir/data-reporting/factbook/enrollment.html

Figure 1.4

Rockefeller Center Co-Curricular Program Participants by Race Since 2014

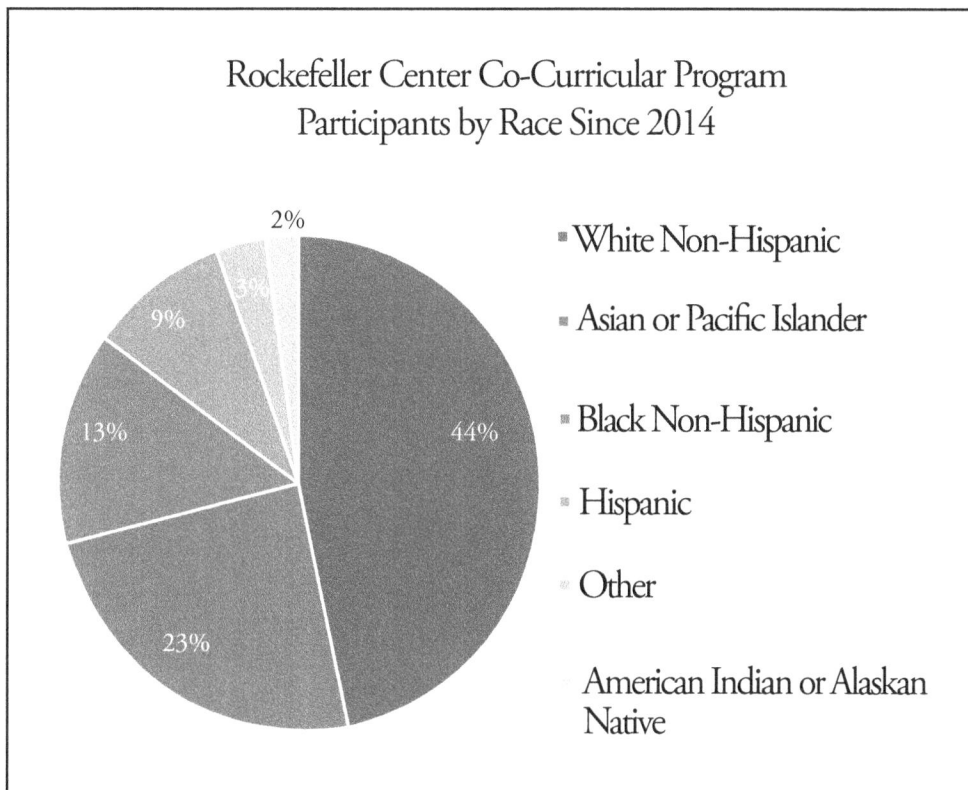

Rockefeller Center Co-Curricular Program Participants by Race Since 2014

- White Non-Hispanic
- Asian or Pacific Islander
- Black Non-Hispanic
- Hispanic
- Other
- American Indian or Alaskan Native

Note. Data and categories provided by the Office of Institutional Research, Dartmouth College.

Whom Is This Book For?

The five major leadership programs have been designed for participants in different stages of development, maturity, and experience. While these programs were designed for an undergraduate audience, the underlying principles of each program are applicable for those that are interested in teaching leadership skills and attitudes across a wide range of fields. The intended readers and users of this book include the following:

- ➤ Educators and students at all levels
- ➤ Professionals in education
- ➤ Professionals in nonprofit and for-profit organizations
- ➤ Managers and leaders from business to government

Here are some suggestions on how you might adopt, adapt, and adjust our continuum of programs to bring about positive changes in your department or organization, as well as in society and the world. Table 1.3 outlines each program, the stage of the learner, the overall goal, and key components. For your applications in your own programs, find your own hook to the book!

Table 1.3

Adopting, Adapting, or Adjusting Program for Any Field of Endeavor

Program Name	Stage of Learner	Overall Goal	Key Components
Dartmouth Leadership Attitudes and Behaviors (D-LAB)	All levels	Understanding yourself, how you work with others, and your community or organization's mission	• Value and behavior clarification • Professionalism • Working with others • Understanding your organization's goals and principles
First-Year Fellows Program (FYF) Four Components: • Formal course work • Dartmouth Leadership Attitudes and Behaviors • Civic Skills Training • Fellowships	Entry level	Entry-level preparation for success in the workplace	• Curricular course work or industry-specific information • Value and behavior clarification • Professionalism • Technical skills (project management, advocacy writing, research, etc.) • Understanding workplace culture and industry • Formal and informal leadership • Mentorship • Reflection
Management and Leadership Development Program (MLDP)	Intermediate (2–4 years of experience)	Enhanced hard and soft skills for success in the workplace	• Verbal and written communication • Values clarification • Personal leadership challenge • Difference between management and leadership, and personal strengths analysis • Negotiation • Intergenerational communication • Diversity, equity, and inclusion in teams • Value of networks and building professional relationships • Reflection

Program Name	Stage of Learner	Overall Goal	Key Components
Rockefeller Global Leadership Program (RGLP)	Intermediate to advanced (2–4 years of experience) Senior-level management	Development of intercultural communication and leadership skills	• Intercultural understanding • The Developmental Model of Intercultural Sensitivity • Understanding others by developing self • Global leadership and consciousness • Values and customs through multicultural lenses • Cultural Intelligence and multicultural toolkit • Needs of underrepresented populations • Intercultural conflict resolution • Reflection
Rockefeller Leadership Fellows Program (RLF)	Mid to senior management level (4+ years of experience)	Self-awareness, working on teams, and working within an organization to achieve societal good	• Reflective practices • Awareness of one's strengths and weaknesses • Enhanced communication skills, including framing difficult conversations • Team dynamics and teamwork • Organizational behavior • Development and growth • Change management • Developing and articulating a leadership philosophy

The details in Table 1.3 will help you to pick a session, a part of a program, a mix of sessions based on your needs, or the program in its entirety. Think about how you might use the continuum of programs provided in this book—given your resources, time, and human capacity, as well as constraints you might face in your own situation.

I get many personal accounts from alumni and colleagues who are using information they have learned from the programs, either personally or professionally. My first example is from Jenny P. from the class of 2016, who, at the time of this writing, plans to introduce the lessons learned from the Management and Leadership Development Program (MLDP) in her new position as a leadership resident in a program for women in Cambodia. She wants to create a program based on the design of the MLDP, in which she hopes to establish an atmosphere of trust and open communication. She plans to build strong relationships with her students from her first day of work and is unafraid to make mistakes and take risks. She believes that modeling this behavior "will hopefully inspire these young women to continue their work towards becoming leaders in their respective fields."[17]

The second example is from Sarah Morgan, a former employee of the Center, who has chosen to adapt the selection process used in the Rockefeller Leadership Fellows (RLF) program in her entrepreneurship student leadership board. In this program, current senior student leaders develop a rigorous application, interview, and selection process to determine who their successors will be for the next year. Sarah tells us why she chose this approach:

> The RLF selection process inspired me when I worked at the Rockefeller Center. When I started working with our entrepreneurship student leadership board, I knew that we should adopt similar principles for succession. Our challenge is that our leadership board includes multiple Dartmouth undergraduate class years and graduate students. Students take great pride in creating the application and interview process and want to ensure that the process is fair and equitable. Students are thoughtful as they evaluate applicants and make sure that the newly selected leaders share the same leadership spirit and will fold in well with the student leaders already on the board. The interview and evaluation process is a valuable professional development experience for the outgoing seniors. The student leaders recognize the honor given to them to select their successors and are committed to selecting a diverse set of students with complementary skill sets. The senior leaders deliberate on the final list, present their list to me, and we discuss their decisions. I make suggestions, but it is the senior student leaders that make the final decisions. Our process differs from the RLF process as decisions are made in the winter term and outgoing seniors transition into the role of senior advisors for the spring term. Senior advisors lead the new student orientation and the spring term retreat. They are available as advisors to then field questions about programming. Senior advisors are empowered and committed to not only choose their legacy but also help nurture incoming student leaders.[18]

The third example is from Brenna C., who is now a chief resident in pediatrics in a well-known hospital. She is currently trying to develop a leadership curriculum for the pediatric residency program she is involved with based on her experience participating in the RLF program. Brenna reached out to the Center because she remembered the excellent use of simulations to teach and reinforce key leadership skills such as interprofessional teamwork and conflict resolution. Being in the healthcare setting, these skills are used daily, if not hourly, and she was hoping to create an opportunity for the pediatric trainees to gain hands on practice through simulation.

To date, I have also adapted sessions from our program for public health associations, a leadership academy, and an international NGO. I have also selected reviewers from all fields of endeavor to review the manuscript of this book and was pleased to receive feedback that most of them can see how these sessions might be applied in their specific contexts.

Our process is **just one way** in which programs can be designed, planned, implemented, monitored, and evaluated. There are many other ways to create such programs. In thinking about the combination of creative minds that created these programs, I concluded that it would be critical for me to share this book, so that you—my readers—might adopt, adapt, and adjust the ideas herein to your own circumstances and reality.

Organization of This Book

Most of this book provides descriptions of each of the five major programs that form the continuum of leadership and management offerings for participants in different developmental stages, maturity, and experience. The programs described here are as follows:

➢ Dartmouth Leadership Attitudes and Behaviors Program (D-LAB)
➢ First-Year Fellows Program (FYF)
➢ Management and Leadership Development Program (MLDP)
➢ Rockefeller Global Leadership Program (RGLP)
➢ Rockefeller Leadership Fellows Program (RLF)

This book is divided into 10 chapters. If you have come this far, you are almost finished with **Chapter 1**!

Chapter 2 of this book focuses on considerations for program design and implementation. You will learn how to conceptualize a program, develop it, and assess and evaluate it. It also includes a few thoughts about speaker selection criteria and implementation of sessions.

Chapter 3 contains information about the Dartmouth Leadership Attitudes and Behaviors Program (D-LAB). You will learn about how to facilitate discussions on character, values, and working with others, as well as principles that guide a community and an individual's role within it.

Chapter 4 highlights information related to the First-Year Fellows Program (FYF). You will learn about how to structure a program that focuses on technical competence and, at the same time, how to identify management and leadership work for a fellowship or a workplace.

Chapter 5 focuses on the Management and Leadership Development Program (MLDP). This program will allow you to explore management and leadership skills, tips, tools, and strategies, and reflect on ways to apply them immediately.

Chapter 6 features the Rockefeller Global Leadership Program (RGLP). This program will prepare you to think about cross cultural and intercultural skills needed to be successful in a culturally diverse yet interdependent world.

Chapter 7 contains the program description for the Rockefeller Leadership Fellows (RLF). You will reflect on what it takes to be self-aware and to work with others and within organizations to meet their mission. You will be able to articulate your leadership philosophy.

Chapters 3–7 provide session descriptions of the current iteration of the five major leadership programs that were implemented in the fall of 2019 through the first couple of weeks in the spring of 2020. I have also included a few sessions from past programming, as well as future program iterations. COVID-19 has added a new reality and, where relevant, I have shared thoughts and experiences on online learning. Each program description ends with a reflection from our current program officers.

Each one of the programs featured in *Leadership Blueprints* begins with a program overview, jointly constructed by our team—consisting of our program officers responsible for programs, my Program Assistants who have also participated in the programs, and me.

Our team selected a "participant reflection" that represents the general perception of the session in which it appears. You will notice that these reflections refer to the term in which the participant took part in a given program and do not provide that participant's name. This is because many programs or sessions included within this book collect anonymous feedback. Reflections from alumni who have participated in these programs are also included. Finally, each session description contains supplemental resources that you can refer to when you want to adapt a session to meet your program's needs.

Chapter 8 offers ideas for developing an online program. You will learn about considerations for online programming, how to develop an online presence, and ways in which you can build an online community. Virtual learning has fostered innovative ways to expand programs and strengthen participant learning and empowerment. Most, importantly, it is teaching all of us to deal with unpredictability and ambiguity, factors that effective leaders need to be able to navigate.

Chapter 9 contains suggestions for measuring effectiveness and impact at several levels (participant, program, organization, and institution). It is designed to make you think about how you would measure success and how you would create an environment that supports continuous quality improvement.

Chapter 10 concludes with my overall reflections and personal takeaways for being a good manager, leader, and follower. It comes full circle and creates a space for you, as the reader, about how you might adapt these programs to educational, nonprofit, for-profit, or government settings. It also contains reflection questions related to self-awareness, working in teams, and questions related to organization growth and development.

My co-authored book, *Teaching Leadership: Bridging Theory and Practice* is referenced several times throughout this book. *Leadership Blueprints* is not a companion book. While it covers overviews of concepts and ideas in *Teaching Leadership: Bridging Theory and Practice*, this book primarily focuses on the "how to" of implementing leadership programs.

A word about data presented in this book. Unless otherwise noted, the figures and statistics throughout *Leadership Blueprints* reflect Rockefeller Center participant data from the fall of 2014 through the spring of 2020. Although we have data for the five programs since their inception, the 2014–2015 academic year serves as the starting point because information was gathered more consistently across this reporting period. An academic year in Dartmouth terms begins in September of a given year and concludes in August of the following year. Unique to our institution is also the "D-Plan," which allows students to curate their on- and off-campus experiences.[19] This is why programs like MLDP and RGLP, which are open to all students on campus, are offered each term, three times in a given academic year.

I hope you enjoy the thought process behind each program and find the sessions inspiring and relevant. I invite you to use these designs to create or revise your own program. When working with the friends and colleagues in your community who share your zest for developing a program that meets your participants' needs, it's your creativity in action!

Notes

[1] However, others like Bennis and Nanus (1985, p. 21) drew a subtle distinction between both when they proposed, "managers are people who do things right and leaders are people who do the right thing."

[2] Allio, 2005.

[3] Reichard & Walker, 2016.

[4] Kellerman, 2004, and Lipman-Blumen, 2006.

[5] Avolio & Hannah, 2008.

[6] Heifetz & Linsky, 2017, p. 123.

[7] Indeed, 2020, December 2.

[8] The Nelson A. Rockefeller Center at Dartmouth College, 2019.

[9] This background behind the development of the leadership programs has been excerpted and adapted from *Teaching Leadership: Bridging Theory and Practice* (Perruci & Hall, 2018).

[10] L. Fowler, email communication, March 30, 2017.

[11] As Komives et al. (2011) discuss in *The Handbook for Student Leadership Development*, programs must be evaluated based on institutional and staffing considerations with regard to the feasibility of the program.

[12] Dartmouth College Office of Residential Life, 2016.

[13] Dartmouth Undergraduate Admissions (n.d.).

[14] Warner et al., 2018.

[15] Dartmouth College Office of Institutional Research, *Interactive Fact Book.*

[16] According to the U.S. Department of Education Federal Student Aid Office (2021), Pell Grants are U.S. federal scholarships that are "awarded only to undergraduate students who display exceptional financial need and have not earned a bachelor's, graduate, or professional degree." We use Pell Grants as proxy indicators for socioeconomic status.

[17] Jenny P., class of 2016, personal communication, November 11, 2020.

[18] S. Morgan, personal communication, February 6, 2021.

[19] The D-Plan is Dartmouth's quarter academic system which enables students' flexibility in choosing their enrollment pattern. Students pick 12 terms to graduate.

References

Allio, R. J. (2005). Leadership development: Teaching versus learning. *Management Decision*, 43, 1071–1077.

Avolio, B. J., & Hannah, S. T. (2008). Developmental readiness: Accelerating leadership development. *Consulting Psychology Journal: Practice and Research, 60*(4), 336.

Bennis, W. G. & Nanus, B. (1985) *Leaders: The strategies for taking charge* (1st ed.). Harper & Row.

Dartmouth College Office of Institutional Research (n.d.). *Interactive fact book*. Retrieved February 6, 2021, from https://www.dartmouth.edu/oir/data-reporting/factbook/index.html

Dartmouth College Office of Residential Life. (2016, August 23). *About the house system*. Office of Residential Life. https://students.dartmouth.edu/residential-life/house-communities/about-house-system

Dartmouth Undergraduate Admissions. (n.d.). *Glossary terms: D-Plan*. Dartmouth Admissions. Retrieved February 6, 2021, from https://admissions.dartmouth.edu/glossary-term/d-plan

Garrison, D. R., Anderson, T., & Archer, W. (2000). Critical inquiry in a text-based environment: Computer conferencing in higher education. *The Internet and Higher Education, 2*(2–3), 87–105. https://doi.org/10.1016/S1096-7516(00)00016-6

Heifetz, R., & Linsky, M. (2017). *Leadership on the line, with a new preface: Staying alive through the dangers of change*. Harvard Business Press.

Indeed. (2020, December 2). *What is management? Definitions and functions*. Indeed Career Guide. https://www.indeed.com/career-advice/career-development/what-is-management

Kellerman, B. (2004). *Bad leadership: What it is, how it happens, why it matters* (1st ed.). Harvard Business Review Press.

Komives, S. R., Dugan, J. P., Owen, J. E., Slack, C., & Wagner, W. (2011). *The handbook for student leadership development*. John Wiley & Sons.

Komives, S. R., Owen, J. E., Longerbeam, S. D., Mainella, F. C., & Osteen, L. (2005). Developing a leadership identity: A grounded theory. *Journal of College Student Development, 46*(6), 593-611. doi:10.1353/csd.2005.0061.

Lipman-Blumen, J. (2006). *The allure of toxic leaders: Why we follow destructive bosses and corrupt politicians—and how we can survive them*. Oxford University Press.

McLeod, S. (2017). *Kolb's learning styles and experiential learning cycle.* SimplyPsychology. https://www.simplypsychology.org/learning-kolb.html.

The Nelson A. Rockefeller Center at Dartmouth College. (2019). *2018-2019 Annual report.* https://rockefeller.dartmouth.edu/sites/rockefeller.drupalmulti-prod.dartmouth.edu/files/rocky_annualreport_18-19_final.pdf

Perruci, G., & Hall, S. W. (2018). *Teaching leadership: Bridging theory and practice.* Edward Elgar Publishing.

Reichard, R. J., & Walker, D. O. (2016). In pursuit: mastering leadership through leader developmental readiness. *New Directions for Student Leadership, 149,* 15–25. https://doi.org/10.1002/yd.20158

Senninger, T. (2000). *The Learning Zone Model..* ThemPra Social Pedagogy. http://www.thempra.org.uk/social-pedagogy/key-concepts-in-social-pedagogy/the-learning-zone-model/

U.S. Department of Education Federal Student Aid Office. (2021). *Federal Pell Grants.* https://studentaid.gov/understand-aid/types/grants/pell

Warner, J., Ellmann, N., & Boesch, D. (2018, November 20). *The women's leadership gap.* Center for American Progress. https://www.americanprogress.org/issues/women/reports/2018/11/20/461273/womens-leadership-gap-2/

Figure 1.1

Summary of Curricular & Co-Curricular Programs at the Rockefeller Center

Start Here!

FIRST-YEAR-FELLOWS PROGRAM
Learning & Living Public Policy

· PBPL 5 Introduction to Public Policy (Winter)

· Dartmouth Leadership Attitudes and Behaviors (Winter)

· STATISTICS or METHODS PREREQUISITE in any social science department (Fall, Winter, or Spring)

· CIVIC SKILLS TRAINING (Spring & Summer)
WASHINGTON, DC INTERNSHIP
Unique placements working with Dartmouth alumni mentors (summer)

PUBLIC POLICY COURSES
· PBPL 5 Introduction to Public Policy (*Required*)
Two policy methods classes, such as:
   · PBPL 40 The Economics of Public Policymaking
   · PBPL 41 Writing and Speaking Public Policy
   · PBPL 42 Ethics and Public Policy
   · PBPL 43 Social Entrepreneurship
   · PBPL 45 Introduction to Public Policy Research
   · PBPL 46 Policy Implementation

   Customized policy tracks in health, education, environment, leadership, poverty, law, urban issues, or a topic of your own design

   · PBPL 85 Topics in Global Policy Leadership
   · PBPL 91 Independent Study in Public Policy

ENGAGE
· First-Year Fellows · Rockefeller Public Events
· First-in-the-Nation NH Primary & General Election
· Mentoring Opportunities and Model UN

RESEARCH
· The Class of 1964 Policy Research Shop
· Dartmouth Oxford Exchange at Keble College

TRAIN
· Leave-Term Internship Advising and Funding
· Public Policy Minor · Student Workshops

LEAD
· Dartmouth Leadership Attitudes and Behaviors Program
· Rockefeller Global Leadership Program
· Management and Leadership Development Program
· Rockefeller Leadership Fellows Program

YOUR GATEWAY TO PUBLIC POLICY

In your four years at Dartmouth, there are countless ways to engage with the Rockefeller Center. For some of you, this will start with First-Year Fellows. Others will start with public police courses or leadership programming. Mix and match our tremendous curricular and co-curricular opportunities to create your own unique roadmap.

LIFE BEYOND DARTMOUTH

LAW

RESEARCH

POLITICS

ADVOCACY

EDUCATION

PUBLIC SERVICE

JOURNALISM

DEVELOPMENT

POLICY ANALYSIS

ENTREPRENEURSHIP

CIVIC LEADERSHIP

INTERNATIONAL DEVELOPMENT

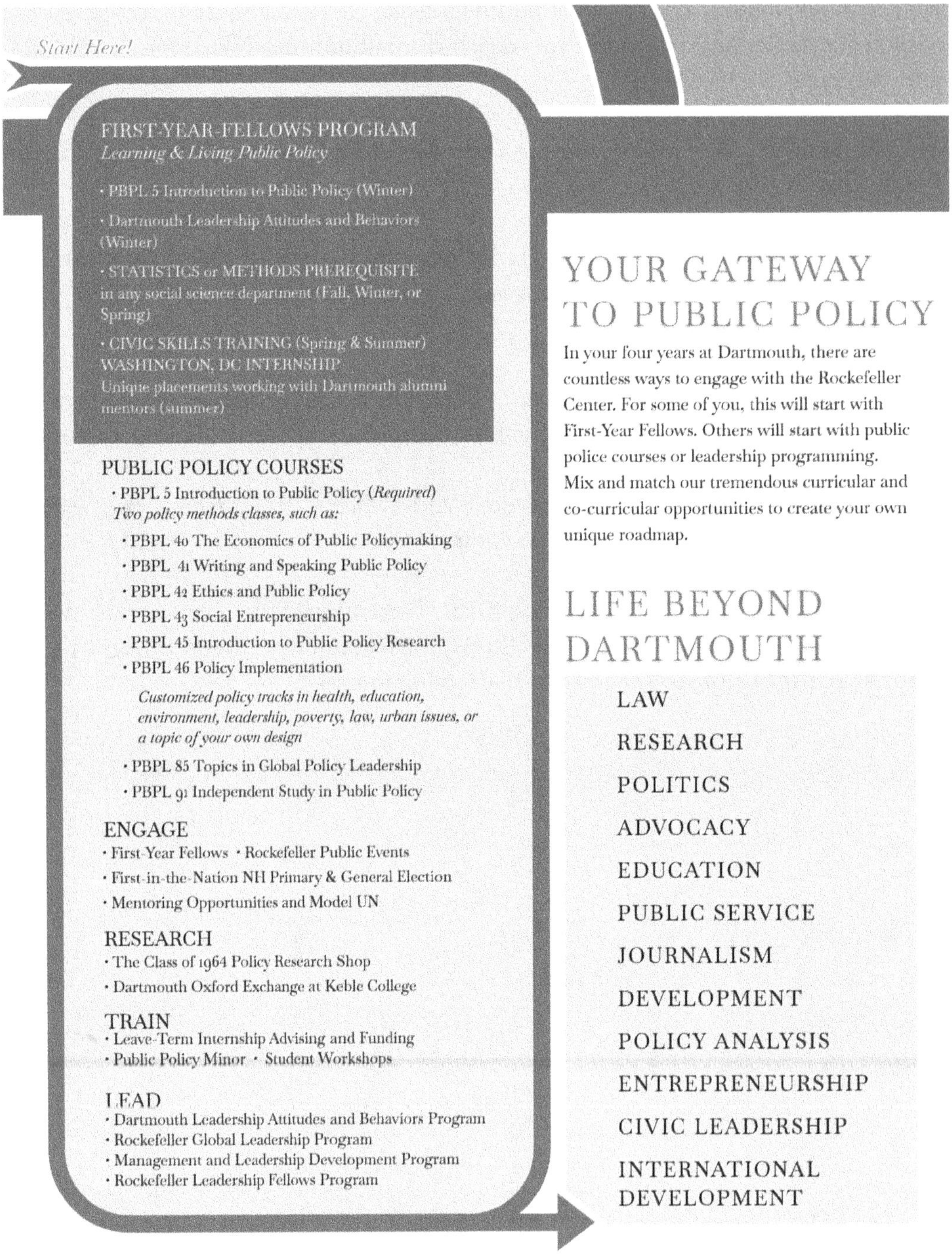

Rockefeller Center Leadership Competencies

At the Rockefeller Center, we define leadership as the process that influences people to mobilize resources to address an identified problem and come up with innovative solutions toward accomplishing an identified goal. It is about developing relationships between leaders and followers to engage joint efforts to become larger than the sum of their parts. Based upon the core values of integrity, authenticity, ethical and appropriate behavior, and responsibility to community, leaders create the conditions to empower others to make lasting impact. The Rockefeller Center believes that participants can be assisted to develop the following leadership competencies through intentional programming:

Collaboration

- Builds and maintains partnerships based on shared purpose
- Acknowledges and listens to different voices when making decisions and taking action
- Facilitates collective action toward common goals
- Encourages, supports and recognizes the contributions of others
- Fosters a welcoming and inclusive environment

Effective Communication

- Writes and speaks after reflection
- Clearly articulates ideas in a written and spoken form
- Exhibits effective listening skills
- Influences others through writing, speaking, or artistic expression
- Acknowledges and appropriately communicates in situations with divergent opinions and values

Management

- Develops and implements a plan for goal attainment
- Develops appropriate strategies for capitalizing on human talent
- Stewards and maximizes all resources
- Manages multiple priorities
- Prepares for leadership transition
- Develops appropriate strategies for effective teamwork
- Evaluates efficacy of current course(s) of action
- Identifies structure and culture of organization
- Demonstrates effective and appropriate use of technology
- Demonstrates financial, task, and resource management skills

Self-Knowledge

- ➢ Continually explores and examines values and views
- ➢ Understand social identities of self and others
- ➢ Demonstrates realistic understanding of one's abilities
- ➢ Seeks opportunities for continued growth
- ➢ Takes appropriate action towards potential benefits despite possible failure
- ➢ Shows self-respect and respect for others
- ➢ Moves beyond self-imposed limitations
- ➢ Practices self-compassion, friendliness, ease with self, and vulnerability

Principled Action

- ➢ Identifies and commits to appropriate ethical framework
- ➢ Demonstrates congruence between actions and values
- ➢ Demonstrates personal responsibility
- ➢ Appropriately challenges the unethical behavior of individuals or groups
- ➢ Bases actions on thoughtful consideration of their impact and consequences
- ➢ Seeks appropriate and mutually beneficial solutions when conflict or controversy arises

Intercultural Mindset

- ➢ Contextualizes social identities and experiences
- ➢ Understands, communicates with, and respectfully interacts with people across cultures
- ➢ Actively engages in opportunities to expand world view
- ➢ Applies intercultural knowledge and skills in local, national, or global contexts

2 | Program Design and Implementation

Excellence is never an accident. It is always the result of high intention, sincere effort, and intelligent execution; it represents the wise choice of many alternatives—choice, not chance, determines your destiny.

—Aristotle

If you ask me about what I love most about my job, it would unreservedly be just how energized I feel when designing new programs and revising existing ones. It would be the enjoyment I derive working with my colleagues to keep learning and refining our approach to teaching leadership. It would be the joy I feel when I see participants in our programs transformed in the process. As a result of all these experiences, I have become a lifelong learner, filled with curiosity, and the desire to make something better.

As described in the introduction, as an academic center, our co-curricular leadership programs serve the entire institution. Starting from one program offered for undergraduate seniors, we have developed a continuum of programs that meets the needs of students in various stages of maturity and development. This chapter describes the way we have conceptualized program design to get to this point and explores such questions as: What are some key elements of program design that we should always think about in designing and implementing programs? What are the Eight Pillars of Program Design and how do they help in creating a meaningful program that guides its participants to learn and grow? The chapter ends with tips for implementation of programs.

The Planning and Implementation Process

Thinking about the overall program design at the outset results in rich dividends. Excellent planning often leads to great outcomes. As leaders and managers, we should devote as much time as possible to conceptualizing a program design. It is true: A lack of planning on our part as leaders and managers should not constitute an emergency for others!

The three stages (conceptualization, development, and assessment) outlined in Figure 2.1 in this chapter encompass a complete program design and are followed by a determination of what is required, what outcomes are sought, and what can take the program to a higher level the next time around. The *conceptualization* stage involves identifying the needs of the audience being considered for the program. These needs can be determined through primary and secondary sources, focus groups, and discussions with stakeholders. I highly recommend setting up a team informally or formally that deliberates on those needs, considers the resources necessary to enact the vision, and conducts research on what other similar programs have done. The *development* stage involves understanding the goals and learning outcomes that are a part of the new program and using the Eight Pillars of Program Design as the foundation upon which to build. Finally, the *assessment* stage involves asking the key questions about this process using assessment tools at the participant, program, organization, and institutional levels. At this time, please recognize that the questions are not set in stone; they simply provide a vision for how we might measure success and outcomes. These can be revised as the program goes into the implementation phase. Please consider this idea as well: Although it is a temptation to collect data, it means nothing if you do not have the time or the capability to analyze it. Less is more! Develop the key questions, the process by which you will collect information, and the tools you will use (e.g., survey, focus groups, interviews).

Figure 2.1

Roadmap for Effective Program Conceptualization and Development

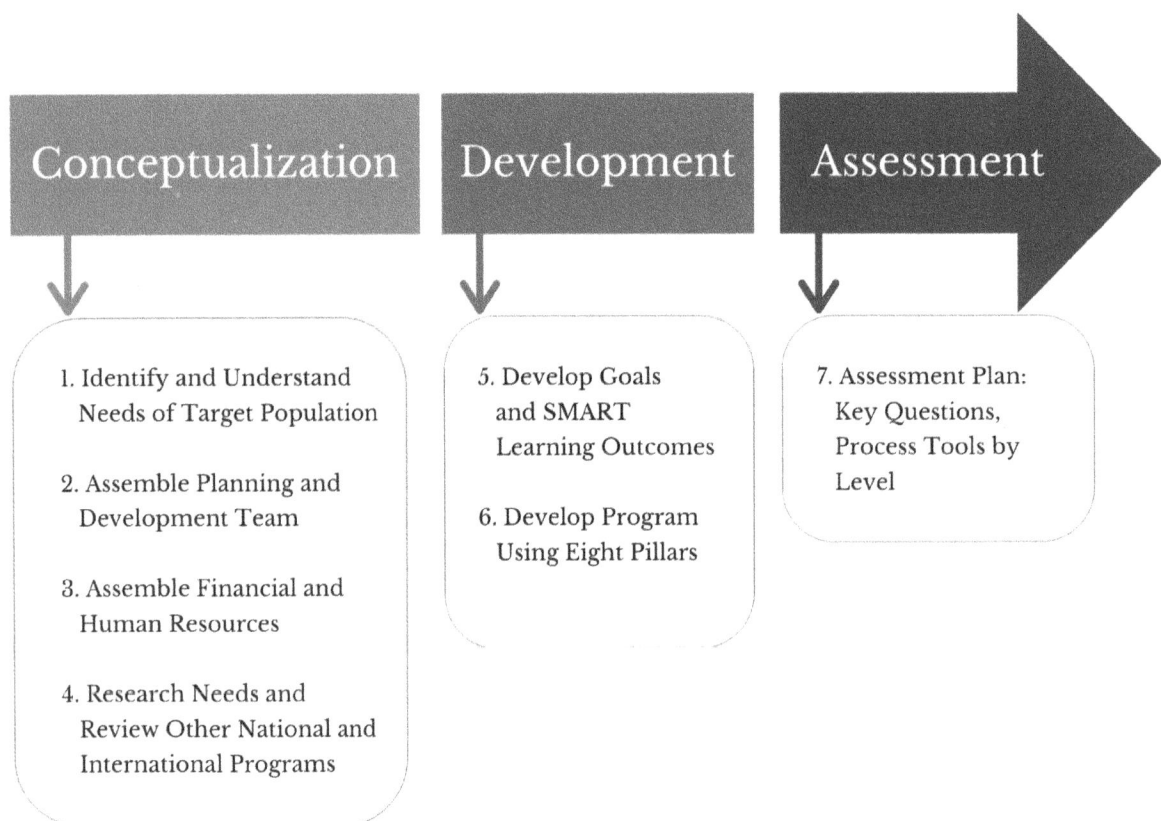

Note. Adapted from *Teaching Leadership: Bridging Theory and Practice* (p. 130) by G. Perruci & S. W. Hall, 2018, Edward Elgar Publishing. Copyright © 2018 by Gama Perruci and Sadhana Warty Hall

Eight Pillars of Program Design

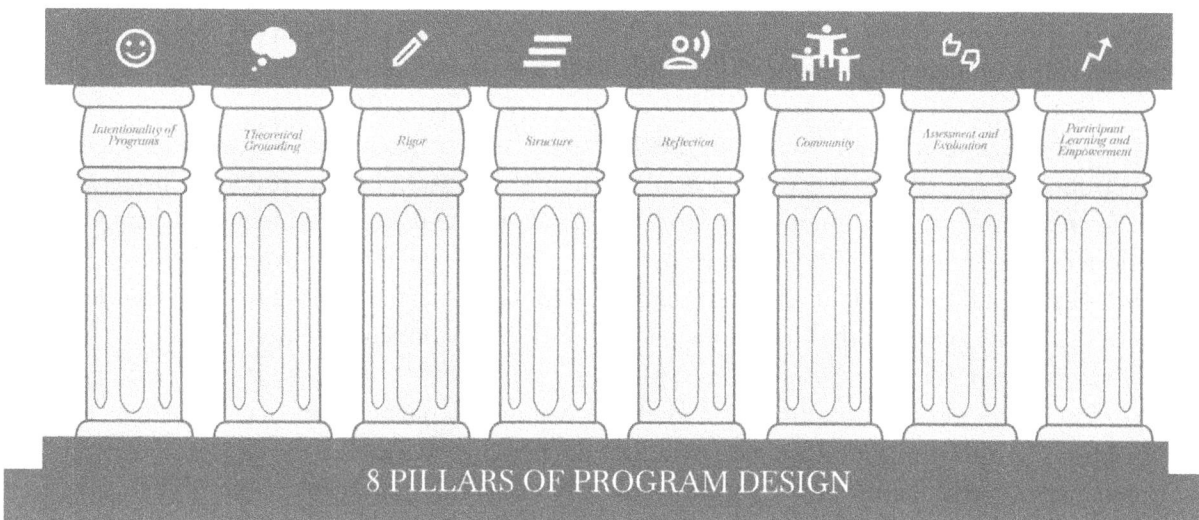

The heart of all these programs pulsates with the idea that leadership is a process in which participants are self-aware of their place within their leadership role, work effectively in teams, and understand how to meet their organization's mission to achieve societal good. All the programs described in this book also share a common structure, using the framework Perruci and I described previously as the "Seven Pillars of Program Design" in *Teaching Leadership: Bridging Theory and Practice*. Paying attention to the seven pillars often helps to create thoughtful learning in a structured yet adaptable way and paves the path for transformational changes in habits, attitudes, practices, and behaviors. These pillars, along with an eighth one that I have added recently, are shown in Figure 2.2.

Figure 2.2

Eight Pillars of Program Design

8 PILLARS OF PROGRAM DESIGN

I have summarized thoughts about these pillars as outlined in that book and share some additional thoughts about them. The eighth pillar that I added—Participant Learning and Empowerment— is introduced at the end of this chapter. Please know that while these pillars are mentioned independently, they are interrelated.

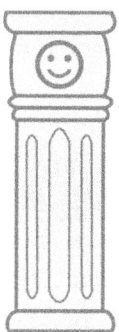

Pillar One, **Intentionality of Programs,** asks us to begin or continue to understand the background of participants for any program we are designing. We also want to think about ways to intentionally select and reach out to potential participants when we are designing a cohort-based program to create as diverse a group as possible. Diversity is all-embracing of identities and differences, which include race, ethnicity, religion, disability, sexual orientation, gender identity, national origin, tribe, and socio-economic status. All people are unique and bring something different to the table based on their experiences. Different backgrounds, experiences, and perspectives can deepen the conversations and the learning. It is important not only to recognize those differences but also to value them.

How do we ensure this diversity in programs? We reach out to potential participants through various departments in the institution and gather nominations from past participants and student organizations on campus. This is a practice you can incorporate in your own organization. In this way, being intentional about who should be in the programs invites participants from different backgrounds and perspectives, while creating an environment that promotes a vibrant exchange of ideas and opinions.

We should also think about participant demographics related to cultural styles. For example, do they come from individualist societies or societies that put collectivity first? To what scale are participants tolerant of ambiguity and uncertainty? What is their orientation toward time? For instance, do they take a long view of a plan or a challenge or do they expect results quickly? Does the group of participants have any group memberships (e.g., political, religious, service group, or other association)? Although we currently do not have data or a way to collect this information systematically, we recognize this is a gap we need to address moving forward. Nonetheless, in many of our programs, participants explore this concept of cultural difference and practice self-reflection to determine the things that have influenced their perspectives. While it may be difficult to determine this data on cultural difference externally, we encourage participants to take this inward exploration.

Intentionality also asks us to create an intellectually supportive environment that includes a demonstration of respect for everyone, a nonjudgmental mindset, and the ability to listen and not refute. Such an environment is conducive to learning. The challenge for educators, managers, and practitioners is to create curiosity for mutual learning. We also need to embrace "inclusion" in our program design and think about all the myriad ways in which participants genuinely feel that their personal situations are seen, their opinions valued, and their voices are heard.

Paying close attention to the attitudes, beliefs, or values of participants sets the stage for rich conversations. For example, do you know whether participants are interested or uninterested in the topic selected for discussion? Are they favorable or unfavorable to your position? What is their motivation to participate? Are they part of the program because their organization requires them to participate? Also, consider your participants' beliefs and attitudes toward you as a facilitator or toward other participants. I have learned a lot about my program participants by listening carefully to the stories they tell about their fortunes or misfortunes. Embedded in those stories and concerns are the clues that make me ask the question "Why?" and help me to understand how their background has shaped how they think, act, do, or feel.

This pillar is deeply connected with all the other pillars. We need to be intentional in everything we do in designing a program!

The second pillar, **Theoretical Grounding,** invites us to help participants translate theory into action. The programs in this book use Kolb's Cycle of Experiential Learning (Figure 2.3 and Handout 2.1), in which students participate in a planned activity, and review and reflect on the experience, draw conclusions, practice the new learning, and apply what was learned.[1] The programs also incorporate ideas from Bandura's Self-Efficacy Model (Handout 2.2) and the Leadership Identity Development Model (Handout 2.3) into the content of sessions offered.[2] These programs are built on developing SMART (specific, measurable, attainable, realistic, and time-bound) learning outcomes with Bloom's Taxonomy as the basis.[3] This taxonomy describes cognitive, affective, and behavioral domains of learning. Learning then is scaffolded and, as a result, moves along from simple to complex levels along these three domains.

Figure 2.3

Kolb's Cycle of Experiential Learning

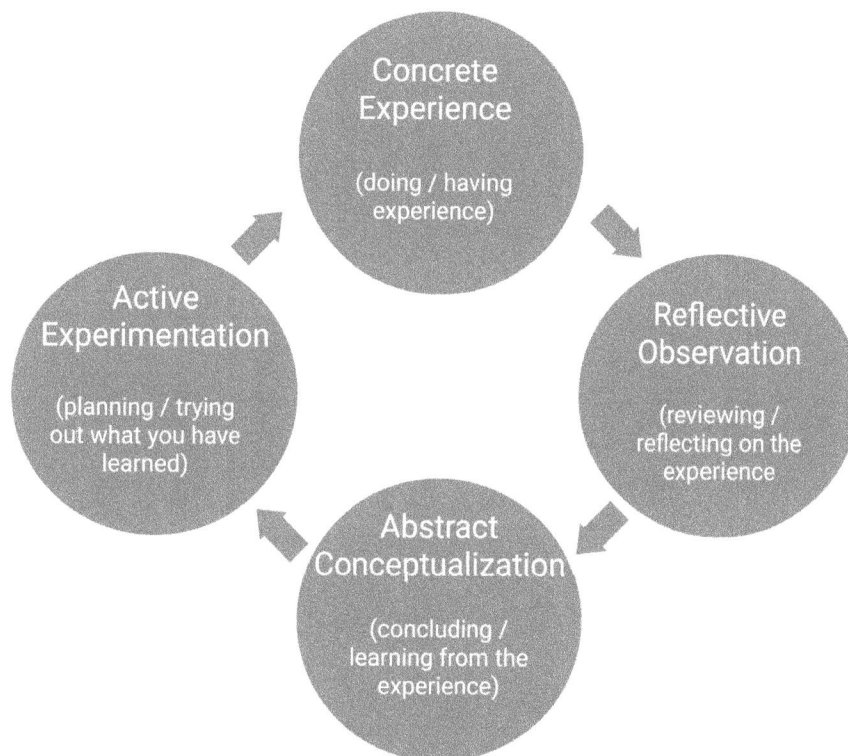

Note. Adapted from *Kolb's Learning Styles and Experiential Learning Cycle* by S. McLeod, 2017, https://www. simplypsychology.org/learning-kolb.html.

The Learning Zone Model (Figure 2.4 and Handout 2.4) that underpins participant learning is used in covering program content.[4] This model, developed by Tom Senninger, suggests that when we are in our **Comfort Zone**, we are in a familiar environment, feel comfortable, and are not obliged to take any risks. To learn something new, however, we need to leave this comfort zone and enter a **Learning Zone**. The Learning Zone requires us to consider new experiences that bring us into unknown territory and make us uncomfortable. As the name suggests, this is where we stretch ourselves to learn. I believe we need to be in the Learning Zone for most of the time if we want to continue learning new ideas, concepts, and skills in order to practice the habits of a lifelong learner. Returning to the Comfort Zone every now and again gives us an opportunity to reflect and make sense of things we have learned. Senninger proposes that there is also a **Panic Zone** that exists beyond the Learning Zone. If participants move abruptly into this zone, learning simply stops, which often results in anxiety, stress, or distress. Signs of participants being in a panic zone are often physical disengagement or withdrawal from participation. As educators, we need to maintain a balance between these zones and to scaffold learning (move from a current level of understanding to an advanced level) in an intellectually supportive environment in which participants learn about complex information that may have seemed out of their reach. Please note that these zones are experienced differently for each person.

Figure 2.4

The Learning Zone Model

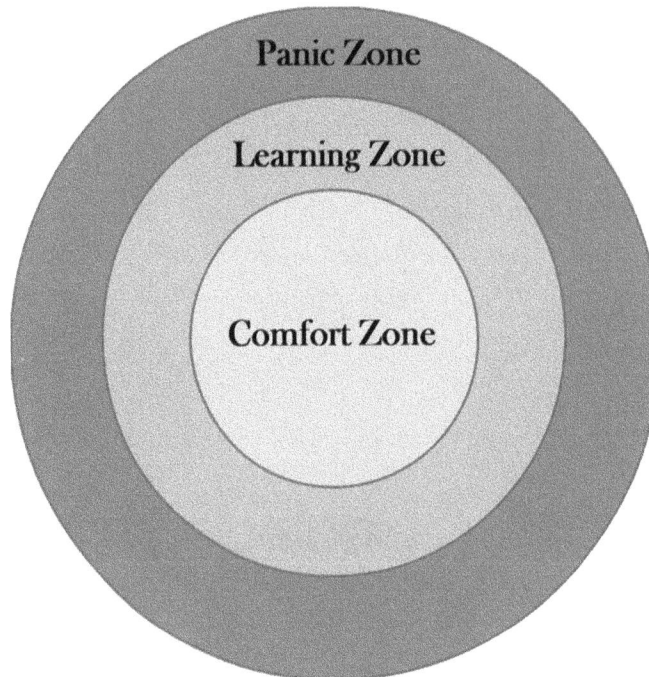

Note: Adapted from *The Learning Zone Model* by T. Senninger, 2000, ThemPra Social Pedagogy. http://www. thempra.org.uk/social-pedagogy/key-concepts-in-social-pedagogy/the-learning-zone-model/.   Copyright © 2015-2021 ThemPra Social Pedagogy.

Rigor, the third pillar, invites us to do rigorous research to identify topics and content that need to be covered in our programs. Rigor points to the work done before a program even begins and the research and analysis that needs to take place to create the definitions within a program. For example, at the Center, we study and draw our inspiration from information made available by other institutions such as the International Leadership Association (ILA), the National Association of Campus Activities (NACA), and the National Clearinghouse for Leadership Programs (NCLP). We talk to participants' internship supervisors about the types of management and leadership skills and competencies required for people entering the workforce. We also check the National Association of College Employers (NACE) surveys to assess how our program competencies relate to those outlined in their surveys. The World Economic Forum reports provide further insight. Podcasts such as *The Leadership Educator* help us to keep abreast of new directions in leadership development and education.[5] There are many more resources in addition to the ones listed above. The simple idea is this: Find all the information you can to make your programs rigorous. The term rigor cuts through all the pillars, and we need to be rigorous and intentional in our approach.

Thoroughness of content coverage as well as learning processes or approaches applied should be considered when thinking about this pillar. It is a start to developing a "culture" of rigor within an institution. Rigor also refers to having financial and administrative systems in place. Such systems should be dynamic, and we should review them periodically to see whether the programs provide the information we need to efficiently assess whether the programs are responsive to participant as well as workplace needs.

Maintaining rigor in the quality of a program also requires selecting speakers very carefully and intentionally. The Center's programs select scholars, practitioners, and alumni who have demonstrated expertise in their field. Diversity (e.g., age, race, perspectives) is another consideration. Speakers should be willing to deliver content using the theories you have identified in the second pillar. For example, we select speakers who are willing to adopt Kolb's Cycle of Experiential Learning and understand why it is important to allocate their session time with at least 70% allocated for structured interactive activities and the remaining time allocated for presentation of content. Speakers we select, despite being accomplished, are humble. They are engaged and engaging, embrace the idea of continuous quality improvement, show commitment, and understand how management and leadership shows up in their area of expertise. They understand the importance of creating a structure in which students can wrestle and engage with the content and decide how it relates to their current and future experiences. Finally, the commitment of the program officers and the speakers to continually improve their sessions speaks of their determination to make programs or sessions stronger with each passing year.

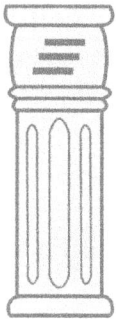

Structure, the fourth pillar, is perhaps the most visible to participants. When programs are clearly structured and well organized, short- and long-term credibility is established with participants. In this pillar, please pay close attention to these questions: Why are you offering the program? What need(s) does it address? How will it take place? What does the physical layout of each program session look like and is it conducive to offering an intellectually supportive environment? Have you selected a time and place that is convenient for the participants? Are activities within a program, as well as a series of programs, sequenced in such a way that they build upon each other and become successively more complex as a continuum of offerings? How do the programs relate to one another? What is the evaluation methodology that should be used?

Participants are and always should be at the center of developing programs. I refer to establishing an intellectually supportive environment often in this book. In addition to creating a respectful environment, consider how you might set ground rules and norms for your activities. Consider privacy of participants, being open to each participant's perspective or story, and always keep personal information participants share with you confidential. Think about ethical considerations for using tests and inventories in your programming.[6] Look for discussion about this in Shankman and Gigliotti's forthcoming publication, *Using Inventories to Enhance Leadership Development.*

At the Center, we use a document called the Session Proposal Form (see Handout 2.5) which allows us to keep track of essential information related to speakers and a session. I constantly think about how we deliver session content within a program. Each session will be very focused if speakers have thought about the key concepts that cover "essential-to-know" information within the time allotted for the session. The "good-to-know" information can be provided through handouts. The "nice-to-know" information is covered through supplemental resources that are either suggested by the speaker or are the result of additional research related to the topic. In this book, every session embraces this approach, with clear methodologies and well-planned experiences that reinforce learning.

You probably think that all of this is just common sense, but I am continually surprised by programs I have observed that do not take many of the questions listed in this pillar into consideration. By the time we are planning logistics, we should have clarity about the needs of the participants in a program. Program logistics matter, for when a program is organized and accessible, its reputation and popularity grow.

Reflection, the fifth pillar, is a critical component of our program design. Nowadays, given our busy lives, we really do not take enough time to reflect on what we are doing or learning. Incorporating Kolb's Cycle of Experiential Learning in leadership programming helps to build reflective practices and provides participants the time to process the new information and apply it. The Reflection Pillar is a mandatory component in the sessions of each program in this book. When reflection questions are well crafted, it is inspiring to see how participants enjoy reflecting on their learning. Creating an abundance of spaces and places for reflection is critical for personal and professional growth as managers and leaders. Think about techniques, including journaling, one-minute papers or other timed reflections, drawing concepts, think-pair-share, e-portfolios, small-group discussions, or free-form individual reflections. There are many more, and I have learned that anything works, from a five-minute conversation to an hour-long discussion or activity! It is not when or where it happens that is important, but rather the fact that reflection is planned for and does happen that matters most.

I also believe that building relationships that help participants and educators reflect together about programs creates an environment that allows for deep connection. These relationships, built on trust and friendship, are long lasting.

The sixth pillar, **Community**, is my favorite pillar. It speaks to the need for all of us to create environments and networks where we learn from one another and create long-lasting relationships and friendships of support. It also builds a space to mentor and to be mentored. We work hard to provide leadership programs that create community cohesion. This thought from Chris J., class of 2022, helps us to understand this from a participant's perspective:

I participated in the Rockefeller Center's Civic Skills Training (CST) program. Initially, I was skeptical about whether I would find myself transformed into a radically different individual or leader by the end of the sessions. I was unconvinced that leadership was a trait that could be taught or learned.

What I immediately realized about the program was that it was not simply designed to improve ourselves as individuals but also to create relationships between one another. When we began the sessions, I did not know a single member of my cohort. Through each challenge, activity, and lesson we shared one another's thoughts and beliefs, inevitably becoming closer as a result. In one of our sessions, we shared stories about what motivates [us] and we learned highly personal details about our backgrounds. Moments like these taught me that leadership isn't about an individual, though we may often assume it to be the case.

Chris' observation is supported by political scientist, Robert Putnam (2000), who coined the concept of "social capital," which can be understood in two ways: the value of a network to a society and the value of a network to an individual. Putnam believes that strong social networks are valuable.[7] They establish the ability to address personal, community, and societal issues because of the presence of such things as trust, collaboration, cooperation, and joy in being together, thus building "social capital."[8] It is natural that we seek to establish relationships with like-minded people, a concept Putnam refers to as "bonding." In addition to encouraging bonding, I believe that a program should bring together people with different backgrounds and perspectives, as described in the first pillar. Putnam refers to this concept as "bridging." Creating a sense of community using bridging is difficult, but both exciting and possible.

We have used bonding and bridging strategies in all the programs we offer. Are we 100% successful in creating lasting social networks? Absolutely not. But we are excited about those instances in which program participants continue to communicate using messaging apps either individually or in groups after program completion. For example, the 2016 cohort of the Rockefeller Leadership Fellows Program still stays in touch. In a recent message from Bill K., class of 2016, he explains its impact:

> On another note, there is an RLF virtual reunion/catch-up session planned for available 2016 Fellows next week! This speaks to the formidable staying power and enduring impact of your program. The GroupMe was recently reflecting on how RLF was a highlight of our Dartmouth experience. This continues to be a special group. Almost five years on, this network of highly intelligent, motivated, and compassionate folks is going strong.

In addition to building networks for students, presenters also become part of the Center's professional network. I asked four presenters that regularly facilitate sessions about why they keep coming back, despite their busy schedules. Two themes jumped out at me and I share them with you through these quotes:

Joy derived from working with students

Serving in this capacity has been an amazing opportunity to give back to a community that has given so much to me. Having taken advantage of many Rockefeller Center programs as an undergrad, I can attest to the lasting impact that these programs can have, especially in the early years of entering the workforce. I felt much more prepared for professional life in the "real world" because of Rocky programming, and I am honored to have the opportunity to help the next generation of students feel equally as prepared, if not more.

—Ariel Murphy Bedford, Alumna and presenter in MLDP and CST

I enjoy engaging with current students and learning from their experiences, worldviews, and generational perspectives. Their commitment to excellence, growth, and development—their own, as well as each other's—makes them a joy to teach.

—Kate Hilton, Alumna and presenter in MLDP and RLF

The quality of discussion and engagement from the students was impressive. They were curious, deep thinkers who were leading in organizations, with communities, and for inspiring purposes.

—Kerry Priest, presenter in RLF

Teaching is a passion of mine. And I always find that I learn at least as much from the students as they do from me. When I was asked to teach in a leadership program, I saw it as an opportunity to be more intentional and to distill the critical aspects of negotiation as they relate to leadership.

—John Garvey, presenter in MLDP

Working with the Programs and Staff of the Center

Institutional buy-in is a critical component to the success of any initiative. The dedication of the Rockefeller Center staff in providing meaningful professional development experiences for students continues to be inspiring and a source of motivation for returning year after year as a session speaker.

—Ariel Murphy Bedford, presenter in CST and MLDP

Working with them connects me to an ever-growing Dartmouth community. This includes the Rockefeller Center program staff, who support continuous improvement and contextualization to make each and every session more relevant and rewarding than the last.

—Kate Hilton, presenter in MLDP and RLF

The faculty and students showed me incredible hospitality, the campus is beautiful, and I loved learning more about the school's history and regional culture. I was honored to be asked to facilitate an RLF session. The purpose and mission of this program, along with the intentional format, aligned with my own values as a leadership educator and practitioner. And I was excited to engage in the learning process with this group of talented, diverse students.

—Kerry Priest, presenter in RLF

From these quotes and my personal experience of working with all speakers, I have learned how passionate and committed they are about creating vibrant learning environments for students. Kerry Priest represents this passion for all speakers when she describes her desire to help students to generate new perspectives geared toward their own purpose and practice of leadership: "We situate leadership as an activity that is driven by a challenge—a vision or hope for a better future, a more just and equitable world. And we explore ideas, behaviors, and practices that can help them [the students] to engage and mobilize others in the face of uncertainty and complexity." I was also impressed with the commitment of alumni to "give the work back" as in the case of Ariel Bedford, Kate Hilton, and many others.[9] All four, as well as other speakers in the programs, demonstrate the qualities of a lifelong learner.

Building community and fostering understanding of one another play an important role in our program offerings. We monitor the research and observe trends in the workplace, which allow us to remain nimble and responsive to what our participants need to know. These workplace trends and the impact of politics on communities, both domestically and globally, support our emphasis on the importance of excellent communication skills, including the ability to have difficult conversations. These skills are critical for building community cohesion. Furthermore, our conversations with professors, supervisors, alumni in different fields, and employers emphasize the need to foster effective intergenerational communication and thus we also include this topic in our program offerings.

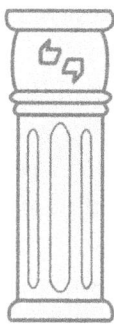

Assessment and Evaluation is the seventh pillar. Leadership programs must have clear assessment and evaluation processes in place for the learners, the programs, and the institution. In our case, we place emphasis on individual participants and on all aspects of the programs being offered, including how a program meets organizational and institutional missions, and how alumni benefit from it. As a result, a few things happen. First, we articulate learning objectives to capture participants' personal and professional growth. Next, we learn about the strengths and weaknesses of our programs, also noting opportunities for program improvement. Additionally, we map leadership competencies, thereby capturing the emphases of our programs and tying them to our research and practice. Finally, we acknowledge things that are out of our control, which provides greater clarity and context to the environment within which we operate.[10]

We also discuss how our program offerings meet our organizational mission. The Rockefeller Center's mission is to "educate, train, and inspire the next generation of public policy leaders in all fields of endeavor, through multidisciplinary education, public policy-oriented research across the social sciences, leadership training, and public lectures by visiting scholars and dignitaries."[11] If you keep this mission in mind as you read this book, you will notice the various ways in which we work toward accomplishing this mission.

The Center is also concerned with how it meets the institutional mission. Dartmouth College "educates the most promising students and prepares them for a lifetime of learning and of responsible leadership, through a faculty dedicated to teaching and the creation of knowledge."[12] As you will notice throughout this book, our leadership programs and offerings strive to bring this mission to life.

A final word about assessment and evaluation, and its influence on the organizational context where these programs live, breathe, and grow. When consistent evaluation systems are put in place, the idea of continuous quality improvement takes on a life of its own and becomes a way of being, particularly when we want to experiment with a new idea or when we think of mistakes that we will inevitably make when we innovate. But both assessment and evaluation present us with the opportunity to grow and become lifelong learners. I believe, however, that there is a systematic approach to how we think of "making a mistake." The first time a person makes a mistake, it truly is a mistake. The second time the same person makes the same mistake, the person should determine whether it is a systems issue. This includes examining the organizational system supporting it, making changes, testing the system, and making sure it works. After the system is fixed, the third time the same person makes the same mistake, it is time for a difficult conversation. In their book, *Crucial Conversations*, Patterson et al. (2012) provide us with insight into what conditions create difficult conversations and what to do about them.[13] My colleagues do not fear implementing an innovative idea into their leadership programming that takes them out of their Comfort Zone, because they have embraced the view that mistakes (or failures) are important to Rockefeller Center program development. We have followed the systematic approach outlined above to test innovative thoughts and ideas. Over the past fifteen years, I have noticed that it has created a culture of continuous quality improvement, which has put all of us on the path to becoming lifelong learners as well.

Participant Learning and Empowerment is the new and eighth pillar in program design. We have always placed a priority on participant learning and empowerment in our programs. The transition to virtual teaching and learning as a result of the pandemic, however, has forced all of us to consider ways in which educators and participants can stay engaged as part of a vibrant community of learners. In every sense, we have all become participants in learning how to navigate our new reality. We are learning about how to use technology together. We are learning about self-care together. We are learning about how to support each other through virtual platforms so that we can replace the loss of human contact, and the yearning for it, with empathy, laughter, compassion, humor, and joy. As we learn these lessons together, relationships become less hierarchical and less limited by knowledge differentials. COVID-19 has given educators an increasingly intense urgency to explore ways in which we can empower participants to direct their own learning and foster their own small communities.

Conversations with colleagues from all fields have shown me that they, too, are looking for ways in which they can continue to grow personally and professionally. Further, they are committed to helping their program participants to do the same. Our world is remarkably complex, yet full of opportunities, and so participant learning and empowerment deserves a pillar of its own.

So how do our programs allow participants to discover themselves as leaders, followers, and learners? Meet Meghna R., from the Dartmouth College class of 2020. She majored in quantitative social science with a concentration in global health and sustainable development. At Dartmouth, in addition to various Rockefeller Center programs, Meghna was involved with Dartmouth Emergency Medical Services, the Political Violence Lab, and the John Sloan Dickey Center for International Understanding. She is now working as a healthcare consultant and hopes to pursue a Ph.D. in Epidemiology in the future.

Here is Meghna's reflection on her growth with the Rockefeller Center, or Rocky, as students fondly refer to it:

> Rocky's leadership programs awaken the seed in students and give them the resources and skills to grow as leaders. When I first joined Rocky, I lacked confidence in myself and thought I could never be as strong of a leader as some of my extroverted peers. Through Rocky, I met leaders with a diverse range of work habits, leadership

styles, and personal experiences. These conversations helped me realize that there is no one recipe for creating a perfect leader. More importantly, the best leaders are dynamic and can adapt to the ever-evolving economic, social, and political environment.

Good leaders can thrive in a variety of contexts and work with many different types of people to create effective teams. During the Rockefeller Leadership Fellows fall retreat, Jay Davis '90 facilitated the "Compass Points" exercise to help us identify our personal strengths as leaders. Jay also discussed how we could best meet the needs of those who identified as other "points" on the compass. Jay's session helped me recognize my, as well as others', strengths as leaders, and how to adapt my work style to meet each team member's compass direction. Being cognizant of different leadership styles can help us mitigate misunderstandings and minimize differences to create effective teams. Our distinct leadership competencies are complementary, and as leaders, we should try to take advantage of the diversity of work styles.

I can now recognize when personalities in a team are seemingly clashing, and how I can delegate responsibilities and create compromises that will play to each team members' strengths. This has been critical to successful collaboration on academic group assignments, working on professional teams to meet client deadlines, and even in my personal life with friends and family. In addition, I am now more confident and aware of my own assets as a leader and a team player. The journey to becoming a strong leader, however, is ongoing. My time at the Rockefeller Center has nurtured my seed and kindled a desire to always want to grow and learn from those around me.

Meghna's reflection is an example of the development of self-awareness, the meaning of working with team members and styles, and the birth of her new ideal of lifelong learning. In my personal conversations with her, I know that she has much more to say. Through such reflections, though, I have become particularly sensitive to the learning needs of introverts and the methods we might use to engage them to make them feel confident about their skills and abilities, and to help them develop a clear vision of being a good manager, leader, and follower.

I have seen many other narratives like Meghna's over the past fifteen years. My colleagues and I aspire to work with current participants and program alumni on igniting inspiration to become self-aware, learn to work with others, understand team behavior, and grasp how to meet their organizational missions. As managers, leaders, and followers, our goal is to achieve societal good.

But a program design is only good if it is implemented. The Rockefeller Center programs not only follow program design steps but also incorporate the Eight Pillars of Program Design to implement programs. Chapter 3–7 describe the programs in more detail, but for now here are some general program implementation tips for your consideration.

Tips for Implementing Programs

➤ Plan your approach using the Eight Pillars of Program Design.

➤ Use an outreach strategy that reaches out to diverse audiences.

➤ Anecdotal information suggests fatigue with electronic communication. Use other methods (informal coffee hours, information sessions, peer-to-peer discussions) to create awareness about the benefits of the program for personal and professional growth.

➤ Select speakers carefully and think about how they might help you to meet program goals and objectives.

➤ Logistics, Logistics, Logistics! Pay close attention to details.

➤ Evaluate your program at these levels: participant, program, organization, and institution.

Notes

[1] McLeod, 2017.

[2] Lopez-Garrido, 2020, Aug 09; and Komives et al., 2006.

[3] Bloom, 1956.

[4] Senninger, 2000.

[5] Jenkins & Bullock, 2019–present.

[6] Shankman & Giogliotto (in press).

[7] Putnam, 2000.

[8] Heath, 2007.

[9] This observation is linked to "Part Two: The Response" in section 6, p. 123 of *Leadership on the Line* (Heifetz & Linsky, 2017).

[10] Combs et al., 2008.

[11] The Nelson A. Rockefeller Center at Dartmouth College, 2019.

[12] Dartmouth, 2013.

[13] Patterson et al., 2002.

References

Anderson, L. W., Krathwohl, D. R., Airasian, P., Cruikshank, K., Mayer, R., Pintrich, P., & Wittrock, M. (2001). *A taxonomy for learning, teaching and assessing: A revision of Bloom's taxonomy.* Longman Publishing.

Bandura, A. (1997). *Self-efficacy: The exercise of control.* W.H. Freeman.

Blink, R. (2016). *Leading learning for digital natives: Combining data and technology in the classroom.* Routledge.

Bloom, B. S. (1956). *Taxonomy of educational objectives, Handbook 1: Cognitive domain* (2nd ed.). Addison-Wesley Longman Ltd.

Berrett-Koehler Publishers. *The ultimate guide to DEI: Investing in diversity, equity, and inclusion in your organization.* https://ideas.bkconnection.com/ultimate-guide-to-dei

Bolger, M. (2020, May 24). Diversity, Inclusion & Equity in Tech: Understand the Difference. *General Assembly Blog.* https://generalassemb.ly/blog/diversity-inclusion-equity-differences-in-meaning/

Combs, K. L., Gibson, S. K., Hays, J. M., Saly, J., & Wendt, J. T. (2008). Enhancing curriculum and delivery: Linking assessment to learning objectives. *Assessment & Evaluation in Higher Education, 33*(1): 87-102.

Covey, S. R. (2020). *The 7 Habits of highly effective people* (30th anniversary ed.). Simon & Schuster. (Original work published 1989)

Dartmouth. (2013, June 5). *Mission statement.* Dartmouth College. https://home.dartmouth.edu/mission-statement

Heath, R. (2007). Rethinking community collaboration through a dialogic lens: Creativity, democracy, and diversity in community organizing. *Management Communication Quarterly, 21*(2), 145–171. https://doi.org/10.1177/0893318907306032

Heifetz, R. (1994). *Leadership without easy answers.* Belknap Press of Harvard University Press.

Heifetz, R., & Linsky, M. (2017). *Leadership on the line, with a new preface: Staying alive through the dangers of change.* Harvard Business Press.

Jenkins, D., & Bullock, L. (2019, November–present). *The leadership educator podcast* [Audio podcast]. https://theleadershipeducator.podbean.com/

Kolb, D. A. (1984). Experiential Learning: *Experience as the Source of Learning and Development* (1st ed.). Prentice Hall.

Kolb, A. Y., & Kolb, D. A. (2005). Learning styles and learning spaces: Enhancing experiential learning in higher education. *Academy of Management Learning & Education, 4*(2), 193–212.

Komives, S. R., Longerbeam, S. D., Owen, J. E., Mainella, F. C., & Osteen, L. (2006). A leadership identity development model: Applications from a grounded theory. *Journal of College Student Development, 47*(4), 401–418.

Lopez-Garrido, G. (2020, Aug 09). Self-efficacy theory. *Simply Psychology*. https://www.simplypsychology.org/self-efficacy.html

McLeod, S. (2017). Kolb's learning styles and experiential learning cycle. *Simply Psychology*. https://www.simplypsychology.org/learning-kolb.html

Office of Planning, Evaluation and Policy Development. (2016, November). *Advancing diversity and inclusion in higher education: Key data highlights focusing on race and ethnicity and promising practices*. Office of the Under Secretary, U.S. Department of Education. https://www2.ed.gov/rschstat/research/pubs/advancing-diversity-inclusion.pdf

Patterson, K., Grenny, J., McMillan, R., & Switzler, A. (2012). *Crucial conversations: Tools for talking when stakes are high* (2nd ed.). McGraw-Hill.

Perruci, G., & Hall, S. W. (2018). *Teaching leadership: Bridging theory and practice*. Edward Elgar Publishing.

Putnam, R. (2000). *Bowling alone: The collapse and revival of American community*. Simon & Schuster.

Putnam, R., & Feldstein, L. (2004). *Better together: Restoring the American community*. Simon & Schuster.

The Nelson A. Rockefeller Center at Dartmouth College. (2019). *2018-2019 Annual report*. https://rockefeller.dartmouth.edu/sites/rockefeller.drupalmulti-prod.dartmouth.edu/files/rocky_annualreport_18-19_final.pdf

Saska, S. (2019, November 5). How to define diversity, equity, and inclusion at work. *Culture Amp Blog*. https://www.cultureamp.com/blog/how-to-define-diversity-equity-and-inclusion-at-work/

Shaiko, R. G. (2013, June 9). *Admissions is just part of the diversity puzzle*. The Chronicle of Higher Education. https://www.chronicle.com/article/admissions-is-just-part-of-the-diversity-puzzle/

Shankman M.L. & Giogliotto, R. (in press). Using inventories to enhance leadership development. *New Directions for Student Learning*, 170.

Senninger, T. (2000). *Abenteuer leiten-in Abenteuern lernen: Methodenset zur Planung ud Leitung kooperativer Lerngemeinschaften Für Taining und Teamentwicklung in Schule, Jugendarbeit und Betried.* [Leading adventures - learning adventures: A set of methods for planning and managing cooperative learning communities for training and team development in schools, youth work and companies]. Ökotopia-Verlag.

Schmutte, K. & Harte, S. Y. (2019). *How do we push the boundaries of the learning zone without dipping into the panic zone?* d.school Public Library. https://dlibrary.stanford.edu/ambiguity/learning-zone-reflection-tool

YWBoston (2019, March 26). *Beyond the DE&I acronym: What are diversity, equity, and inclusion?* YW Boston Blog. https://www.ywboston.org/2019/03/beyond-the-acronym-dei/x

Kolb's Cycle of Learning and Its Connections with Bloom's Taxonomy

The Experiential Learning Cycle, also known as Kolb's Cycle of Learning, developed by David Kolb and published in 1984, is in essence <u>a model of the learning process consisting of four distinct but interconnected stages through which the learner passes repeatedly.</u>

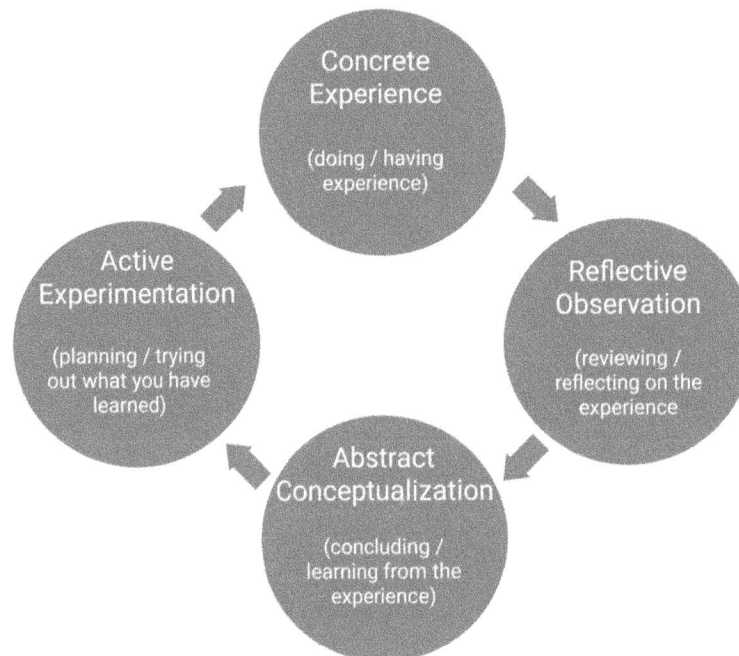

Note: Adapted from *Kolb's Learning Styles and Experiential Learning Cycle* by S. McLeod, 2017, https://www.simplypsychology.org/learning-kolb.html.

The cycle underscores the ongoing nature of learning by illustrating that a learner might enter the process at different stages; however, in order for knowledge acquisition to be effective and sustainable, the learner must engage with each of the four elements. Usually, a learner would first enter the **Concrete Experience** stage, which is attributed to the brain's sensory cortex. During this period, the learner would encounter a new concept or environment. As a consequence, they would enter the second stage of the cycle—**Reflective Observation**. During this stage, the learner not only indicates that they have experienced something unknown or unusual, but more importantly, tries to reflect on how this encounter impacts their personality, well-being, emotional state, and world view. Once they have identified such changes, the learner is ready to enter the third stage of the cycle—**Abstract Conceptualization**. The role of this stage is to allow for the reflection to give rise to a change in the learner's thought process and views by triggering the formulation of a new idea or the revision of an old one. As a result, the learner can enter the **Active Experimentation** stage of the cycle where they have the opportunity to apply in practice what they have just conceptualized in theory. The experiment is essentially the learner's attempt to integrate their new views in the world around them, which can cause several main outcomes. If the new idea clashes with other beliefs of the learner, it would trigger a set of novel experiences, bringing them back to Stage 1. If the idea neither gives rise to conflicts nor fits well, it would lead back to the Reflection stage and force the learner to rethink the way in which they have reflected on the experience. In the case where the idea works well within the learner's set of views and practices, it would open up the way for them to focus on other new experiences that need reflection. In any of these cases and many more, Kolb's Cycle provides a model of learning that has no final stage—just as the process itself is never-ending and constantly enhanced by the learner's interaction with the world around them.

Another systematic classification of the learning process is Bloom's Taxonomy. Developed by Benjamin Bloom and published in 1956, the taxonomy is in essence <u>a framework of the levels of knowledge acquisition presented in a hierarchical structure in accordance with the order of mastery.</u>

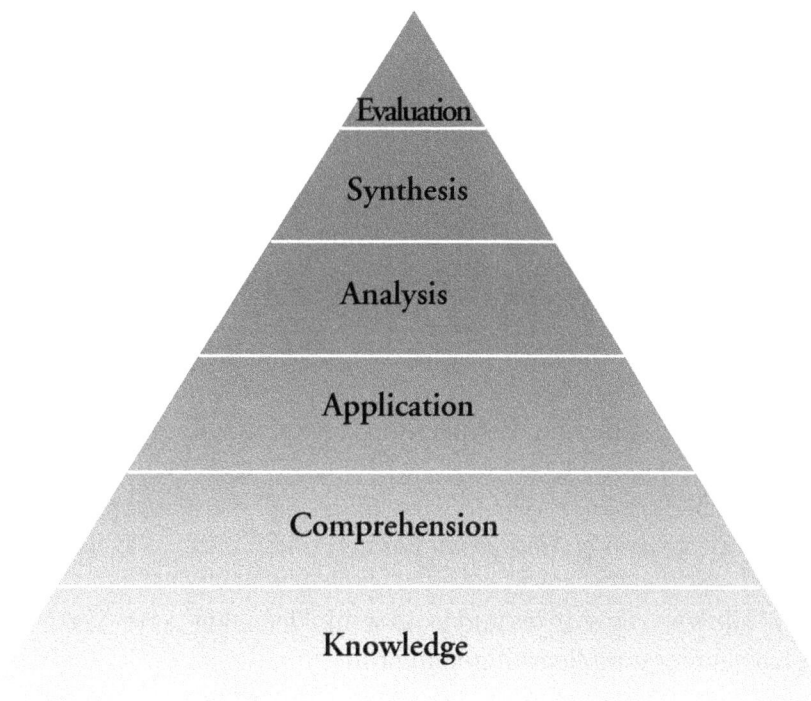

Note: Adapted from *Emerging Perspectives on Learning, Teaching and Technology* (p. 43) by M. Orey (Ed.), 2005. Copyright © 2010 by M. Orey.

It has to be noted that despite having become representative of Bloom's work, this is only one of three domains, with the other two being the affective and psychomotor ones. In short, the bottom three levels are of lower order and are much easier to master. They are mainly concerned with the learner's ability to recall relevant knowledge, construct meaning out of it, and implement the newly obtained information in other situations. When compared to Kolb's cycle, these levels seem to fall within the *Concrete Experience* and *Active Experimentation* stages. The top three levels of the taxonomy, defined as being of a "higher order," require more time to grasp. Concerned with skills such as breaking concepts into pieces and analyzing them or constructing judgments, these levels relate to the *Reflective Observation* and *Abstract Conceptualization* stages. This suggests that learners often struggle more with contemplating their experience and formulating new views, which is why practices such as reviews and feedback are very important. Even under Krathwohl and Anderson's (2000) revised taxonomy, which places the emphasis on the student outcome rather than the activity, the connections remain closely the same. Both Kolb's Cycle and Bloom's Taxonomy in its original and revised versions prove that successful learning is attainable only when attention is paid to physical and cognitive processes as complementary rather than opposite.

References

Anderson, L., Krathwohl, D., Airasian, P., Cruikshank, K., Mayer, R., Pintrich, P., Raths, J., & Wittrock, M. (2000). *Taxonomy for learning, teaching, and assessing: A revision of Bloom's taxonomy of educational objectives, abridged edition* (1st ed.). Pearson.

Bloom, B. S. (1956). *Taxonomy of educational objectives, Handbook 1: Cognitive domain* (2nd ed.). Addison-Wesley Longman Ltd.

Chiu, S. K. (2019). Innovative experiential learning experience: Pedagogical adopting Kolb's learning cycle at higher education in Hong Kong. *Cogent Education*, *6*(1). https://doi.org/10.1080/2331186X.2019.1644720

Forehand, M. (2005). Bloom's taxonomy: Original and revised. In M. Orey (Ed.), *Emerging perspectives on learning, teaching, and technology (pp. 40–47). The Global Text Project*. https://textbookequity.org/Textbooks/Orey_Emergin_Perspectives_Learning.pdf.

Kolb, A. & Kolb, D. (2005). Learning styles and learning spaces: enhancing experiential learning in higher education. *Academy of Management Learning & Education*, *4*(2), 193–212.

McLeod, S. (2017). Kolb's learning styles and experiential learning cycle. *Simply Psychology*. https://www.simplypsychology.org/learning-kolb.html

University of Puget Sound. (n.d.). *Kolb's learning cycle*. https://www.pugetsound.edu/academics/experiential/create-experiential-learning-opportunities/available-resources/creating-critical-reflection-assignments/design-models/kolbs-learning-cycle/

Tomkins, U. (2015). Oh, was that 'experiential learning'?! Spaces, synergies and surprises with Kolb's learning cycle. *Management Learning*, *47*(2), 158–178. https://doi.org/10.1177/1350507615587451.

Watson, P. (2019). Using Kolb's Learning Cycle to Improve Student Sustainability Knowledge. *Sustainability*, *11*(17), 4602–4621. https://doi.org/10.3390/su11174602.

Handout created by Kristabel Konta, class of 2024

Bandura's Model of Self-Efficacy

The Self-Efficacy Model, developed by Albert Bandura and first introduced in 1977, is in essence a framework encompassing the characteristics of people with high and low levels of self-confidence, plus strategies to build and sustain this trait.

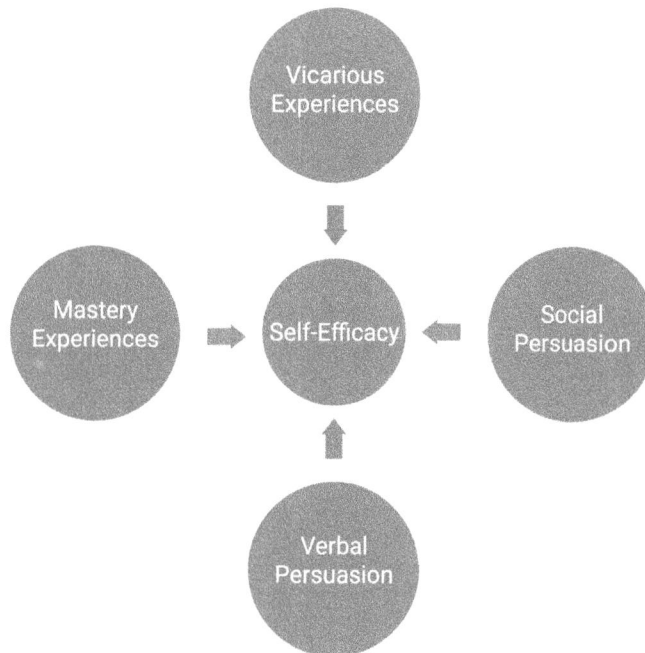

Note: Adapted from *Self-efficacy Theory* by G. Lopez-Garrido, 2020, https://www.simplypsychology.org/self-efficacy.html.

Following the features of the realm in which Bandura dedicates a significant portion of his work—social cognitive psychology—the term *self-efficacy* considers one's belief in the efficacy of their own actions. He has identified four sources of influence, which if utilized correctly, can increase the levels of self-confidence and lay the foundation for a person's high motivation and sense of accomplishment.

The first source is **Mastery Experiences**—capabilities obtained in the past after a person has invested time and effort in challenges they eventually succeeded in. This latent knowledge, however, is often not enough to boost a person's confidence, which is why a strategy to increase the likelihood of good performance is reminding individuals about their previous achievements. Prompting people to recall prior success in similar situations could elevate their self-confidence by reminding them that they already possess the necessary skills to complete the task.

The second motivator is **Vicarious Experiences**—knowledge obtained by observing others who succeed in certain situations. Consciously or not, everybody is a role model and those who accomplish what someone else is aiming at automatically become their positive role models. Therefore, increasing one's self-efficacy can be achieved by introducing them to environments where they are surrounded by other successful people. A valuable strategy for utilizing this source of influence is thus to reduce people's anxiousness through a demonstration of what others are doing well.

Third in the list, Bandura introduces **Social Persuasion**—encouragement, which if administered at as young an age as possible, can effectively improve one's self-efficiency. Techniques, such as verbal motivation and positive self-talk, applied while a person is struggling with a complicated problem, can persuade them that they indeed have the necessary set of skills to overcome the current challenge.

Lastly, Bandura proposes that a significant source of motivation is one's personal **Emotional State**. Depression or anxiety could prove detrimental to building self-confidence, which is why it is crucial to track people's well-being as it affects their perception of themselves and their scope of influence as opposed to others. However, an even more important remark he makes is that it is not the emotional state by itself but the way it is interpreted that affects a person's performance. Bandura explains that a state of arousal could be viewed as both an incentive and counterincentive. Therefore, simple somatic arousal techniques, such as taking deep breaths, can be used to reduce anxiety's negative influence.

Based on these factors, there are several traits that people exhibit, which can help identify them as either possessing high or low self-efficacy. Characteristic of confident people are possessing a sense of power, approaching challenges, and having perseverance even in cases of failure. On the other side, those with low self-efficacy tend to adopt a behavior of avoidance and easy surrender before complex situations because of their anxiety and fear of failure.

It can therefore be concluded that by placing emphasis on peer modeling, seeking and offering feedback, and encouraging people to accept challenges, one can increase the levels of self-efficacy and thus unlock a sense of motivation previously restricted by lack of self-confidence.

References

Bandura, A. (2011). On the functional properties of perceived self-efficacy revisited. *Journal of Management, 38*(1), 9-44. https://doi.org/10.1177/0149206311410606

Bandura, A. (1997*). Self-Efficacy: The exercise of control*. Freeman.

Lopez-Garrido, G. (2020, Aug 09). Self-efficacy theory. *Simply Psychology*. https://www.simplypsychology.org/self-efficacy.html

PsychologicalScience. (2013, Dec 20). *Inside the Psychologist's Studio with Albert Bandura* [Video]. YouTube. https://www.youtube.com/watch?v=-_U-pSZwHy8&ab_channel=PsychologicalScience

Handout created by Kristabel Konta, class of 2024

Leadership Identity Development Model

The Leadership Identity Development Model (LID), developed by Komives et al. and published in 2006, is in essence a roadmap to fostering the formation of a leader's personality in a holistic approach through various learning opportunities.

Awareness → Exploration Engagement → Leader Identified → Leadership Differentiated → Generativity → Integration Synthesis

Note: Summarized from "Developing a leadership identity: A grounded theory," by S. Komives, S. Longerbeam, F. Mainella, L. Osteen, & J. Owen, 2005, *Journal of College Student Development, 46(6), p. 599.*

The model itself is stage-based, following a person's lifelong development from early childhood to post-college experiences. The LID model is based on the grounded theoretical findings of scholars who have identified six categories of strong influence on leadership development: "broadening view of leadership, developing self, group influences, developmental influences, and the changing view of self with others." As a result, a model of six stages is constructed with each stage including an analysis of the person's interaction with adults, peers, and changes in engagement with the community. Another key element is the transition between stages which is characterized by an observable shift in thinking.

Stage One: Awareness

➢ **Essence:** being exposed to the concept of leadership and beginning to recognize authority figures
➢ **How to foster it:** using more explicit language revolving around terms such as *leaders, leadership, accomplishing goals,* and *leadership styles* by adults

Stage Two: Exploration/Engagement

➢ **Essence:** taking on responsibilities and joining groups as a member/follower
➢ **How to foster it:** helping students get involved with new activities and building self-confidence by affirming a person's strengths

Stage Three: Leader Identified

➢ **Essence:** taking on managerial roles within groups, practicing different leadership styles and implementing delegation, valuing interdependence
➢ **How to foster it:** helping students identify organizations and groups that match their values; designing experiences that openly promote positional leadership roles

Stage Four: Leadership Differentiated

➢ **Essence:** learning to be effective in both positional and non-positional roles; exploring group processes and how systems work; valuing interdependence
➢ **How to foster it:** teaching skills, such as teamwork, handling group conflict, active listening; creating environments that encourage commitments beyond self-interest

Stage Five: Generativity

➢ **Essence:** being committed to sustainability and group growth, identifying potential personal passions, valuing interdependence
➢ **How to foster it:** assisting in finding personal passions; encouraging students to appreciate mentoring younger peers' work within the system but beyond the individual group

Stage Six: Integration Synthesis

➢ **Essence:** recognizing leadership as a lifelong development process and being interested in role modeling
➢ **How to foster it:** helping people identify personal strengths they can utilize beyond college and in diverse environments

---

References

Komives, S., Longerbeam, S., Mainella, F., Osteen, L., & Owen, J. (2005). Developing a leadership identity: a grounded theory. *Journal of College Student Development, 46*(6), 593–611. https://doi.org/10.1353/csd.2005.0061.

Komives, S.R., Longerbeam, S.D., Owen, J.E., Mainella, F.C., & Osteen, L. (2006). A leadership identity development model: applications from a grounded theory. *Journal of College Student Development 47*(4), 401-418. https://doi.org/10.1353/csd.2006.0048

Martinelli, E. (2017). Public relations leadership development cycle: A cross-cultural perspective. *Public Relations Review, 43*(5), 1062–1072. https://doi.org/10.1016/j.pubrev.2017.09.002.

Zheng, M. (2015). Embracing leadership: a multi-faceted model of leader identity development. *Leadership & Organization Development Journal, 36*(6), 630–656. https://doi.org/10.1108/lodj-10-2013-0138.

Handout created by Kristabel Konta, class of 2024

The Learning Zone Model

The Learning Zone Model, developed by Tom Senninger, is in essence <u>a synthesis of the lifelong process of learning.</u> The model is constructed of three distinct circular layers whose boundaries are dynamic and can be expanded through one's experience.

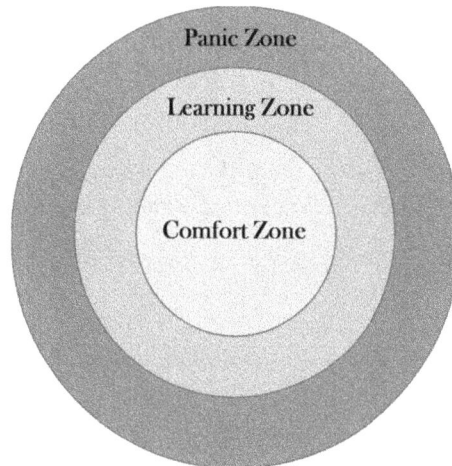

Note: Adapted from *The Learning Zone Model* by T. Senninger, 2000, ThemPra Social Pedagogy. http://www.thempra.org.uk/social-pedagogy/key-concepts-in-social-pedagogy/the-learning-zone-model/. Copyright © 2015-2021 ThemPra Social Pedagogy.

The innermost layer—the **Comfort Zone**—is the familiar environment. It is the place where everyone feels the most confident without having to take any risks; however, if stuck within it for too long, the person can never discover and develop. This zone's importance lies within its role as a point to return to, providing security and a place to reflect.

The middle layer—the **Learning Zone**—is the most desirable area to devote the majority of a person's time and energy to. It lies beyond the Comfort Zone as its environment is unknown and provides opportunities for growth and learning. However, as it forces the person to explore the limits of their skills and to acquire additional ones, the Learning Zone is also a place that can easily become a part of the Comfort Zone once the learner feels confident and familiar enough with the newly discovered environment.

An excessive amount of energy put into moving throughout the Learning Zone, however, might bring the person within the third circle—the **Panic Zone**. What makes this area problematic is that the learning process becomes impossible when it is blocked by the person's attempts to avoid any traumatic experiences that may be caused by uncertainty. However, just as one can expand their Comfort Zone, they can also apply the right amount of pressure to break through the Learning Zone boundary and stretch it throughout the Panic Zone. It is important to understand that the fluidity of the boundaries can be used to one's benefit only when they are *invited* rather than *pushed* to move from one layer of the model to the next.

References

Azulay, H. (2013). *Learning beyond the comfort zone: stretch and job rotation assignments allow employees to develop and build their skills and organizations to retain and engage good talent at minimal cost.* Association for Talent Development. http://en.atdchina.com.cn/magazines/td-magazine/learning-beyond-the-comfort-zone

Palethorpe, W. (2011). Learning in the panic zone: Strategies for managing learner anxiety. *Journal of European Industrial Training, 35*(5), 420–438. https://doi.org/10.1108/03090591111138008

Schmutte, K. & Harte, S. Y. (2019). *How do we push the boundaries of the learning zone without dipping into the panic zone?* d.school Public Library. https://dlibrary.stanford.edu/ambiguity/learning-zone-reflection-tool

Senninger, T. (2000a). *Abenteuer leiten-in Abenteuern lernen: Methodenset zur Planung ud Leitung kooperativer Lerngemeinschaften Für Taining und Teamentwicklung in Schule, Jugendarbeit und Betried.* [Leading adventures - learning adventures: A set of methods for planning and managing cooperative learning communities for training and team development in schools, youth work and companies]. Ökotopia-Verlag.

Senninger, T. (2000b). *The Learning Zone Model.* ThemPra Social Pedagogy. http://www.thempra.org.uk/social-pedagogy/key-concepts-in-social-pedagogy/the-learning-zone-model

Handout created by Kristabel Konta, class of 2024

Session Proposal Form

2019–2020 Session Proposal Form

PROGRAM "TITLE"

SPEAKER NAME

Thank you for contributing to the success of our program. Please complete the following Session Proposal Form, which ensures consistency throughout our programming and facilitates in the overall assessment of our program's learning objectives and competencies. Co-curricular programs at the Rockefeller Center follow the Kolb Cycle of Learning: theory-based knowledge, experiential learning, reflection, and concrete application.

Program Specific Criteria:

- Session Date(s):
- Session Duration:
- Target Complexity Level (basic, intermediate or advanced):
- Audience (describe audience):
- Primary Point-of-Contact:
- For more information about (name of program), please visit (insert relevant URL here):

Part 1. Speaker Information, Session Administration, and Logistics

Your Name

Your Title

Your Institution or Affiliation

Brief Bio

Please provide a brief bio of 200 words or less.

Photo

Please provide a photo to be used in our program information. The picture should be high resolution, 300 dpi or more. Please insert the photo here and resize to a height of 2.5 inches, if needed.

Required Required Materials

Please list your A/V or classroom needs. Additionally, please specify if your slide presentation includes multimedia such as video clips to ensure audio will be setup for this purpose.

Dietary Restrictions (if any)

Part 2. Session Proposal

Session Title

Maximum of 10 words.

Session Description

Please provide a brief description of the session, maximum 150 words.

Learning Objectives:

Objectives should be SMART:

Specific,

Measurable,

Appropriate,

Realistic, and

Time-bound.

Please limit to 3 objectives.

Key Concepts and Definitions

Please list up to 3 key concepts that your session will focus on and how you define those concepts. Examples of key concepts may include authenticity, integrity, empowerment, creativity, risk taking, results, autonomy/independence, accuracy, growth, excellence/mastery.

Reflection Questions

What questions should our
students be asking themselves
when the session is over? Please
limit to 3 questions.

Session Outline or Lesson Plan: *Please provide an outline of how you will use the time to present your material. What types of activities will you utilize, and in what order will you use them? See the example provided. Total programming should not exceed the session duration listed on page 1.*

Time Required (*Minutes*)	**Description**
minutes	
minutes	
minutes	
minutes	
minutes	
minutes	
minutes	

**Required
Readings (*Optional*):**

*Please limit required reading to a
total of 20 pages.*

Additional Resources:

*What resources would you
recommend on this topic? Please
feel free to include books, articles,
websites, multimedia, TedTalks,
etc.*

Leadership Competencies Addressed: *Please indicate which of the following leadership competencies **your session focuses on** and seeks to develop within students. Please select a maximum of six competencies.* **Double click** *on the box to check it.*

Collaboration

- ❑ Builds and maintains partnerships based on shared purpose
- ❑ Acknowledges and listens to different voices when making decisions and taking action
- ❑ Facilitates collective action toward common goals
- ❑ Encourages, supports, and recognizes the contributions of others
- ❑ Fosters a welcoming and inclusive environment

Effective Reasoning

- ❑ Employs critical thinking in problem solving
- ❑ Employs creative thinking in problem solving
- ❑ Develops personal reflective practice
- ❑ Engages in inquiry, analysis, and follow-through
- ❑ Integrates multiple types of information to effectively solve problems or address issues

Self-Knowledge

- ❑ Continually explores and examines values and views
- ❑ Understands social identities of self and others
- ❑ Demonstrates realistic understanding of one's abilities
- ❑ Seeks opportunities for continued growth
- ❑ Takes appropriate action toward potential benefits despite possible failure

Effective Communication

- ❑ Writes and speaks after reflection
- ❑ Clearly articulates ideas in a written and spoken form
- ❑ Exhibits effective listening skills
- ❑ Influences others through writing, speaking, or artistic expression
- ❑ Acknowledges and appropriately communicates in situations with divergent opinions and values

Management

- ❑ Develops and implements a plan for goal attainment
- ❑ Develops appropriate strategies for capitalizing on human talent
- ❑ Stewards and maximizes all resources
- ❑ Manages multiple priorities
- ❑ Prepares for leadership transition
- ❑ Develops appropriate strategies for effective teamwork
- ❑ Evaluates efficacy of current course(s) of action
- ❑ Identifies structure and culture of organization
- ❑ Demonstrates effective and appropriate use of technology
- ❑ Demonstrates financial, task, and resource management skills

Principled Action

- ❑ Identifies and commits to appropriate ethical framework
- ❑ Demonstrates congruence between actions and values
- ❑ Demonstrates personal responsibility
- ❑ Appropriately challenges the unethical behavior of individuals or groups
- ❑ Bases actions on thoughtful consideration of their impact and consequences
- ❑ Seeks appropriate and mutually beneficial solutions when conflict or controversy arises

- ❏ Shows self-respect and respect for others
- ❏ Moves beyond self-imposed limitations
- ❏ Practices self-compassion, friendliness, ease with self, and vulnerability

Intercultural Mindset

- ❏ Contextualizes social identities and experiences
- ❏ Understands, communicates with, and respectfully interacts with people across identities
- ❏ Actively engages in opportunities to expand worldview
- ❏ Applies intercultural knowledge and skills in local, national, and/or global contexts

3 Dartmouth Leadership Attitudes and Behaviors (D-LAB)

A highly developed values system is like a compass. It serves as a guide to point you in the right direction when you are lost.

— Idowu Koyenikan

In creating the continuum of Rockefeller leadership programs, we set as our priority ensuring that first-year students would learn and practice the art of civil discourse and value clarification. Today, this art has proved to be indispensable in the face of the heated debate that has replaced civil conversation. Partisanship and miscommunication flourish in this state of divisive discord. To address this need, we developed the Dartmouth Leadership Attitudes and Behaviors Program (D-LAB). Although this has been developed for students in the first year of their undergraduate experience, the content is applicable to all fields.

Program Goal

D-LAB is a six-week program for first-year undergraduates. In small-group discussions led by upper-class student facilitators, the program aims to assist participants to explore their values in the context of leadership and community. Together they identify their individual values, understand their place in the community, and tie their realizations to the College's mission. D-LAB also provides these participants with a space to practice having difficult conversations early in their careers.

Program Prerequisites

Offered as a campus-wide program in collaboration with the Office of Student Life and the Office of Residential Life, this program is a prerequisite for those hoping to meet all requirements to qualify for the Rockefeller Center's First-Year Fellows (FYF) Program, which is described in Chapter 4. Because of this, many of the students who participate in D-LAB are interested in FYF, and a subset of 20–25 of these students are selected to participate in it.

D-LAB is also open to all first-year students on campus. The collaboration between the Office of Student Life and the Office of Residential Life came about because both partners believed in the value of the FYF program and pooled their resources to expand campus reach. Professional staff from both departments work closely with student assistants and student facilitators to plan and implement the program. Planning takes place over the six-month period leading up to the D-LAB start date.

This program is unique because all group discussions for the first-year students are facilitated by students who are in their second, third, and final year of their undergraduate experience.

Program Participation

As a young program that aims to have an outreach campus-wide, D-LAB attracts a range of students across campus. Each first-year student has different interests; our program is designed to help students build community and meet others they would not have otherwise met during their first winter on campus. Because of the experimental nature of this program, its specifics have varied over time. For instance, the number of sessions offered has changed since 2015, as have the corresponding number of sessions required to complete the program.

As seen in Figure 3.1, the number of students who have signed up for D-LAB has increased significantly over the past five years. However, the number of students who have completed the program each year has remained largely consistent. This is because a lower percentage of participants completed the program in more recent years. Attrition in the program has been a challenge, and the next few years will be devoted to developing strategies to mitigate attrition.

Figure 3.1

D-LAB Participant and Completion Data 2015–2020

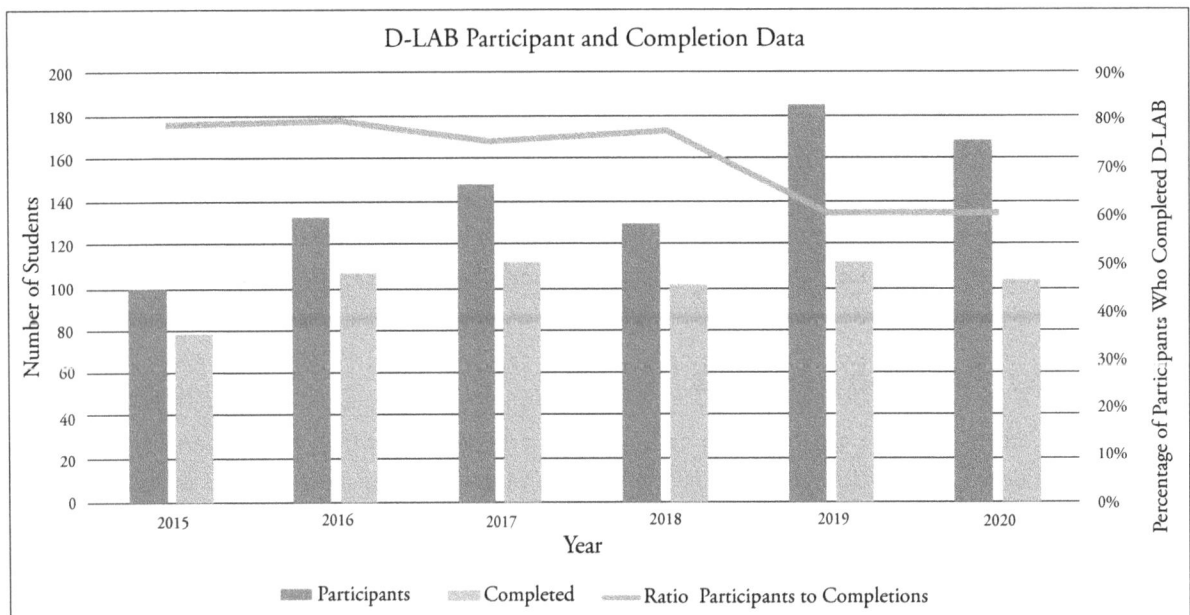

Key Program Elements

➤ Small group discussions led by trained student facilitators
➤ Informal physical spaces that are conducive to frank and collegial conversations
➤ The establishment of collaborative partnerships with other parts of the institution
➤ The opportunity to explore personal and professional development

Program Description

D-LAB began in the winter of 2014 and, since then, has hosted 699 participants. It has been led by 184 upper-class student facilitators. The program has grown since its inception, and adjustments in budget, staff capacity, and student input have been made to accommodate this growth. To assess and evaluate the program, a series of reflections and surveys are distributed throughout its six-week duration.

The connection of first-year students to their upper-class peers helps to build community between class years while encouraging an open and honest dialogue on values, working with others, and the principle of community. The Rockefeller Center, Office of Student Life, and the Office of Residential Life decided to train upper-class students to facilitate these discussions because we found that participants are often intimidated by the perceived "authority" of a professional staff member. Trained peer leaders help them feel comfortable about expressing their opinions and practicing civility when there are differing views. To enhance the participant experience, these discussion groups meet in various student community spaces across campus. These are areas familiar to the participants and help them to feel comfortable when engaging with their peers. These upper-class student facilitators are recruited from all areas across campus. Some are D-LAB alumni; others join because they are interested not only in the program but also in making the campus a better place.

Key Leadership Competencies

D-LAB focuses on collaboration, effective communication, effective reasoning, self-knowledge, principled action, and building an intercultural mindset.

Possible Adaptations

In addition to higher education, this program can be applicable to nonprofit organizations, for-profit organizations, government institutions, and anyone working within communities. It is also applicable for K-12 audiences. Managing oneself as a leader or a follower is common to all these institutions. Some ideas to adapt this program are as follows:

➤ Identify your audience and their needs. Research what is known or not known about these needs.
➤ Use the Eight Pillars of Program Design to develop your concept.
➤ Make sure the content you cover matches the experience and maturity level of your audience.
➤ Develop activities for individual and group reflections.
➤ Select facilitators well versed in value clarification, discussions related to self-awareness, congruence of values with behaviors, and community building and empowerment.

Session 3.1 Leadership from Within— Character (Part I)

Session Description

In this session, participants will work together in their discussion groups to complete the Mission to Mars Activity and present their results. Participants will engage in discussion to analyze how what they chose to "bring to Mars" can be reflective of what they value. Participants will discuss how they see themselves versus how others might see them and explore the importance of diverse personalities in a group setting.

Learning Objectives

Participants will do the following:
- Name three of their important personal values
- Explore three or more factors that influence their values and personality
- Identify at least three attributes of their core identity and three attributes of their social identity

Leadership Competencies Addressed

Collaboration
- Encourages, supports and recognizes the contributions of others

Intercultural Mindset
- Contextualizes social identities and experiences

Effective Reasoning
- Develops personal reflective practice

Self-Knowledge
- Shows self-respect and respect for others

Key Concepts and Definitions

Self-awareness   Conscious knowledge of one's own character, feelings, motives, and desires.

Identity   The descriptive characteristics, qualities, and abilities that people use to define themselves.

Required Materials

- Participant Folder, including program schedule and weekly agenda
- Handout 3.1.1 D-LAB Values List
- Handout 3.1.2 "Where I'm From" Poem Activity, with George Ella's poem as an example: http://www.smithsonianeducation.org/educators/professional_development/workshops/writing/george_ella_lyon.pdf. Retrieved on Nov. 14, 2020.
- Mission to Mars Activity instructions and set of photos

- Individual writing utensils
- Group chart paper and markers

Session Outline

Session duration: 2 hours

Time Required		Description
20 minutes	Introduction	As participants enter, give them their folder with their name and their assigned discussion group number on it and direct them to locate and mingle within their discussion groups. Introduce the program. Briefly discuss the value of participants' involvement in the program. Ask them to consider what they intend to get out of the program and how they will hold themselves accountable to this goal. Remind participants that "what is said here stays here," and "what is learned here leaves here." Emphasize that all participants must respect confidentiality. Direct facilitators and participants within each discussion group to introduce themselves and mention what areas of campus they each represent.
35 minutes	Activity 1	In participants' folders is a handout with instructions for the Mission to Mars Activity. Ask them to read the following prompt on it: *You and your team have been selected as members of the very first general settlement on Mars. NASA has constructed the basic infrastructure and has provided the essentials for survival on the red planet. Now you as a group need to consider what is important as you build a functioning society. As a group, choose five photos from among those provided to represent the foundations of the society you would like to establish on Mars. Why are these helpful or even critical for establishing a society on Mars? Adequate shelter, water, basic food, and any necessary medical supplies are already provided.* Instruct each group to take a few minutes to silently look through all the photos and write or take notes before discussing as a group. Give them approximately 15–20 minutes to discuss and reach a decision on the five photos. The photos are purposely ambiguous, and each group will need to determine what they represent. They are allowed only five photos per

Time Required		Description

team, not per person. In the large group, guide participants through the following discussion questions and ask participants to share out. Ask the following:

What was that experience like? What made the activity difficult? Why did you select the photos you did? How did you decide what each photo is about? What do the photos you chose reveal about what your new society might value? Were those values rooted in values of your existing community/culture? How did you do as a group adhering to the expectations and standards we just set before this?

Seek a few volunteer groups to present their Mission to Mars choices.

45 minutes   Activity 2   Introduce George Ella Lyon's poem titled "Where I'm From." Tell participants that they will be writing their own poem, inspired by "Where I'm From," about the people, places, and experiences that have shaped them. Ask volunteers to read some examples. Give each participant at least 10 minutes to work on their poems. Once everyone has had the opportunity to come to a stopping point (not necessarily completion), ask a few volunteers to share their work within their groups.

Make sure they know that their poems do not have to be complete, and that they can share as much or as little (including not at all) from their poems. Within each discussion group, have participants discuss the following reflection questions:

Does anyone want to explain more about something they wrote— provide more context? What places did you think about, what people? What memories from your childhood came back as you reflected? What parts of "where you are from" were easy to identify, and which were more difficult? Why? Are there any parts of "where you are from" that are hard to share with people? When you were writing this, what made you decide to include some things over others? How do you think this piece looks different today than it would have a year ago? How do the things you wrote about shape how you see the world and what you value? How have they shaped your leadership and how you work with others?

Time Required		Description
15 minutes	Framing	Introduce the Bridge Activity, which will bridge today's activities with the next session. In this activity, participants will analyze how personality traits and individual values influence each other. They will each craft a list of their individual values, rank them, and explain why they prioritize some over others. Referring to the values list in their participant folders, ask them to select 10 that are the most important to them and 10 that are the least important.
5 minutes	Conclusion	Rejoin as a large group for a recap of the session activities and the major takeaways of the session. Ask participants to complete the session evaluation using your desired format. Close the session by thanking the participants and facilitators.

Reflection Questions

- How have my experiences and identities shaped my values?
- How does my current context (e.g., first year in college) impact my identities and values?

Supplemental Resources

Avolio, B. J., & Locke, E. E. (2002). Contrasting different philosophies of leader motivation: Altruism versus egoism. *The Leadership Quarterly*, *13*(2), 169–191. https://doi.org/10.1016/S1048-9843(02)00094-2

Urs Bender, P. (1998a). The five steps to leadership. *The Canadian Manager*, *23*(3), 21–22.

Urs Bender, P. (1998b). *Leadership from within* (3rd ed.). Stoddart.

Participant Reflection

Looking back on the D-LAB experience, writing my "I Am From" poem and listening to others read theirs aloud remains one of the most impactful activities from the program. As a freshman in college, it was not only emotional but enlightening to consider the parts of my background that had formed me into who I am, and the sharing portion of the session gave me the chance to better understand my peers and their pasts. As a senior now, I still lead with the knowledge that it's important to show empathy to others as you can never truly know where they are "from."

D-LAB Winter 2018

This session has been formatted and revised for consistency and clarity. The original session in the Dartmouth Leadership Attitudes and Behaviors Program was facilitated by program alumni.

D-LAB Values List

This is the Values List included in the participant folder and referenced throughout D-LAB. Fill in values not listed.

Advancement Getting ahead; ambitious; aspiring to higher levels	**Community** Living where neighbors are close and involved	**Forgiveness** Able to pardon others and let go of hurt
Adventure Seeking excitement; novel or unusual experiences; often with some risk	**Compassion** Showing sympathy to others' distress and a desire to help alleviate it	**Health/Wellness** Maintain and enhance physical, mental or emotional wellbeing
Aesthetic Appreciation of beauty in art, nature, surroundings	**Competence** Being good at what I do; capable	**Helping/Hospitality** Taking care of others; doing what they need; serving others
Appearance Looking good; dressing well; keeping fit	**Courage** Standing up for your beliefs; overcoming fear	**Honesty** Sincere; truthful
Authenticity Genuineness; true to oneself; representing one's true nature	**Creativity** Finding new ways to do things; innovative	**Loyalty** Faithfulness to commitments
Authority/Power Having control/influence over events or people	**Diplomacy** Finding common ground with difficult people and situations; resolving conflict	**Humility** Modest; not prideful or arrogant
Belonging Being connected to and liked by others	**Environment** Respecting the future of the earth	**Independence** Not subject to obligations or control by others
Challenge Testing physical limits, strength, speed, agility, and intellect	**Fairness** Respecting everyone's rights; ensuring equality for all	**Neatness/Order** Tidy; orderly
Collaboration/ Teamwork Cooperating with others toward a common goal	**Friendship** Connection to another by affection or esteem; on-going relationships	**Peace** Seeking harmony; inner harmony, security and order

Communication Open dialogue; exchange of views	**Prosperity** Flourishing; well-off; able to afford what I want	**Perseverance** Pushing through to the end; completing tasks
Personal Growth Continual learning; development of intellectual status, new skills	**Rationality** Consistent, logical, clear reasoning	**Self-Control** Self-disciplined; able to manage one's actions
Play Fun; light-hearted; spontaneous	**Recognition** Getting noticed for efforts	**Spiritual Growth** Relationship to higher purpose; divine being
Intimacy Deep emotional, spiritual connection	**Respect** Demonstrating consideration; regarding with honor	**Tradition** Respecting the way things have always been done
Personal Knowledge Seeking intellectual enjoyment; new ideas, truth	**Stability** Security	**Self-Acceptance** Tolerance; self-respect

"Where I'm From" Poem Activity

Often, the values that inform our leadership are informed by our experiences and histories. Loosely following the idea of George Ella Lyon's poem "Where I'm From," take the next 10–15 minutes to write a short piece rooted in the people, places, experiences and memories that have shaped who you are. This will only be a start to get you thinking—you will have the opportunity, but not the obligation to share at the end of this time.

Use the following categories to list specific details related to you. The key is making this as specific and personal as possible. Use nicknames or words that only you or your family use. Don't worry about readers not knowing what you're talking about.

CONSIDER:

- Parent's names and significant relatives
- Special foods or meals
- Family-specific games or activities
- Nostalgic songs
- Stories, novels or poetry that you'll never forget
- Phrases that were repeated often
- The best things that you were told
- The worst things that you have been told

- Ordinary household items
- Family traditions, traits, and tendencies
- Religious symbols or experiences
- Stories about a specific family member that influenced you
- Accidents or traumatic experiences
- Losses and joys
- Location of memories, pictures, or mementos

Select from your lists the items you want to include in your poem. You do not have to include everything that you listed, and you can always add more categories or items to include in your poem. You can stick to or break from the format of the original in whatever way you wish. To help get you started if you are feeling some writer's block, you will find a "mad libs" style template in your folder.

Session 3.2 Leadership From Within— Character (Part II)

Session Description

In this session, participants will work within their small groups to challenge their understanding of how values can be "lived" through actions, behaviors, and experiences. Participants will evaluate how their schedules reflect their values and connect their actions to who they are. Participants will engage in a discussion about the nature of integrity and how they uphold integrity.

Learning Objectives

Participants will do the following:
- Identify their top 10 core values
- Assess how their values translate into behavior through three real-life examples
- Identify three ways to uphold their values authentically in everyday life

Leadership Competencies Addressed

Effective Reasoning
- Develops personal reflective practice.

Effective Communication
- Exhibits effective listening skills

Self-Knowledge
- Continually explores and examines values and views

Principled Action
- Demonstrates congruence between actions and values

Key Concepts and Definitions

Authenticity   Being authentic means that you act in ways that show your true self and how you feel. Rather than showing people only a particular side of yourself, you express your whole self genuinely. That means to succeed in being authentic, you first must know who your true self is.

Congruency   The dictionary definition of congruence is "identical in form; in agreement or harmony." When one lives with congruency, their actions coincide with their thoughts, values, and beliefs.

Integrity   "Living with integrity means: not settling for less than what you know you deserve in your relationships, asking for what you want and need from others, speaking your truth, even though it might create conflict or tension, behaving in ways that are in harmony with your personal values, making choices based on what you believe, and not what others believe."
— Barbara De Angelis[1]

---

[1] De Angelis, B. (2006). *How did I get here?: Finding your way to renewed hope and happiness when life and love take unexpected turns* (1st ed.). Griffin.

Required Materials

- Handout 3.2.1 Integrity Scenarios (2 copies per group)
- Goal Setting Frameworks Sheet (1 copy per participant)
- Loose leaf paper for schedule activity (enough for each participant)

Session Outline

Session duration: 2 hours

Time Required		Description
15 minutes	Introduction	As participants enter, direct them to their facilitation groups and allow them to mingle until everyone arrives. Within their groups, facilitators ask their participants to share one of their role models and describe their core values.
15 minutes	Framing	Based on the Bridge Activity from the previous session, ask participants to share their top three individual values with a neighbor, arranged in order of importance. Have facilitators ask the following questions of their participants: *As you are comfortable, share your thoughts on why you selected the values you did, keeping in mind that your partner may have a very different list. What people or experiences have shaped your lists? Were there some items that were easier to select than others? Why?*
15 minutes	Discussion	Prompt participants to think about a time when they acted in opposition to their values or failed to live up to them. Provide the following reflection questions: *What are some reasons that you did not live up to your values? Which of your values did you violate? What positive outcome did you stand to gain from your actions? Why is it sometimes hard to live your values?* Review the following key takeaways after some discussion in the groups: Even people from similar backgrounds (e.g., age, race, socioeconomic status) can have very different values. Our values are constantly evolving, and they are shaped by our experiences. We do not always live up to what we value the most in life (e.g., individuals who value honesty might not

Time Required		Description
		always tell the truth). "Living your values" is not automatic, and it is not easy. Individuals must constantly be aware of how small, everyday actions can translate into the composition of their character.
25 minutes	Reflection	Direct participants to write down their entire schedule from the past weekend (Friday, Saturday, and Sunday). Ask them to think about events, activities, and interactions (e.g., study groups, time spent with friends).
		Ask if any of their individual values play a role in their schedule (activities, interactions, etc.) and when. Discuss for 10 minutes.
		Ask if they think about their values every day and why or why not. Discuss for 5 minutes.
		Finally, discuss whether values are context dependent. In their groups, participants should discuss their personal goals and whether their schedules are working toward any of these goals. Ask: *What are the pros and cons to working hard at one thing vs. trying to achieve many things?*
		Discuss the following key takeaways: We have opportunities to live our values every single day. The most last-minute decisions we make on a daily basis all add up to our character and shape our identity as a leader. Therefore, if we can strive to think more critically about every word we say and every action we take, we will have a better chance of living with integrity.
20 minutes	Activity 1	Explain that now facilitation groups will practically think about making decisions that uphold our integrity through a set of relatable scenarios. Group facilitators read one of the "Integrity scenarios" provided on Handout 3.2.1 and try to answer the question: *Is this person acting with integrity?*
		In groups, participants reflect on the following discussion questions: *Discuss the merits of the above scenarios… do you agree with some or all of these parts? What's missing? What's challenging about living with integrity? What if you can't keep your word? How does living with integrity play into our creation of goals? How will you pursue your goals with integrity?*

Time Required		Description
		Review the following key takeaways after the small group discussions: Living with integrity means keeping your word to yourself and to others. Incidents of incongruence don't make you a bad person, rather congruence should be a goal we strive to achieve. What we do about incongruence afterward is more important. Integrity includes being accountable to yourself and others if you can't keep your word.
20 minutes	Activity 2	Explain that goal setting can be an effective step in living more congruently and intentionally. In this activity, participants will set goals for themselves and use a framework to help think through that goal more effectively. In their groups, facilitators will introduce two goal-setting frameworks. First, facilitators challenge participants to set a goal of some sort. It should be something they want to do, accomplish, or grow in—not necessarily change. Once participants have articulated their goals and shared them with a partner, briefly introduce the "SMART goal" framework (refer to Handout 5.1.3 in Chapter 5). Using examples, explain the acronym SMART (specific, measurable, attainable, relevant, and time-bound). Ask participants to rewrite their goals using the SMART framework. In pairs, have participants share how their goal is a SMART goal.
5 minutes	Framing	Introduce the Bridge Activity, which will bridge today's activities with the next session. Ask participants to choose a close friend and set up a time to meet and discuss each other's values. Based on shared experiences, Person A (the participant) will identify the top five values of Person B (the close friend) and vice versa. Then, both should identify and discuss overlap in values and how they complement/supplement one another.
5 minutes	Conclusion	In the large group, recap the session. Ask participants to complete the session evaluation using your desired format. Close the session by thanking the participants and facilitators.

Reflection Questions

- What leads to incongruence between values and behaviors?
- What are our core values?
- What does integrity mean to us?

Supplemental Resources

Kraemer, H. (2011). *The values-based leader* [Video]. Kantola Productions. https://dartmouth. kanopy.com/video/values-based-leader

Lehman, D. W., O'Connor, K., Kovács, B., & Newman, G. E. (2019). Authenticity. *Academy of Management Annals*, *13*(1), 1–42. https:// doi.org/10.5465/annals.2017.0047

Stanley, D. (2008). Congruent leadership: Values in action. *Journal of Nursing Management*, *16*(5), 519–524. https://doi.org/10.1111/j.1365-2834.2008.00895.x

This session has been formatted and revised for consistency and clarity. The original session in the Dartmouth Leadership Attitudes and Behaviors Program was facilitated by program alumni.

Participant Reflection

Considering each of the "integrity scenarios" really helped me visualize how I could practice integrity in my own life at Dartmouth. Each one was specific and thought provoking, and they all seemed true-to-life—like things a real college student would encounter. It was also valuable to be able to discuss the scenarios with my peers, as we were able to bring diverse perspectives into the conversation and weigh different values that were at play in each situation. At times, I feel like throwing words like "integrity" around can lead to vague conversations and limited understanding. Putting the concept into concrete terms made it seem like something I could see myself practicing.

D-LAB Winter 2018

Integrity Scenarios

Scenario A. After the Activities Fair in the fall term, Alex is excited about jumping into extracurricular life at Dartmouth. Alex has signed up for four clubs, each of which has a weekly meeting and additional time commitments throughout the term. It's a lot of work, but Alex valued being active outside of the classroom in high school and wants to maintain this track record in college. However, once week five rolls around and midterms begin, Alex begins to realize that these commitments aren't sustainable. With his grades suffering, Alex doesn't know what to do. Alex wants to maintain these commitments, but he knows that academics should be the priority. In the end, Alex officially resigns from one of the clubs and just stops showing up to another. This allows Alex more time to focus on his academic work, and he receives decent grades for the term.

Scenario B. Sally and her roommate, Liz, are getting ready to go out when Ellen stops by their dorm room. After chatting with them, Sally and Liz convince Ellen to go out to the frats [or some commonly visited social space] with them, though Ellen had been planning on spending her Friday night studying for her MATH11 exam on Monday. Fast forward to a few hours later, when Ellen seems to have lost track of Sally, and Liz has passed out from drinking. Ellen is worried about Liz and thinks she should call for someone who can help; she goes to find an upperclassman to help, leaving Liz alone in a bedroom. When Ellen comes back, Sally is there and is trying to get Liz to walk downstairs; Liz can barely stand or open her eyes. Sally is adamant that Ellen shouldn't call for medical professionals to take care of Liz and becomes angry that Ellen would try and save *her* friend, who isn't even that good of friends with Ellen. Liz still isn't really conscious, and this worries Ellen, but she knows that Sally knows Liz relatively well and doesn't want to interfere. Ellen bites her lip and ends up leaving Sally and Liz to go home and sleep. The next morning, Ellen texts Sally if she wants to get coffee; Sally responds saying that she's in the emergency room with Liz after Liz had woken up with a broken ankle after drunkenly falling down some stairs.

Scenario C. Tim had a hard time making friends when he started at Dartmouth his freshman fall. This term, he starts hanging out with a new group of friends. He enjoys having people to hang out with, but sometimes he feels like they drink and go out more than he would want to. Tim's friend Paul has been invited to party at an upperclassmen's fraternity on Wednesday and is bringing along their whole friend-group. Tim is excited to go, but he has an important chemistry midterm the next day. He wants to maintain his new friendships and meet new people, but he's worried that his academic performance might suffer. He decides that he'll go out for a little bit before going home to study. At the party, he drinks a few more beers than he was planning, but he still leaves by 11 pm to go to his room to study; he feels guilty leaving when Paul gives him a hard time about heading out, but he wants to stick to his plan to study. Back in his dorm, Tim feels kind of lousy and decides to wake up early to study. The next morning, Tim wakes up, feeling worse than the night before, but tries to study anyway. Midway through the exam, Tim has to leave and throw up in the bathroom. He finishes the exam, but a week later receives his worst grade yet since arriving at Dartmouth.

Scenario D. Laura entered Dartmouth confident that she wanted to become a doctor and major in chemistry. But, after her first term of chemistry classes, and 10 years of pre-med ambitions, she finds herself uninspired and bored. Laura really likes her fall term professors and teaching assistants (TAs), but for some reason chemistry is not making her feel excited the way she thought it was going to during orientation. She thinks she wants to explore some other academic departments, but her parents keep telling her friends and family how proud they are of Laura for pursuing a medical degree; she keeps getting emails from relatives and her parents' friends congratulating her on pursuing her studies at Dartmouth. Laura wonders if her parents would be as proud of her if she took a geography course instead of the next chemistry sequence course next term. During course election, she initially signs up for the geography course and leaves out the chemistry course, but before course election is due, she switches back to chemistry. Over winter break, she talks herself into being excited about chemistry again, and she loves telling her parents about how interesting her classes and professors are. But when she's back at Dartmouth, Laura finds herself bored and feeling apathetic towards her chemistry classes. She doesn't know how to tell her parents that she doesn't like chemistry anymore, so she suffers through it. She starts feeling anxious and has trouble sleeping; her grades start slipping, which heightens both the anxiety and the insomnia. After pulling her grades up by the end of the term, her parents reiterate how proud they are of her over spring break. She signs up for the next chemistry requirement for the spring term.

Scenario E. Amber is inviting some of her friends to go out to dinner for her upcoming birthday. She has been planning this for weeks, and has worked hard to find a date that works for all of her friend group. One of her invited friends, Liam, cannot afford to eat off-campus. Liam is not very open about his financial situation, and Amber is not among those in the know. Elizabeth wonders if she should say something to Amber, because she would likely change her plans if she knew that the dinner would be hard for Liam to afford. On the other hand, Elizabeth is worried that she would violate Liam's trust by sharing information about his financial situation. She ends up saying to Amber that she thinks they should switch the birthday plan to an on-campus get-together to be more financially inclusive; she offers to get a special treat from the café with the extra money left on her meal plan. Amber says that's fine but wants to know if there's someone in particular that she should know about to prevent being financially exclusive in the future. Seeing her motives as nothing but kind, Elizabeth discloses Liam's name. Somehow, ostensibly through Amber, this disclosure gets back to Liam. He sends Elizabeth an emotional and harsh text saying that she broke his trust and violated his privacy. Liam goes to Amber's birthday celebration, but Elizabeth notices that he starts to pull back from the group, avoiding their friends more frequently, particularly Elizabeth.

Scenario F. It's 2:30 a.m. in a campus cafe and Max is finishing studying for a midterm exam that he'll take in nine hours. As he's getting ready to head out, he sees a friend of a friend, Olivia, quietly crying at the end of one of the tables as she appears to be working on a paper. Max doesn't know Olivia well, but he saw on Facebook that her father recently passed away. He really wants to get some rest before his exam tomorrow, which he's heard is notoriously difficult, but he feels like he should say something, though he doesn't know what he could say to help. He ends up going to bed without talking to Olivia; he has a big day the next day and doesn't think she would appreciate him saying something anyway.

Scenario G. Louisa has been friends with Sam since Orientation Week, and he made her transition to Dartmouth so much easier when she was overwhelmed and homesick. Now, a term in, Louisa feels a lot more comfortable meeting new people and figuring out what she wants to do at

Dartmouth. However, as she becomes more excited to meet new people, Sam seems more reserved and reluctant to branch out socially. He keeps inviting himself to plans that Louisa made with other people, even when she is trying to be more independent. She feels like he's continuing to rely on her when she's actively trying to make new relationships and expand her friendships. She of course values her friendship with Sam, but she also wants to make new friends. Louisa feels like she should talk to Sam in person, but she is anxious about having that hard conversation. She settles for a lengthy text in which she details why she feels a bit smothered by his friendship while emphasizing how much she values their relationship. Sam doesn't respond until the next day, at which point he replies tersely that he will try to stop getting in the way of her budding social life. Louisa apologizes profusely, still over text, but Sam stops responding. She ends up developing a new friendship with some folks from her art history class, but whenever she sees Sam around campus, she has a sinking feeling in her stomach.

Scenario H. When Hannah gets out of class, she sees that her friend Lauren texted her multiple times to ask if Hannah can come by her room because she's not feeling well. When Hannah goes to check on her, Lauren has clearly been crying but doesn't want to talk about why she's upset. It's been like this for weeks, if not months. Hannah has tried to gently suggest that Lauren talk to someone at the Student Wellness Center, the counseling office, or even talk to an upperclassmen mentor, but Lauren resists and argues that Hannah is the only person she trusts. Hannah wants to help Lauren, but she's also worried about how being there for Lauren affects her own well-being, academics, and mental health. Hannah doesn't want anything to happen to Lauren, so she starts spending more time with Lauren to try to support her. After spending most of the day being essentially on-call for Lauren, Hannah stays up late to finish her homework and averages about 30 hours of sleep per week. By the end of the term, Hannah's grades have slipped; she hasn't seen friends other than Lauren in weeks; and her parents worry that she's too exhausted when Hannah comes home from school for spring break.

Scenario I. After three full weekends of going out in the frats, Mikayla thought she'd feel less lonely. She thought that she would make the group of friends she always dreamed of having in college, but she somehow feels more alone. She doesn't like how everything smells like beer and how the drunkest people yell over one another so that they are also the loudest, but she doesn't know where else to go to make friends or to be social. Dartmouth students rave about the frat scene, and Webster Ave seems to be the place to be on the weekends, but Mikayla feels like she'd rather be anywhere else. One night, as she's getting ready to go out, she sees some of her floormates playing Risk in their common room. She pokes her head in and shyly asks if she can join, to which they reply, "Sure!" Some other floormates come by to try and persuade Mikayla to join them at the frats, but she says she'll stay here for the time being but might meet up with them later. A few hours later, Mikayla's still there, hanging out in the common room with her floormates. This is the happiest she's been at Dartmouth since she's arrived.

Session 3.3 Leadership with Others

Session Description

In this session, participants will discuss how their values interact with the values of individuals in their immediate communities. Participants will analyze real-world scenarios in which values came into conflict to reflect on the dissonance that lies at the core of ethical dilemmas. Participants will frame their conversations in the language of "intent" and "impact" to clarify these conflicts and their own reactions.

Learning Objectives

Participants will do the following:
- Analyze the impact of their interactions with others through reflecting on past experiences
- Define the relationship between intent and impact
- Identify two ways to apply an understanding of intent and impact to experiences in their everyday lives

Leadership Competencies Addressed

Effective Reasoning
- Develops personal reflective practice

Effective Communication
- Acknowledges and appropriately communicates in situations with divergent opinions and values

Self-Knowledge
- Continually explores and examines values and views

Principled Action
- Demonstrates congruence between actions and values
- Bases actions on thoughtful consideration of their impact and consequences

Key Concepts and Definitions

Intent/Impact   One's intent does not always match the impact of their actions. Whether or not you intend the consequences of your actions to be a certain way, you must always take responsibility for their impact. This is because the values that inform one's actions are unique to their experience and will often differ from the experiences and values of others.

Action/Reaction   Like intent/impact, the actions of one can affect the reactions of others in unpredictable ways. If you are the sum total of your reactions, then your actions will reflect the way you see and respond to the world. It is important to be aware of the factors that may influence one's actions. This knowledge will help one to control their reactions and consider their response more thoughtfully.

Required Materials

- Selected scenarios relevant to the context of the participants (i.e., first-year college students)

Session Outline

Session duration: 1 hour 50 minutes

Time Required		Description
10 minutes	Introduction	In their discussion groups, group facilitators give an overview of the session outline and review or set any ground rules for participating, as necessary.
20 minutes	Framing	In their groups, participants discuss these reflection questions based on last session's Bridge Activity:
		What was it like to have someone else identify what they thought you valued? Where were they right? Where were they wrong? What actions, behaviors, or insights shaped their selection of your values? Did you share values? How did/didn't your values complement each other?
		In the large group, review the following key takeaways: The values we believe we have might be different from the values others believe we have. Our actions might not always reflect our espoused values. We can appreciate the differences in our values, and we can also acknowledge the tensions that can arise when members of an immediate community do not share the same values.
15 minutes	Discussion	Use the following questions to guide a discussion on immediate community:
		How do our friends in various stages in our life (e.g., high school, college, workplace) differ, and how does this impact us? How do our friends reflect on us, and how do they shape our values, opinions and actions? How would you describe how you fit in during this current stage of your life?
		Read the prompting quote: *"You are the average of the five people you spend the most time with"* (attributed to motivational speaker, Jim Rohn). You may also wish to provide the quote on a piece of paper in each participant's folder. Discuss whether participants agree or disagree and why. Discuss if, how, and why we act differently with different people.

Time Required		Description
		Review the following key takeaways: Our values and behaviors are often shaped by those around us. Going to new places and surrounding ourselves with new people often calls our own identity into question. In adjusting to a new community, we might feel pressure to minimize our own values to fit into a perceived norm.
20 minutes	Activity	Each facilitator will have selected a few scenarios prior to the session to discuss with their group. Participants will evaluate scenarios of conflict relevant to their first year and new college environment (e.g., roommate conflicts, social pressure, group projects). Provide discussion questions for each individual scenario.
		Review the following key takeaways: In difficult ethical situations, often it is not just our values conflicting with another's values, but several of our own values conflicting (e.g., If a friend acts in a way you disagree with, you might feel conflicted between acting on your value of integrity to call out the friend, and acting on the value of friendship to prioritize the relationship you have with this person). It is easy to talk about our values in isolation, but living our values may become much more complicated when we must navigate the many complex communities we are a part of. Sometimes, our core values do not align with our behavior, but this does not make us bad people because congruity is something we strive for.
30 minutes	Discussion	Each group will define intent/impact, action/reaction for themselves. Facilitators can use the following guiding questions to develop the conversation: *In scenarios of misunderstanding, hurt or harm, does intent matter? Does positive intent absolve a negative impact? Even if you had positive intent, should you still rectify the harm? How can our behavior affect others? How might others perceive our behavior differently from how we perceive it?*
		Facilitators should ask participants to draw on relevant examples of conflicts that reflect clashes in values or misunderstandings and consider whether they were related to a dichotomy of intent/impact. Ask: *What were the actions, perceptions and/or misperceptions that led to that conflict? How did people react to negative consequences? Where does fault lie? What is your opinion as an observer of this situation versus if you were taking part in it?*

Time Required		Description
		In the large group, read the following prompting quote: *"Every man is the sum total of his reactions to experience"* (attributed to writer Hunter S. Thompson). Ask participants what this means, whether they agree or disagree, and why. Review the following key takeaways: You can't always control your immediate emotional response to a situation, but you can control how you react and channel that response. We should own our impact, regardless of our intent; part of owning our impact and intent is recognizing that what we do does not always define us. Seek to understand the influence your personal experiences have on your reactions and to understand where someone else's reactions are coming from.
5 minutes	Framing	Introduce the Bridge Activity, which will bridge today's activities with the next session. Read the prompt: *Consider the values you see on display in the current community in which you live and submit three photos representing each of these "lived" values.*
10 minutes	Conclusion	End the session with a summary of how the discussions tied to the objectives of this session. Ask participants to complete the session evaluation using your desired format. Close the session by thanking the participants and facilitators.

Reflection Questions

- How do my experiences and identities influence the way I react to situations?
- How do clashes in values influence the climate we're living in?

Participant Reflection

This session's emphasis on examining my values and the values of those around me has had a profound lasting impression on me. I learned how my surroundings influence me, and how I may influence my surroundings. Even two years later, I distinctly remember the conversation I had with the friend I asked to do my "bridge activity" with. By taking a moment to consider the values that bond me with my friends and my community, I felt more connected than ever to those who mattered most to me.

D-LAB Winter 2019

Supplemental Resources

Crowley, M. (2020, June 5). *How to build and rebuild trust* (No. 50) [Audio podcast]. http://markccrowley. com/frances-frei-how-to-build-and-rebuild-trust/

Dasborough, M. T., & Ashkanasy, N. M. (2002). Emotion and attribution of intentionality in leader– member relationships. *The Leadership Quarterly*, *13*(5), 615–634. https://doi.org/10.1016/S1048- 9843(02)00147-9

This session has been formatted and revised for consistency and clarity. The original session in the Dartmouth Leadership Attitudes and Behaviors Program was facilitated by program alumni.

Session 3.4 Leadership for Others (Part I)

Session Description

In this session, participants will explore the community and institutional values that influence their experiences in their current life stage (e.g., high school, college, workplace). They will discuss the ways these values interact with their own values and how to navigate differences that may exist. Participants will analyze their institution's values as stated in its mission statement and definition of community and discuss how these stated values relate to the values they observe every day. Students will engage in a discussion about integrity and will broaden previous conversations about how individuals live their values in order to examine how institutions live their values.

Leadership Competencies Addressed
Principled Action   • Identifies and commits to appropriate ethical framework   • Demonstrates personal responsibility   • Appropriately challenges the unethical behavior of individuals or groups

Learning Objectives

Participants will do the following:
- Articulate the values they perceive in their communities
- Assess how their personal values interact with their community as a whole
- Identify at least three ways in which they can help make their community a community of integrity

Key Concepts and Definitions

Integrity   Integrity is demonstrated through actions that are in accordance with established values. This is true on the individual and institutional levels. Integrity is a matter of your word—nothing more, nothing less. If you break your word to someone, you are out of integrity. This results in lack of trust and confidence. That further results in loss of credibility. If you are a leader, people will follow you because of your positional authority and not your moral authority. You can always say you are sorry to those you broke your word to and tell them how you will fix the mess you made. Then fix the mess you made! The person who has fixed the mess often ends up regaining trust and credibility. So, try to keep your word— to yourself and to others.

Required Materials

- Photo packet for each facilitation group with its members' submissions from the previous Bridge Activity
- Printouts of Organizational Mission Statement, Core Values Statement, and Definition of Community for any organization of your choice
- Post-its (variety of colors)
- Writing utensils
- Chart paper for each group
- Specific materials for writing activity, if requested

Session Outline

Session duration: 2 hours 10 minutes

Time Required		Description
10 minutes	Introduction	As participants join their facilitation groups, have facilitators distribute to them their photos from last session's Bridge Activity. Share the session agenda and its objectives and thank participants for submitting their photos. Begin with a short discussion about why they have been talking about values in the context of leadership. Review the key messages from the previous three sessions.
50 minutes	Framing	Facilitators will ask participants to lay out all the photos from the Bridge Activity and take notes on their thoughts, interpretations, and reactions. One participant will volunteer to identify one of their three photos. Facilitators will use the following questions to guide discussion: *What did you take a picture of? Why did you choose this? How does it represent your organization's lived values? If you had to assign it a word or brief phrase, what would it be? What else did you consider photographing to represent the same value?*
		After they have explained their photo, ask if there are other participants who took photos to represent the same value or concept. Have them group these photos together. Another participant should go next and select one of their photos that represents a value or idea that has not already been discussed.

Time Required	**Description**
	Follow the same process as above. Continue until all participants have shared about at least one of their photos. If you reach a point where all remaining photos have already been grouped together, remaining participants should select any one of their photos to discuss.
	After the photo identification exercise, facilitators will guide a discussion about their reactions to this exercise and how the institutional values come into relation with their own individual values. Participants will answer the following questions: *When you viewed the photos without explanation at the beginning of the exercise, did you interpret them the same way as the photographer? If yes/no, why do you think that is? As you are comfortable, share your thoughts on why you selected the values you did (and potentially, why did you choose to represent it with the photo you did?). What observations or experiences here have shaped your responses? Were there any of the photographs or explanations that surprised you, and why?*
	Looking over this full collection of photographs, do you think that it accurately captures the values expressed in your institution? Does it paint too rosy/grim of a picture? Are there ways in which the collage we've created is incomplete or misleading? Does anyone feel like it doesn't reflect their reality in the institution?
	Connect back to individual values: *How do these communal values reflect YOUR values…or not? How would a collage representing your personal values look similar or different? How is the community you just described similar to/different from a community that would align with your individual values? What are the challenges you experience in living your values here? How do we navigate differences between these values? How do you see individuals shaping the community's values? Conversely, how do you see this community shaping your/others' individual values? What is the effect of dissonance between your individual values and your community's values? Given this dissonance, what does it mean for you to "live authentically" wherever you are?*

Time Required	Description
	In the large group, review the following key takeaways: Our differing identities and affiliations shape the way we experience our community, and our experiences shape the way we perceive our institution's values. Our individual values may not align with the institutional values we perceive, so we must navigate this tension between our core values and the core values of the larger institutions of which we are a part. Our institution's perceived values influence us as individuals, but we as individuals can also influence the way our institution lives its values. The ways we experience values different from our own may challenge our integrity or the ease with which we live our values.
50 minutes Discussion	Have participants now examine their institution's Mission Statement, Core Values Statement, and the Definition of Community (or any similar materials in your specific context). Looking at these documents, what would they identify as their institution's primary "espoused" values? In their facilitation groups, participants will discuss these values. Facilitators should choose the format for discussion—pairs, triads, small groups, or full group discussion. It is suggested that facilitators vary strategies for exploring these questions: *What values did you identify as your institution's espoused values? Is there an incongruence between what your institution states as its values and what people experience as the community's values? Who is responsible for that? Who can impact it? How does an institution demonstrate or "live" its values?*
	Review the following key takeaway in the large group: We as a community should invest in taking responsibility for the incongruence between what the college states that it values and what people experience as the community's values.
	In their groups, facilitators read the following and discuss: *We talked in our second session about what it means for an individual to act with integrity. What does it mean for a community or institution to act with integrity? How does it relate to espoused vs. experienced values? What makes it hard for an institution to act with integrity? What role do we as members of our community have in helping our institution act in line with its values? What if we disagree with the institution's values? How do we represent this institution and its values to those outside our institution?*

Time Required		Description
		In the large group, review the following key takeaways: Just as individuals struggle to live their values with integrity, so do institutions. We as community members are responsible to help our institution to act in line with its values; we are also responsible to challenge the way our institution lives its values. Reflecting on our own integrity allows us to better connect to the idea of institutional integrity.
10 minutes	Activity	Facilitators read the following writing prompt to their participants: *Over the last few weeks, we've explored our values and how they influence our behaviors and interactions with others. We've explored how our friends and associations shape us, and the impact we can have on them in return. We've talked now about your individual values, as well as our institutional values. What have these activities and conversations provoked for you? How will you demonstrate integrity here? How will you shape our institution's values, and how will you let its values shape you? What action steps can you take to lead and live with integrity and authenticity?*
		Participants are free to write but are encouraged to use an open-ended form like poetry or drawing to express their ideas. They will discuss their work in pairs.
5 minutes	Framing	Introduce the Bridge Activity, which will bridge today's activities with the next session. Participants will submit problems or issues at their institution or in their community that they have seen or confronted. This would be institutional/community-level problems rather than specific individual incidents.
5 minutes	Conclusion	Ask participants to complete the session evaluation using your desired format. Close the session by thanking the participants and facilitators.

Reflection Questions

- How do community values and individual values interrelate and influence one another?
- What is my role in helping my community live its values?

Participant Reflection

Being able to see pictures taken by my peers of what our community means to them was a privilege. This session allowed me to learn from my peers about how our values can manifest in different ways within the same community or even the same experience. Gaining insight by listening to everybody's stories and learning something new about them that I wouldn't have picked up from simply by looking at their picture was particularly meaningful. Since this session, I've approached situations thinking about how someone with different values might be thinking differently from myself.

D-LAB Winter 2020

Supplemental Resources

Etzioni, A. (2018). *Law and society in a populist age: Balancing individual rights and the common good.* Bristol University Press. https://doi.org/10.2307/j.ctv56fgtg

Kraemer, H. M. J. (2011). *From values to action: The four principles of values-based leadership.* Jossey-Bass.

Sternbergh, B., & Weitzel, S. (2001). *Setting your development goals: Start with your values.* Center for Creative Leadership.

This session has been formatted and revised for consistency and clarity. The original session in the Dartmouth Leadership Attitudes and Behaviors Program was facilitated by program alumni.

Session 3.5 Leadership for Others (Part II)

Session Description

In this session, participants will discuss community concerns through an exercise of collectively ranking their peers' submissions. They will consider how their identities and experiences connect to the ways they prioritize these concerns and what the resulting implications are for community membership. They will reflect on their own role in shaping the future of these problems through their leadership, attitudes, and behaviors.

Learning Objectives

Participants will do the following:
- Analyze how their perceived top concerns relate to their identities and experiences
- Prioritize personal concerns first, and then community concerns collectively while navigating intersections of identity and experience
- Devise a plan to act as community agents with the power to influence the status quo

Leadership Competencies Addressed

Collaboration
- Acknowledges and listens to different voices when making decisions and taking action

Effective Communication
- Acknowledges and appropriately communicates in situations with divergent opinions and values

Effective Reasoning
- Integrates multiple types of information to effectively solve problems or address issues

Principled Action
- Bases actions on thoughtful consideration of their impact and consequences

Intercultural Mindset
- Understands, communicates with, and respectfully interacts with people across identities

Key Concepts and Definitions

Ranking	We are effectively ranking the realities participants face and should be sensitive to the fact that problems are not abstract but directly related to participants' lives.
Interdependence	These community concerns aren't issues in isolation and therefore addressing one of these concerns is often linked to addressing others.
Intersections of identity	We can acknowledge that different identities and experiences often lead to a different set of priorities when it comes to community concerns;

however, we can still engage respectfully with participants whose priorities are different from our own. We often understand and prioritize only the problems that directly affect us. It is paramount to widen our perspectives to overcome privilege and address all community concerns.

Agency

Addressing these community concerns may seem daunting, yet our interpersonal interactions and our interventions in our smaller communities always have an impact on the larger community. While we can't always control our emotional reactions to these problems, we can be intentional about what we do next through our leadership, attitudes, and behaviors.

Acknowledging community imperfections

It's possible to love your community and acknowledge that it still has problems. It's also okay to not love it all the time.

Required Materials

- List of all submitted community concerns from the previous Bridge Activity printed for each participant

Session Outline

Session duration: 1 hour 55 minutes

Time Required		Description
5 minutes	Introduction	Recap the previous session and highlight key points. Discuss issues that came up that need further clarification.
60 minutes	Framing	In their facilitation groups, give each participant a list of community concerns compiled from participants' submissions from last session's Bridge Activity. Have them brainstorm any additions to the list and individually rank their top 10 perceived problems from most important to least important. Ask participants to share their thoughts in pairs, focusing specifically on their top three problems. Ask how their values intersect with these community concerns. Facilitators now ask their group to reach a consensus after they have rank-identified community concerns based on their importance or perceived severity. Facilitators read the following before beginning the group discussion: *As you engage in this attempt*

Time Required		**Description**
		to rank these problems, please remember that your peers and group members may feel differently or experience these problems in different ways than you have. We ask that you engage in honest but respectful discussion as you attempt to prioritize these community concerns, but most importantly we ask that you listen to each other with open minds.
		Facilitators decide ahead of time whether they would prefer their group to rank all problems or just the top five. They should consider the sensitive nature of ranking these problems and assess what kind of activity would be most appropriate for their group. This is intentionally designed to be difficult for participants. By the end of this session participants should recognize that their peers may have different but equally valid concerns about community concerns. Offer support to facilitators in preparing for this conversation.
40 minutes	Discussion	Debrief with the following discussion questions: *Reflect on the process of ranking values: Was consensus easy or difficult to achieve? What made this task difficult? Were any concerns you see as primary issues missing from this list? What are the different perspectives surrounding each problem? How do those perspectives arise? What values/conflicts created these problems? Were there differences in problem rankings among different people? What might account for those differences? How did you feel if someone ranked a problem that was important to you as not so important? What is the use of trying to rank these problems? How does this parallel the way we engage with these problems in our actual lives?*
		What are possible resolutions to the problems we discussed above? Where does responsibility lie? What do you think is your role in addressing these problems? Sometimes serious issues and concerns can seem insurmountable; can you think of times when small actions created noticeable changes in collective understanding, the environment, or lived experiences? This could be a time when you addressed something or someone else addressed your behavior.
		When discussing these questions, make sure to cover the key concepts and definitions.
5 minutes	Framing	Introduce the Bridge Activity, which will bridge today's activities with the next session. Participants will answer the following questions: *From a leadership lens, what matters to me and*

Time Required		Description
		why? What do I want my personal and community experiences to look like? How will it engage with my values? How have these discussions about community problems impacted my goals for my role in my community?
		Participants should also be prepared to comment and reflect on their progress towards the goals they set for themselves in Session 3.2.
5 minutes	Conclusion	Remind participants to strive to collaborate with each other on issues, even if it's not what they are most passionate about. Progress for one is progress for all. Urge them to have real conversations about these problems in their communities, to engage with each other respectfully, and recognize their personal agency in shaping the future of these concerns. Ask participants to complete the session evaluation using your desired format. Close the session by thanking the participants and facilitators.

Reflection Questions

- How does my identity expose and protect me from different problems in my community or institution?
- What can I do as an empowered individual to help improve issues in the community?

Supplemental Resources

Battilana, J. (2016). Agency and institutions: The enabling role of individuals' social position. *Organization*. https://doi.org/10.1177/1350508406067008

Plank, K. M. (2019). Intersections of identity and power in educational development. *New Directions for Teaching and Learning, 2019*(159), 85–96. https://doi.org/10.1002/tl.20351

Skillsoft YouTube. (2017, July 7). *Prioritizing tasks to pinpoint your priorities* [Video]. YouTube. https://www.youtube.com/watch?v=Ftf1kMZN-HQ&ab_channel=SkillsoftYouTube

Participant Reflection

This session was the first time that I ever felt comfortable being honest in openly criticizing Dartmouth. I learned that there are ways to both appreciate the opportunity I have in attending this institution while also actively trying to find ways to improve upon its shortfalls at the same time because of our values. It was grounding to learn from my peers about concerns and adversity that they had faced that I had barely given any thought to despite the fact that we share this community and the experiences that come along with it.

D-LAB Winter 2020

This session has been formatted and revised for consistency and clarity. The original session in the Dartmouth Leadership Attitudes and Behaviors Program was facilitated by program alumni.

Session 3.6 Leadership in Practice

Session Description

In this session, participants shift their focus to next steps. With a deeper sense of self and community, participants will examine a decision about which they may be uncertain. The session will begin with a panel discussion from group facilitators on what they find meaningful in their own organizations and experiences, and the insights that a few years have brought. The rest of the time in the program will be spent with the participants looking introspectively at a decision they are contemplating.

Learning Objectives

Participants will do the following:
- Reflect on a decision or change they have been considering and determine the desire, ability, reasons, and need for this possible change
- Evaluate the opportunities presented in the facilitator panel and determine which ones are applicable to their own lives

Leadership Competencies Addressed

Collaboration
- Encourages, supports, and recognizes the contributions of others

Principled Action
- Demonstrates personal responsibility

Effective Reasoning
- Engages in inquiry, analysis, and follow-through

Management
- Develops and implements a plan for goal attainment

Self-Knowledge
- Seeks opportunities for continued growth

Key Concepts and Definitions

Your place within a community

You can imagine your place within a community in two ways: the way you interact with it and the ways it influences you. This external engagement can look like the activities, organizations, physical spaces, and social interactions you are a part of. On the other hand, one can find their place through a process of self-reflection: reflecting on your personal impact on community and reflecting on the community impact on your personal values and experiences.

Required Materials

- Panelists' tables and chairs set up in a row facing the room
- Handout 3.6.1 Turning Points Activity (printed for each participant)

Session Outline

Session duration: 2 hours 5 minutes

Time Required		Description
5 minutes	Introduction	This session will begin with all participants together, instead of in their facilitation groups. Provide an overview of the program thus far: Participants reflected on their individual values and examined whether these values inform their daily life, engaged their values with their friends and evaluated values in situations of conflict, and navigated their values in the context of their wider community and sought integrity within this context. Introduce the purpose of Session 3.6, thereby linking the effort that participants have put into knowing what is important to them with acting on what's important to them.
40 minutes	Discussion	Turn attention to the facilitator panel. Some of the facilitators will speak about their most meaningful experiences during their time at their institution. Two facilitators will moderate the panel with the discussion questions below: *Describe the activities you are involved in. How do these involvements allow you to impact your community? How have they impacted your sense of community? How did you find your spaces within your organization? How do the spaces you inhabit impact your values? How do your values impact those spaces? Have your values changed at all over your time in your institution? How so? How have the people you spend your time with influenced your values? Have your values been challenged within your institution? How so? What advice would you give to your younger self? Tell us about an unexpected experience you have had in your organization that changed you. Can you tell us about a goal you set for yourself and how you accomplished that goal? Can you tell us about the impact your community has had on your experience? How do you think you've impacted your community? How do you engage with this community?* After the discussion, participants return to their facilitation groups.

Time Required		**Description**
45 minutes	Activity	Facilitators should divide their groups into groups of four or five participants. Then introduce the Turning Points Activity with the following prompt:

As you go through your time at your institution, there are moments and decisions that will steer your experience in different directions. These turning points are places where you have the ability to choose in which direction you want to go.

Different parts of this program may have touched on what these turning points could be for you. For instance, we discussed how our lived values may not reflect our lived experience; we touched on the concept of integrity and what it means to live with integrity; and we discussed and explored issues in this community.

A large goal of this program is to help you be more intentional with the choices you make. In this exercise we are going to explore ideas of how you choose to spend your time. This could be a change you want to make, a practice you want to incorporate, an experience you may want to have, or a transition away from activities you find less fulfilling.

Tell participants to take five minutes to think about what this idea/experience/desire/transition is for them. It needs to be something they are willing to share and discuss, and something that is not necessarily a quick or easy decision. Tell participants that each person will have an opportunity to share their idea. Then the rest of the group will, in turn, each ask a question from Handout 3.6.1 to help the individual reflect. Facilitators hand out one question sheet to each person. The questions are designed to help think through this potential change or shift. The group will need one person to volunteer to go first. To begin, they will introduce the turning point they have been considering and explain its context. The group will listen to their thoughts, and then the person to their right will ask the first question. The group will continue around the circle until all of the questions have been asked. It is okay if one person ends up asking multiple questions.

Time Required		Description
10 minutes	Debrief	In the large group, explain that the questions in the Turning Points Activity were intended to help them think through the desire, ability, reason(s), and need to make this possible change or articulate the next step in their lives. Review the following reflection questions: *How would you have answered these questions differently if this were the first week of the program? In what ways is talking about your own personal circumstances different from looking at others? Think about scenarios, examples shared, issues discussed. How can you apply introspection and self-knowledge when you are leading others?*
15 minutes	Reflection	Facilitators will now ask some final reflection questions in their facilitation groups. Facilitators, having led their group for five weeks now, may come up with their own questions. The primary themes for participant reflection are reflecting on learning from this program and considering their future plans. Facilitators may use the following reflection questions: *What did you learn about yourself from the past few weeks? What is something you learned or heard from someone else that has made you think differently or more deeply about your experience? Looking at the goals you set for yourself earlier in the program, how successful do you think you were in achieving them? How do you feel about that? And why? Were they realistic goals? Reflecting on your core values and goals we discussed early in the program, do your goals address the values you are struggling to live by? Do you want to reconsider which values you are hoping to address? Looking forward to the coming years in your organization, can you answer this question, "What matters to me and why?" How will the answer to this question impact your leadership? Reflecting on your experience within your organization so far, what are you doing that aligns with your values? Do some things serve another purpose? Anything you want to reconsider? What is missing?*
10 minutes	Conclusion	Conclude this program by thanking participants for their participation. Highlight key discussions participants had related to self-awareness, values clarification, working with others, building a community mission, and addressing an organizational goal. Ask participants to complete the program evaluation using your desired format. Close the program by thanking the participants and facilitators one last time.

Reflection Questions

- What do I want my experience in this current stage of my life to look like?
- What have I learned about myself and others from being a part of this program?

Supplemental Resources

Cefrey, Holly. (2000). *Everything you need to know about the art of leadership: How to be a positive influence in your home, school, and community* (1st ed.). Rosen Pub. Group.

Talks at Google. (2017, August 28). *Inclusion: Diversity, the new workplace & the will to change | Jennifer Brown | Talks at Google* [Video]. YouTube. https://www.youtube.com/watch?v=06-Js35QwPY&feature=youtu.be&ab_channel=TalksatGoogle

Venkataraman, B. (2019, April). *The power to think ahead in a reckless age* [Video]. TED Conferences. https://www.ted.com/talks/bina_venkataraman_the_power_to_think_ahead_in_a_reckless_age

This session has been formatted and revised for consistency and clarity. The original session in the Dartmouth Leadership Attitudes and Behaviors Program was facilitated by program alumni.

Participant Reflection

As D-LAB concludes with this session, it is clear to me how much I have learned about myself over the course of the program. D-LAB has trained me to be more intentional with my actions and to be mindful of how I affect those around me. Compared to six weeks ago, I see significant growth in terms of how I set my goals and expectations for myself. Now that I know myself and my values better, as well as the factors that influence each, I feel prepared to participate and lead meaningfully in my communities.

D-LAB Winter 2019

Turning Points Activity

(Desire)   Why would you want to make this change?

(Ability)   How might you go about it in order to succeed?

(Reason)   What are the three best reasons for you to do it?

(Need)   How important is it for you to make this change, and why?

Summarize what has been said, and then ask:

(Commitment)   So, what do you think you'll do?

D-LAB Program Officer Reflection

By Hannah Andritsakis

In January of 2020, I joined the Rockefeller Center as the Dartmouth Leadership Attitudes and Behaviors (D-LAB) program transitioned from its planning phase to the implementation phase. In those following weeks I carried a small purple notebook all around campus. During team meetings, facilitator training, and sessions, I captured my observations, as well as what I was thinking and feeling in those moments.

When I first met the student facilitators, I was moved by their desire to be mentors to their first-year peers. I noticed how they provided each other with constructive feedback during their training, in which they had the opportunity to try shortened versions of sessions. In my opinion, these facilitators were well selected because they were coachable and eager to learn.

D-LAB is a collaborative program. At its core lives the partnership between Student Life, Residential Life, and the Rockefeller Center. I observed this partnership as it fulfilled a variety of purposes. First, it helped to expand the reach of the program to a greater student audience. Second, it helped expand the locations where the program takes place. Third, it helped to expand resources, time, money, and people power. Fourth, it helped everyone involved to have a full picture of the student journey.

In the transition to remote work caused by the COVID-19 pandemic in March of 2020, the D-LAB team felt uncertain. We wondered how we should be moving forward. What would the program look like in Winter 2021? Would we be in-person, hybrid, or virtual? These questions swirled as we tried to press on. We evaluated the recent program feedback on the assumption that regardless of the upcoming format, at least some of it would be useful to us. As the weeks progressed and administrative decisions unfolded it became clear that if D-LAB were to take place, it would need to be a virtual program. We now had a direction in which to channel our energy.

I became excited by the opportunity to redesign and launch yet another virtual program! As a team, we constructed a timeline to visualize our weeks until program launch. We then identified and focused on our three primary concerns: learning outcomes, time, and recruitment.

We reviewed the D-LAB curriculum. With Zoom fatigue in the back of our minds, we determined what to adapt for either synchronous or asynchronous delivery and what to put aside for now. We arrived at eight weekly, one-hour sessions with 15 minutes of asynchronous exercises. D-LAB would be offered at various times each week to accommodate time zones. We decided to use tools such as Slack, OneNote, and Miro.com to help us deliver this program in an interactive, user-friendly, secure manner.

The program rolled out in January 2021 and I am proud of the work we have accomplished. However, there are some things I would do differently based on the lessons I have learned.

I transitioned into leading the D-LAB team remotely without having met everyone in person, being unsure of the direction of the program, and being unsure of whether I was taking the lead. In the first few meetings, I struggled to find my footing. Looking back, I should have met with my professional staff colleagues and defined our roles before our first team Zoom meeting. This would have reduced the ambiguity of navigating a virtual collaboration earlier in the planning process. I should have set up separate check-in meetings with team members to get to know everyone outside of our team Zoom meetings and do a pulse check. I should have done team builders or engaged in before- or after-meeting small talk earlier in the process. I value efficiency and staying on task. I enjoy being part of a team, but I can have a hard time being present and engaging in team builders or small talk because I want to maximize working time. In person, I have relied on being able to share meals or aligning myself with a colleague or student assistant who complements my skills.

This experience has shown me the value in making intentional time for well-placed team builders and small talk. I found making the time for your team to connect with one another helps you all be more productive, innovative, and creative during working time. I now value connection and efficiency more than ever. I see they are not an either/or but a powerful combination that leads to more fulfilling work. Moving forward, I will embrace conversations about role clarity earlier and make efforts for team connection both virtually and in person.

As we move forward with D-LAB in the coming years I would like us to expand our reach and reduce our attrition. The lessons learned from our remote transition might just be able to help us. Some ideas for consideration are as follows:

> ➢ Time offered: Can we remove the barrier to participation due to such things as time zone differences or internet connectivity by thinking more innovatively now?
> ➢ Intent: Can we develop asynchronous videos that review the intent behind a session and how it connects to leadership?
> ➢ Community-building: What are some of the ways we can cultivate community and connection after a time of disconnection?

4 First-Year Fellows (FYF) Program

In an age where community involvement and partnerships with civil society
are increasingly being recognized as indispensable, there is clearly a growing
potential for cooperative development and renewal worldwide.

-Kofi Annan

Program Goal

The program goal is to prepare participants to understand the importance of public policy and leadership for its intended population and to practice the skills and competencies they need to have as managers and as leaders. It is the first step they take to develop personal and professional practices to grow as leaders. This program is also important in cultivating interest in the Center's public policy minor and other co-curricular programs offered by the Center.

Program Prerequisites

There are three prerequisites for First-Year Fellows (FYF): successful completion of the Rockefeller Center's Introduction to Public Policy course; participation in D-LAB; and one introductory statistics course.

Program Participation

Like all the co-curricular offerings, this program values diversity. For instance, since the 2014–2015 cohort, we have attracted students who intend to major in 19 different fields, ranging from the humanities and arts to STEM. Though this data represents what students expect to study at Dartmouth, a retroactive analysis of FYF participants suggests that these students largely continued to pursue their intended majors. Table 4.1 outlines the top 10 intended majors for FYF participants. Since the summer of 2015, the five most popular (intended) majors for fellows were, in descending order: government, economics, history, computer science, and quantitative social science.

Table 4.1

Ten Most Popular Expected Majors for FYF Participants (2015–2020)

Intended Major	Number of Participants
Government	68
Economics	29
History	5
Computer Science	5
Quantitative Social Science	4
Geography	3
Environmental Studies	2
English	2
Middle Eastern Studies	1
Philosophy	1

FYF has served 81 female and 81 male participants since the spring of 2015. The effort to achieve gender balance is intentional and allows for robust discussions during the program.

The number of participants who completed FYF from 2015 to 2020 ranged from 22 to 26. There have been no dropouts since the program's inception except for one student. Evaluations suggest that the students find this program rigorous, relevant, and well organized. Students also report developing a strong sense of community as a result of participating in the program. Only a few international students participate in this program due to the visa and regulatory issues in the U.S. and the resulting inability of this program to place them in congressional or other organizations. Each year, the program is revised based on feedback received from participants and mentors.

Key Program Elements

➤ Prerequisites designed to give participants a strong foundation of industry-specific information and skills
➤ Opportunities for participants to practice the skills gained in Civic Skills Training (CST) prior to the start of their placements with mentors
➤ Committed mentors and organizations that will provide participants with engaging, meaningful internship placements and provide timely feedback
➤ Continued assessment and evaluation from multiple stakeholders, including program participants

Program Description

The First-Year Fellows Program was established in 2007 and is designed for students in the first year of their undergraduate experience. Each year, 20–25 students are selected for summer placement in a diverse range of policy fellowships in Washington, D.C. with Dartmouth alumni mentors. Some examples include fellowships in senate offices, think tanks, national and international NGOs, and media. The program aims to prepare participants for their first professional experience and reinforce their commitment to and interest in public policy.

FYF is an ideal stepping stone for students interested in developing their leadership skills and gaining early exposure to policy and government. During their fellowships, students gain valuable professional experience, live with their peers, and develop leadership, writing, and critical thinking skills. Fellowships, in any field, are especially valuable to students entering the workforce or holding an internship for the first time.

The prerequisites for FYF give all applicants the necessary background for entering a summer fellowship with an organization in Washington D.C. These serve as foundational learning experiences, even for those who do not get selected for a fellowship. If selected, they also complete the Civic Skills Training (CST) Program before their fellowship with alumni mentors in government, nonprofit institutions, and media.

The introductory policy course provides first-year participants with a combination of the necessary theoretical frameworks related to the public policy-making process prior to further studies and hands-on work in the field.

The Dartmouth Leadership Attitudes and Behaviors (D-LAB) Program highlighted in Chapter 3, engages first-year participants in critical thinking and reflection about their own leadership capacities and their respective communities; it requires that participants consider the ways in which they are impacted by and have the potential to impact their cultures and communities, both at Dartmouth and as leaders elsewhere.

Finally, the introductory statistics course gives students the opportunity to develop the increasingly critical data science skills in a content area of their interest (e.g., public policy, economics, government, mathematics, psychology, sociology, quantitative social science, geography, education) necessary to succeed in a policy fellowship.

Before their fellowships begin, students selected as First-Year Fellows attend four Civic Skills Training sessions on campus during the spring term and an additional five days of training in Washington, D.C. The training includes meetings and sessions around the city, including a visit to Dartmouth alumni serving in the U.S. Senate and House of Representatives. To broaden their network and to practice their networking skills, they participate in a Dartmouth Student and Alumni Reception in Washington, D.C. The curriculum builds cumulatively in order to provide a comprehensive and coherent picture of the public and nonprofit sectors. Training sessions include topics such as public speaking, networking, professional communication strategies, team building, advocacy writing, project management, and professionalism. Participants enjoy additional activities such as learning from young alumni about their experiences in the civic sphere and attending a dining experience that teaches participants about professional etiquette related to networking, lunches, and dinners. At the conclusion of the Civic Skills Training Program, Fellows begin their 8-week fellowships. Mentors and fellowship placement organizations commit to providing the students meaningful work, first-hand experiences in the policymaking process, and advice about potential career placement possibilities.

Key Leadership Competencies

These competencies are for the entire program, consisting of the curricular and co-curricular components which include D-LAB, CST, and Summer Fellowships. The program focuses on self-knowledge, communication skills, principled action, effective reasoning, and collaboration.

Possible Adaptations

Using these key elements, you could adapt FYF for participants who are entering the workforce in any field. Whether you are in a profit or nonprofit organization or institution, you could do the following:

> ➢ Develop an in-person or online course covering essential information and technical skills needed for an employee to excel at the job. You could also create handouts or reference lists for additional "good-to-know" information. You might then develop a series of sessions related to values, professionalism, and practical experiences for incoming employees.
> ➢ Create networking opportunities and emphasize their relevance to learning and fund-raising.
> ➢ Develop a mentoring program (in person or online) for new hires, with mentor participation from within or without the organization to aid in their transition to your workplace. Mentoring programs can also be developed for personnel moving into new positions.
> ➢ Have new hires participate in interactive sessions that explain your workplace culture, norms, and expectations.
> ➢ Develop or revise a framework for assessing and evaluating results.

You could adapt every aspect of this program or you could selectively adapt aspects depending on what practices you already have in place.

Important Note

A full description of D-LAB (a prerequisite for this program) is provided in Chapter 3. This chapter ends with the program officer's reflection on CST and Summer Fellowships, with some brief thoughts about D-LAB. The following pages describe each of these two remaining components.

FYF: Civic Skills Training (CST)

Program Goal

To help participants learn about the public policy process, develop and practice communication, management, and leadership skills, gain professional experience, and live and work independently with their peers in Washington, D.C.

Program Prerequisites

Open only to First-Year Fellows who have completed Public Policy 5: Introduction to Public Policy; a social science statistical methods course; and the Dartmouth Leadership, Attitudes, and Behaviors Program (D-LAB).

Key Program Elements

➢ Alumni expertise and involvement
➢ Participants interested in Public Policy as a career
➢ Creation of a simulated workweek by intentionally setting training day times and assigning work during and between sessions
➢ Interactive innovative sessions and experiences centered around essential, industry-specific knowledge, technical skills, workplace culture, norms, and professionalism, with sessions incorporating needs identified by mentors
➢ Cohort-building to develop relationships and set the stage for a living learning team

Program Description

CST is a component of the First-Year Fellows (FYF) Program. The roots of this program can be traced back to when it was offered four times a year as a standalone program in Washington, D.C. for 12 to 15 students from all class years. It was designed to inform students about the structures and processes of the political world and provide them with technical skills necessary to excel in their internships and beyond. After evaluation and deliberation, it was determined that the program would need to be scaled down to once a year and offered only to participants selected for the First-Year Fellows Program. The program needed to become cost efficient and be built to address the maturity and experience of one student group instead of trying to be everything to everyone.

Participants selected as First-Year Fellows attend four on-campus training sessions during the spring term and an additional five days of training in Washington, D.C. before their fellowships begin. The on-campus sessions provide an opportunity for the selected students to get to know each other and build a sense of community.

In Washington D.C., the training includes meetings and sessions around the city, including a visit to Congressional offices in which alumni serve senators and members of the House of Representatives. The program also hosts a networking reception for alumni, friends of the program, and participants in Washington, D.C. The curriculum builds cumulatively in order to provide a comprehensive and coherent picture of the public and nonprofit sectors. It also creates an understanding of the relationship between for-profit and nonprofit institutions in the civic sphere.

Training sessions facilitated by Dartmouth alumni and the Center's staff include topics such as public speaking, networking, professional communication strategies, team building, advocacy writing, project management, professionalism, and research methods.

One of the many silver linings that has resulted from our exploration into virtual programming is the possibility of returning CST to its roots. For example, we are looking at creating a virtual conference-style program for internship preparation that would be offered to a larger group of students across campus. A virtual offering will be more cost efficient, and the flexible nature would allow us to meet different levels of maturity and experience.

Key Leadership Competencies

CST is the glue that binds curricular and co-curricular components of FYF. It is informed by public policy courses and D-LAB in preparation for Summer Fellowships. The competencies are: self-knowledge, communication skills, principled action, effective reasoning, and collaboration.

Possible Adaptations

While CST is especially tailored for participants interested in public policy, it can be adapted to any field of endeavor through the following adaptations:

➤ Create a program within your community. Select community members, local leaders, or alumni to conduct sessions you select.
➤ Use professional development funds to create a training. If you do not have funds allocated for this purpose, use resources such as TED Talks, webinars, and Coursera to learn about concepts included in this component of the program.
➤ Choose community members and your local office representatives to design a program that uses selected sessions or adopt the program design in its entirety.

Session 4.1 Orientation

Session Description

In this session, the facilitator will introduce participants to the Civic Skills Training (CST) Program. This session will provide a comprehensive overview of CST program expectations and then move on to focus on professionalism and professional dress in the workplace. These topics will be covered through a series of activities designed to maximize participant engagement and community building.

Learning Objectives

Participants will do the following:
- Define examples of appropriate dress for three experiences or occasions in their near future
- Describe at least three scenarios of professional behavior in CST and the workplace
- Identify two personal strengths for building living learning teams

Leadership Competencies Addressed

Collaboration
- Builds and maintains partnerships based on shared purpose; fosters a welcoming and inclusive environment

Management
- Identifies structure and culture of organization

Principled Action
- Identifies and commits to appropriate ethical framework

Intercultural Mindset
- Contextualizes social identities and experiences

Key Concepts and Definitions

Professionalism	The set of behaviors, standards, and practices that are acceptable norms within a profession.
Professional Dress	A dress code that is expected to be followed within a workplace or professional setting.
Living Learning Team	A group of individuals that identify common goals, understand team skills, and harness them for personal and professional growth.

Required Materials

- PowerPoint slides and appropriate technology (optional)
- Audio system for music and space for runway and dancing
- Flip charts and markers for each small group
- Various attire for runway volunteers

Session Outline

Session duration: 2 hours and 45 minutes

Time Required		Description
20 minutes	Introduction	Begin with an icebreaker of your choice that is designed to introduce participants past a superficial level. An example can be as follows: Ask participants to get into groups and each complete the sentence, *"You will know me if…."* Ask participants to share what they learned about each other.
35 minutes	Framing	Explain the purpose and overview of Civic Skills Training. It is designed as a crash course to the "civic sphere" and our place within it. It also provides the personal and professional skills necessary to excel in internships and the workplace. Discuss basic concepts related to teams and teamwork, which will be dealt with in greater detail later in the session. Explain how the purpose of the program is to promote a sense of lifelong learning. Discuss any logistics related to the program (travel, housing, etc.).
		Explain the constituent letter assignment, to be completed throughout the duration of the program. The assignment requires participants to write a letter to their member of Congress about an issue they care about and wish to see changed. Explain that there will be one checkpoint during the program where they will send in a draft for edits.
30 minutes	Activity 1	Divide participants into small groups. Ask participants to use flip charts to answer this prompt: *What does professionalism mean to your group, and what advice would you give to others to uphold high standards of professionalism?* Give participants five minutes to answer the question. Then give them another ten minutes to do a "gallery walk" to learn about the opinions of other participants. In a large group, ask participants what surprised them and discuss key concepts related to integrity, honesty, transparency, and the importance of these concepts for personal and professional leadership.
30 minutes	Dinner Break	Break for dinner. Ask participants to talk about where they grew up and any family details they feel comfortable sharing over dinner.

Time Required		Description
25 minutes	Activity 2	In a "runway show," instruct former participants or volunteers to dress in a variety of styles, each with different levels of formality. As they "walk down the runway," discuss with participants what occasion is appropriate for each dress style. Emphasize that work culture dictates dress code. Invite participants to reach out to their workplace supervisors to clarify their dress code if confused.
15 minutes	Discussion	Open the floor for participants to ask advice from CST alumni. Divide participants into groups and assign two former Fellows to each group. Ask them to discuss how professionalism showed up in their specific workplaces.
5 minutes	Activity 3	If your program has a mentorship/internship component, invite participants to reach out to their mentors/supervisors to introduce themselves and thank them for the opportunity. Emphasize the importance of gratitude. Help participants draft this introductory message.
5 minutes	Conclusion	Ask participants to complete the session evaluation using your desired format. Close the session by thanking the participants.

Reflection Questions

- What choices regarding professionalism will I realistically face during this summer?
- What parts of my workplace dress code am I still uncertain about?
- What are the strengths of my team members?
- What are the norms or behaviors we collectively adopt for our personal or professional growth together?
- What are the implications of these concepts for leadership and management?

Participant Reflection

The first CST session set the bar high for the entire program. Professionalism is about how you carry yourself, and this session showed me how we can control and improve our professionalism every day. The part about professional dress offered very practical advice and the activities were engaging not just because of the discussions, but also because it allowed me to hear from my fellow students about their perspectives. To this day, I apply the practical professionalism skills I learned during this session in my professional life, from the value of being on time (or rather, early!) to dressing professionally.

CST Summer 2018

Supplemental Resources

Clayton, L. (2019, April). *The true power of a good outfit* [Video]. TEDx Exeter. https://www.ted.com/talks/lucy_clayton_the_true_power_of_a_good_outfit

Dartmouth. (2011, August 2). *Anna Post: "Professionalism in the 21st century"* [Video]. YouTube. https://www.youtube.com/watch?v=YEV44sbAGOQ&ab_channel=Dartmouth

Romme, G. (2016). *The quest for professionalism: The case of management and entrepreneurship.* Oxford University Press. https://doi.org/10.1093/acprof:oso/9780198737735.001.0001

This session has been formatted and revised for consistency and clarity. The original session was facilitated by Sadhana Hall, reached at Sadhana.W.Hall@dartmouth.edu, and Ronald Shaiko, reached at Ronald.G.Shaiko@dartmouth.edu. Many sessions in the Civic Skills Training Program are now facilitated by alumni of the First-Year Fellows Program.

Session 4.2 Communication in the Workplace

Session Description

In this session, participants are provided with a comprehensive overview of workplace communication from the perspectives and experiences of their peers. This session will focus on two types of communication skills: *hard skills,* those that can easily be learned and acquired, and *soft skills,* those that are adapted from and unique to one's personality. They will also discuss three mediums of workplace communication: virtual (e.g., email, social media), phone (e.g., calls, voicemails), and in-person (e.g., meetings, "water-cooler" interactions). These topics will be covered through a comprehensive presentation, panel, and Q&A featuring Fellows from the Rockefeller Leadership Fellows Program with a diversity and depth of workplace experiences, as well as interactive scenarios and discussion facilitated in small groups by each panelist.

Leadership Competencies Addressed

Self-Knowledge
- Shows self-respect and respect for others

Effective Communication
- Influences others through writing, speaking, or artistic expression;
- Acknowledges and appropriately communicates in situations with divergent opinions and values

Management
- Identifies structure and culture of organization:
- Demonstrates effective and appropriate use of technology

Learning Objectives

Participants will do the following:
- Craft three messages based on common workplace scenarios
- Analyze customs of communication across academic, professional, and personal settings

Key Concepts and Definitions

Authenticity	The ability to communicate with and relate to other people in the workplace without compromising one's identity and/or personality, even in challenging situations.
Autonomy/ Independence	The ability to communicate with peers, colleagues, and superiors in the workplace without depending on approval and/or guidance from one's direct supervisor.

Required Materials

- PowerPoint slides and appropriate technology
- Choose five panelists for their ability to relate to participants. They should have 3–5 years of work experience.
- Participant's constituent letters
- Facilitator may use their creativity to create a "Do's and Don'ts" handout for common professional communication methods (virtual, phone, face-to-face).
- Facilitator may also create a workplace communication scenario handout.

Session Outline

Session duration: 2 hours and 20 minutes

Time Required		Description
10 minutes	Introduction	Introduce the session. Ask the Rockefeller Leadership Fellows panelists to introduce themselves and list their workplace experiences.
25 minutes	Framing	Panelists present slides outlining key takeaways from the two types of communication skills (i.e., hard and soft) and the three mediums of workplace communication (i.e., virtual, phone, in-person). Panelists conduct an interactive discussion of "do's and don'ts" of workplace communication and etiquette and answer frequently asked questions about workplace communication and etiquette. Ask participants if they have any more specific questions they would like answered.
60 minutes	Activity	Divide participants into smaller groups of four in which they will talk through three communication scenarios. Each group will be led by one of the panelists. They will oversee each group and challenge cliché responses. The first scenario will review the constituent letters participants wrote in the first session of the program. In pairs, each participant will give feedback. The second scenario will consist of an informal, vague request from a supervisor to do research. The third scenario will focus on asking for help in an internship position where they must consult with a supervisor, mentor, or other resource available. Small groups will discuss each scenario, craft a collective response, and share in the large group.

Time Required		Description
15 minutes	Reflection	In the large group, debrief the responses from the small groups. With participants, discuss the differences between professional and informal communication and why we do not always use professional communication. Encourage participants to share their own communication practices and why they prefer to communicate the way they do.
25 minutes	Discussion	Invite the panelists to sit at the front of the room to answer general questions about their internship experiences. These questions will not solely be limited to workplace communication but can be related to anything the participants are feeling particularly concerned about.
5 minutes	Conclusion	Reviewing key takeaways, emphasize the importance of intergenerational communication. Ask participants to complete the session evaluation using your desired format. Close the session by thanking the participants and panelists.

Reflection Questions

- How does communication in the workplace differ from communication in personal and/or academic settings?
- How can I learn to communicate authentically while respectfully adhering to the customs of workplace communication?
- How should the way I communicate with my peers (e.g., fellow interns) compare to the way I communicate with my superiors (e.g., supervisors, mid-level managers, upper-level executives)?

Participant Reflection

Prior to this session, communicating with my superiors in the workplace was probably what I was most nervous about going into my summer internship. Breaking communication down into "hard skills" and "soft skills" and then into the "three mediums"—virtual, phone, and in-person—made the topic seem more digestible and easier to tackle. I also really appreciated getting to hear from young alumni about their own experiences communicating in the workplace, as it reminded me that even if I were to make a mistake, I could recover and go on to be successful in the office.

CST Summer 2018

Supplemental Resources

Coffelt, T. A., Grauman, D., & Smith, F. L. M. (2019). Employers' perspectives on workplace communication skills: The meaning of communication skills. *Business & Professional Communication Quarterly*, *82*(4), 418–439. https://doi.org/10.1177/2329490619851119

Keyton, J. (2017). Communication in organizations. *Annual Review of Organizational Psychology and Organizational Behavior*, *4*(1), 501–526. https://doi.org/10.1146/annurev-orgpsych-032516-113341

Miller, K. I. (2007). Compassionate communication in the workplace: Exploring processes of noticing, connecting, and responding. *Journal of Applied Communication Research*, *35*(3), 223–245. https://doi.org/10.1080/00909880701434208

This session has been formatted and revised for consistency and clarity. Many sessions in the Civic Skills Training Program are facilitated by alumni. This session is now organized by fellows of the Rockefeller Leadership Fellows Program.

Session 4.3 Cohort-Building and Teamwork

Session Description

In this session, participants will engage in activities designed to help them understand the stages of a group's life, the advantages and possible pitfalls of group living, and potential solutions to problems that may arise. They will discuss the significance of community, then jointly design an agreement that will prevent many of the pitfalls they may experience as they live together as a cohort.

Learning Objectives

Participants will do the following:
- Identify their own living styles and describe their expectations
- Identify the five stages in a group's life
- Build a working community by designing an agreement to accommodate the various styles of its members

Key Concepts and Definitions

Leadership Competencies Addressed

Collaboration
- Acknowledges and listens to different voices when making decisions and taking action

Management
- Develops appropriate strategies for effective teamwork

Self-Knowledge
- Shows self-respect and respect for others

Principled Action
- Demonstrates personal responsibility
- Bases actions on thoughtful consideration of their impact and consequences

Tuckman Stages of Group Development   The stages are forming, storming, norming, performing, and adjourning. *Forming* is the stage when team members are still getting to know each other and may be anxious about beginning to work together. *Storming* is the phase where team members may face conflict in working with each other due to working styles, roles within the teams, or doubts surrounding overall objectives. After storming, *norming* comes next, where team members begin to resolve differences and appreciate each other's strengths. *Performing* is the stage where team members can work hard to achieve their mutual goal. Finally, *adjourning* is the last phase where teams that are not permanent may disband.

Expectations   A clear articulation of behaviors that are acceptable and unacceptable. Group expectations will be in the form of a written agreement crafted by its members. It is a living document that changes as the group adapts to one another and develops norms, moving through the stages of group development.

Required Materials

- PowerPoint slides and appropriate technology (optional)
- Community Agreement template (optional)
- Paper and writing utensils for each group

Session Outline

Session duration: 2 hours

Time Required		Description
20 minutes	Introduction	Explain the connection between teamwork and living as a cohort. Describe some scenarios of sharing living spaces done right and some examples of it gone wrong. You may choose to use anecdotes from your personal experience. Ask participants to share some of their own experiences living with family or roommates and some of the conflicts that arose in those living situations. The purpose of this discussion is to illustrate why teamwork is important and applicable to living with others.
35 minutes	Discussion	Divide participants into their pre-assigned living arrangements. Ask participants to introduce themselves to one another: their internship, daily schedule, habits and preferences, things they do for fun, things they do when they are having a bad day, and core values. Encourage participants to add anything they feel is important. Someone in the group should take note of items that members feel strongly about, align with, or disagree with.
15 minutes	Framing	Explain that groups will craft their community agreement document based on the information they just shared. Their notes will serve as the framework for developing group expectations. Define expectations and the Tuckman Stages of Group Development. Explain that defining group expectations is crucial in moving through the storming, norming, and performing stages with success.
35 minutes	Activity	In the same groups, ask participants to write their community agreement. You may wish to develop a template for them to follow or encourage them to make it their own. Remind fellows to consider daily scenarios and unexpected events, as well as writing rules they want to have and norms they want to establish.

Time Required		Description
15 minutes	Conclusion	Ask each group to share one thing they realized that will be important to their success. Identify commonalities and differences between groups. Invite participants to ask questions about unclear situations they might have discussed. Ask participants to complete the session evaluation using your desired format. Close the session by thanking the participants.

Reflection Questions

- What can I do to ensure a positive living arrangement for the summer?
- How can I help group members to do their parts in this endeavor?
- How can we all accommodate the changes and unexpected situations that will certainly arise?

Supplemental Resources

Burke, R., & Barron, S. (2012). *Project management leadership: Building creative teams.* (2nd ed.). John Wiley & Sons, Incorporated. https://doi.org/10.1002/9781119207986

Edmondson, A. (2017). *How to turn a group of strangers into a team* [Video]. TED Salon Brightline. https://www.ted.com/talks/amy_edmondson_how_to_turn_a_group_of_strangers_into_a_team

Hedman, E., & Valo, M. (2015). Communication challenges facing management teams. *Leadership & Organization Development Journal, 36*(8), 1012–1024. https://doi.org/10.1108/LODJ-04-2014-0074

> **Participant Reflection**
>
> *This session was one of the most practical and helpful ones because it allowed us to be intentional about creating a healthy living environment in which we all felt comfortable. By being honest about each other, about our preferences, and about what's important to each of us, we were able to write a community agreement that helped us all get on the same page. By taking time to discuss these things honestly and respectfully, we were able to prevent any unnecessary conflict from arising! And it turns out, it actually worked!*
>
> **CST Summer 2018**

This session has been formatted and revised for consistency and clarity. The original session in the Civic Skills Training Program was facilitated by Sadhana Hall, reached at sadhana.w.hall@dartmouth.edu.

Session 4.4 Leadership in D.C.

Session Description

In this session, participants will discuss professionalism and how to maintain a professional example in the workplace—in other words, the ways they lead themselves. The facilitator will start by describing the unique aspects of D.C. culture as they see them and what the Fellows should expect for their internships this summer. Participants will explore examples of exemplary behavior as well as things to avoid, then break up into smaller groups to consider what might be challenging about their work.

Learning Objectives

Participants will do the following:
- Identify what a professional introduction is and begin to form their own introductions
- List eight behaviors to avoid and eight behaviors to model
- Define what constitutes professional and unprofessional conduct

Leadership Competencies Addressed

Intercultural Mindset
- Understands, communicates with, and respectfully interacts with people across identities

Management
- Identifies structure and culture of organization

Self-Knowledge
- Understands social identities of self and others;
- Shows self-respect and respect for others

Principled Action
- Demonstrates personal responsibility

Key Concepts and Definitions

Professionalism   Presenting yourself to be effective and to make a positive impression based on workplace culture and expectations.

Conscientiousness   Being mindful of the interplay of context, culture, and how one's engagement impacts others.

Required Materials

- Flipcharts and markers for your own and small group use

Session Outline

Session duration: 1 hour 20 minutes

Time Required		Description
10 minutes	Introduction	Provide an in-depth overview of your background and discuss the ways you engage with the civic space in D.C. Model your own "elevator pitch" introduction and explain that in today's session, participants will begin to craft and practice their own professional introductions.
15 minutes	Activity	Ask four pre-selected participants to introduce themselves with an "elevator pitch." Give positive and constructive feedback for the rest of the group to take note.
25 minutes	Discussion	On a flip chart, generate 8–10 examples of "what not to do" and challenges to professionalism. An initial list could include the following: *items related to conduct*—for example, avoiding a sense of entitlement, navigating professional relationships, encountering off-putting individuals, and drinking at work events; *items related to performance*—for example, lack of responsiveness, overly informal communication, poor job performance, and giving or receiving feedback; and *items related to culture*—for example, dress code for all genders, expressing political views in the wrong setting or tone, ignoring the process or chain of command, intergenerational communication, ensuring you're included in a social situation even if you don't have the resources (e.g., time or money) to join.
20 minutes	Activity	Divide participants into three break-out groups to brainstorm their own challenges to professionalism. Ask them to consider the situations that might arise that would require them to be thoughtful and avoid some of the common mistakes mentioned in the earlier discussion. How should they handle them? Alternatively, each group may draft a "code of conduct" that would work for general best practices in their upcoming professional settings. After 15 minutes, bring the smaller groups together to share their thoughts.

Time Required		Description
10 minutes	Conclusion	Discuss the connections between professionalism and leadership, and the importance of understanding the unique things about every individual workplace culture. Ask participants to continue to reflect on how they can best lead themselves into and around professional settings. Ask participants to complete the session evaluation using your desired format. Close the session by thanking the participants.

Reflection Questions

- How can I introduce myself with a strong and authentic personal introduction?
- How can I use these lessons to handle challenging workplace situations appropriately?

Supplemental Resources

Bakker, A. B., Demerouti, E., & ten Brummelhuis, L. L. (2012). Work engagement, performance, and active learning: The role of conscientiousness. *Journal of Vocational Behavior, 80*(2), 555–564. https://doi.org/10.1016/j.jvb.2011.08.008

Glamrs. (2016, May 22). *How to introduce yourself effectively in professional situations—professional introduction* [Video]. YouTube. https://www.youtube.com/watch?v=7E1JOuAVlz4&ab_channel=Glamrs

Participant Reflection

Going into my internship, I was obviously hoping to make the best impression possible, but I was worried about knowing exactly what to do and what to avoid being an ideal member of the office. This session was really useful in identifying some behaviors and qualities to try to model over the summer and keeping those lessons throughout the summer helped me shape my experience into one in which I made a real impact and formed lasting connections. Three years later, as I approach my first full-time position, I am revisiting the lessons I learned during this session, and I look forward to continuing to apply them.

CST Summer 2018

Harris, K., Mike, A., Roberts, B. W., & Jackson, J. J. (2015). Conscientiousness. In J. D. Wright (Ed.), *International encyclopedia of the social & behavioral sciences* (2nd ed., pp. 658–665). Elsevier. https://doi.org/10.1016/B978-0-08-097086-8.25047-2

This session has been formatted and revised for consistency and clarity. This session in the Civic Skills Training Program is facilitated by program alumni.

Session 4.5 Advocacy Writing with Precision

Session Description

In this session, the facilitator will discuss the key components of advocacy writing: clear and simple writing, a target audience, an analysis of an issue or problem, and a recommendation for some position or solution. Whether for an audience internal or external to an organization, advocacy writers are attempting to convince the reader to agree with or adopt their proposal. This session will review the basic questions to establish a succinct approach. By the end of the session, participants will have provided feedback and suggestions to a peer and advanced lessons learned in the group.

Learning Objectives

Participants will do the following:
- Discuss the major questions to consider when approaching an advocacy writing project
- Draft a short, written piece advancing a solution, opinion, or idea for a specified audience
- Provide feedback on letters to the editor and tweet threads advancing a solution or position

Leadership Competencies Addressed

Intercultural Mindset
- Understands, communicates with, and respectfully interacts with people across identities

Effective Communication
- Clearly articulates ideas in a written and spoken form;
- Influences others through writing, speaking, or artistic expression

Effective Reasoning
- Integrates multiple types of information to effectively solve problems or address issues

Key Concepts and Definitions

Writing clearly   Writing in easy-to-understand language that accentuates and does not muddle your point, with the appropriate level of detail for the audience.

Advocacy   Working to convince others of an opinion, idea, solution, or approach.

Required Materials

- PowerPoint slides and appropriate technology
- A computer or appropriate writing materials

Pre-session Assignment:
- Choose a topic of interest and research 2–5 recent news stories, long-form articles, or academic papers about your topic.

Session Outline

Session duration: 1 hour and 20 minutes

Time Required		Description
5 minutes	Introduction	Introduce yourself and your background. Ask participants to introduce themselves and provide a very brief summary of the topic they chose to research for the session.
10 minutes	Framing	Review the definitions of *advocacy* and *precision*. Share the learning objectives and outline of the session. Explain that advocacy writing is all about what you are writing about, why you are writing, to whom you are writing, what you want to tell them, and in what form you are writing.
25 minutes	Discussion	Explain that they might consider asking these questions when approaching an issue that they want or need to write an advocacy piece on: *What is the problem or conflict? What is your position, opinion, or recommended solution? What is the supporting evidence or information that informed your chosen position or idea? What are other opposing or simply other ideas, solutions or positions?* First, one must determine the purpose of their writing. Explain that emphasizing the importance of the purpose is crucial and that this is best achieved through understanding the audience. Ask: *What do you know about them? What do they already know and think about this subject? Where are they hearing about this subject on the news? from their neighbors? elsewhere? How is it being characterized there? How would you like them to think about this subject? What do they know about you?* Review the different types of advocacy writing and the basics for each.
20 minutes	Activity 1	In the large group, share a few recent examples of advocacy writing. With participants, identify the audience, message, and supporting points or story. Ask participants to discuss their thoughts on the effectiveness of the argument for the chosen audience.

Time Required		Description
40 minutes	Activity 2	Divide participants into groups of two or three to share their research and provide peer feedback and suggestions based on their new understanding from the session. Each group should then decide which topic they want to advocate for based on their research. They will identify the position/solution, purpose, audience, message, and main points. Then, each group will draft their message in either the form of a tweet thread or a letter to the editor referencing a recent news story. The product cannot be longer than 200 words.
10 minutes	Conclusion	Ask participants to share their experience of the advocacy writing exercise: *What did they like about it? What do they find challenging? What are their key takeaways? What is the importance of being a good advocacy writer?* Ask participants to complete the session evaluation using your desired format. Close the session by thanking the participants.

Reflection Questions

As it relates to your topic or issue of choice, consider the following:
* What is the supporting evidence or information that informed your chosen position or idea?
* What are other ideas, solutions, or positions?
* What people would you like to convince about your idea and what might be the best form in which to reach them?

Participant Reflection

In this session, we examined real examples of writing in order to better understand how to improve upon our own writing, especially in professional settings. Paying particular attention to tone and understanding how it might be interpreted by others is a valuable skill that I have continued to work on since this session. Skills that I learned from the speaker to ensure that I am respectfully and purposefully conveying my message.

CST Summer 2020

Supplemental Resources

Cohen, D. S. (1977). Ensuring an effective instructor-taught writing and advocacy program: How to teach the teachers comments. *Journal of Legal Education, 29*(4), 593–612.

National Consumer Voice for Quality Long-Term Care. (n.d). Crafting an effective advocacy message. *Advocacy Toolkit.* Retrieved November 27, 2020, from https://theconsumervoice.org/uploads/files/issues/Crafting_an_Effective_Advocacy_Message_han.pdf

TEDx Talks. (2015, December 11). *Demand to understand: How plain language makes life simpler | Deborah Bosley | TEDxCharlotte* [Video]. YouTube. https://www.youtube.com/watch?v=OXcLwlZOE1s&ab_channel=TEDxTalks

This session has been formatted and revised for consistency and clarity. The original session in the Civic Skills Training Program was facilitated by Matthew H. Davis, reached at matthew.davis.01@gmail.com.

Session 4.6 Fundamentals of Project Management

Session Description

In this session, the facilitator discusses the fundamentals of project management. Project management is the art and science of utilizing personal and team knowledge, skills, material, and financial resources to produce a unique product, service, or result in a finite period. This session will cover some key principles, techniques, and processes of project management that participants will be able to apply immediately in their internship placements. Participants will also begin to prepare a presentation they will give the next day.

Leadership Competencies Addressed

Self-Knowledge
- Continually explores and examines values and views

Collaboration
- Builds and maintains partnerships based on shared purpose;
- Facilitates collective action toward common goals

Principled Action
- Identifies and commits to appropriate ethical framework

Learning Objectives

Participants will do the following:
- Write two SMART objectives for their summer
- List at least seven skills of effective project managers
- Identify five factors to consider as project managers
- Practice developing a plan for a project
- Discuss how to develop a project during the eight-week fellowship placement

Key Concepts and Definitions

E-W-N-S working styles	"East" is the approach of looking at the bigger picture. "West" is the approach of looking at details. "North" is the action-oriented approach, and "South" is the feelings and process approach. There is a tendency to favor one working style in most people, but this is flexible depending on the situation.
SMART (specific, measurable, attainable, realistic, time-bound)	This is a framework commonly used for goal-setting.

Time management	What timeline are you going to use? Use a backwards-planning technique for time estimation. Begin with the end in mind. Use Gantt charts for identifying the task, person(s) responsible, and deadlines. Task sequencing and "critical path" strategies are useful for outlining one step to the next. These are all organizing principles for project management.
Budgeting	This is a process to estimate what the project is going to cost. It should be based on similar experiences and actual costs that will be incurred. It is important to monitor and evaluate the budget before, during, and after the project.
Monitoring and evaluation	What is going well? What problems can you anticipate and how will you address them? How will you measure success? Qualitatively and quantitatively? SWOT (strengths, weaknesses, opportunities, threats) analysis is a helpful tool for evaluation.

Required Materials

- PowerPoint slides and appropriate technology (optional)
- Loose paper and pens for each participant
- Flipchart and markers for each group
- Index cards

Session Outline

Session duration: 1 hour and 40 minutes

Time Required		Description
10 minutes	Introduction	Begin by taking a poll of the room: Ask participants if they know how to or have ever managed a project before. Most of them will likely raise their hand. Ask for some volunteers to define what project management, program management, and/or portfolio management are. Explain that though most people have done project management to some degree, there is much to know and learn about it. Define management as the ability to use knowledge and skills to effectively channel time, talent, and resources towards the achievement of an identified goal.

Time Required		Description
5 minutes	Activity 1	Ask participants to think about the organizational structure of the Rockefeller Center: Who runs programs and how are they run? Instruct participants to draw an organizational chart for the Center, including projects, programs, and portfolio management. The best chart wins!
25 minutes	Discussion	Explain that when we are responsible for a project, we need to understand our personal workstyle and the workstyle of others who will be participating in it. Discuss the E-W-N-S model of working styles. Read out the information for each style and ask participants to go and stand under the sign that best fits their work style. In their working style groups or during some personal reflection time, ask participants to answer these questions: *What are four adjectives that describe the strengths of this style? What are four adjectives that describe the limitations of this style? What style do you find most difficult to work with and why? What do people from the other "directions" or styles need to know about you so you can work together effectively? What do you value about the other three styles? What are the implications of this discussion for project management?*
20 minutes	Framing	Explain that when you do project planning and management, you begin with the end in mind. Define the key concepts and mention that these are all important tools for management. Give examples, verbally or visually, of these tools. For example, you may compare these two statements to illustrate SMART goals: *By December 2022, participants will be aware of the health status of NH citizens.* vs. *By December 15, 2022, at least 80% NH citizens 18–25 years old will be able to identify four symptoms of Diabetes Type II.* Provide a list of some of the services and tools you can't live without, such as Google apps, Google Chrome, Dropbox, Slack, Trello, and paper notebooks. Encourage participants to add to this list of resources with their own favorite tools.
10 minutes	Activity 2	Instruct participants to develop two SMART objectives for themselves based on what they have learned so far in CST. Ask them to share with the person next to them once they have finished.

Time Required		Description
20 minutes	Activity 3	Divide participants into teams of four or five. Read them the following prompt: *You have $15,000 for an audience of XXX (you decide). Please develop a project focused on a social cause that your group feels strongly about. You will present your project plan.* Encourage them to use any of the tools discussed in the session to develop this project and deliver a creative 10-minute presentation. Their presentation should include these project components: a goal, SMART objectives, qualitative and quantitative measures of success, a Gantt chart, problems they can anticipate and how they will address them, a budget including services and tools needed for the project, and anything else the team would like to highlight. Teams may begin planning this project and presentation during the session but will have to continue their work outside of the session time. Presentations will occur at a time that is appropriate in the program schedule. Allot time for participants to work in their teams. Inform the participants that visiting alumni will judge the presentations based on the proficiency of the project components and the presentation skills.
10 minutes	Conclusion	Provide an index card for each participant. On one side, ask them to write the program management skills that they possess and feel confident about. On the other, ask them to write the skills they want to work on. Ask participants to complete the session evaluation using your desired format. Close the session by thanking the participants.

Reflection Questions

- What are my skills as a project manager? What do I need to focus on?
- How well do I use my critical thinking skills in outlining assumptions and becoming proactive about anticipating problems?
- How do I rate myself on my ability to plan, implement, monitor and evaluate a project?

Participant Reflection

The project management session was incredibly helpful. It might seem simple, but if you don't understand your organization's organizational structure, you can't be successful in it. The interactive activity of coming up with a project using concrete tools such as SMART objective and Gantt charts was very eye-opening because it taught me that even the most daunting task can be achieved by breaking it down into bits and using proven techniques to tackle the different parts. In fact, I still use these concepts in my class projects and internship experiences! It has allowed me to be more effective.

CST Summer 2018

Supplemental Resources

Audy, J. (2019, May). *Project management applied to life | Jorge Audy | TEDx Laçador* [Video]. TEDx Conferences. https://www.ted.com/talks/jorge_audy_o_gerenciamento_de_projetos_aplicado_a_vida

Carvalho, M. M., Patah, L. A., & de Souza Bido, D. (2015). Project management and its effects on project success: Cross-country and cross-industry comparisons. *International Journal of Project Management, 33*(7), 1509–1522. https://doi.org/10.1016/j.ijproman.2015.04.004

Taylor, J. (2016, June 17). *A guide for setting SMART goals* [Video]. YouTube. https://www.youtube.com/watch?v=fY-1UGhBXLE&ab_channel=JamesTaylor

This session has been formatted and revised for consistency and clarity. The original session in the Civic Skills Training Program was facilitated by Sadhana Hall, reached at sadhana.w.hall@dartmouth.edu.

Session 4.7 Advanced Public Speaking—On Becoming Engaged and Engaging

Session Description

In this session, the facilitator covers advanced concepts of public speaking related to framing a concept or idea to persuade and provoke thought, rather than merely to debate the substantive merits of an argument.

Learning Objectives

Participants will do the following:

- Describe the four key concepts that serve as a basis for designing speeches
- Demonstrate at least three approaches to framing a message to engage and persuade the audience
- Give and receive feedback in peer presentations

Leadership Competencies Addressed

Self-Knowledge
- Demonstrates realistic understanding of one's abilities
- Shows self-respect and respect for others

Effective Communication
- Clearly articulates ideas in a written and spoken form
- Influences others through writing, speaking, or artistic expression

Key Concepts and Definitions

Presence	The ability to be completely in the moment and be flexible to handle the unexpected.
Reaching out	The ability to build relationships with others through empathy, listening, and authentic connection.
Expressiveness	The ability to express feelings and emotions appropriately by using all available means—words, body, face—to develop a congruent message.
Self-knowing	The ability to express yourself, to be authentic, and to reflect your values in our decisions and actions.

Required Materials

- PowerPoint slides and appropriate technology (optional)
- State Farm commercial "Jacked Up." This video is available on YouTube (https://youtu.be/k29ogXL_S2U).

- Handout 4.7.1 Developing a Message and Handout 4.7.2 Feedback Rubric printed for participants
- Index cards for each participant
- Writing utensils
- Assistants to record and time speeches

Session Outline

Session duration: 2 hours

Time Required		Description
10 minutes	Introduction	Introduce the main ideas that will be explored in this session. Ask participants to think about what ideas they would like to propose in persuasive public speech, what problems they would solve, and why the audience should care. Introduce some of the tools that orators use to frame their speeches: the way in which they present assertions, arguments, supporting evidence, data, and a narrative to achieve a particular end.
10 minutes	Framing	Introduce the "mechanics of public speaking": *message* (how clear is your message? why should the audience care?); *key points* (the essential-to-know, good-to-know, nice-to-know information in the presentation); understanding *audience needs* and how you can tailor the message to meet them; *intentional vocabulary*; *dialogue* vs. *debate*; and *integrity* (how your values play into the authenticity of a message).
5 minutes	Activity 1	Pass out the "Developing a Message" worksheet (Handout 4.7.1). Ask participants to write a clear message about a public policy issue they care about. It should focus on essential-to-know information either backed by data they know or a suggested credible source where one could receive this information.
10 minutes	Discussion	Present the State Farm Commercial, "Jacked Up." Ask participants what they observed about the differences in the characters. The key point of this exercise is to express that with body language and tone, the meaning of the same exact words can be changed. The key is to practice making message, tone (which expresses emotions), and body language congruent.

Time Required		Description
15 minutes	Activity 2	Ask participants to write down a common problem they experience or have seen others experience in public speaking on one side of an index card. Explain that participants will walk around the room, collecting solutions from other participants and offering solutions. On one side of the index card is the problem, on the other side, participants will write at least three solution suggestions from other participants. Ask participants to share the most helpful or most creative solutions to their problems. You may collect these cards and compile a list of solutions for common problems to return to participants or use as a helpful, collaborative resource.
60 minutes	Activity 3	Pass out and explain the Feedback Rubric (Handout 4.7.2) participants will be using for the next activity. Divide participants into three groups. Each participant will give a two-minute speech about a public policy issue they care about. They should end with a call to action: *Why should others care about this issue?* Ask session assistants to time and record each participant for their personal reflection later. Four group members will give oral feedback based on persuasiveness and rhetorical techniques: two positive and two constructive. The rest of the group will hand in their written feedback using the rubric. After each participant has given a speech and has had the opportunity to give oral feedback, end the activity with some examples of excellent feedback from the groups.
10 minutes	Conclusion	Reflect with participants about the session. Ask participants to complete the session evaluation using your desired format. Close the session by thanking the participants.

Reflection Questions

- What are my strengths as a speaker?
- How deliberate am I in considering audience needs when speaking?
- How do I express myself authentically and with consideration of the needs of others?

Participant Reflection

I found this session to be really valuable because it addressed both speech content and speech delivery rather than considering either one in isolation. The portion of the lesson that centered around crafting a message helped to center the process for constructing the content of a speech, and then delivering our speeches and having them recorded (and being forced to watch them back) really aided in identifying the strengths and weaknesses of my own public speaking capabilities. While the activity was a bit nerve-wracking, it was comforting to be surrounded by a small group of my peers who were facing the same challenges.

CST Summer 2018

Supplemental Resources

Cuddy, A. (2012, June). *Your body language may shape who you are* [Video]. TED Conferences. https://www.ted.com/talks/amy_cuddy_your_body_language_may_shape_who_you_are

McGrath, C. (2006). The ideal lobbyist: Personal characteristics of effective lobbyists. *Journal of Communication Management, 10*(1), 67–79. http://dx.doi.org.dartmouth.idm.oclc.org/10.1108/13632540610646382

Phillips, D. J. (2018, September). *The 110 techniques of communication and public speaking* [Video]. TEDxZagreb. https://www.ted.com/talks/david_jp_phillips_the_110_techniques_of_communication_and_public_speaking

Rossette-Crake, F. (2020). 'The new oratory': Public speaking practice in the digital, neoliberal age. *Discourse Studies, 22*(5), 571–589. https://doi.org/10.1177/1461445620916363

This session has been formatted and revised for consistency and clarity. The original session in the Civic Skills Training Program was facilitated by Sadhana Hall, reached at sadhana.w.hall@dartmouth.edu.

Developing a Message

Write a message about a public policy issue you care about for a two-minute presentation. It should have three main points. It should focus on essential-to-know information backed by data you know or at least citing the authentic source you would go to for this information.

Write your SMART Objective for a two-minute presentation:

Outline your Message (essential-to-know information, data and sources, and 3 main points)

Feedback Rubric

CIVIC SKILLS TRAINING
STUDENT PRESENTATION ASSESSMENT

Criteria for Assessment	1=Poor; 6=Outstanding					
Tone • *inflection, confidence*	1	2	3	4	5	6
Message • *clarity, organization, consistency*	1	2	3	4	5	6
Body Language • *eye contact, posture, absence of fidgeting/pacing*	1	2	3	4	5	6
Audience Engagement • *interaction with audience, openness to questions*	1	2	3	4	5	6
Notes:						

Session 4.8 What to Expect on the Hill

Session Description

In this session, the facilitator will provide an overview of the structure, key procedures, and players in Congress. By the end of the session, participants will have a firm understanding of these concepts from the Hill: the legislative process, constituent service, press and communications, and the role of congressional committees.

Learning Objectives

Participants will do the following:
- List the differences between the House of Representatives and the Senate
- Outline a day in the life of a Hill staffer
- Describe the legislative process, constituent service, press and communications, and the role of congressional committees

Leadership Competencies Addressed

Collaboration
- Acknowledges and listens to different voices when making decisions and taking action

Management
- Develops and implements a plan for goal attainment
- Develops appropriate strategies for capitalizing on human talent
- Identifies structure and culture of organization

Key Concepts and Definitions

Constituent	The people that members of Congress and Senators represent.
Constituent service	This is a general term for the service that an elected official provides to their constituents.
Press Shop and Communications	The press shop is the hub of public relations. They are responsible for building and maintaining lines of communication between Congress members, constituents, and the public.
House vs. Senate and the role of legislative staff	The House and Senate are separate but equal partners in the legislative process. While legislation cannot be enacted without the consent of both, each chamber has unique powers granted by the Constitution. The Senate ratifies treaties and approves presidential appointments while the House initiates revenue-raising bills. Legislative staff conduct legal research, handle communication and public relations, or handle administrative tasks.
Bipartisanship	The spirit of consensus-building between the parties in legislation and working together to serve the American people.

| *Legislative calendar* | The legislative calendar is used to plan business during a legislative session. There are two legislative sessions in the year. At the end of the session, the calendar is cleared. Bills are often reintroduced in the second session if they are not passed in the first. |

| *Committees and Subcommittees* | The thousands of bills and resolutions handled by Congress are referred to Senate committees, which are further divided into subcommittees, depending on complexity or volume. |

| *Legislative process* | Bills drafted in Congress are introduced in either the House or Senate and are then sent to committees. Committees decide whether to further the bill and make edits, then vote to report the bill to the floor. On the floor, either chamber debates, then votes. Then the bill must pass through the same process in the other chamber. Finally, once issues are resolved, the President may veto or sign, and the bill becomes a law. |

| *Role of lobbyists* | Lobbyists try to influence legislation, regulation, or other government decisions, actions, or policies on behalf of a group or individual who hires them. They can be professionals hired on behalf of businesses and corporations, individuals, or nonprofit organizations. |

Required Materials

- PowerPoint slides and appropriate technology (optional)

Session Outline

Session duration: 1 hour 40 minutes

Time Required		Description
10 minutes	Introduction	Introduce yourself and your role on the Hill. Ask participants to introduce themselves and to share their areas of interest. Share the learning objectives and the session outline.
20 minutes	Framing	Provide an overview of the structure of the Hill. Discuss the respective roles of the House and the Senate and the role of legislative staff. Define and explain committees and subcommittees, the press shop and communications, the legislative calendar, legislative process, constituent service, and the role of lobbyists.

Time Required		Description
55 minutes	Discussion	Discuss the climate in Washington today and the importance of bipartisanship as tensions rise and issues continue to get more and more polarized. Describe "a day in the life" on the Hill. Discuss staff delegations and receptions. Talk about the influence that you may have as an individual that leads in any role. Give D.C.-specific internship and career advice, like tips for networking, doing a good job on the first day, etc. Answer questions from participants.
15 minutes	Conclusion	Summarize the discussions from the session. Conclude your thoughts by talking about the role that every person must play in making the American democracy run smoothly and encourage participants to think about the big picture. Discuss the implications for leadership and our role in preserving and encouraging consensus, progress, and efficiency. Ask participants to complete the session evaluation using your desired format. Close the session by thanking the participants.

Reflection Questions

- What issue areas am I the most interested in?
- Would I be a good fit for the legislative, press and communications, administrative, or committee staff?
- What are the pros and cons of working on the Hill?

Supplemental Resources

Grabowski, S. (2006). Acquainting yourself with the office. In N. Folk (Ed.), *Congressional intern handbook: A guide for interns and newcomers to Capitol Hill* (pp. 15–40). Congressional Management Foundation.

Macneil, N., & Baker, R. A. (2013). *American Senate: An insider's history.* Oxford University Press USA - OSO. http://ebookcentral. proquest.com/lib/dartmouth-ebooks/detail.action?docID=1179550

Participant Reflection

No matter whether you're interning on the Hill or with any organization focused on public policy, a thorough understanding of how Congress operates is crucial to being effective at your job. I did my fellowship with a trade association, and on a daily basis I applied the things I learned about Congress from this session. Hearing from alumni with jobs on the Hill really got me thinking about my own career and inspired me to do something related to public policy. Their advice is very applicable because many of them have gone through CST themselves!

CST Summer 2018

Martinez, D. (2009). Who does what, and where, in Washington. In *Washington internships: How to get them and use them to launch your public policy career* (pp. 7–36). University of Pennsylvania Press.

This session has been formatted and revised for consistency and clarity. This session in the Civic Skills Training Program is facilitated by alumni.

Session 4.9 Conducting High-Quality Research in the Workplace

Session Description

In this session, the facilitator will discuss the importance of high-quality research for sound policy making. In the workplace, participants may be asked to summarize and synthesize evidence on a particular topic to inform a policy decision. Given the enormous amount of information and resources available, it can be challenging to determine the most reliable resources for a given topic or to organize and present the evidence they gather in a way that highlights the most important aspects. This session will discuss strategies for conducting effective research, with an emphasis on techniques tailored to common research tasks in professional settings.

Leadership Competencies Addressed

Effective Reasoning
- Employs critical thinking in problem solving
- Employs creative thinking in problem solving
- Engages in inquiry, analysis, and follow-through
- Integrates multiple types of information to effectively solve problems or address issues

Effective Communication
- Clearly articulates ideas in a written and spoken form

Learning Objectives

Participants will do the following:
- Formulate research plans for different types of research projects
- Identify reputable research sources
- List three reasons that being meticulous is important in conducting research

Key Concepts and Definitions

Synthesis	Bringing together different sources, identifying the most important information, and developing a coherent argument.
Audience	Being aware of your audience means matching your research approach to the purpose for which it will be used.
Objectivity	Avoiding bias in choice of sources and interpretation of findings.

Required Materials

- PowerPoint slides and appropriate technology (optional)
- Excerpts from two different blogs on the same topic, for example, parental leave or wage inequality

Session Outline

Session duration: 1 hour and 35 minutes

Time Required		Description
15 minutes	Introduction	Introduce yourself and provide an overview of the session objectives. Discuss the role and expectations for research in the workplace; in public policy, research is fast-paced and focused on influencing decision-making. Define the key concepts.
10 minutes	Discussion	List and explain the main types of research projects: fact-finding and gathering of research, paragraph syntheses, "blogs," and research papers. Participants are more likely to encounter broader and succinct research projects in their fellowships, due to the nature of workplace research. Explain how each type of project is designed to most effectively use the appropriate research.
10 minutes	Activity 1	Divide participants into groups of four or five. Assign each group with a social problem and explain that the groups will spend 5 minutes evaluating it for a solution. Provide the following prompt for the activity: *Articulate the problem you're solving from the perspective of your target population: "As a _____, I want to_____, so that I can _____." Then dissect the previous statement and brainstorm solutions. Lastly, identify your stakeholder groups (sponsor, target population, collaborator, opposition).*
10 minutes	Discussion	Ask participants to share general thoughts about the previous activity. Ask them how framing the problem from the perspective of the target population shaped their discussion. Talk about understanding the landscape of a topic and how to ensure you are asking the right questions. Discuss ways to do this, like asking experts in the organization or by utilizing Google Scholar to conduct a quick literature review. A good strategy to follow is to write out the "so what," articulate and test assumptions, get feedback from colleagues, and prioritize the most important questions.

Time Required		Description
10 minutes	Activity 2	Within the same groups from Activity 1, ask participants to: summarize the 1–3 most influential sources of literature on the social problem that they are trying to solve and why they chose them; summarize the existing solutions for this problem; develop a prioritized list of research questions, along with their hypotheses for each; and identify potential primary sources that will help them answer the above questions.
10 minutes	Discussion	Ask participants to consider the pros and cons of some of the sources they identified. Choose volunteers to share their thoughts. Present on recognizing the quality of different sources. High-quality resources typically are non-partisan and non-political; end with ".org" or ".gov" or ".edu"; and have credible sources.
10 minutes	Activity 3	Present the "About" statement from the websites of three credible research sources that are concerned with the same social issue. For example, Citizens for Tax Justice, the Urban-Brookings Tax Policy Center, and the Tax Foundation. In small groups of three or four, ask participants to discuss the following questions: *What do you notice about these different research organizations? How would you feel about citing the organizations in different contexts? What are the strengths of these organizations from the narrative you have read about them?*
5 minutes	Discussion	Ask participants to share thoughts from their discussion. Present on best practices for collecting data and synthesizing sources. Discuss bias and how to recognize it, in your own research and in sources.
10 minutes	Activity 4	In the same groups from the previous exercise, ask participants to review two blogs you have selected on a particular topic and discuss these two questions: *To what extent does the blog accurately synthesize the original research? Can I identify any bias? What are alternative sources that might be helpful?*

Time Required		Description
5 minutes	Conclusion	Review the key takeaways from the session: Workplace research is fast-paced and focused on influencing decision-making; the people around you may be your biggest asset in research; invest the time to ask the right questions to focus your research; and always evaluate your sources to recognize bias. Answer any remaining questions from participants. Ask participants to complete the session evaluation using your desired format. Close the session by thanking the participants.

Reflection Questions

- How do I ensure that the research I'm producing meets the need in my organization?
- How do I avoid bias, both as a producer and a consumer of research?

Supplemental Resources

Fiedler, S. (2014, July 18). *Navigating the research process with TED speaker Uri Alon | SciTech Connect.* Elsevier SciTech Connect. http://scitechconnect.elsevier.com/find-c/, http://scitechconnect.elsevier.com/find-c/

Pannucci, C. J., & Wilkins, E. G. (2010). Identifying and avoiding bias in research. *Plastic and Reconstructive Surgery, 126*(2), 610–625. https://doi.org/10.1097/PRS.0b013e3181de24bc

Participant Reflection

Two pieces of advice really stuck out to me. One, ask questions from the beginning about the expectations, scope, and purpose of the research assignment. Good writing is so context dependent, and the research we produce can only be good insofar as it fulfills the need of the organization. Second, include your supervisor in the drafting process and ask questions to ensure what you have produced already is still meeting expectations. I want to try to draft outlines and other mini-stages of the assignment, which I can show and get feedback on.

CST Summer 2020

TED. (2014, June 12). *Uri Alon: Why truly innovative science demands a leap into the unknown* [Video]. YouTube. https://www.youtube.com/watch?v=F1U26PLiXjM&feature=emb_logo&ab_channel=TED

University of Texas at Arlington, & University of Wollongong, Australia. (2020, November 16). *Subject and course guides: Research process :: Step by step: Evaluate sources.* University of Texas at Arlington Libraries. https://libguides.uta.edu/researchprocess/sources

This session has been formatted and revised for consistency and clarity. The original session in the Civic Skills Training Program was facilitated by Mary Peng, reached at mpengottowa@gmail.com.

Session 4.10 The Art of Notetaking

Session Description

In this session, the facilitator will outline the skill set of notetaking. Using a mix of exploratory discussions and activities, the facilitator will introduce participants to the key steps of notetaking, as well as other tips and tricks for professional writing. This session points to the importance of notes as a reminder to oneself, a source, or even as a public record. The facilitator will also stress how good notetaking requires identifying a purpose, participating in the appropriate manner while taking notes, and compiling the information in a relatable way for the correct audience.

Leadership Competencies Addressed

Effective Reasoning
- Engages in inquiry, analysis, and follow-through

Effective Communication
- Clearly articulates ideas in a written and spoken form
- Exhibits effective listening skills

Learning Objectives

Participants will do the following:
- Identify and evaluate forums for notetaking and forms of notetaking for recording large amounts of new information quickly and accurately through exercises and discussion
- Practice taking notes for different situations and evaluate their notes, as well as the notes of a partner
- Discern general best practices of effective notetaking in different situations

Key Concepts and Definitions

Purpose	The end goal of an action and/or the on-going effect of an action.
Expectations	The baseline actions and efforts desired from you by your colleagues, superiors, and clients, as well as your own ideas and beliefs about a situation or project; understanding "the ask" from your supervisor and colleagues to avoid unnecessary rework.
Professionalism	Defined in the Merriam-Webster Dictionary as "the skill, good judgment, and polite behavior that is expected from a person who is trained to do a job well." One can never be too professional.
Resilience	The ability to recognize an activity stressor, take a brief step away from the activity, remind yourself that you are capable of completing your task, and continue working on the activity with a positive and energetic attitude.

Required Materials

- PowerPoint slides and appropriate technology (optional)
- Audio (and optionally video) for 2-3 speech examples
- Paper and writing utensils
- Handout 4.10.1 The Art of Notetaking
- Any debate video, perhaps from C-SPAN or Youtube

Pre-session Assignment:

- Watch Prince Ea's "A Brand New Ending." This video is available to watch on YouTube (https://youtu.be/2e2mwoIXv8Q).

Session Outline

Session duration: 1 hour 30 minutes

Time Required		Description
20 minutes	Introduction	Play 2–3 short audio or video clips and ask participants to take thorough notes of what is said during each. Find a diversity of clips, for example one may be very wordy and another very fast or boring. Ask participants what these videos have in common. Highlight that these examples may resemble some of the meetings or events participants may be asked to attend and take notes at during internships; some will be more exciting than others, but each assignment will be equally important. Review the primary session objectives and agenda items. Pass out Handout 4.10.1.
15 minutes	Discussion	Give examples of the different forums for notetaking: in-person meetings, phone/video conferences, events, interviews, etc. Invite participant contributions when making this list. Discuss the different forms of notetaking (laptops/tablets, cell phones, voice recorder, pen and paper, etc.) and their pros and cons (speed, technical difficulties, efficiency, space, etc.). Ask participants to contribute to these lists.

Time Required		Description
15 minutes	Framing	Speak about best practices of effective notetaking: establishing the purpose of the event and the purpose of the notes (i.e., private consumption vs. public consumption); do homework and find context to be best prepared to take notes (i.e., what meetings have already taken place and what were the action items coming out of those meetings; is the topic a high/low-priority issue); note the title, date, location, participant names, number of participants, and, when necessary, mood in the room; collect handouts and scan after the meeting, event, etc.; focus on capturing the major points of the conversation (i.e., paraphrase); use abbreviations and/or graphics, whenever possible; when taking notes using a pen(cil) and notepad, use neat handwriting and do not waste time erasing; keep notes organized using a system that works for you (i.e., separate sections/notebook for different topics); identify questions and next steps from the meeting, event, etc.; if notes are for public consumption, prepare notes and get the proper approval for distribution. Ask participants to contribute to the list once you have finished.
15 minutes	Activity	Play the Debate video clip and ask participants to take thorough notes during the video.
20 minutes	Reflection	Ask participants to reflect independently for three minutes on the quality of their own notes and why they feel the way they do. Have participants exchange their notes with a partner and evaluate that partner's work independently for three minutes. Then, partners should discuss bright spots and areas of growth for four minutes. With the entire group, discuss which tools and strategies could make their notetaking more effective and how their notes compared to each other's in terms of content (i.e., did you and your partner capture the same or different ideas). Highlight the strategies discussed earlier in the presentation and emphasize the importance of working with other interns/colleagues to make sure that all major points are captured—teamwork can be another great strategy for taking effective notes. The bottom of the last page of Handout 4.10.1 lists the general reflection questions.
5 minutes	Conclusion	Ask participants to complete the session evaluation using your desired format. Close the session by thanking the participants.

Reflection Questions

- Do I understand the purpose of my notetaking assignment?
- Do I have the right tools to take effective notes?
- Have I done my homework to learn as much as I can about the session?
- Do I have a professional mentor or role model with whom I can check in, ask questions, receive feedback, and be honest about my struggles and concerns?
- How can I integrate what I learned today about effective notetaking into other areas of my life?

Supplemental Resources

Donohoo, J. (2010). Learning how to learn: Cornell notes as an example. *Journal of Adolescent & Adult Literacy, 54*(3), 224–227.

Dyer, J. W., Riley, J., & Yekovich, F. R. (1979). An analysis of three study skills: Notetaking, summarizing, and rereading. *The Journal of Educational Research, 73*(1), 3–7. https://doi.org/10.1080/00220671.1979.10885194

Fisher, D., & Frey, N. (2013a). Gradual release of responsibility instructional framework. *IRA E-Ssentials.* https://pdo.ascd.org/lmscourses/pd13oc005/media/formativeassessmentandccswithelaliteracymod_3-reading3.pdf

Fisher, D., & Frey, N. (2013b). *Better learning through structured teaching: A framework for the gradual release of responsibility* (2nd ed.). ASCD.

This session has been formatted and revised for consistency and clarity. The original session in the Civic Skills Training Program was facilitated by Ariel Murphy Bedford, reached at ariel@ambnational.org.

Participant Reflection

Notetaking is something so seemingly simple yet so fundamentally important. I have been able to apply these skills in the workplace and it has been incredibly effective. It doesn't only save time when you're able to go back through your notes and find exactly what you need from that particular meeting you had yesterday, but it also shows your coworkers that you care. In fact, I've had multiple supervisors compliment me on my extensive notetaking. It has quite literally helped me make a good impression! This also led me to be more credible in the workplace.

CST Summer 2018

The Art of Notetaking

Notetaking Comparison Exercise

VERSION A

Date	Start	End
8/16/21		

Meeting	Agenda
Purpose of the Meeting	**A list of topics, presenters, and time allotment**
Prep: Leadership Trip Retreat	
Attendees	

Action Item Review

Were all items implemented as planned?

_____
_____
_____
_____

Action Plan (Tasks assigned during the meeting. The 3W-rule: What, Who, When)

Action Item	Delegated To	Deadline

Notes

- April
  - Project planning + milestones (review)
- Spring Leadership Retreat
  - Consultant (Emily H.)

Outcomes
- Clarity around roles + responsibilities
- Structures that help us move forward (discussion)
- Balance discussion + creation of work product
- Comprehensive plan for team
- Project management tool
  - Workstreams

STRENGTHS	AREAS OF GROWTH

VERSION B

Date	Start	End
7/24/21	11:00 am	11:30 am

Meeting	Agenda
Purpose of the Meeting	**A list of topics, presenters, and time allotment**
Data collection, monitoring, and allocations	Data Tracker for Talent Office - update
Attendees	
Hannah, Ariel, Sara, Jennifer, Dannielle & Nicole	

Action Item Review

Were all items implemented as planned?

_____

_____

_____

Action Plan (Tasks assigned during the meeting. The 3W-rule: What, Who, When)

Action Item	Delegated To	Deadline
★ Clarify what data should be collected, when & how	JT	Next mtg
★ Check w/ Rebecca/Litsy re: Her data collection efforts	AM	Next mtg
★ Develop recs for platform decision ★ Mtg (30 min) wo Hannah to discuss	AM	Next mtg

Notes

Background:
- Meet 3 times/week
- Paint clear picture of numerical streams + TIF allocations
- Danielle leads w/ Jennifer + Nicole contributing
- See Google spreadsheet: "Talent Data Tracker"

Updates:
★ "Questions/Priorities" tab (Column C: Relevant Data)
★ Categorizing where data is coming from
    ○ Line 20 + up must be finalizes still
★ Focus on clarifying what should be collected, when and how, which impacts callout plans

★ Check w Litsy/Rebecca rec: additional data collection efforts on their end and see if consultation can happen (don't need to leep w every office)
   ○ FYI: Data team gives each office access
      ▪ Low-coding queries that our team could access would be helpful (i.e. mse hive is fluid review)
★ Timeline/calendar re: what data collections are recorder + when
★ "Platform" tab
   ○ We need to select a platform (mse hive is fluid rev)
   ○ Must see recommendations budget, options, pros/cons
      ▪ Historical data input capability in mse hive (+)
      ▪ 30 min mtg w/ Sara to further discuss

STRENGTHS	AREAS OF GROWTH

Notetaking Template 1: Inspired by Uncommon Schools

Meeting: _____   Date: _____

Questions	Meeting Notes

Action Item	Owner	Deadline

Notetaking Template 2: The Cornell Notetaking System

Meeting: _____   Date: _____

Key Points	Details
	_____
	_____
	_____
	_____
	_____
	_____
	_____
	_____
	_____
	_____
	_____
	_____
	_____
	_____
	_____
	_____

Summary

_____
_____
_____
_____
_____
_____
_____
_____
_____
_____
_____
_____
_____
_____
_____
_____
_____

Notetaking Template 3: Inspired by Action Day Meeting & Action Notebook

Date	Start	End

Meeting	Agenda
Purpose of the Meeting	**A list of topics, presenters, and time allotment**
	_____
	_____
	_____
	_____
	_____
Attendees	_____
	_____
	_____

Action Item Review

Were all items implemented as planned?

_____

_____

_____

_____

Action Plan (Tasks assigned during the meeting. The 3W-rule: What, Who, When)

Action Item	Delegated To	Deadline
_____		
_____		
_____		
_____		

Notes

_____

_____

_____

_____

_____

_____

_____

_____

Final Notetaking Exercise:
Take notes for the debate video clip you are about to watch.

_____
_____
_____
_____
_____
_____
_____
_____

Independent Reflection:
How strong are my notes and why?

_____
_____
_____
_____

Partner Reflection:
How strong are my partner's notes and why?

_____
_____
_____
_____

Whole Group Reflection:
What other tools/strategies could be used to make the notes more effective?

_____
_____
_____

How do my notes compare to my partner's notes in terms of content?

_____
_____
_____
_____

General Reflection Questions to Keep in Mind:

- Do I understand the purpose of my notetaking assignment?
- Do I have the right tools to take effective notes?
- Have I done my homework to learn as much as I can about the session?
- Do I have a professional mentor or role model with whom I can check in, ask questions, receive feedback, and be honest about my struggles and concerns?
- How can I integrate what I learned today about effective notetaking into other areas of my life?

_____

_____

_____

_____

_____

_____

_____

Session 4.11 Networking—Presenting Your Best Self

Session Description

In this session, the facilitator will guide participants toward a better understanding of networking and its purpose. The facilitator will also discuss the broader scope of social connections, the benefits of strong social connections in today's culture, and how confidence and authenticity in ourselves can increase connections. This session will incorporate role-plays of networking scenarios, as well as time for reflection and small group discussions on topics such as authenticity, confidence, and anxiety. The session will end with a mock networking experience in preparation for any event designed to highlight networking.

Leadership Competencies Addressed

Collaboration
*   Fosters a welcoming and inclusive environment

Effective Communication
*   Exhibits effective listening skills

Self-Knowledge
*   Practices self-compassion, friendliness, ease with self, and vulnerability

Learning Objectives

Participants will do the following:
*   Identify at least three people in their existing networks
*   Describe at least three differences between inauthentic and authentic approaches to networking
*   Explain at least three ways to build confidence in networking
*   Practice networking methods through mock scenarios and a mock networking activity

Key Concepts and Definitions

Networking   Interacting with other people to exchange information and develop contacts, especially to further one's career.

Authenticity   Vulnerability that allows us to let go of the demands of perfection we place on ourselves and allows us to build trust and connection with other human beings.

Required Materials

* PowerPoint slides and appropriate technology (optional)

Pre-session Assignment:
* Ted Talk by Amy Cuddy, "Your Body Language Shapes Who You Are." This video is available on the TED website (www.ted.com).

Session Outline

Session duration: 1 hour and 25 minutes

Time Required		Description
15 minutes	Introduction	Introduce yourself to participants as you would if you were networking. Use this as an introduction to the session and some of the things that will be covered. Discuss networking with the following points in mind: Networking is about creating and nurturing sustainable two-way relationships; networking is not transactional; there are many opportunities and platforms for networking (events, email, social media, etc.); strong networks are based on commonalities and shared interests. Ask participants what their purpose is while they network.
25 minutes	Framing	Ask participants to think about their existing personal networks: Whom do they interact with regularly and every day? Whom do they interact with occasionally? These people include but are not limited to family, friends, coworkers, and peers. Ask participants to consider that the context of these relationships may be bigger than they seem now; someone could even be a potential bridge between people. Ask participants what organizations or people they really want to connect with and how they can take the proper steps.
		Discuss signs of confidence and the importance of playing to one's strengths as an introvert or extrovert. Cover the following concepts: vulnerability and being genuine allows us to build trust and connections with others; listening is the key to building relationships; body language can make you appear more confident, if not actually improve your confidence; strong body language is eye contact, a firm handshake, uncrossed arms, good posture, and a relaxed expression.

Time Required		Description
		Take a poll of the introverts in the room. Explain that though large events can be draining for them, they have specific strengths in networking, such as listening and a preference for one-on-one conversations. Ask all participants to think about how they can be their most authentic selves.
15 minutes	Activity 1	Pair up the participants and present these two scenarios for them to work through: Scenario 1. You want a job in a new field but don't know many professionals in that field. There is an upcoming networking event that would be a great opportunity to get your foot in the door, so you decide to attend. At the event, you meet someone who works at a company you've been interested in. What is your approach to networking with this individual? Scenario 2. You learn that a friend of a friend whom you've met once just launched a new project and you would really love to be a part of it. Your friend shares this individual's email with you and tells you to reach out. What do you write in your email?
10 minutes	Reflection	Ask participants to share their thoughts or concerns after roleplaying the scenarios. Open the floor for participants to ask you more specific questions about tips or approaches to networking.
15 minutes	Activity 2	Ask participants to network with each other, using the lessons from the session. Note: You can create further practice of this skill by setting up subsequent networking sessions, for example a reception for students and alumni, peers, and colleagues.
5 minutes	Conclusion	Ask participants to complete the session evaluation using your desired format. Close the session by thanking the participants.

Supplemental Resources

Menon, T. (2017, March). *The secret to great opportunities? The person you haven't met yet* [Video]. TEDxOhioStateUniversity. https://www.ted.com/talks/tanya_menon_the_secret_to_great_opportunities_the_person_you_haven_t_met_yet

TEDx Talks. (2018, February 15). *How to hack networking | David Burkus | TEDxUniversityofNevada* [Video]. YouTube. https://www.youtube.com/watch?v=xFrqZjIDE44&ab_channel=TEDxTalks

Weaver, A. C., & Morrison, B. B. (2008). Social networking. *Computer, 41*(2), 97–100. https://doi.org/10.1109/MC.2008.61

Participant Reflection

Catherine told us that authenticity is having the vulnerability to let go of the pursuit of perfection. This means that when I show up as an intern, I should be honest and ask questions when I need help. By sharing myself without feeling like I need to be perfect, I will be able to build trust and more genuine connections with the people I will be working with this summer.

CST Summer 2020

This session has been formatted and revised for consistency and clarity. The original session in the Civic Skills Training Program was facilitated by Catherine Miller, reached at catherineannettemiller@gmail.com.

FYF: Summer Fellowships

Key Program Elements

➢ Methodical mentor selection based on these criteria: Do they have a substantive project? Are they developmentally focused? Do they have time to meet with a participant?
➢ Completion of a fellowship with at least one concrete technical skill they can demonstrate
➢ Understanding of workplace culture, industry, and professionalism
➢ Participants establish a network of professionals

Program Description

The FYF Summer Fellowships, the fourth component of the First-Year Fellows Program, ties together participant experience with prerequisite courses, D-LAB, and Civic Skills Training through an eight- to ten-week fellowship in the public policy arena with Dartmouth alumni mentors in Washington, D.C. Fellows gain valuable professional experience and early exposure to policy and government, live with their peers, and develop leadership, writing, and critical thinking skills during the fellowships. Since program inception, participants in this program have been placed in government, nonprofit, and media organizations.

Placements and mentors are selected by the Rockefeller Center using a two-pronged approach. In the first approach, we look to see if there are alumni in organizations in which we would like to place our Fellows. In the other, we look to see if there are alumni we know in the D.C. area who would make great mentors. We then establish contact and determine their interest in participating in the program by meeting them in person or through a video conference. This gives us a sense of their engagement and investment in participants. During this conversation, we gauge their interest in participating in the program as a mentor and their ability to offer a fellowship. If they are willing and able to host a fellow, we move on to the confirmation form (Handout 4.1).

Full completion and the return of the confirmation form by a given time serve as the official confirmation for the mentor. The placement is then added to the list of potential mentors for a given year. In rare cases, we have a great placement at an organization, but the alumnus/alumna who served as a mentor previously does not work there anymore. In such cases, we pair the fellow with a supervisor within the organization and an alumnus mentor outside of the organization who works in a similar field. All mentors must be willing to invest time and energy in their Fellows to make this a developmental experience.

We use the mentor confirmation form as a discussion guide with mentors and to gather all necessary information in one place. One of the hallmarks of a fellowship is an eight-week project assigned and selected by their mentor. The project needs to be substantive and have some contribution to the mission of the organization. Mentors outline the project in their confirmation form, provide a description of what they are looking for in a Fellow, provide information about specific organizational requirements, and include other additional information such as dress code and institution-specific needs. This provides us with clarity about mentor expectations for Fellows who will be placed with them and helps the mentors to visually assess the commitment.

Fellows live together in D.C. in apartment-style housing. This opportunity to live together while learning together provides them with an established support network in what might otherwise be an entirely new experience.

Three weeks into the program we do a mid-term check-in. We fly down to D.C. and meet with each Fellow to learn about the progress they are making in their fellowship and what they are learning. We also give them an opportunity to develop strategies to address challenges they are facing.

At the end of the program, Fellows and mentors fill out surveys evaluating their experience. They are asked to reflect on different aspects of their experiences in the program and to assess their likelihood to recommend the placement to another Fellow next year or their likelihood to return as a mentor.

Four weeks after the program concludes, we gather Fellows to do a debrief on their experience. During this time, we come together and reflect on all the learning that has taken place, share stories, and explore learning opportunities that are on the horizon for these students.

As you will imagine, this year was different because of COVID-19. However, it gave us opportunities to expand the program to 26 Fellows. Twenty-six mentors (some returning and some new) willingly and enthusiastically worked with us to offer remote placements. Being remote in 2020 and 2021 provided us the opportunity to host a variety of different style check-ins throughout the weeks of the program.

First-Year Fellows Program Mentor Confirmation Form

Fellowship Dates	
Organization	
Physical Address	
City, State Zip	
Phone Number	
Mentor	
Position	
Email	
Phone	
Bio	
Daily Supervisor (if different from mentor)	
Position	
Email	
Phone	
Intern Coordinator (point of contact if Rocky needs to coordinate directly)	
Position	
Email	
Phone	
Host Organization Description / Website	
Description of the fellowship responsibilities/tasks	
Description of the office environment	

Desired skills and qualities (e.g., second language, coding skills)	
Specific organization requirements (e.g., U.S. citizenship, pre-approval required by HR)	
Internal host organization's approval process requirements (e.g., online application)	
Office dress code	

FYF Program Officer Reflection

by Hannah Andritsakis

I joined the Rockefeller Center in January 2020 eager to continue cultivating the next generation of leaders equipped with skills to excel amid 21st century demands. As someone interested in neuroscience, social emotional learning, and instructional scaffolding as they relate to leadership development, I was immediately captivated by the First-Year Fellows Program with its intentional framework, relevant learning objectives, and seemingly boundless opportunities.

The First-Year Fellows Program consists of prerequisites and 20–26 fellowships. This program seeks to build a strong foundation of public policy, leadership, and work experience for its participants. There are both curricular and co-curricular components.

The first curricular component includes an introduction to the public policy course and a statistical methods course. These help participants develop industry-specific building blocks.

The three mandatory co-curricular components are Dartmouth Leadership Attitudes and Behaviors (D-LAB), Civic Skills Training (CST), and Summer Fellowships. In D-LAB, participants engage in crucial conversations about beliefs, values, and differing perspectives. In CST, participants develop and practice the skills necessary to excel in their internships and beyond. In their fellowships, participants put all their learning into action by engaging in a policy fellowship under the mentorship of a Dartmouth alum.

I believe that to develop as leaders, we need to hold ourselves accountable for building our internal and external self-awareness by practicing reflection and dialogue. However, I think taking time to connect with our thoughts to become intimate with our values and then to articulate them requires intentional effort. I find engaging in this work can feel daunting if we aren't disciplined because we have a world of distractions at our fingertips. While acclimating to the Center, I witnessed the facilitator training and the six sessions of D-LAB unfold. I was also given the opportunity to lead the facilitator debrief. I observed how D-LAB helped students to carve out that intentional time. They worked together to build a practice that is still imprinted in the minds of alumni. The following quote from a participant in the D-LAB program in the winter of 2020 summarizes participant learning in this program: "The program's meticulously designed and thoughtfully facilitated sessions helped me better define my values and connect them to the academic and extracurricular opportunities I chose to pursue throughout the remainder of my college experience."

In late March, the First Year Fellows staff members at the Rockefeller Center made the decision to offer remote fellowships and CST in response to the COVID-19 pandemic. Together, they took on the challenge of preparing students to work in a remote office setting in unprecedented times. Already inspired by online learning and the Community of Inquiry (CoI) Model referenced in Chapter 8 of this book, I found myself excited by the prospect of transferring and translating the purposeful design of these programs into our new virtual world.

As we navigated, the change questions naturally surfaced. How would a remote fellowship compare to an in-person one? Would they feel lonely? What additional skills or information do Fellows need to know to be successful remote workers? As a result, the modality and some of the CST content had to change. An adaptation of CST materialized that consisted of both synchronous and asynchronous components. It was during this process that I appreciated how imperative it was to have a system that documented the "what" and the "why" behind a program. To that end, the session proposal forms that you see adapted throughout this book are essential, and even more so in helping us turn CST virtual. The proposal form (see Handout 2.5 in Chapter 2) gave us all a clear picture of what sessions took place and why. Even though I had never seen a CST session in person, I could extrapolate this information because of these documents. They helped to guide our decisions about session delivery and content so we could make strategic changes to the program that do not sacrifice learning outcomes. Our content highlighted best-practices for remote work, hard and soft skills students needed for their fellowship experience, and student reflections of their remote learning habits—all of which were used to inform the ways in which their individual needs could be related to their remote fellowship placements.

Then in mid-June, the fellowships began and at the end of eight weeks, each student had learned at least one transferrable hard skill that they could identify with pride. However, what intrigued me more was the learning they did that went beyond a bullet point on their resume.

For instance, one day in early July my phone rang, and it was a student calling to seek some advice. She was completing her workplace tasks faster than they were being assigned to her. Could she ask for more work? Would that be rude? Should they be taking her longer? Her supervisor was busy, and she did not want to be a burden. We talked through some strategies that she could use when she talked to her supervisor next. Armed with confidence and a few possible solutions to this problem, she met with her supervisor. She came out of that meeting with an action plan to increase her workplace contribution and visibly track her tasks. She learned how to advocate for herself.

In mid-July I checked in with another student who was having regular one-on-ones with her mentor. She told me how, during their second meeting, her mentor stopped shortly to explain that she should come prepared to guide these meetings with her updates and questions. She was completely puzzled by this. She assumed that because the mentor was in a position of power, they should always be leading meetings. She learned about workplace culture.

It was in these moments I recognized students were still having transformative learning experiences despite the program's remote nature. The final mentor and Fellow evaluations reaffirmed this thought. If you are looking to adapt the fellowship portion of this program, it would be crucial to have developmentally focused and willing mentors who are providing real work opportunities and engagement. I have been told being a mentor is rewarding, but it is undoubtedly additional work. A committed mentor makes all the difference in the participant's experience.

During our final debrief in September, a peculiar feeling overtook me as I hovered over the end-meeting icon for the last time. I felt both heavy and light, the way I normally feel when I finish working with students in person. Sad to see them go, but grateful for the time we shared. It was then that I realized I felt like I knew them in person. As these thoughts rattled in my brain, a participant wrote in the chat something along the lines of "I feel like this was in person." They felt it too! This led me to question what defines a quality relationship. Does merely being in person truly mean a better-quality relationship? After this experience, I don't think so. I think it's the effort and mindset you and the other party approach the relationship with that is most important, not the modality of that relationship.

If you want to adopt a program such as FYF, practicing participant-centered design is essential. At the heart of all the Rockefeller programs is the student voice. Hearing the phrase "What do the students think?" is not uncommon. That is why D-LAB is facilitated by students in student spaces. It's why when adapting CST, we checked in with our students using surveys at several points throughout the planning and implementation process. This provided them the opportunity to offer feedback on our content or delivery. It's why we do a mid-term check-in and debrief during the fellowships. As a result, the program is more relevant to our participants and they feel invested in the success because we included them in the process.

Having to quickly adapt these programs in turbulent times made me realize how much I value being a part of an organizational culture with a commitment to trust and authentic conversations. The timeline to produce this program was tight, and I had a background in developing online orientations and trainings from my previous work experience. There were several instances in which I was tasked with making decisions quickly, such as determining in what platform this or that program would live. This level of trust in my abilities not only helped to enhance the program but it also helped me feel like my experience was valued. This trust encouraged me to continue to go above and beyond in my role for our students and team. In addition, throughout this process I was able to engage in genuine discussions with my colleagues about our successes, challenges, strengths, and weakness. They were reflective and mission driven in nature. These exchanges enhanced our collaboration by helping us to divide up tasks and set personal growth goals. Without this culture, I believe our adaptations would not have been as strong or successful.

5 | Management and Leadership Development Program (MLDP)

Management is doing things right and leadership is doing the right things.

—Warren Bennis and Burt Nanus

The Management and Leadership Development Program (MLDP) is a one-term program offered three times a year. This program was developed because the Civic Skills Training Program, which was open to many students, had to be absorbed into the First-Year Fellows Program and, as a result, had created a gap for students seeking to build their management skills. Another reason was that the Center was turning away many students who had applied for the selective Rockefeller Leadership Fellows Program.

Program Goal

The program's goal is to develop practical competencies and capacities that participants can apply in real time within their leadership and management roles on campus, during internships, and in their careers after they graduate.

This program is open to all students campus wide, especially participants with some previous leadership or professional experience looking to develop management and leadership competencies common to corporate, public, and nonprofit sectors. MLDP is designed to help participants become self-aware and understand the context and situation within which they operate. We hope they will demonstrate integrity, authenticity, ethical and appropriate behavior, and responsibility to community. In addition, they also need to work well in teams both as leaders and followers, be technically competent, and demonstrate professionalism. Participants come away with new and improved management and leadership skills, which they can then apply to roles within campus organizations, internships, projects, and entry-level careers.

Program Prerequisites

MLDP is open to all students on campus except for participants in their first year in college. This is because many of them do not have work or internship experiences, and this program is for higher levels of maturity, development, and experience.

Program Participation

The program values diversity and works intentionally to invite participants from different majors and different parts of campus. Since the fall of 2014, we have attracted students who intend to major in 38 different fields of study, ranging from the humanities to STEM and the arts. Table 5.1 represents what MLDP participants had declared as their majors while they were completing the program. The five most popular majors for MLDP participants are, in descending order: government, economics, history, psychology, and geography.

Table 5.1

Ten Most Popular Majors for MLDP Participants, Fall 2014–Spring 2020

Major	Number of Participants
Government	139
Economics	138
History	30
Psychology	29
Geography	27
Computer Science	26
Biology	26
Sociology	23
Neuroscience	19
Engineering	19

MLDP attracts more female than male participants; since 2014, 55% of the students who successfully completed MLDP identified as female. MLDP also serves a considerable number of international students. Historically, 10.9% of MLDP participants are international students who collectively represent 29 different countries. MLDP also directs its energy toward developing partnerships with the First-Year Student Enrichment Program (FYSEP) and the Athletics program to expand on diversity and inclusivity. The FYSEP program on Dartmouth's campus serves low-income and first generation first-year students. Second, third, and final year undergraduates who have participated in FYSEP are invited to participate in MLDP.

MLDP has developed definitions for what constitutes completion of the program as well as criteria for completing the program with excellence. These definitions have been consistently applied across years, which allows the program to clearly articulate expectations to students and implementors alike. We strictly adhere to our attendance policy of two excused absences, but we also direct our efforts to offering make-up sessions for sessions participants miss. Additionally, participants must complete a Personal Leadership Challenge (PLC). This is also a way to maintain the quality of the program and participant learning. Finally, students who have completed MLDP may receive special recognition if peers or staff have nominated them at least twice during the program for the "with Excellence" designation.

On average, 34% of participants who completed MLDP received the "with Excellence" distinction from Fall 2014 through Spring 2019. Although the program aspires to educate as many participants as possible, we found that there were high dropout rates in the earlier years of the program due to the less competitive nature of the application process. Completing MLDP "with Excellence" was introduced in 2014 to encourage students to participate more intentionally, and this has proved to be a very successful strategy to reduce attrition.

As seen in Figure 5.1, the number of MLDP registrants has decreased, on average, from Fall 2014 to Spring 2019, but the number of participants who completed MLDP during the term they were originally assigned has remained quite consistent. This is because the percent of registrants who complete the program has increased from about 60% in Fall 2014 to nearly 100% in Spring 2019. In this same time frame, the number of students who completed the program each term has varied from 33 (Spring 2019) to 54 (Spring 2015). The average number of participants who completed MLDP from 2014 to 2019 was 42 students, and the average number of registrants during this time period was 60 students.

Figure 5.1

MLDP Participant and Completion Data Since 2014

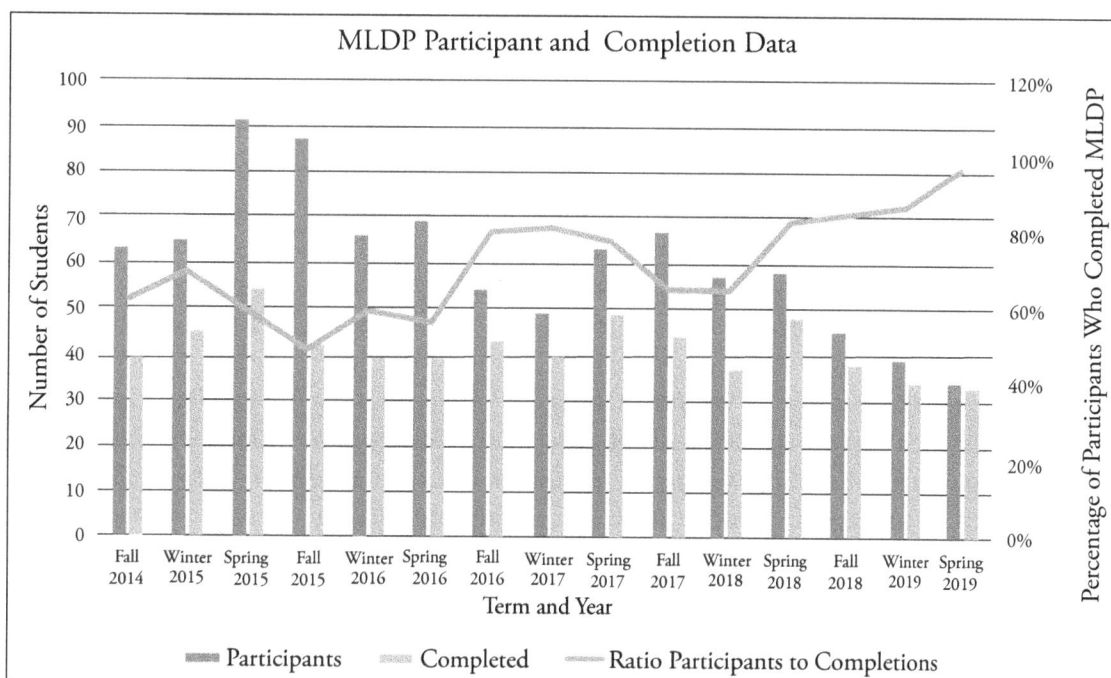

Key Program Elements

> ➢ The skill-focused speaker-led sessions
> ➢ The Personal Leadership Challenge
> ➢ A coaching session with a staff member
> ➢ Participant-led dinner discussions
> ➢ The off-campus experience session
> ➢ The opportunity to complete the program "with Excellence"

Program Description

MLDP is managed by a program officer and student assistants who play an important role in helping with the logistics and working with participants to build a sense of community. Each Tuesday evening throughout the term, accomplished guest speakers lead discussions and learning exercises on vital elements of management and leadership. Session content focuses on competencies described by the National Association of College Employers (NACE) survey for students to be successful in the workplace. Some of these are self-awareness, team-building and interpersonal communication, public speaking, negotiation, and professionalism in communication. Session content is also based on research findings from program comparison with peer institutions, alumni input, and suggestions from supervisors of students who receive internship funding from the Rockefeller Center.

MLDP offers a "Personal Leadership Challenge," or PLC (see Handout 5.1.2), which is a way for learners to craft their own leadership challenge in the beginning of the program. Participants demonstrate their learning and evaluate their progress through goal-setting frameworks, accountability groups, and personal reflection. At least once during the term, participants meet with a trained career and life coach to discuss their PLC. During the coaching session, the coach asks questions to dig beneath the surface and discover the participants' motivations, triggers, values, and limiting beliefs that drive their behavior. Participants work with the coach to set personalized SMART goals (see Handout 5.1.3) to address their challenge. Throughout the term, participants check in with each other to learn from their peers' experiences and to hold each other accountable. The PLC culminates in a 2–3 page written reflection.

One venue for participants to check in with each other is through the participant-led dinner discussions. Trained student program assistants run small-group discussions over dinner that focus on practical ways to incorporate program content or reflect on it. Participants stay in the same small groups throughout the term, which creates relationships that last well beyond the program.

Another important component of the program is the off-campus excursion. Participants can see how the concepts they explore in the classroom translate to local organizations. All participants are given a choice to visit a nonprofit or for-profit organization. Learners identify the mission and values of the organization, see how the practices of that organization connect to its mission and values, and discuss with organizational leadership the challenges and successes they encounter. Examples of organizations that host visits are a local homeless shelter and food pantry, a food cooperative, and a small local theatre. Although the program introduces participants to the organizations, it is their personal choice if they wish to stay engaged after program completion.

MLDP outreach relies on word-of-mouth spread by past program participants and intentional outreach to all parts of campus spearheaded by student assistants and the program officer, who are assisted in this effort by program ambassadors. Ambassadors are participants who have successfully completed the program and encourage others to apply for it. Given that the size of the program every term is large, the program is divided into two sections that are offered back-to-back and led by the same guest speakers. Once participants decide to join a section, they cannot switch sections. This is to ensure that each cohort may become closely acquainted and that every participant is offered ample interaction with facilitators.

Successful completion of MLDP is a prerequisite to become a student program assistant at the Center. It also strengthens students' applications for funding offered by the Rockefeller Center for unpaid internships in the field of public policy, as well as selection into other Rockefeller Center programs, such as the Rockefeller Leadership Fellows Program.

Key Leadership Competencies

The key leadership competencies the program focuses on are self-knowledge, effective communication, and management. MLDP helps participants recognize their strengths and weaknesses, and learn about management, professionalism and work ethic.

Possible Adaptations

In addition to higher education, this program can be applicable to nonprofit organizations, for-profit organizations, government institutions, and anyone working within communities. It is also applicable for K-12 audiences. Managing oneself as a leader or a follower is common to all these institutions. Some ideas to adapt this program are as follows:

- ➢ Identify your audience and their needs. Research what is known or not known about these needs.
- ➢ Use the Eight Pillars of Program Design to develop your concept.
- ➢ Make sure the content you cover matches the experience and maturity level of your audience.
- ➢ Create a structure within which you will sequence the content.
- ➢ Make sure you have enough time for individual and group reflections.
- ➢ Consider how to use alumni, colleagues with expertise, and committed leaders in the community as guest speakers and for promotion of programs.

Session 5.1 What's Your "Why" of Management and Leadership?

Session Description

In this session, the facilitator will clarify expectations and give opportunities to practice some of them right away with the help of a student-led improv group. Participants will begin to explore an integral part of MLDP, the Personal Leadership Challenge (PLC), and learn to craft SMART goals to address their challenge. By the end of the session, participants will have experience writing their own SMART goals and a plan to complete their leadership challenge by the conclusion of the program.

Learning Objectives

Participants will do the following:
- Identify three ways that they can take responsibility for their own learning throughout the program
- Analyze an example of a PLC and write one to three SMART goals for it
- Develop a work plan for the PLC example

Leadership Competencies Addressed

Collaboration
- Fosters a welcoming and inclusive environment

Management
- Develops and implements a plan for goal attainment

Effective Reasoning
- Develops personal reflective practice

Principled Action
- Demonstrates personal responsibility

Self-Knowledge
- Shows self-respect and respect for others

Key Concepts and Definitions

Risk taking	Taking action toward some desired result, despite uncertainty of achieving it.
Growth	A positive, measurable change that can occur externally or internally.
Defining expectations	The crucial statement of limits and goals that can help one achieve their objectives.
Courageous leadership	This is required of people who must make difficult decisions. Courageous leaders are willing to push through uncomfortable situations and do not back down when things get hard.

Extroversion/ introversion	A personality trait that describes where a person's energy is derived. Extroverts are energized from being around other people. Introverts are energized from being alone.
Gantt chart	A chart for project planning which shows tasks needed to be done, a timeline for these tasks, and person(s) responsible.
SMART goals	This is a framework for goal setting. SMART is an acronym for Specific, Manageable, Attainable, Realistic, and Time-bound. A SMART goal is 1–2 sentences and has all five components.

Required Materials

- MLDP folders including: schedule, program information, Handout 5.1.1 Examples of the Differences Between Introverts and Extroverts, Handout 5.1.2 Personal Leadership Challenge, and Handout 5.1.3 SMART Goals Worksheet

Session Outline

Session duration: 1 hour and 30 minutes

Time Required		Description
35 minutes	Introduction	Introduce yourself and ask participants to introduce themselves to those around them. Introduce the Management and Leadership Development Program and give a brief history of the program. Ask participants to discuss in small groups the concept of a curious and active learner and the behaviors that such a learner would exhibit.
		Ask for examples from the small groups and discuss with participants. Ask participants to discuss in their small groups how the program expectations relate to the attributes of a curious and active learner. Ask for small groups to share and discuss with participants. Emphasize the importance of face-to-face interactions as a way of practicing hard conversations and active participation and ownership of one's own experience.
		Discuss how the excellence nomination process can become a popularity contest and how to avoid that. Discuss the leadership examples to look for when nominating your peers: putting others before oneself, owning mistakes, leading with empathy, courageous leadership, showing vulnerability, being fully present, and active listening.

Time Required		Description
		Discuss the introversion/extroversion dynamic and how to engage introverts (Handout 5.1.1). Introduce the improv group and remind participants that this is an opportunity to practice stepping out of their comfort zone and supporting each other.
25 minutes	Activity 1	The next activities are being led by Casual Thursdays (student-led improv group on Dartmouth campus). Participants will practice walking around the room in different ways (e.g., on a beach, on a busy NYC street). Do this for five minutes. For the next activity, arrange participants around the room in a large circle. A volunteer will shout out a problem and people around the circle will respond with solutions. After each solution is proposed, the entire circle must yell either yes or no. Do this for five minutes. For the third activity, divide participants into three groups. Two volunteers from the group will begin to improv a scene and the rest of the group forms a line that will rotate through the exercise. After about a minute, the scene is stopped and the acting participants freeze in place. One person is tapped out of the scene by the next person in line, who enters the same position as the participant they just tapped. When the scene starts again, the new pair improvises a completely new scenario.
25 minutes	Discussion	Once the improv activities end and groups return to the main room, pass out Handout 5.1.2 and introduce the Personal Leadership Challenge (PLC). Discuss how the PLC is an example of leadership education through experiential learning and how it is tied into the program. Invite prior participants to share their PLC's or share different types of projects people have had in the program history. Introduce SMART goals (Handout 5.1.3). Explain that SMART goals help one think through the goal setting process with questions such as: *What exactly do I want to achieve? Where? When? With whom? What are the conditions and limitations (cultural, logistical)? What are my resources (skills, people, money, time, training available to me)? Why exactly do I want to reach this goal? What will be the outcome of achieving this goal?* In their small groups, ask participants to make a few SMART goals for one of the previous PLC examples. In the large group, introduce the GANTT chart model (activity, person responsible, and timeline) as a framework for building a workplan. Explain that a workplan provides a detailed timeline that is useful in groups or for personal purposes. Participants start to build an accountability structure with the end in mind. Emphasize that a workplan is flexible, but SMART goals are not. Ask participants to complete Handout 5.1.3.

Time Required	Description	
5 minutes	Conclusion	Ask participants to complete the session evaluation using your desired format. Close the session by thanking the participants.

Reflection Questions

- Which leadership skills or competencies would I like to develop during MLDP? How can I take ownership over that development?
- What can I expect from this program and what can the MLDP program staff expect from me?
- Which people can I collaborate with to learn about and address my leadership challenges? Who or what can help me to develop?
- How should I integrate skills I learn in MLDP into my life?
- Where in my life can I improve as a manager/leader?

Supplemental Resources

Cain, S. (2012, February). *The power of introverts* [Video]. TED Conferences. https://www.ted.com/talks/susan_cain_the_power_of_introverts

Lucas, K. (2015, November). *In defense of extroverts* [Video]. TED @ State Street Boston. https://www.ted.com/talks/katherine_lucas_in_defense_of_extroverts

Sternbergh, B., & Weitzel, S. (2001). *Setting your development goals: Start with your values.* Center for Creative Leadership. https://www.oreilly.com/library/view/setting-your-development/188219764X/

Participant Reflection

Although I was excited about meeting my cohort, I was really nervous and anticipated taking the back seat during the first session. However, participating in the Improv activity pushed me to step out of that mindset and my comfort zone. Fully engaging in the activity made me realize how integral active learning is to growth. Later, I was able to extensively practice active learning in my internship, which required me to strike a balance between being resourceful and asking questions when needed. Overall, I have found active learning to be a valuable skill both within the classroom and the workplace.

MLDP Spring 2020

This session has been formatted and revised for consistency and clarity. The original session in the Management and Leadership Development Program was facilitated by Robin Frye, reached at Robin.T.Frye@dartmouth.edu.

Examples of the Differences Between Introverts and Extroverts

Extroverts generally

- Are seen as "go-getters" or "people persons"
- Feel comfortable and like working with groups
- Have a wide range of acquaintances and friends
- Get energy from being around people
- Think out loud
- Are comfortable taking risks
- Are comfortable being the center of attention
- Prefer to solve problems by collaborating
- <u>Can sometimes</u> jump too quickly into an activity and not allow enough time for reflection
- <u>Can sometimes</u> forget to pause to clarify ideas that give aim or meaning to their activities

Introverts generally

- Are seen as calm and "centered" or reserved
- Feel comfortable being alone and like solitary activities
- Like being around people but need time alone to recharge
- Prefer fewer, more intense relationships
- Prefer to speak when they have a fully thought-out response
- Are better listeners and more observant
- Ask thoughtful questions
- Prefer to solve problems thinking deeply by themselves
- <u>Can sometimes</u> spend too much time reflecting and not move into action quickly enough
- <u>Can sometimes</u> forget to check in with the outside world to see if their ideas really fit with others' experiences

<u>Note: People are complicated, everyone is different, and the way we behave can change depending on the situation.</u>

Adapted from *Quiet: The Power of Introverts in a World That Can't Stop Talking* by S. Cain (2012), Crown Publishing Group. Copyright 2012, 2013 by Susan Cain.

Personal Leadership Challenge

The purpose of the Personal Leadership Challenge is to further your growth as a manager and leader. The process of identifying and then working through a personal and professional challenge is powerful. This challenge is meant to be just that— a challenge. Think about an area of your current campus experience that puts you outside of your comfort zone. What skill, habit, or competency would improve that experience?

A meaningful PLC will have the following characteristics:

- Focuses on a specific aspect of your campus experience
- Pushes you to learn a new skill, practice a new habit, or develop a new competency
- Has a measurable outcome: You will recognize success when you see it.
- Achievable within the term (or at least a significant start)

When identifying a PLC, consider all areas of your life, especially areas that impact others: class projects, sports teams, Greek life, a campus job, clubs, or other campus activities.

Here are some examples:

- Establishing a leadership presence within a group
- Preparing for a leadership role
- Addressing group dynamic issues
- Learning a new skill or doing something for the first time
- Joining a new group
- Starting a new group
- Succession planning for a group you lead
- Building intentional professional relationships with peers or professors
- Finding your voice, through planned or impromptu speaking
- Securing a research position, an internship, or a job

By the end of week three, have a 20-minute coaching session.

Schedule a 20-minute mini-coaching session with the program officer where we will dive a little deeper into your PLC. We'll discuss why it's important to you and how you envision the outcome. We will also go over your SMART goals, workplan, and any other questions or concerns.

Assignment due Saturday of week three: Identifying Your MLDP Personal Leadership Challenge

Write 2–3 double-spaced pages using these prompts:

- Briefly describe the challenge you would like to address. Please provide the context and how this challenge pushes you into new territory. Why this challenge? Why now?
- Write one or two SMART goals to address your challenge (see the SMART goal worksheet).

> ➤ Write a workplan. How do you plan to address your SMART goals? (see the SMART goal worksheet).

Throughout the term, various check points

You will be asked periodically to reflect on your challenge and SMART goals. This may be done within the sessions, the online reflection, or through the dinner activities.

Assignment due Saturday of week eight: Your MLDP Personal Leadership Challenge Reflections

Use the questions below as a guide to help you reflect on your MLDP PLC. Write two to three double-spaced pages.

Start by briefly outlining your PLC and SMART goals. Be sure to note any changes to your challenge or goals if necessary.

> ➤ Think about the MLDP sessions in which you participated. Outline how you were able to use the knowledge and skills you gained through MLDP to address your challenge.
> > ○ Be sure to include specific examples of how you addressed each challenge.
> ➤ What advice did your colleagues in MLDP give you that you have been able to apply to your challenge? What happened as a result?
> ➤ What worked and what didn't?
> ➤ Do you feel that you were unsuccessful reaching your goals at any time? What did you learn as a result?
> ➤ What did you learn about yourself by taking on this challenge?
> ➤ What did you learn about leadership and/or management through this process?
> ➤ What did you learn about working with others during the challenge?
> ➤ What aspects of the experience were the most uncomfortable? Why?
> ➤ What are your next steps?

In the wrap-up session, prepare for a three-minute presentation on your Personal Leadership Challenge Reflections

Practicing the public speaking techniques you learned in MLDP, give a short three-minute presentation on the process you went through to address your PLC, what you learned about yourself, and lessons learned about management and leadership. This will take place in a small-group format, just like the public speaking session.

SMART Goals Worksheet

If you can't measure a goal, you can't manage it.
What makes a goal **SMART**?

S – Specific: What exactly do you want to achieve? The more specific, the better. Use action words and be straight-forward! You will feel motivated by a specific as opposed to a general goal.

M – Measurable: How will you know you have achieved your goal? What will you see, feel, hear when you've reached your goal? Establish quantifiable criteria and you are more likely to stay on track.

A – Attainable: Your goal should be a stretch just out of your comfort zone but not overwhelming. It's ok to shoot for the stars, but plan smartly. Weigh your effort, time, and other costs against the outcome. Ask, "Do I really want to do this? Why do I want to do this?" Only you can decide what's attainable.

R – Realistic: Your goal must be "do-able." What is the objective behind the goal, and will this goal really achieve that? Consider your resources, conditions, and limitations. Do you have the skills, money, people, and authority needed to achieve your goal? Is it the right time? Are people on board with you? Please also consider the culture and the context in which you are working.

T – Time-bound: Creating a deadline allows you to stay motivated and accountable toward achieving your goal. Make sure it's not too stringent and not too loose. You want to push yourself, but not unreasonably.

Note: There are other versions of the SMART acronym, and other words that you can imagine fit the mold—the key here is to use a SMART goal or objective to frame the tasklist or workplan you'll need to put in place in order to achieve your goal.

In one or two sentences, write your goal. Make sure it has ALL five components of a SMART goal.

Now break it down!

Once you set the goal, it's important to break it down into smaller, more manageable tasks with shorter deadlines. This can be used for one person or multiple people. If used in a group, it can help create an easy accountability structure.

MLDP Workplan Template

Number	Task	Person Responsible	Deadline
1.			
2.			
3.			
4.			

Session 5.2 Using Your Strengths for Effective Professional Communication

Session Description

In this session, the facilitator will introduce the the concepts behind the *Social Compass Survey* and teach participants about their social styles and natural strengths. Participants will learn how to better influence and motivate others, increase their ability to improve communication, and strengthen their effectiveness in the workplace. They will also gain an understanding of the challenges of their own style and identify areas where they can further develop strengths that will lead to success in the workplace and other aspects of their lives.

Learning Objectives

Participants will do the following:
- Describe the differences between the four social styles
- Identify three ways to improve their ability to communicate with, influence, and motivate others they work with
- Identify two personal strengths and two professional development opportunities
- Practice describing their strengths and areas of growth using an interview activity

---

Leadership Competencies Addressed

Collaboration
- Acknowledges and listens to different voices when making decisions and taking action

Effective Communication
- Influences others through writing, speaking, or artistic expression

Self-Knowledge
- Demonstrates realistic understanding of one's abilities
- Seeks opportunities for continued growth

Key Concepts and Definitions

Effective communication	The ability to adapt communication styles to meet the needs of others, resulting in stronger relationships, mutual respect, ability to collaborate, and the ability to get things accomplished.
Self-understanding	Understanding one's own strengths, contributions, challenges, and developmental needs. In a leader, this skill will support professional development and growth.
Tolerance	Understanding how people differ and recognizing how those differences contribute to work-group effectiveness. In a leader, this appreciation for different ways of being can result in less judgement and greater ability to tap into the strengths of the group.

Required Materials

- PowerPoint slides and appropriate technology (optional)
- Participants in groups based on the primary social style results of the *Social Compass Survey*
- Four poster papers available on the table for each of the four groups
- Flipchart and markers at each table

Pre-session Assignment:

- Use the link provided by the facilitator to complete the *Social Compass Survey* prior to the session (link provided by Dr. Pamela Skyrme, reached at pameralskyrme@gmail.com). Students should complete the survey 48-hours prior to the session.

Session Outline

Session duration: 1 hour and 35 minutes

Time Required		Description
10 minutes	Introduction	Introduce yourself and begin outlining the learning objectives of the session. Using the data from the *Social Compass Survey*, which participants completed prior to the session, they will learn how to adjust their communication style for optimal performance based on their innate strengths, possible areas of weakness, and the communication preferences of themselves and others.
5 minutes	Activity 1	Based on the pre-session survey, group participants according to their *Social Compass Style*. This is an icebreaker and a chance for the participants in each group to find ways in which they are similar. Ask each group to work together on their flipchart paper to write down five words that they feel describes them all. Each word must be unanimously agreed upon. Encourage participants to speak up against a word if it does not describe them; it should not be included on the flipchart.
35 minutes	Framing	As each group shares their flipchart work, tell them about their *Social Compass Style* (Navigator, Explorer, Social Servitor, Worker). After the mini-lecture, ask each group whether they feel that what was shared describes them accurately. Discuss how secondary styles may show up depending on group make-up. Participants should take notes during the discussion of the things that caught their attention or surprised them.

Time Required		Description
20 minutes	Activity 2	In their *Social Compass Style* groups, request participants to work together for 10 minutes to summarize their communication preferences. You may wish to provide a worksheet that asks several questions that prompt them to think about how they prefer to receive communication. For example: "If I am your boss, how do you like to be recognized?" Ask the groups to share their preferences within the larger group so participants can identify similarities and differences and appreciate the values and preferences of each style.
5 minutes	Reflection	Ask participants to reflect on the following questions and write down their responses: *What kind of job would you most like to have? What kind of organizational culture would be important to you? What are your greatest strengths for this kind of job? What do you think are your professional development areas?*
15 minutes	Activity 3	Request participants to pair with someone from a different primary style group. Each pair will interview each other one after the other. Ask participants to be mindful of the time so that both can have equal time answering questions. You may also wish to announce when participants should switch roles. The interview is based on the previous reflection questions. Interviewers are asking: *What kind of job would you most like to have? What kind of organizational culture would be important to you? What strengths do you bring to the table for this kind of position? Can you give me an example of when you have used these strengths recently? If I am your manager, what do you most want me to know about you?*
5 minutes	Conclusion	Ask participants to complete the session evaluation using your desired format. Close the session by thanking the participants.

Reflection Questions

- How does what I just learned about myself match the activities that come easily to me professionally and personally?
- How can I use my strengths to address my SMART goals for my Personal Leadership Challenge?
- How does what I just learned about myself match the activities that I am struggling with personally and professionally?
- How can I use the language of the *Social Compass* to describe myself to an interviewer?

Supplemental Resources

Ahlquist, J. S., & Levi, M. (2011). Leadership: What it means, what it does, and what we want to know about it. *Annual Review of Political Science, 14*(1), 1–24. https://doi.org/10.1146/annurev-polisci-042409-152654

Choren, A. (2015). The Importance of Communication in the Workplace. *IEEE Potentials, 34*(3), 10–11. https://doi.org/10.1109/MPOT.2014.2331793

Schnurr, S. (2012). Leadership. In *Exploring Professional Communication: Language in Action* (pp. 150–174). Routledge. https://doi.org/10.4324/9780203095324

This session has been formatted and revised for consistency and clarity. The original session in the Management and Leadership Development Program was facilitated by Dr. Pamela Skyrme, reached at pamelaskyrme@gmail.com.

Participant Reflection

This session allowed me to learn about my social communication style and natural strengths, as well as those of my peers. Dr. Skyrme taught us how to use this information to better motivate, communicate, and understand others in a professional environment. The idea that adapting to other people's styles is equally as important as understanding your own was eye-opening. By also learning about my communication weaknesses, I was better able to communicate at a club meeting I led the following week by relaxing my rigid schedule and connecting with my peers on a personal level.

MLDP Winter 2021

Session 5.3 Understanding Your Strengths in the Context of Management and Leadership

Session Description

In this session, the facilitator will explain how managers and leaders are critical contributors to the success of any organization. Participants will learn about the unique set of strengths that managers and leaders possess to enhance organizational performance. This session provides an overview of key concepts related to management and leadership, and challenges participants to evaluate their strengths in those two areas. Through an interactive group activity, participants will assess their strengths and determine the degree to which they fall under the manager or the leader side of a continuum. This session employs interactive group activities and challenging values-based discussion.

Learning Objectives

Participants will do the following:
- Identify their top five strengths related to management and/or leadership
- Determine how strengths may be categorized into the areas of management, leadership, or a combination of both management and leadership
- Choose their top three values and one non-negotiable value and evaluate how that relates to leadership
- Interpret how their strengths and values are interrelated and what that means for their leadership development

Leadership Competencies Addressed

Collaboration
- Acknowledges and listens to different voices when making decisions and taking action

Effective Reasoning
- Develops personal reflective practice

Self-Knowledge
- Continually explores and examines values and views
- Understands social identities of self and others

Intercultural Mindset
- Actively engages in opportunities to expand worldview

Key Concepts and Definitions

Strengths   The natural inclinations of an individual in terms of ways of thinking, feeling, and behaving.

Manager   A person who is responsible for planning, directing, monitoring, and assessing the work of a group or a team.

Leader   A person who has a vision and the necessary commitment and skills to achieve that vision.

Required Materials

- PowerPoint slides and appropriate technology (optional)
- Handout with a list of the strengths of managers and leaders for each participant
- All strengths printed and cut out to hang up on white board or wall
- Index card and writing utensil for each participant

Session Outline

Session duration: 1 hour and 40 minutes

Time Required		Description
10 minutes	Introduction	Introduce yourself and your personal and professional background. Highlight leadership and management roles you have had and share some humorous stories about the challenges you faced in either role. Invite participants to share some of their leadership or management roles and ask them to share some short anecdotes of their most challenging or triumphant moments.
10 minutes	Framing	Display a painting that will allow participants to identity people acting in leadership and management roles (e.g., the 1851 painting *Washington Crossing the Delaware*). Ask participants to identify the leaders and the managers in the painting. Lead a discussion about the roles of managers and leaders based on the key concept definitions. Ask participants what their assumptions were based on when they identified roles. Explain leadership and management as part of a process.
5 minutes	Activity 1	Pass out a handout that lists strengths of leaders and managers, without identifying which strengths are for which role. Ask participants to choose their top five strengths from the handout and write them on an index card. Tell them to set it aside for later.

Time Required		Description
5 minutes	Discussion	Ask participants which role is more important, manager or leader? Explain that there is value in both, and often the cultural cue in the U.S. is to value leaders. Lead a discussion about how cultural cues regarding leadership and management may vary across cultures.
30 minutes	Activity 2	Divide participants into five groups. Ask each group to categorize each of the strengths on the list passed out earlier as traits of either a leader or a manager using a digital poll or online form. While the groups are discussing, mark a continuum on the board with management on one end and leadership on the other. In between, create six categories: 5/0, 4/1, 3/2, 2/3, 1/4, 0/5. Once all the groups have submitted their categorization of the strengths, call everyone's attention. Display the strengths on the board based on the results from the online form. For example, if three groups out of five thought commitment was a management trait, place commitment at 3/2 on the continuum. At the end of this activity, a single "spread" on the board will be created. This final spread will show which strengths fall under each of the six rating scales above according to this unique cohort.
10 minutes	Reflection	Ask participants to categorize themselves as manager or leader based on the five strengths they wrote on their index card. Where do they stand in the continuum? Are they surprised? Why or why not?
20 minutes	Discussion	Ask participants to choose their top three values and one non-negotiable value that they would never compromise. In pairs, the participants discuss one of the following questions: *Do you see a direct correlation between your values and your strengths? Explain why that might be; or pick one value and describe why that might be a top value for you based on your background.* How is an understanding of values and particularly non-negotiable values related to management and leadership? At the end of the discussion, you may choose to share a personal story about a time when your non-negotiable value was tested. Ask volunteers to share their non-negotiable value through a real-life experience.

Time Required		Description
10 minutes	Conclusion	Review key points with the participants: remind them to always pay attention to context, align with their strengths, do the right thing (leadership) and do it right (management). Ask participants to complete the session evaluation using your desired format. Close the session by thanking the participants.

Reflection Questions

- Where am I along the manager/leader continuum?
- What does my position along the continuum mean for me?
- Considering my understanding of my strengths and my position along the continuum, do I want to change course or proceed? Why?
- What are my values and how are they related to my strengths?
- How can I address my areas of improvement?

Supplemental Resources

Arnold, F. (2011). Part 3: Managing people. In *What makes great leaders great: Management lessons from icons who changed the world* (chaps. 25–56). McGraw-Hill. https://learning.oreilly.com/library/view/what-makes-great/9780071770514/

Participant Reflection

In this session, Dr. Gama Perruci illustrated the difference between management and leadership skills by allowing us to categorize various strengths along a management/leadership spectrum. The session helped me realize that the difference in the way we perceive these terms is due to societal factors that place importance arbitrarily. In reality, both management and leadership are equally important in executing a project successfully. While I previously considered myself more leadership driven, realizing I had strong management skills as well has allowed me to take on roles I would have previously been afraid to accept.

MLDP Winter 2021

Las Marias, S. (2016). What makes a great leader? *SMT007 Magazine*, *4*(10), 100.

Sullivan, C. (2013). *The clarity principle: How great leaders make the most important decision in business (and what happens when they don't)*. Jossey-Bass. https://search.library.dartmouth.edu/permalink/01DCL_INST/134hn0f/cdi_safari_books_9781118630686

This session has been formatted and revised for consistency and clarity. The original session in the Management and Leadership Development Program was facilitated by Gama Perruci, reached at perrucig@marietta.edu.

Session 5.4 Mindful Presence to Masterful Presentation

Session Description

In this session, the facilitator highlights how greater awareness of our mindset, behaviors, and interactions can impact our presence, whether sitting in a meeting, interviewing for a job, or public speaking to an audience of 500. Participants will learn about controlling presence in different contexts, aligning mind-body-spirit in effective communication, and maximizing natural strengths and social styles when presenting in different situations, particularly in public speaking settings. Participants will also practice presenting to others through story crafting of their Personal Learning Challenge and receiving feedback.

Leadership Competencies Addressed
Self-Knowledge • Demonstrates realistic understanding of one's abilities • Moves beyond self-imposed limitations **Effective Communication** • Clearly articulates ideas in a written and spoken form • Exhibits effective listening skills • Influences others through writing, speaking, or artistic expression

Learning Objectives

Participants will do the following:

- Identify the three concepts of mindful presentations: mindfulness, presence, and emotional contagion
- Reinforce understanding of these concepts by presenting in small groups and giving and receiving feedback while being recorded
- Review video recordings and set at least two goals to improve presentations

Key Concepts and Definitions

Mindfulness	A state of being in which one is aware of what is happening moment by moment without trying to control what is happening.
Presence	The ability to have others take notice by simply being in the room; a product of internal mindset, external behavior, and interactions with others.
Emotional contagion	The concept of triggering similar emotions and behaviors in others by exhibiting or conveying one's own emotions and behaviors.

Required Materials

- PowerPoint slides and appropriate technology (optional)
- Notepaper and writing utensils
- Assistants and appropriate technology to record presentations

Session Outline

Session duration: 1 hour and 15 minutes

Time Required		Description
20 minutes	Introduction	Introduce yourself and lead participants through a deep breathing activity to focus attention on the session. Explain that being connected to your breath is a way of building mindfulness. Ask the audience when they are most conscious of their breathing: When is it slow and deep or fast and shallow? If participants do not offer public speaking as an answer, suggest this.

Ask participants where and when they are most and least comfortable public speaking. Form a list with participants of things in public speaking situations that are controllable, like yourself, or uncontrollable, like the audience.

Introduce mindfulness and presence. As the facilitator, you must embody "being in presence" and presenting with confidence and mastery to convey the same authenticity being asked of the participants. Ask participants to imagine a big mindful presence and a big mindless presence and discuss the differences, particularly in body language. Introduce the concept of emotional contagion. |
| *5 minutes* | Activity 1 | Divide participants into groups of three. Each participant will have a role: speaker, listener, and distractor. The speaker will talk for one minute while one group member listens and another tries to distract the speaker. You can provide a list of distracting activities or have participants think of their own. After one minute, the roles switch and a new distraction will be acted out. After everyone has played all the roles, discuss in the large group whether the distractor got the speaker's attention or the distractor was ignored by the speaker, and why. |

Time Required		Description
5 minutes	Discussion	Give some public speaking tips and provide demonstrations. Be sure to discuss eye contact and body language. Some tips are to look someone in between their eyes rather than into them, standing near distracted audience members—but not looking at them—to command their attention while maintaining yours, and avoiding the "lighthouse" by not scanning the room too much.
15 minutes	Activity 2	Explain that words such as "like" and "um" are filler words; they do not provide any context or substance to the content and are often a crutch for uncomfortable speakers. Divide participants into groups of three. This will be an exercise to become mindful of filler words and comfortable with pauses. One participant will speak about their Personal Leadership Challenge for three minutes while the other two group members listen for filler words. When they hear one, group members should snap at the presenter and the presenter must restart the sentence or thought. After all participants have given their 3-minute speech, bring the groups back together to discuss the power of a pause in a speech and building presence with space. This session should be adapted to be most immediately applicable and relevant to participants; if you find that there is a presentation that the class is working towards, the practice exercises can be tailored towards that as well.
20 minutes	Activity 3	Divide participants into the same groups of three and ask them each to find a space where they can give their 3-minute speech and watch a recording of themselves. After each speech, the rest of the group can provide feedback. They may choose to write this down on a note paper for the speaker to keep. Ask groups to keep the videos to send to their group mates after the session.
10 minutes	Conclusion	Bring the groups back together. Ask participants to complete the session evaluation using your desired format. Close the session by thanking the participants.

Reflection Questions

- How might I increase my impact with my audience by understanding myself as a facilitator?
- How might I use the range of my facilitation tools to impact the group with whom I am working?
- What techniques might I consider using to ensure each member of my audience feels included, heard, and safe to share?
- What are the next steps I should take to ensure that my speaking will be clear and coherent?
- What techniques should I learn to eliminate fill-ins such as "um" and "like"?

Supplemental Resources

Antonakis, J. (2012). Transformational and charismatic leadership. In D. V. Day & J. Antonakis (Eds.), *The nature of leadership* (2nd ed., pp. 256–288). SAGE Publications. https://serval.unil.ch/resource/serval:BIB_3576DF50B587.P001/REF.pdf

Bateman, A. (2012). Mindfulness. *The British Journal of Psychiatry, 201*(4), 297–297. https://doi.org/10.1192/bjp.bp.111.098871

Cuddy, A. (2012, June). *Your body language may shape who you are* [Video]. TED Conferences. https://www.ted.com/talks/amy_cuddy_your_body_language_may_shape_who_you_are

Hatfield, E., Cacioppo, J. T., & Rapson, R. L. (1993). Emotional contagion. *Current Directions in Psychological Science, 2*(3), 96–99.

Participant Reflection

Dr. Chiu's tips on mindfulness made me reflect deeply on how I've typically dealt with stressful situations. I think when I'm in situations that I know will likely be emotionally charged, taking a step back and mentally preparing myself to be calm despite all that would be helpful. When you prepare yourself for an emotional situation ahead of time and process what your gut reaction will be to a variety of outcomes, it becomes easier to temper those emotional responses in the moment. I left with her session brainstorming how to adapt her strategies in ways that worked for me.

MLDP Spring 2020

This session has been formatted and revised for consistency and clarity. The original session in the Management and Leadership Development Program was facilitated by Dr. Belinda Chiu, reached at belinda@hummingbirdrcc.com.

Session 5.5 Authentic Exchanges—The Science & Art of Building Relationships

Session Description

In this session, the facilitator explores the nature of developing relationships as a leader. Participants will learn the strength of basing these relationships on shared values and a mutual exchange of resources toward a shared purpose. This session will introduce participants to strategies for building authentic relationships and provide practice for putting these strategies to the test.

Learning Objectives

Participants will do the following:
- Describe a "relationship," why relationships are the foundation for authentic exchanges, and the five-step process
- Practice the five-step process through an interactive activity
- Identify two people with whom they will apply the five-step process in a one-to-one meeting

Leadership Competencies Addressed

Collaboration
- Builds and maintains partnerships based on shared purpose

Effective Communication
- Exhibits effective listening skills

Principled Action
- Demonstrates congruence between actions and values

Management
- Stewards and maximizes all resources

Self-Knowledge
- Understands social identities of self and others

Key Concepts and Definitions

Relationships	The relationships that leaders aim to develop are intentional and public, grounded in shared values, a mutual exchange of skills and resources, and result in growth and learning.
The five steps	A relationship-building process for conducting a one-to-one meeting: (1) selection, (2) purpose, (3) exploration, (4) exchange, and (5) commitment.
Co-creation	An act that occurs by identifying one another's values, interests, and assets, which enables us to make mutual exchanges and commitments to one another.

Required Materials

- PowerPoint slides and appropriate technology (optional)
- Handout 5.5.1 One-to-One Meetings

Session Outline

Session duration: 1 hour and 30 minutes

Time Required		Description
10 minutes	Introduction	Ask participants to discuss in groups of four or five why building relationships is important as leaders. After a few minutes, define leadership in such a way that highlights that it is inherently a relationship with other people. Discuss the differences between personal and public relationships and ask participants for examples of both. Ask participants to think of someone they would like to be in a public relationship with. Explain that relationships are founded on shared values, shared interests, and an exchange of assets.
15 minutes	Framing	Introduce the five-step process for one-to-one meetings: (1) Selection and Attention—whom should I ask?; (2) Purpose—being upfront about the purpose of the meeting; (3) Exploration—most of the time in the meeting is spent doing this; find out the values and what motivates the other person; (4) Mutual Exchange —listening and strategizing, finding a way there; (5) Commitment—what are the next steps, how to make an ask, and how to respond if you receive a "no."
10 minutes	Activity 1	Ask for a volunteer who will demonstrate with you a five-step one-to-one meeting. Stand with the volunteer in front of the participants and lead a five-minute conversation that goes through the steps. After the conversation, thank the volunteer and identify where the five steps took place.

Time Required		Description
20 minutes	Activity 2	Pass out Handout 5.5.1 to participants. At each table, instruct participants to pair up with the person sitting across from them. After 10 minutes, participants will shift one seat to their right to make a new pair. Explain that every participant will have the opportunity to practice the five-steps in a 10-minute conversation. During the first 10 minutes, all participants on one side of the table will drive the conversation. In the second 10 minutes, participants on the other side of the table will drive the conversation. After each conversation, discuss briefly how well the five steps were executed. Offer a purpose for the one-to-one meetings if needed. For example, find out what others value about the program and how they are applying the skills; see if there is an exchange to make around supporting each other's learning.
30 minutes	Reflection	In the large group, ask participants what values, interests, and assets surfaced during the one-to-one meetings and what commitments people made to one another. Ask participants how conducting a one-to-one meeting is different from other approaches to building relationships. Ask participants to identify one person with whom they can have a one-to-one meeting this week.
5 minutes	Conclusion	Ask participants to complete the session evaluation using your desired format. Close the session by thanking the participants.

Reflection Questions

- What is the value of building relationships through the five-step process of a one-to-one meeting? How does it differ from other approaches?
- How could the five-step process of a one-to-one meeting affect your leadership in your organizations and/or endeavors?
- Who can you have a one-to-one meeting with this week?

Participant Reflection

In this session, Kate Hilton taught us how to be more intentional in meeting new people and forming connections. My biggest takeaway was that at the end of any conversation, you need to make a commitment. After this session, my lunches with my peers grew more purposeful and productive as I was better able to facilitate a mutual exchange of ideas and interests. Most importantly, I made sure to leave each conversation with a clearly defined next step.

MLDP Fall 2019

Supplemental Resources

Brodin, T. M., & McLaughlin, M. K. (2019). Creating powerful personal and professional relationships through effective communication. *Journal of Family & Consumer Sciences*, *111*(2), 17–24. https://doi.org/10.14307/JFCS111.2.17

Schindler, E. (2016). *The secrets behind great one-on-one meetings*. O'Reilly Media, Inc. https://learning.oreilly.com/library/view/the-secrets-behind/9781491995112/

TEDx Talks. (2014, July 28). *Successful leaders build and sustain long-term relationships | Steve Cockram | TEDxABQSalon*. YouTube. https://www.youtube.com/watch?v=DQzyCbIuIII&ab_channel=TEDxTalks

This session has been formatted and revised for consistency and clarity. The original session in the Management and Leadership Development Program was facilitated by Kate Hilton, reached at kate.b.hilton@gmail.com.

One-to-One Meetings

PRACTICE: Conduct a one-to-one meeting! Build or further develop relationships with your project leaders, community members, or supporters.

During the one-to-one, move through the five steps:

Step #1: Get the person's attention.
Reach out by email, phone, or in person to schedule intentional time together.

Step #2: Describe your purpose. Be clear about your reason for the meeting. For example, "I am working to improve our community's health. I'd like to find out about your interests, tell you a little bit about the effort, and see if you'd be interested in playing a role." Establish how much time you have together so you are clear on when the meeting will end.

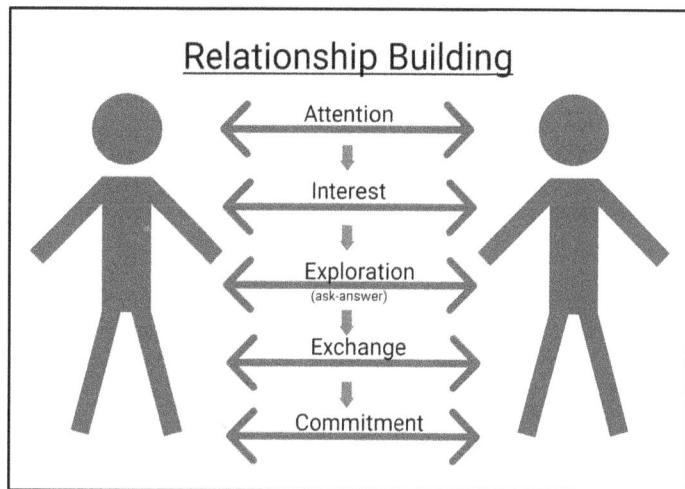

Relationship Building

Attention

Interest

Exploration (ask-answer)

Exchange

Commitment

Step #3: Elicit and Explore. Learn about the other person's **values, interests, skills,** and **resources**. Create space to listen. Probe with open-ended "Why?" questions to get to choice points and specific experiences that shaped their life. Briefly share your own story and make connections to commonalities and differences. Be specific. Avoid talking about things in an abstract way. Get to lived experiences around why you care about the things that you want to do something about, and the resources that come from each of your experiences.

> **Story:** Why do you care about our community's health? Where did you learn these values?
> **Hope:** What's your vision of how things could be different?
> **Challenge:** What keeps you from action?
> **Resources:** What skills do you bring to this work?

Step #4: Make an Exchange. As you listen, take mental notes about what you are discovering, and think strategically about possible exchanges of resources. It may not be the same exchange that you originally imagined. Also, be explicit about articulating the exchanges happening during the meeting such as sharing information, support, appreciation, challenge, and insight.

Step #5: Seek a Commitment. Make a specific and genuine "ask" of the person with whom you are meeting. Put a date and time on it as a way to secure the commitment. If the person does not want to get involved directly, will they introduce you to others? Look for ways in which you might find points of synergy and seek a commitment. Follow up.

What Did You Learn?

At the end of each one-to-one meeting, be sure you can answer the following four questions:

- ➤ What does this person **value**? What is their history acting on their values?
- ➤ What **interests** does this person have? How can my efforts support their interests?
- ➤ What **skills** and **resources** do they bring to this work?
- ➤ When will we **meet again** and/or **what will we do next** to take action and continue building this relationship?

Reflection Questions

- ➤ How does doing one-to-ones compare with other types of conversations you have? How is it different from an interview? How is it different from a sales pitch?
- ➤ What is most challenging about conducting a one-to-one meeting? Most rewarding?
- ➤ How can you further employ this relationship-building tactic to engage others on your team, in your student groups, in your classes, and/or in the community?

Adapted from the works of Marshall Ganz, Harvard University; modified by Kate B. Hilton.

Session 5.6 Benefiting from the Richness of Diversity, Equity, and Inclusion in Teams

Session Description

In this session, the facilitator will discuss the benefits of diverse teams. Teams that balance the concepts of diversity, equity, and inclusion (DEI) well understand how to have crucial conversations across differences. Through the mastery of open and honest questions, participants will learn how to create intellectually supportive environments for teamwork that encourage the expression of differing perspectives and allow the richness of diversity to be fully realized.

Learning Objectives

Participants will do the following:
- Identify two ways in which DEI opens opportunities for effective communication within teams
- Use open and honest questions to understand different perspectives
- Identify two ways to apply their learning to team environments going forward

Leadership Competencies Addressed

Collaboration
- Fosters a welcoming and inclusive environment

Effective Reasoning
- Exhibits effective listening skills

Self-knowledge
- Understands social identities of self and others

Management
- Develops appropriate strategies for effective teamwork

Intercultural Mindset
- Understands, communicates with, and respectfully interacts with people across identities

Key Concepts and Definitions

Diversity in teams	Socially constructed experiences based on characteristics including but not limited to race, gender, or background influence perspective and frame how you see the world. Diversity (in thought, geography, race, religion, etc.) ensures a richness in problem solving and goal achievement.
Equity in teams	Having a diverse team does not automatically make the experiences of members equitable and inclusive. Equity and equality are not the same thing. For instance, equality is giving everyone a size ten pair of shoes, whereas equity is giving everyone a pair of shoes that fits. To make teams equitable, you must get to know your teammates and their needs.

Inclusion in teams	Being part of a team does not necessarily mean that an individual feels included. Inclusion enriches the experience of the whole team/community, but only if everyone in the community is willing to participate in the inclusive experience. In teams, we must recognize our own biases and be curious about other perspectives. This requires a mindset shift from a "fixed" mindset to a "growth" mindset as stated by Carol Dweck (2007/2006). Different perspectives make people uncomfortable, which encourages growth.
Open and honest questions	These types of questions are rooted in curiosity about the other and are nonjudgmental. As Steven Covey (1989/2020) states, you must seek to understand before seeking to be understood. Open and honest questions require effective listening skills in which an individual listens to understand and not merely to respond to what is being said.

Required Materials

- PowerPoint slides and appropriate technology (optional)
- Handout 5.6.1 Open and Honest Questions
- Handout 5.6.2 Open and Honest Conversation Instructions
- Writing utensil and paper
- Watch "Inclusion Makes the World More Vibrant." This video is available on Youtube. https://www.youtube.com/watch?v=QXY5TyCUTlo

Session Outline

Session duration: 1 hour and 15 minutes

Time Required		Description
5 minutes	Introduction	Introduce yourself and give some anecdotes of experiences where diversity, equity, and inclusion were crucial to effective teamwork. Identify the elements of that team that helped or hampered teamwork.

Time Required		Description
20 minutes	Framing	Explain the key concepts of diversity, equity, and inclusion in teams. Share a relevant example that demonstrates a difference in perspective through a minority group experience, for example, the selection of "nude" tones available for non-white people (on Band-Aids for example). Share "Inclusion Makes the World More Vibrant," a video of a child going to an art museum with his blind mother. Discuss how the video highlights that everyone in a community benefits from inclusion.

Explain the concept of open and honest questions and give some examples (see Handout 5.6.1). |
| *40 minutes* | Activity | Divide the participants into groups of four. Provide a pen and paper for each participant and explain the ground rules of an intellectually supportive space: ask open and honest questions; respect others and conduct yourself with integrity; replace judgment with genuine curiosity; and keep what is said in the group confidential.

Explain and follow the instructions from Handout 5.6.2. |
| *10 minutes* | Conclusion | Ask participants to share how the experience was for them and their group. Ask if there were any changes of perspective or if they were able to change a negative statement into a positive. Ask participants to complete the session evaluation using your desired format. Close the session by thanking participants. |

Reflection Questions

- How did this process feel as opposed to other conversations about similar topics?
- How were you able to change what could be perceived as negative into positive?
- Where can this process be used in my life today?

Supplemental Resources

Covey, S. R. (2020). *The 7 Habits of highly effective people* (30th anniversary ed.). Simon & Schuster. (Original work published 1989)

Dweck, C. S. (2007). *Mindset: The new psychology of success* (Illustrated ed.). Ballantine Books. (Original work published 2006)

Kreamer, L., & Rogelberg, S. (2020). Leadership & professional development: Evidence-Based strategies to make team meetings more effective. *Journal of Hospital Medicine, 15*(4), 236–236. https://doi.org/10.12788/jhm.3294

Parker J. Palmer (2004). *A hidden wholeness: The journey toward an undivided life.* Jossey-Bass

Palmer, P. J. (2007). *The courage to teach: Exploring the inner landscape of a teacher's life* (10th anniversary ed.). Jossey-Bass.

Participant Reflection

In this session, we learned about the importance of diversity and acceptance in groups through answering and asking our peers open and honest questions. These questions demanded vulnerability, and while answering was nerve-wracking at first, they led to amazing conversations. My peers and I were able to share advice with each other about sensitive topics I rarely would have spoken about, let alone to students I barely knew. Learning about equity and acceptance through powerful conversations taught me that there is strength in vulnerability, and speaking out in an honest way creates a path for inclusion and understanding.

MLDP Winter 2021

Parker, G. M. (2008). *Team players and teamwork: New strategies for developing successful collaboration* (2nd ed.). John Wiley & Sons, Incorporated. http://ebookcentral.proquest.com/lib/dartmouth-ebooks/detail.action?docID=331599

Talgam, I. (2009, July). *Lead like the great conductors* [Video]. TED Conferences. https://www.ted.com/talks/itay_talgam_lead_like_the_great_conductors/transcript

This session has been formatted and revised for consistency and clarity. The original session in the Management and Leadership Development Program.was facilitated by Anthony Johnson, reached at ajohns15@gmail.com.

Open and Honest Questions

What is an open, honest question?

➢ The best single mark of an open, honest question is that the questioner could not possibly anticipate the answer to it.

➢ Ask questions aimed at helping the other person come to a deeper understanding.

➢ Ask questions that are brief and to the point without adding background considerations and rationale—which turn the question into a speech.

➢ Ask questions that go to the person as well as the problem or story—for example, questions about feelings as well as about facts.

➢ Trust your intuition in asking questions, even if your instinct seems off the wall: "What color is your present job, and what color is the one you have been offered?"

➢ Try to avoid questions with yes-no, right-wrong answers.

➢ If you feel the subtle pull of hoping for a certain answer to a question, it's probably not open and honest! (Sit in discernment to avoid asking a question that is really advice in disguise!)

Adapted from A Hidden Wholeness: *The Journey Toward an Undivided Life*, by P. J. Palmer, 2004, Jossey-Bass. Copyright © 2004 by John Wiley & Sons, Inc.

Open and Honest Conversation Instructions

PART I (Statements) 15 minutes

Team members will take turns completing the statements listed below. Do not move on to the next statement until each team member has completed the prior statement.

Statement 1: People judge me because…
Statement 2: I am [fill in the blank with your political affiliation OR religious belief] because…
Statement 3: People may not like me because…
Statement 4: Sometimes I cry because…

*NOTE: AS INDIVIDUALS ARE MAKING THEIR STATEMENS, OTHER TEAM MEMBERS ARE **NOT** TO COMMENT OR ASK QUESTIONS. THIS IS YOUR TIME TO PRACTICE ACTIVE LISTENING. YOU WILL ALSO BE USING THIS TIME TO TAKE NOTES (SEE BELOW).

Note Taking

> As mentioned above, you will be taking notes while your other team members are speaking. Write down some open and honest questions that you could ask in Part II. Remember: Be curious and non-judgmental.
> Take note of how you feel and consider why you might feel that way.
> For statements that may be perceived as negative, or different from your own, write down how they can be perceived as positive or how they can make that person an asset to the team.

PART II (Open and Honest Questions) 25 minutes

In this portion of the activity, you will open the floor for the team to ask questions about their teammates' statements in Part I. Everyone will have the opportunity to be in the "hot seat." It's very important that these conversations do not turn into arguments about "right" and "wrong." They are meant to be discussions fueled by curiosity and open-mindedness.

Rules are simple:
The person in the hot seat will field one open and honest question.
The person in the hot seat will then choose another team member and ask them a question.
Once everyone has answered a question, continue rotating out of the hot seat until the time expires.

Examples of Open and Honest Questions
Instead of this: Did that make you feel sad?
Say this: How did that make you feel?

Instead of this: Did your parents make you choose that class?
Say this: What made you choose that class over some of the other options?

PART III (Share) 5 minutes

Take a few minutes for each person to share one thought from the activity that reflects a change in perspective. It can be a moment where they changed a statement from negative to positive or showed how the team could benefit from someone's attributes or how they now have a deeper understanding of another person.

Session 5.7 Effective Teams That Inspire Change

Session Description

In this session, the facilitator will illustrate how being part of an effective team can be inspiring and energizing. In contrast, being part of an ineffective team can become a grueling experience. By the end of the session, participants will know 10 rules that an effective team must follow to inspire change.

Learning Objectives

Participants will do the following:
- Identify the 10 Rules of Effective Teams
- Demonstrate some of the 10 rules through an exercise
- Identify three ways that their teams can and do embody the 10 rules

Leadership Competencies Addressed

Collaboration
- Facilitate collective action toward common goals

Effective Reasoning
- Employ creative thinking in problem solving

Self-Knowledge
- Take appropriate action towards potential benefits despite possible failure

Management
- Develop appropriate strategies for capitalizing on human talent
- Develop appropriate strategies for effective teamwork

Key Concepts and Definitions

Open and Honest Communication	Communication with trust, clarity, and courage.
Law of Significance	Nothing of significance has ever been achieved alone.
Embrace diversity	All types of diversity are a tenant of effective teams. Diversity can be broadly defined through race, ethnicity, thoughts, or opinions for example.
Law of the Niche	The right person in the right place yields maximum effectiveness.

Autonomy	Effective teams acknowledge that people crave flexibility and the desire to be themselves.
Team-Before-Self	An effective team has members that put the team ahead of themselves and their personal gain.
Accountability Through Compassion	Accountability must be void of judgment.
Own Failure & Recognize Achievement	Owning one's failures builds trust, while recognizing achievement builds team morale.
Operate with Integrity	Integrity should be the backbone of action. Decisions require reflection on values and mission.
Remove the Armor	Vulnerability creates an environment where members of a team have the potential to grow into the best versions of themselves.

Required Materials

- PowerPoint slides and appropriate technology (optional)
- Handout 5.7.1 10 Rules of Effective Teams
- Handout 5.7.2 Conversation prompts printed for each table

Session Outline

Session duration: 1 hour and 40 minutes

Time Required		Description
5 minutes	Introduction	Introduce yourself and give some anecdotes of experiences where effective teamwork was crucial to success. Identify the elements of that team that ultimately led to successful or failure.
15 minutes	Framing	Share the 10 Rules of Effective Teams (Handout 5.7.1).
10 minutes	Activity 1	Role play a coaching session with a participant where any of the 10 rules can be applied. Demonstrate vulnerability as the facilitator to encourage participants to do the same. Talk about coaching and best practices.

Time Required		Description
5 minutes	Discussion	Establish the ground rules for the next activity: Ask participants to practice authentic listening, to be completely open and honest, have respect for one another, and replace judgment with curiosity and compassion. Encourage participants to coach each other and stay in the moment. Discuss with participants how a conversation using coaching techniques differs from their past conversations with friends and peers.
40 minutes	Activity 2	Divide participants into small groups of four or five. Ask them to refer to the Prompts for Deep Conversations handout provided to guide their discussion (Handout 5.7.2).
15 minutes	Reflection	Ask participants for their initial thoughts after the activity. Ask participants how they were able to "remove the armor." Emphasize that vulnerability precedes trust. Ask participants to discuss in their groups what other rules were on display.
5 minutes	Discussion	Demonstrate vulnerability by answering all questions from the participants.
5 minutes	Conclusion	Ask participants to complete the session evaluation using your desired format. Close the session by thanking participants.

Reflection Questions

- What does it take for a group to work effectively? What are the necessary conditions?
- Who needs to be at the table? Who is responsible for making this happen and how?
- What steps will I take to become a more effective team member?

Participant Reflection

I grew up with the motto "Order and Discipline" and it has stuck with me, so it's hard not to want to have control over the things I'm involved with. I will try practicing autonomy with my groups because it will help me trust people and their skills more.

MLDP Winter 2020

Supplemental Resources

Appleman, J. E. (2009). *10 Steps to successful business writing.* Association for Talent Development. https://www-proquest-com.dartmouth.idm.oclc.org/publication/686463?accountid=10422

Cavanor, N., Meirowitz, C., & Covey, S. R. (2013). *Learn good business writing and communication (collection)* (1st ed.). Pearson. https://learning.oreilly.com/library/view/learn-good-business/9780133577785/

TEDx Talks. (2017, November 30). *The power of written communication in a technological age | Ashley Davis | TEDxCharlotte* [Video]. YouTube. https://www.youtube.com/watch?v=AoZ7qxHXmpI&ab_channel=TEDxTalks

This session has been formatted and revised for consistency and clarity. The original session in the Management and Leadership Development Program was facilitated by Anthony Johnson, reached at ajohns@gmail.com.

10 Rules of Effective Teams

➤ **Open and Honest Communication** It seems self-explanatory, but not exactly. It's important to note that open and honest communication is not a given. It takes courage; leaders are responsible for fostering an environment where this can take place. Effective communication involves trust and clarity. "The single biggest problem with communication is the illusion that is has taken place"—George Bernard Shaw. We must learn how to actively listen. And our desire to understand has to be equal to, or greater than, our desire to be understood.

➤ **Law of Significance** This idea comes from *The 17 Indisputable Laws of Teamwork* by John Maxwell. We have to understand that nothing of significance was ever achieved by individuals acting alone. We also have to put our ego and insecurities aside and let the team work. It's naïve to think we can do it alone. One is too small a number to achieve greatness.

➤ **Embrace Diversity** This is not just about race and gender. It's embracing diversity of thought, methodology, socioeconomic backgrounds, etc. The key word here is *embrace*. We can't just accept it. We have to welcome it and be genuinely open to hearing another perspective. If we open ourselves to ideas that differ from our own, it provides us with the opportunity to see the value in varying beliefs.

➤ **Law of the Niche** Also taken from John Maxwell's book, this law states that people are most valuable where they add the most value. We don't need everyone to be good at everything. Leaders have to put the right people in the right places to optimize team performance. Failure to do this can decrease productivity and result in lower morale.

➤ **Autonomy** Most people in today's culture perform at a higher level when offered flexibility and freedom to be themselves. Many people work in groups or organizations where they feel powerless to make decisions or think outside the box. This hurts morale, stifles creativity, and lowers productivity. Many companies are converting to Results Only Work Environments (ROWEs) where they are allowing their team members as much flexibility as possible; this is allowed as long as the work gets accomplished to standard.

➤ **Team-Before-Self** Borrowed from the Army value of *Selfless Service*, we have to put the team ahead of our own needs and personal gain. This does not mean one must sacrifice everything. It means you must keep the team in mind when you are making choices that affect the team. This requires humility, mindfulness, and self-awareness.

➤ **Accountability (Through Compassion)** The process of holding someone accountable has to be devoid of judgment. We must have compassion and try to understand why someone might not be meeting the standard. It's a leader's job to provide the tools and resources to navigate through that. We must also understand that compassion is not synonymous with tolerance. We can sympathize and empathize with an individual while continuing to hold them to the standard.

➢ **Own Failure & Recognize Achievement** This rule helps strengthen your team in multiple ways. Taking ownership of failure and shortcomings helps build trust and reinforces accountability. Recognizing achievement builds team morale and becomes an infectious behavior. This is also something that takes a lot of humility and self-awareness. Our team needs to know that perfection is not realistic. They also need to feel like their hard work and adherence to team values do not go unnoticed.

➢ **Remove the Armor** Allowing oneself to be vulnerable opens the door for teams to thrive. It requires trust, communication, integrity, and honesty. It allows us to see one another as the humans that we are. If we can stop pretending that we are perfect and without struggle, we can establish an environment that is conducive for everyone to grow and be the best version of themselves. When we allow vulnerability to precede trust, we set the stage for other team members to do the same.

➢ **Operate with Integrity** Above all, operating with integrity is key. We must discuss, as a team, how to conduct business the "right way." As an individual, you can lack some of the necessary skills for a team to function well. But if you are committed to operating with integrity, you will also be committed to doing the required work to sharpen those skills. Operating with integrity also develops a sense of pride within the team dynamic. How we conduct ourselves and treat one another is more important than any specific outcome.

References

Maxwell, J. C. (2013). *The 17 indisputable laws of teamwork*. HarperCollins Leadership. (Original work published 2001)

Prompts for Deep Conversations

Talk about a time when you should have spoken up and didn't. Why didn't you? And how would the person you'd like to be have handled that situation?	What's something you wish you were good at, and why?
What's the best part about being you? What's the worst?	Can you tell the team about something that stresses you out?
What's holding you back (or what habit do you need to change) that's keeping you from becoming the best version of yourself? What can this group do to help hold you accountable?	How would other people describe what it's like to work with you? Would you describe yourself the same way?
What are you most afraid of, and who's to blame?	Describe a time when you thought your parents were 100% wrong but eventually learned they were actually right.
Talk about a time when it was difficult for you to apologize. What made it difficult, and how did you feel afterwards?	What's the most challenging thing that you're dealing with right now?
Whom do you take for granted? How can you better show your appreciation?	When do you feel under the most pressure to violate your own core values?
What are you holding onto that you need to let go of? What makes it so hard to let go?	If you were to die today, what would you most regret not having told someone? Why haven't you told them yet?
When is it ok not to be completely honest? Are you willing to share the last lie you told?	If a crystal ball could tell you the truth about yourself, your life, the past, the future, or anything else, what would you want to know and why?

Session 5.8 Writing and Workplace Etiquette

Session Description

In this session, the facilitator will illustrate the many writing opportunities that we encounter in the workplace and explain the rules and best practices that apply to every piece of professional writing. Participants will explore the ways that technology and text can blur the lines between appropriate and inappropriate, professional and unprofessional, and accurate and inaccurate. Participants will focus on writing with an audience and purpose in mind and will have several opportunities to practice their new knowledge.

Learning Objectives

Participants will do the following:
* Identify the four strategies for approaching challenging writing situations in the workplace: tone, precision, clarity, and format
* Analyze examples of the four strategies for professional writing
* Develop a plan to apply the four strategies of professional writing in their current and future work

Leadership Competencies Addressed

Intercultural Mindset
* Understands, communicates with, and interacts with people across identities

Effective Communication
* Clearly articulates ideas in a written and spoken form
* Influences others through writing, speaking, or artistic expression

Principled Action
* Bases actions on thoughtful consideration of their impact and consequences

Key Concepts and Definitions

General best practices of professional writing	These include keeping track of resources when conducting research, setting deadlines, writing follow-up e-mails, taking notes for personal and public consumption, saving documents using appropriate file names, appropriate ways to begin and end an e-mail for gender-specific or gender-neutral audiences, reaching out for informational interviews with supervisors, professors, and alumni, etc.
Tone	This is a literary device that professionals should use to consider their audience and their workplace environment/approach.

Precision	Generally, less is better. Precise writers keep it simple and still relay all the appropriate and required information.
Clarity	For the writer, it is crucial to understand "the ask" from a supervisor when completing a writing assignment to avoid unnecessary rework. For the audience, clarity is achieved through editing and revising.
Format	This refers to the actual outline and structure of a piece of writing. One may need to consider when to use bullet points, graphics, hyperlinks, and indentations.
Professionalism	The skill, good judgment, and polite behavior that are expected from a person who is trained to do a job well (Merriam-Webster Dictionary). Professionalism can always be improved.

Required Materials

- PowerPoint slides and appropriate technology (optional)
- Handout 5.8.1 Writing and Workplace Etiquette
- Paper, pen, pencil, tablet, or other electronic writing devices

Session Outline

Session duration: 1 hour and 15 minutes

Time Required		Description
15 minutes	Introduction	Introduce the topic using real-world examples. Emphasize that strong writing skills are important, especially for writers who are representing organizational views. Ask participants to consider the increasing importance of various social media platforms. Discuss why good writing matters in an academic or a professional setting.
50 minutes	Activity	Outline the four key strategies of professional writing. These are tone, precision, clarity, and format. After discussion of each strategy, lead participants through the corresponding practice exercise on Handout 5.8.1 that highlights correct and incorrect professional writing practices. Aim to spend 10 minutes on each strategy.

Time Required		Description
5 minutes	Discussion	Discuss the rest of Handout 5.8.1: share the 12 best practices of professional writing; share 10 considerations for format; and discuss with participants four questions to ask when receiving a writing assignment.
5 minutes	Conclusion	Share a list of helpful resources to read or review for improving your writing skills in the workplace. Ask participants to complete the session evaluation using your desired format. Close the session by thanking the participants.

Reflection Questions

- Do I have the tools to write clearly and simply when given an assignment?
- Do I know how to evaluate and define both my target audience and other potential audiences?
- Do I have a professional mentor or role model with whom I can check in, ask questions, receive feedback, and be honest about my struggles and concerns?
- How can I integrate what I learned today about professional writing etiquette into my personal leadership challenge?

Supplemental Resources

Kochan, T. A., & Lipsky, D. B. (Eds.). (2002). *Negotiations and change: From the workplace to society*. Cornell University Press, ILR Press. https://doi.org/10.7591/9781501731686

Pasquier, P., Hollands, R., Rahwan, I., Dignum, F., & Sonenberg, L. (2011). An empirical study of interest-based negotiation. *Autonomous Agents and Multi-Agent Systems, 22*(2), 249–288. https://doi.org/10.1007/s10458-010-9125-6

Weiss, J. N. (2018). Connecting the dots: The nexus between leadership and negotiation. *Negotiation Journal, 34*(2), 207–213. https://doi.org/10.1111/nejo.12224

Participant Reflection

Ariel Bedford led this session with passion and thoughtfulness. We examined several theoretical email exchanges and engaged in a lively critical discussion of what works and what doesn't. We critiqued tone, length, syntax, purpose, context, efficiency, and more. Bedford encouraged us to ask questions and provided thoughtful answers on how tone may shift on different platforms, how we should make decisions when faced with ambiguity, and how to navigate the digital space in a professional manner. As my MLDP experience was in the midst of the COVID-19 pandemic, I found her guidance to be immediately relevant to my everyday life.

MLDP Winter 2021

This session has been formatted and revised for consistency and clarity. The original session in the Management and Leadership Development Program was facilitated by Ariel Murphy Bedford, reached at ariel@ambnational.org.

Writing and Workplace Etiquette

Tone in Action

SCENARIO: Suzanne is interning for a national nonprofit organization and has been drafting a report for the past month. When she initially began the project, Suzanne had multiple conversations with her supervisor and with the director of her office about what they were looking for in the final product. After a third round of revisions, she believes that everyone on her team, including the director, is on the same page. In response to her third draft, however, the director sends Suzanne the following e-mail:

> Hi Suzanne –
>
> The language in this version continues to just be confusing, I think. What are we trying to show here and why? Answering this will help with the labels in our graphs, which need to be more descriptive or precise. Please revise and let me know when it's ready for me to review again.
>
> Thanks,
> Daniel

Suzanne must share the final draft of the report with the Communications team no later than 12 p.m. tomorrow. In addition, the director's schedule is packed and, before the director can review the draft, Suzanne must also find time for her supervisor to review her revisions before sending it to the director. Suzanne responds to the director's e-mail as follows:

> Daniel –
>
> The language that was used in this version to describe the initiative is the language that has been used in previous documents. With the due date of this report pressing at the front of my mind, I'm struggling to understand why we would make changes to language that people are already familiar with. To be very honest, I am feeling a massive sense of urgency here. It is of the utmost importance that we provide the final draft of the report to the Communications team by 12 p.m. tomorrow. I think we should keep it AS IS to avoid confusion. Let me know if helpful to discuss.
>
> Suzanne

What do you think about the tone of Suzanne's' e-mail? Use the margins above and/or the lines below to rewrite all or part of the e-mail.

_____

_____

_____

_____

_____

Precision in Action

MEMO

To: Selection Committee, Fellows Program

From: Frances Houseman, Candidate for 2015 Fellows Program

Date: March 9, 2015

RE: Proposed Modifications to ESEA Section 2112(b) in furtherance of ESEA Title II, Part A

Summary

The Elementary and Secondary Education Act (ESEA) is one of our most comprehensive pieces of federal legislation surrounding elementary and secondary education. Authorized by President Lyndon Baines Johnson in 1965, ESEA was renamed No Child Left Behind (NCLB) when it was reauthorized in 2002, under the Bush administration. Today, under the Obama administration, Secretary of Education Arne Duncan is pushing for reauthorization, yet again, believing that this law still has room for improvement. After reviewing ESEA section 2112(b), I, too, see the need for improvement, especially in furtherance of ESEA Title II, Part A, which grants funding to educational agencies at state and local levels with two express purposes:

(1) "increase student academic achievement through strategies such as improving teacher and principal quality and increasing the number of highly qualified teachers in the classroom and highly qualified principals and assistant principals in schools; and (2) hold local educational agencies and schools accountable for improvements in student academic achievement."[1]

Section 2112(b) enumerates twelve requirements that must be met in a state's application for that state to be eligible for a grant. Overall, this section adequately pushes states to be proactive in thinking about the kinds of strategies and programs they will implement to enhance student achievement and about the levels of oversight they will emplace to ensure compliance with federal law and the fulfillment of their objectives. That said, section 2112(b) could better meet the purpose of ESEA Title II, Part A if states were also required to include the following: (1) a description of previous efforts made to increase student achievement and hold key players at the local level accountable and how those efforts will inform their future plans, and (2) a description of the indicators of academic rigor used to develop content, standards, assessments, and curricula in the state to ensure that activities created in alignment with those indicators will actually enhance academic achievement.

Use the margins above and/or the lines below to rewrite a part or parts of the memo summary.

_____

_____

_____

_____

_____

_____

_____

_____
_____
_____
_____
_____
_____
_____
_____
_____
_____
_____
_____
_____
_____
_____
_____
_____
_____
_____
_____
_____
_____
_____
_____
_____
_____
_____
_____
_____
_____
_____
_____
_____
_____
_____
_____
_____
_____
_____
_____
_____
_____

[1]Elementary and Secondary Education Act of 1965, as amended. Title II, Part A – Teacher and Principal Training and Recruiting Fund. 20 U.S.C. § 2101 (2005). https://www2.ed.gov/policy/elsec/leg/esea02/pg20.html

Clarity in Action: Part One

DIRECTIONS: Your supervisor provides only the following directions for your first assignment: "Start a blog on behalf of the agency to promote our five initiatives."

What are some clarifying questions you would ask your supervisor before starting the assignment?

_____

_____

_____

_____

_____

_____

_____

_____

_____

_____

Clarity in Action: Part Two

DIRECTIONS: Skim the draft one-pager below. What revisions, if any, would you make to this draft?

Educator Preparation in State X

Excellent school systems —internationally and in the United States—are focused on recruiting, preparing, and retaining strong teachers. In direct response to feedback from teachers and from K-12 and teacher preparation leaders, and in line with leading nations' approaches to teacher preparation, the Louisiana Department of Education launched Believe and Prepare in 2014. This nationally recognized teacher preparation pilot program provided grant funds to support closer partnerships between preparation providers and school system leaders to offer aspiring teachers a full year of practice under an expert mentor and a competency-based curriculum. Thus far, over 850 undergraduate teacher candidates have been supported by expert mentors while pursuing certification through a year-long residency program. In October 2016, the Board of Elementary and Secondary Education, with support from the Board of Regents, adopted landmark regulations to expand these practices statewide and, since 2014, have awarded over $9 million in grant awards to teacher preparation providers and their school system partners to advance the shift to full-year residencies for all aspiring teachers.

Recognizing the importance of building a mentor teacher cadre to support new teachers, the Department also launched a paid opportunity in fall 2017 for experienced educators across the state to receive training to become effective mentors. By July 2018, all undergraduate teacher preparation programs in Louisiana will include a year-long residency alongside an expert mentor, and all teacher preparation programs will include a competency-based design (Milestone 1: 2014: The Department releases Partners in Preparation: A Survey of Educators & Education Preparation Programs report and launches Believe and Prepare pilot program; Milestone 2: 2014: Believe and Prepare pilot program launches with 7 participating school systems and 7 participating preparation providers in the first cohort, and expands to over 30 participating school systems and over 20 participating preparation providers by the third cohort (2015-16); Milestone 3: 2016: BESE approves updated regulations to scale yearlong residencies and competency-based teacher preparation curricula statewide; Milestone 4: 2017: The Department launches statewide mentor training for expert teachers; Milestone 5: 2018: All undergraduate teacher preparation programs in Louisiana will include a yearlong residency, and all teacher preparation programs will include a competency-based design; Milestone 6: 2020: The Department's Mentor Teacher cadre expands to 2,500 mentor teachers).

Since the inception of Believe and Prepare, over 850 aspiring teachers have benefited from participating in yearlong residencies, over 820 expert teachers have served as mentors, and over 35 LEAs and nearly all 27 preparation providers in our state have partnered to implement full-year residencies statewide.

"BESE Expands Full Year Classroom Residency for Teachers" See full news release "More Than 500 Louisiana Educators To Be Trained As Mentors To Future Teachers" See full news release "Paving the Way for a New Generation" See full post "Letters: Residencies for teachers good idea" See full article "Clinical Residency Aims to Change Teacher Training in Louisiana" See full article "Professional Reflections of a Mentor Teacher" See full article
Starting in 2017–2018, all teacher preparation providers in partnership with school systems will restructure preparation program designs and curricula to align with state guidelines by July 2018. Over the next three years, Louisiana will establish a cadre of at least 2,500 trained mentor teachers through the Department's Mentor Teacher Training. As a result, these experienced educators will be equipped to support yearlong residents and other new or developing teachers.

Starting in 2017-2018, the Department will focus on teacher workforce strengths and challenges in rural school systems, and work to leverage the role of mentor teachers and yearlong residencies in rural communities to better support the unique needs of rural school systems. (believeandprepare@la.gov https://www.louisianabelieves.com/teaching/believe-and-prepare)

Use the margins above and/or the lines below to edit a part or parts of the draft report.

_____

_____

_____

_____

_____

_____

_____

_____

_____

_____

_____

_____

_____

_____

_____

_____

_____

_____

_____

_____

_____

_____

_____

_____

_____

_____

_____

_____

_____

_____

_____

_____

_____

_____

_____

_____

_____

_____

_____

_____

Formatting in Action

DIRECTIONS: Compare the information from the previous exercise to the information in the following infographic.

Believe PREPARE

PREPARING LOUISIANA'S NEXT GENERATION EDUCATORS

WHAT IS BELIEVE AND PREPARE?

In line with leading nations' approaches to teacher preparation, the Department launched the nationally recognized Believe and Prepare pilot program in 2014. Believe and Prepare programs offer aspiring teachers a full year of practice under an expert mentor and a competency-based curriculum.

In October 2016, the Board of Elementary and Secondary Education (BESE), with support from the Board of Regents (BoR), adopted landmark regulations to expand these practices statewide. As of July 2018, all teacher preparation programs must include a yearlong residency alongside an expert mentor, and all preparation programs must include a competency-based design.

PRIORITY ALIGNMENT
Develop and retain a diverse, highly effective educator workforce.

FOCUS AREA
Intentional partnerships with teacher preparation providers

Timeline

2014-2015
The Department releases Partners in Preparation Survey and launches Believe and Prepare pilot program - expanding from 7 to 30 school systems and from 7 to 20 preparation providers.

2016
BESE approves updated regulations to expand yearlong residencies and competency-based teacher preparation curricula statewide by July 2018.

2017
The Department launches statewide mentor training for expert teachers and grant opportunity to support rural school systems implementing innovative, cost-neutral models of alternate certification preparation, including dedicated time for mentoring.

2018
BESE approves policy requiring ancillary certification for mentor teachers.
All teacher preparation programs aligned to policy or were approved for an innovative model.

2022
All teacher preparation candidates are completing a year-long residency.

WHAT SUCCESS HAS BELIEVE AND PREPARE HAD IN LOUISIANA & NATIONALLY?

In the News

- BESE Expands Full Year Classroom Residency for Teachers *(Louisiana Believes)*
- Louisiana Establishes Credentials for Teacher Leadership Roles *(Louisiana Believes)*
- This State is Reimagining How to Mentor Teachers in Alternative-Certification Programs *(Education Week)*
- Letters: Residencies for teachers good idea *(The Advocate)*

Since the inception of Believe and prepare **over 1,200** aspiring teachers have benefited from participating in yearlong residencies. Since 2016 **over 1,600** teachers have been trained to serve as mentor teachers. **99%** of school systems have trained mentors.

WHAT'S NEXT FOR BELIEVE AND PREPARE?

Louisiana will continue to grow the cadre of paid, trained mentor teachers. The Department will also focus on expanding the number of approved providers offering mentor teacher training.

WHO TO CONTACT?
BELIEVEANDPREPARE @LA.GOV
OR VISIT OUR WEBSITE

Louisiana Believes   *View all of Louisiana's Key Initiatives at: https://www.louisianabelieves.com/resources/about-us/louisiana's-key-initiatives*

How do clarity and formatting go hand in hand?

Formatting Considerations for Professional Writing

Depending on the writing assignment, you may have to consider some of these items. Keep in mind that there is no one-size-fits-all choice, and it is dependent on the situation, context, and workplace specifications. Look at guidelines provided by your organization. Consider the following items:

1. Headings & Subheadings

2. Typeface
   - ➢ Serif Fonts (Print) such as Times New Roman, Georgia, Palatino, and Garamond
   - ➢ Sans-Serif Fonts (Digital) such as Calibri, Arial, Helvetica, and Tahoma

3. Font Size & Color

4. Page Size & Margins

5. Paragraph Alignment

6. Indentation

7. Image Placement

8. Line Spacing

9. Section Breaks
   - ➢ Headers, Footers, Columns, Page Numbers

10. Acronyms & Dates
    - ➢ Management and Leadership Development Program (MLDP)
    - ➢ 2015–16 vs. 2015–2016

Best Practices of Professional Writing

➢ Be mindful of our four key strategies (tone, precision, clarify, and format).
➢ Be consistent (acronyms; punctuation → item one, item two, and item three vs. item one, item two and item three).
➢ Avoid offensive language (e.g., chair or chairperson vs. chairman or chairwoman; client with a disability vs. disabled client)
➢ Avoid passive voice.
➢ Backwards plan and set deadlines that allow for multiple rounds of drafting and revising.
➢ When conducting research, keep track of your sources in a separate folder.
➢ When saving drafts of a writing assignment on your computer, include the title of the assignment, the date that the file was last updated, and the version of the draft (i.e., v1, Final). This works for saving meeting notes, as well.
➢ When taking messages on Post-It notes, be sure to include the date, the time, the purpose of the call, as well as the name, number, and e-mail address of the person reaching out.
➢ When drafting letters on behalf of your supervisor or department head, be sure to include their proper signature line.
➢ When starting and signing off on e-mails, take a cue from the way your supervisor signs off in his/her e-mails. In general, "Dear Mr./Ms. ___" and "Sincerely (your first name)" will work well.
➢ When reaching out to alumni or a potential employer, do a Google search for him or her to confirm his or her gender, and ALWAYS send a follow-up e-mail to thank him or her for his or her time, advice, etc.
➢ When meeting with your supervisors, always bring a pen/pad or a laptop for notes.

Reflection Questions to Keep in Mind

➢ Do I have the tools to write clearly and simply when given an assignment?
➢ Do I know how to evaluate and define both my target audience and other potential audiences?
➢ Do I have a professional mentor or role model with whom I can check in, ask questions, receive feedback, and be honest about my struggles and concerns?
➢ How can I integrate what I learned today about professional writing etiquette into my academic career and personal leadership challenge?

_____
_____
_____
_____
_____
_____
_____
_____
_____
_____

Writing Resources

- Hacker, D. 2006. *A writer's reference* (6th ed.). Bedford/St. Martin's.
- Strunk Jr, W., & White, E. B. (1999). *The elements of style* (4th ed.). Turtleback.
- Roth, E. (2019, December 30). *10 simple design rules for professional Microsoft Word documents*. MUO. https://www.makeuseof.com/tag/design-rules-word-documents/

Session 5.9 Problem Solving Through Negotiation

Session Description

In this session, the facilitator will introduce basic tools and processes available in negotiation which can allow one to systematically identify problems and their desired outcomes, decide what options are available to best achieve the desired outcome, and negotiate with those who must be included in the process of obtaining the desired outcome.

Learning Objectives

Participants will do the following:
- Identify the three basic concepts involved in interest-based negotiation: always be intentional; know yourself and know your opponent; and identify your BATNA
- Practice the negotiation concept of Fair, Firm, and Friendly through an interactive activity

Leadership Competencies Addressed

Principled Action
- Bases actions on thoughtful consideration of their impact and consequences
- Seeks appropriate and mutually beneficial solutions when conflict or controversy arises

Effective Communication
- Influences others through writing, speaking, or artistic expression
- Acknowledges and appropriately communicates in situations with divergent opinions and values

Key Concepts and Definitions

Always be intentional	In negotiation, this means to do research on why one is choosing the path they are.
Know yourself/ Know your opponent	Know your own triggers and negotiation style. Know what your opponent wants and their triggers. Knowing all of this can help you with an intentional strategy of negotiation, as well as prepare you to handle the emotions that may arise.
Best Alternative to a Negotiated Agreement (BATNA)	This term describes the option B that allows one to say no to option A (from Fisher et al., 2011). It is imperative to do research on what one is negotiating for, and to research the other person to discover their own BATNA.

| *Interest-based vs. zero-sum* | These are the two different approaches to negotiation. Interest-based refers to the approach where each negotiator tries to identify the interests of the other person and to meet those interests when possible, so that everyone earns more. Zero-sum implies that when one person earns something, something is necessarily taken away from the other. |
| *Fair, Firm, and Friendly* | This refers to the tone and attitude one should have in the negotiation process. |

Required Materials

- Writing surface and writing utensils
- Room set up for students to face each other in pairs and then split into groups of three
- Compiled results of online personality test. For example, you can purchase the *Thomas-Kilmann Conflict Mode Instrument* or a personality test of your choice.

Pre-session Assignment:
- Take the personality test(s).

Session Outline

Session duration: 1 hour and 30 minutes

Time Required		Description
30 minutes	Introduction	Begin by asking participants where they negotiate now as leaders. Explain that we all negotiated first as babies, bringing in the idea of negotiation as the back-and-forth interaction between two or more parties where some interests are shared, and some are not (Ury, 2007). Define and discuss the key concepts and definitions of negotiation. Explain that all things being equal, it is important to choose the option that keeps the most alternatives open. Go through the personality tests and what they may indicate to each participant when negotiating. Ask the group for their results. Discuss how some of the participants feel about their results, if they ring true, why or why not.

Time Required		Description
5 minutes	Activity 1	Divide participants into pairs. Introduce the arm-wrestling activity. Tell the pairs that each participant should attempt to touch their partner's hand to the table the greatest number of times. After one minute, ask the pairs for their "competition" results. Either, the pair was locked in an arm grip, one partner kept winning, or both realized that they could help each other touch the table as many times as possible. Observe which of these scenarios were acted out by the group. If none of the pairs worked together to have both touch the table as many times as possible, suggest this alternative. Explain that this is an illustration of zero-sum vs. interest-based negotiation.
30 minutes	Activity 2	Select a negotiation simulation in advance. You can create one or obtain one from numerous negotiation programs. The idea should be that the parties negotiating have an opportunity to understand BATNA and to also see how personalities affect the negotiations.
20 minutes	Debrief	Create a grid on the board where you can lay out the results of the different parties in the simulation on the x-axis and the different groups that acted out the simulation on the y-axis. Point out how the participants all got the same instructions, but all or most results are different. The reason is that the negotiators make the difference. Refer back to the personality test results. Ask the participants if their personality made any difference in the way they negotiated. Did their opponent's? Get them thinking about how human factors make a difference in the outcome, so it is important to understand themselves and the people with whom they negotiate. Ask each group what happened, who held power, and how each group negotiated.
5 minutes	Conclusion	Reflect with participants about the importance of having negotiation skills when you are a manager and a leader. Summarize what is important about negotiation and why it matters in personal and professional contexts. Answer any questions. Ask participants to complete the session evaluation using your desired format. Close the session by thanking the participants.

Reflection Questions

- What have I learned about myself and my negotiation skills?
- Are there any personal barriers that might prevent me from being a successful negotiator?
- What negotiation techniques can I use to address the goals of my personal leadership challenge?

Supplemental Resources

Abdallah Ajlouni. (2020, February 27). *Circle of concern and circle of influence | Be proactive | The 7 Habits | Stephen Covey* [Video]. YouTube. https://www.youtube.com/watch?v=tD0aFZkFrFA&ab_channel=AbdallahAjlouni

FranklinCovey. (2018, March 13). *Circle of influence—from The 7 habits of highly effective people* [Video]. YouTube. https://www.youtube.com/watch?v=uj8dmSgQa1c&ab_channel=FranklinCovey

---

Participant Reflection

This week's session on negotiation was eye-opening and allowed me to immediately put my negotiation style into practice. A situation erupted between two friends about securing last minute housing. I was distressed because I was caught in the middle of them. In order to make them happy, I found a way to satisfy their individual wants without canceling our plans entirely. This session affirmed my belief that I am a collaborator who appreciates firm, fair, and friendly means of conflict resolution. Moving forward, understanding my persistent desire to confront interpersonal conflicts head-on without compromising relationships in the long term would be beneficial.

MLDP Spring 2020

Giles, H., Liang, B., Noels, K. A., & McCann, R. M. (2001). Communicating across and within generations: Taiwanese, Chinese-Americans, and Euro-Americans perceptions of communication. *Journal of Asian Pacific Communication, 11*(2), 161–179. https://doi.org/10.1075/japc.11.2.04gil

Fisher, R., Ury, W. L., & Patton, B. (2011). *Getting to yes: Negotiating agreement without giving in.* Penguin.

Miller, K. I. (2007). Compassionate communication in the workplace: Exploring processes of noticing, connecting, and responding. *Journal of Applied Communication Research, 35*(3), 223–245. https://doi.org/10.1080/00909880701434208

Ury, W. (2007). *Getting past no: Negotiating in difficult situations.* Bantam.

Thomas-Kilmann Conflict Mode Instrument by Kenneth W. Thomas & Ralph H. Kilmann. Copyright 1974, 2002, 2007 by The Myers-Briggs Company. All rights reserved.

This session has been formatted and revised for consistency and clarity. The original session in the Management and Leadership Development Program was facilitated by John Garvey, reached at John.Garvey@law.unh.edu.

Session 5.10 Building Bridges Between Generations and Session Reflections

Session Description

In this session, the facilitator will discuss the nature of an intergenerational workplace. For the first time, there are at least four generations working together in some occupations. As a new generation entering the workplace, this session will prepare participants to understand and build bridges between the generations. Participants will also reflect on all previous MLDP sessions and their implications for the workplace.

Learning Objectives

Participants will do the following:
- List at least three identities and beliefs of their generation and at least one other generation
- Describe three strengths in the identities and beliefs of a particular generation to enhance communication in the workplace
- Reflect on the skills learned in MLDP and apply them to their current life and future workplace cultures

Leadership Competencies Addressed

Intercultural Mindset
- Understands, communicates with, and respectfully interacts with people across identities

Effective Communication
- Acknowledges and appropriately communicates in situations with divergent opinions and values

Effective Reasoning
- Develops personal reflective practice

Self-Knowledge
- Understands social identities of self and others

Key Concepts and Definitions

Circle of influence, circle of concern	Covey (1989/2020) writes that the circle of influence is a metaphor for the spaces and ways in which one can make an impact in their life. The circle of concern represents all the things which one concerns themselves with but has no influence over. When one focuses on the circle of influence and the things they can do, they increase their potential for growth and the circle of influence expands. Conversely, if one focuses only on the circle of concern, the circle of influence begins to shrink because there is less time and energy spent in action.
Understand expectations of others and the organization	Every workplace has a unique environment; often when one is new to the workplace culture there are many things that are left unsaid. When you come to a workplace, look around and see what people are doing. This is an act within the circle of influence that can lessen concerns about assimilating or making mistakes.

Make small changes—bring the best influence you can for the best outcome	Another realm within the circle of influence is self-reflection. Asking oneself the following questions can help guide this reflection on being a good influence in the workplace: What about the other generation is adding to the workplace? (e.g. What is the reason they have been there for 30 years?) What do you bring to the workplace? Where could there be some improvements?
Intergenerational communication	It is important to acknowledge that one's identity influences many things about them, including the way that they communicate. The first step in fostering intergenerational communication is understanding the identities and beliefs of different generations and not stereotyping them. This requires using a growth mindset, empathy, listening skills, language, technical competence, and gratitude.

Required Materials

- PowerPoint slides and appropriate technology (optional)
- Flipcharts with MLDP session titles set up around the room
- Markers

Pre-session Assignment:

- Participants should research information about an assigned generation and what we know about them in the workplace.

Session Outline

Session duration: 1 hour and 30 minutes

Time Required		Description
5 minutes	Introduction	Discuss with participants the importance of intergenerational communication in the workplace.
15 minutes	Framing	Review learning objectives and key concepts. Begin a discussion on the characteristics of different generations. Ask the participants to share the things they discovered in their research prior to the session. Ask participants what three things they are proud of about their generation. The purpose of asking participants to name strengths is to bring the group away from stereotypical and negative conversations about generations.

Time Required		Description
25 minutes	Activity 1	Divide participants into groups of four. Ask each group to choose a representative to take notes of their collective discussion. Ask participants to individually list four people they know personally who belong to the four different generations discussed. Based on the characteristics they have observed about each person, participants will share a story with the group that highlights some of the generational characteristics of one person from their list. After each participant takes turns, the group should discuss what they believe to be true or not true about different generations. Participants will individually list three things they can do to be more effective in their communication with other generations, discuss these observations with their group, and conclude their discussion with what they need to be aware of to be effective and successful in their workplace.
10 minutes	Discussion	Bring participants back to the large group. Ask participants what they learned about their strengths. Invite group representatives to share their observations and conclusions about the generations they discussed and what they need to be aware of to be effective and successful in their workplace.
15 minutes	Activity 2	Divide participants into groups of four. Assign each group to a poster paper around the room with a previous MLDP session title on it. Ask each group to write their words of wisdom related to the past session. After they are finished, participants will move to the next flipchart until they have finished including their ideas on every flipchart. If another group has mentioned the same idea, elaborate on it or add other ideas. Ask participants to return to their seats after their group has visited every chart.
10 minutes	Discussion	Ask participants to share what struck them about the words of wisdom that they had not thought about or what was reinforced for them. Share personal thoughts and takeaways from years of being in a workplace. Talk about these key points: elegance, integrity, transparency, honesty, teamwork, and respect. Use this quote: "Despite the differences you may encounter with other [coworkers], there is one underlying principle that is essential for a productive workplace: respect for each other" —Angela Walmsley, author of "Closing the Communication Gap" (2011) and co-author of *Recruiting and Retaining Generation Y Teachers* (2009).

Time Required	Description	
10 minutes	Conclusion	Share the reflection questions for participants to continue considering their circle of influence in the workplace. Ask participants to complete the final session evaluation using your desired format. Close the session by thanking the participants.

Reflection Questions

- What skills do I need to work on to be effective with others—in my current relationships, in the future, or in work with others?
- What do I think about intergenerational differences and what is my place within it?
- What does elegance look like in the workplace?
- You have agency over the environment you create. What is the ideal work environment in your opinion?

Supplemental Resources

Participant Reflection

Sadhana Hall's session gave me a greater understanding of the generational differences between my supervisor and me. I'm now better equipped to meet my supervisor's demands and appreciate their feedback. Adjusting my expectations and actions to accommodate their communication style has allowed our bond to deepen; I finally feel like we're on the same page.

MLDP Spring 2020

Covey, S. R. (2020). *The 7 Habits of highly effective people* (30th anniversary ed.). Simon & Schuster. (Original work published 1989)

McCann, R. M., Dailey, R. M., Giles, H., & Ota, H. (2005). Beliefs about intergenerational communication across the lifespan: Middle age and the roles of age stereotyping and respect norms. *Communication Studies, 56*(4), 293–311. https://doi.org/10.1080/10510970500319286

Myers, K. K., & Sadaghiani, K. (2010). Millennials in the workplace: A communication perspective on millennials' organizational relationships and performance. *Journal of Business and Psychology, 25*(2), 225–238. https://doi.org/10.1007/s10869-010-9172-7

Rebore, R. W., & Walmsley, A. L. E. (2009). *Recruiting and retaining generation Y teachers*. Corwin Press.

Singh, V. (2014). "We are not phobic but selective": The older generation's attitude towards using technology in workplace communications. *Development and Learning in Organizations: An International Journal, 28*(4), 18–20. https://doi.org/10.1108/DLO-10-2013-0082

Tolbize, A. (2008). Generational differences in the workplace. *University of Minnesota Research and Training Center on Community Living*, 1-25. https://rtc.umn.edu/docs/2_18_Gen_diff_workplace.pdf

Walmsley, A. L. E. (2011). Closing the communication gap. *Educational Horizons*, *90*(1), 25–26. https://
     www.jstor.org/stable/42926572

This session has been formatted and revised for consistency and clarity. The original session in the Management and Leadership Development Program was facilitated by Sadhana Hall, reached at Sadhana.W.Hall@dartmouth.edu.

MLDP Program Officer Reflection

by Robin Frye

When I started working at the Rockefeller Center in 2009, the Management and Leadership Development Program (MLDP) had just begun implementing its pilot version. About six months into my tenure, I was charged with implementing the logistics for two of the five leadership programs in this book, Dartmouth Leadership Attitudes and Behaviors and the Rockefeller Leadership Fellows Program. Six years later, I was handed the responsibility of implementing MLDP.

Before I knew it, the Center had become a place where my potential would be realized. I had literally fallen into a career that was meant for me. I would not have stepped into leadership programs without excellent mentorship. The ability to see the potential of others and follow that up with deliberate guidance is something I continue to hone in my own leadership to this day. This has reaped many benefits for MLDP in the ways I work with participants and student program assistants. While I have learned so much in these past few years, I continue to grow. I would like to share some lessons I have learned from these experiences.

When taking over a well-established program like MLDP, I strongly suggest letting it run for a few iterations before making any significant changes. When I first started running MLDP in the winter of 2015, it was already a successful program, and I wanted it to be one of the most respected programs on campus. I spent two terms observing and getting to know MLDP before making any significant changes. The lineup of speakers was great, and the content was excellent. Typically, 65–75 students had signed up for the program, but many would discontinue. In analyzing why this was the case, I realized that the program was open to all and students simply had to sign up for it. As a result, it was not viewed as a selective program by participants. To address this concern, and following the successful recruiting model of the new Rockefeller Global Leadership Program, I implemented an application and student interview process instead of sign-ups. This simple act made students more committed to the program and ensured they had already articulated their purpose in enrolling for it. All that was left for me was to address the attrition rate and level of participation and engagement in the sessions. I introduced the idea of completing the program "with Excellence"—which requires perfect attendance and being nominated by peers for observable qualities such as listening or engaging. As a result of adding this component to the program, attrition levels have dropped, and engagement levels have increased. In this process, I have also learned that participants enjoy being recognized for the effort they put into the program.

In the summer of 2015, I made significant changes to accommodate the large number of participants in an effort to make the program more cohesive and increase engagement. To build cohesion and a sense of community, I divided up the large group of participants into two smaller sections with about 25–30 participants each, running the same content back-to-back with a dinner for all participants held between the two sections. We also changed the physical location from a set classroom layout to a room that enabled small-group work and conversations and increased engagement as a result.

On our campus, we follow the D-Plan, described on our admissions webpage as "Dartmouth's quarter academic system which enables students flexibility in choosing their enrollment pattern." Using this plan, students have options to pick 12 terms to graduate. As a result, the student population turns over each term. For this reason, it is essential to have a long-term plan in which awareness of and interest in the program is maintained. To do that, I suggest striving to have all areas of campus represented in the program. I started looking for ways to reach areas of campus that were not fully represented. I learned from other program officers at Rocky and my student assistants that the key to reaching those groups is through their peers. I have worked hard to continue to maintain diverse representation through a variety of peer-to-peer initiatives, including asking participants to talk about MLDP in their classes, social gatherings, and organizations to which they belonged. They also nominate people they know to apply for the program and send group emails through their affiliations to make the program widely known.

Another change I made was to adapt the program's previously optional Personal Case Study into the mandatory Personal Leadership Challenge (PLC). With the PLC, every participant identifies an area of growth, sets SMART goals, and works towards them throughout the program. The PLC culminates with a written reflection at the end. These are very thoughtful and give great examples of how the program benefits participants specifically. The PLC has been transformative for many participants. Some gain confidence, while others try things they never would have otherwise. Some secure jobs or internships, others learn to step back and let others lead.

One young woman stands out in my mind as an example of how transformations can occur when learners commit to and embrace their articulated challenge fully. She was an African student who was very shy. In her culture, it is easy to build relationships because it is ingrained in the fabric of everyday life. On our campus, she felt that it was much harder to establish relationships. That cultural difference caused her quite a bit of anxiety when trying to get to know people. She was a sophomore with very few friends, all of whom were also African, and she was not involved in any extra-curricular activities. She came to MLDP wanting to change that. She set a goal to broaden her network and talk to people she didn't know in her classes each week or to talk more often with acquaintances. By the end of the 10-week term, as she was saying hello to people she passed on the street, one of her friends commented, "It seems like you know everyone all of a sudden." I think about this student often and how she simply gained the courage to try something in a culture so new and so foreign to her, and how, in a relatively short time, she demonstrated the grit to go beyond her comfort zone.

For a program component like the PLC to be implemented well and be successful, I have learned that participants need a lot of support to set them up for success. I was trained in coaching by the International Coaching Federation, and this has added to the continuous development and improvement of the PLC. Now, MLDP participants are supported with coaching through the identification and goal setting stage of the PLC. When addressing behavior changes, coaching helps them uncover the underlying reasons for their behavior. For example, students who feel they have time management issues may be chronically over-committed. I have also been able to bring the coaching skill into the way I give feedback, how I have difficult conversations, and how I work with my student program assistants.

A concept from Hall and Perucci's *Teaching Leadership: Bridging Theory and Practice* (2018) that resonates with me is the importance of creating a culture of continuous quality improvement. I was privileged to see this culture develop at Rocky, particularly while the Center was developing its assessment plan. When Sadhana [Hall] created the session proposal form (SPF), I first saw it as another form to be filled out by the session's creator, the guest speaker—after all, they are the topic experts. A few years ago, we started using part of our staff meeting to have the program officers present every session proposal form to the team and have a discussion. I then realized that the SPF is better used as a tool for a conversation between the program officer and the speaker as co-creators of the session. The program officer is an expert on the program. I also learned how important it is when developing a new session to start with the learning objectives. And always keep them in mind when making changes. It's tempting to start off talking about the activities and content; that's the fun stuff. But if you start with the learning objectives, you can intentionally tie the session to the program's overall purpose and the Center's mission.

At Rocky, we also embrace the culture of continuous quality improvement and prioritize professional development of students and staff. In assessment venues like participant reflections, peer-to-peer conversations, and regular staff meetings, we take what we feel we can use and adopt, adapt, or adjust for our own programs, as I did with implementing the application and interview process from RGLP. These modes of assessment and collaboration have allowed me to implement ideas that have made the program more cohesive, accessible, and popular.

We can attribute the Rockefeller Center programs' success to a combination of excellent mentorship from senior staff, a growth mindset, and a sense of community within an organization that intentionally pushes its staff to grow alongside its program participants. I have observed that when a program officer has an area of growth, it shows up in the program as well. I remember in my early days, I was avoiding the hard accountability conversations with students. I tried to implement many structures to solve accountability issues, which always led back to a hard conversation. When I finally committed to having those conversations face-to-face, the programs matured, and the students became more committed as a result. Conducting difficult conversations will always be hard for everyone. But as lifelong learners, we continue to look for ways to have them more effectively. This was my biggest motivation to become trained in coaching.

Our Rocky staff members have experienced many changes in our programs due to the COVID-19 pandemic. I compare it to putting sand in our well-oiled machine. With our in-person programming, we became accustomed to relying on that machine, and it allowed us to relax and reflect. Suddenly finding ourselves in profound change put us all back into our learning zones. We proved we could be nimble and get our programs online within two weeks and we were ready to offer them in time for the spring term. That required a positive outlook and collaborative problem-solving.

We also responded rapidly to changes around us. With the Justice for George Floyd and Black Lives Matter protests in the summer of 2020, we joined Dartmouth in its commitment to address racism by changing some of our program content. Those content changes and the challenge of building a community in our programs online are what we are focusing on now. During times like these, we have the opportunity to empower others by bringing them into the process. I have been working with an amazing group of student assistants. They have given great ideas, and they are taking risks and owning the implementation of these risks. It's exciting to see them grow professionally alongside us.

Going forward, further increasing student engagement and empowerment online are on my mind. I will also need to address challenges with outreach because of the silence created by the nature of remote learning. It is hard to not have casual conversations with students in the corridors, which provide you with so much information about them personally as well as the activities on campus.

My work at Rocky has allowed me to grow into a polished and resilient professional. Each challenge I face is met with more grit. I embrace the opportunity to learn and grow. When I started at Rocky, I had never heard of the concepts of personal and professional growth or stepping outside your comfort zone. I look back on the hard work I've done for MLDP and my own professional growth with pride.

6 | Rockefeller Global Leadership Program (RGLP)

Global Dexterity is about learning to adapt your behavior across cultures— No matter what culture you come from, what culture you are going to, or the situation you find yourself in.

—Andy Molinsky

The technological advances in the world have opened doors for businesses and organizations to work across borders. While the pandemic has created challenges, it has also created a unique set of opportunities for organizations to expand their global reach and meet their missions. Working with cultures different from your own requires a special set of skills and competencies. The Rockefeller Global Leadership Program (RGLP) is a nine-week standalone program designed for participants in their second, third, and final years of their undergraduate experience.

Program Goal

The program's goal is to prepare participants for leadership roles in a culturally diverse yet interdependent world. RGLP provides participants with the opportunity to develop greater awareness of their own cultures and the cultures of others, and to develop skills that will help them make a positive impact in their future interactions with diverse individuals, teams, and organizations.

In this program, participants identify the various parts of their cultural identity and those of others and reflect on how this affects leadership in a global context. Some key topics in the program are cultural identity, diversity, globalization, and cross-cultural communication.

Program Prerequisites

RGLP is open to all students on campus except for first-year learners. This is because many of them do not have work or internship experiences. This program is for those with higher levels of maturity, development, and experience.

Program Participation

While diversity, equity, and inclusion are important for all the co-curricular programs, RGLP particularly focuses on these issues, and we attract many participants who want to study these topics in greater depth. It is also suitable for those participants who are preparing for culturally diverse experience, such as a study or work abroad, or for those who have recently completed such an experience.

Since Fall 2014, we have attracted students who intend to major in 39 different fields of study, ranging from the humanities to STEM and the arts. The five most popular majors for RGLP participants are, in descending order: government, economics, geography, neuroscience, and history. Table 6.1 represents what RGLP participants had declared as their majors while they were completing the program.

Table 6.1

Ten Most Popular Majors for RGLP Participants Fall 2014–Spring 2020

Major	Number of Participants
Government	77
Economics	48
Geography	17
Neuroscience	16
History	14
Psychology	11
Sociology	9
Computer Science	8
Environmental Studies	8
Anthropology	8

Like other Rockefeller Center programs, RGLP attracts more female than male participants; since 2014, 59% of the students who successfully complete RGLP identify as female. In addition, RGLP attracts the most international students of the five main co-curricular programs. Historically, 15.8% of RGLP participants are international students who collectively represent 40 different countries. This is not surprising since RGLP appeals to students who are interested in social justice and are committed to learning about different cultures, beliefs, and identities.

The number of students who applied and were accepted into RGLP decreased, on average, from Fall 2017 to Spring 2020. Consistent and accurate completion data were not collected until Fall 2017, which is why this analysis begins there and not in 2014. There are two reasons that may explain this decrease. First, the program is no longer open to first-year students because the content is nuanced and complex, and learners benefit from having more experience in a workplace through internships before participating in this program. Second, the turnover of program staff managing this program has led to varying levels of outreach efforts. The number of students who completed the program each term ranged from 11 in Spring 2020 to 29 in Spring 2017. Figure 6.1 reflects RGLP participation and completion data since Fall 2017.

Figure 6.1

RGLP Participant and Completion Data Since Fall 2017

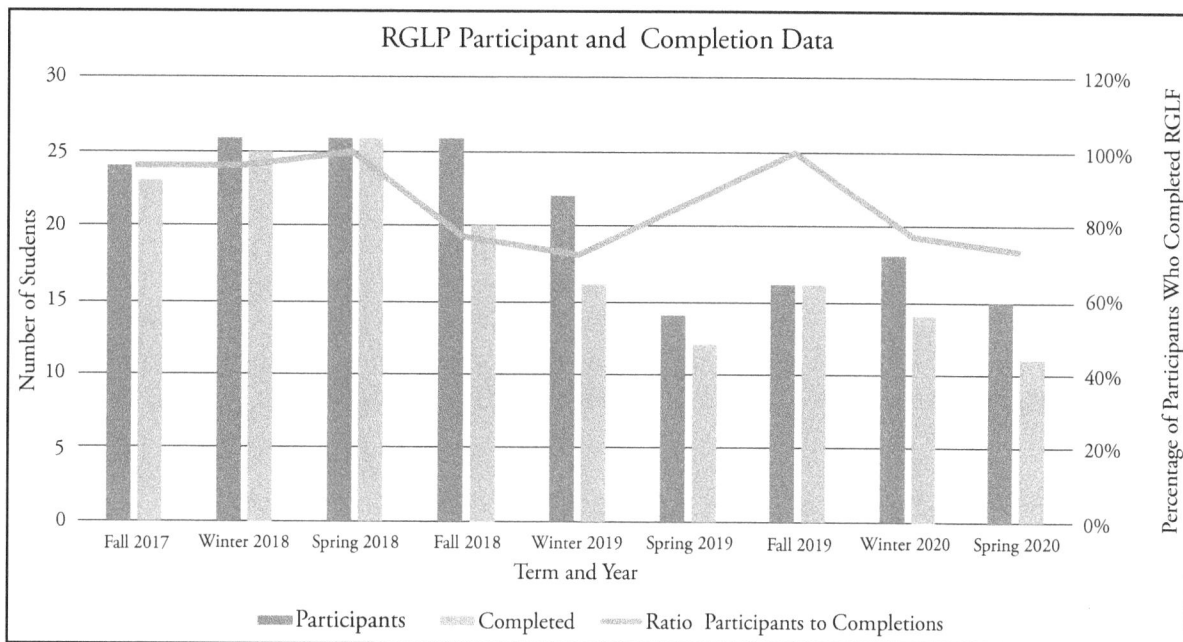

Key Program Elements

➢ Experiential sessions led by diverse guest speakers consisting of in-depth discussions and activities such as roleplays and case study analyses
➢ Development of cultural self-awareness, ambiguity tolerance, intercultural communication skills, and understanding of what it means to be a global leader
➢ Culminating weekend trip to apply lessons learned throughout the program
➢ Group presentations on an intercultural issue or challenge

Program Description

The program consists of 25 or fewer participants each term, which allows for community-building and cohort cohesion. Accountability groups of four to six students are formed at the beginning of program, and these groups engage in dinner discussions each week and prepare a final presentation together. Accountability groups are formed based on random pairing or on interest in a particular content area. Participants also work in pairs and other small groups during the guest speaker portion of the weekly session. This allows all participants to get to know each other and feel comfortable discussing difficult topics. Participants attend eight weekly sessions, each of which consists of a dinner discussion or activity and a speaker-led portion with a short lecture followed by discussion and activities. Participants provide feedback after each session.

Another important component of the program is the experiential weekend trip, which allows participants to apply the concepts explored over the course of the program. The itinerary, apart from departure and arrival times, is deliberately not shared with the participants, which sets the stage for learning how to deal with ambiguity. RGLP has taken trips to Montreal, Boston, and New York City. Examples of activities include attending international film festivals, participating in a deaf workshop, dining in a restaurant run by visually impaired servers, and visiting religious institutions and observing their practices. If you are designing a program of this nature, look for activities in your community or nearby cities that expose participants to diverse experiences that they generally would not have on their own. Travel is not essential. What is important is selecting activities that take participants out of their comfort zone, and these can be found locally as well.

Another essential component of the program is group presentations. At the beginning of the program, participants are tasked with identifying and solving an intercultural issue at the local, national, or global level. Participants work in their accountability groups over the course of the program and in the final session give group presentations on the solutions. The immersion trip also helps participants to reflect on concepts covered during the program.

Key Leadership Competencies

The key competencies the program focuses on are self-awareness, respect for diversity, and intercultural communication skills. RGLP encourages participants to be aware of the ways in which culture permeates every aspect of life and how it influences thoughts and behaviors. By reflecting on their identities and experiences, and hearing about the identities and experiences of their peers and guest speakers, participants develop a more ethno-relative mindset and learn to make a positive impact in their future experiences.

Possible Adaptations

In addition to higher education, the content presented in RGLP can be tailored to and is also applicable to nonprofit organizations, for-profit organizations, government institutions, and anyone working with communities within and across borders. It is also applicable for K-12 audiences. The program is suitable for those who are preparing for a culturally diverse experience such as study or work abroad or for those who have recently completed such an experience. It is also suitable for anyone looking to develop intercultural communication and leadership competencies to better engage with diverse others in their daily lives and post-graduation careers. The program is useful for both participants who have prior intercultural experience and those who do not.

Here are some ideas of how to adapt this program:

> ➤ Identify your audience and their needs. Research what is known or not known about these needs.
> ➤ Use the Eight Pillars of Program Design to develop your concept.
> ➤ Make sure the content you cover matches the experience and maturity level of your audience.
> ➤ Create a structure within which you will sequence the content.
> ➤ Make sure you have enough time for individual and group reflections.
> ➤ Think about an "accountability partner" system and how it might work.
> ➤ Explore whether a weekend trip in person, or virtually, expands understanding related to this content area
> ➤ If resources permit, consider surveys about knowledge, attitudes and practice. Have a group discussion about the results.

Session 6.1 Orientation

Session Description

In this session, the facilitator will kick off the Rockefeller Global Leadership Program (RGLP). After introductions, the cohort will discuss the program learning objectives and expectations. The facilitator will introduce the key concepts that lay the groundwork for the program. Participants will learn about Dr. Milton J. Bennett's Developmental Model of Intercultural Sensitivity (DMIS).

Learning Objectives

Participants will do the following:
- Describe the Learning Zone Model and identify the learning objectives, expectations, and program structure of RGLP
- Identify and define the three conditions necessary for intercultural contact to be constructive: intercultural mindset, skillset, and sensitivity
- Reflect on their own intercultural experiences and where they are on the DMIS continuum, and brainstorm ways they and their peers can move along the DMIS continuum toward a more ethnorelative perspective

Leadership Competencies Addressed

Collaboration
- Fosters a welcoming and inclusive environment

Self-Knowledge
- Understands social identities of self and others

Intercultural Mindset
- Contextualizes social identities and experiences

Key Concepts and Definitions

Learning Zone Model
Tom Senninger suggests that when participants are in their comfort zone, they are dealing with issues familiar to them and do not need to take risks. When they transition to the learning zone, they are presented with possibilities outside of their known experience and outside their comfort zone. Beyond this lies the panic zone, where learning stops as participants find themselves crippled by a fear of the unknown. In such situations, the energy that should be invested in learning is diverted into managing anxiety and distress. Such situations often result in inaction or resistance, which is commonly referred to as flight, fight, or freeze" (from *Teaching Leadership: Bridging Theory and Practice*). When educators create an intellectually and emotionally supportive environment by encouraging them to grow, participants expand their learning beyond their comfort zone.

Intercultural mindset
Recognition of deep differences in cultural worldviews and the potential value of those differences for organizations. Examples include the ability to use generalizations instead of stereotypes or to identify subjective vs objective culture.

Objective culture	What human beings make and what they consciously transmit from generation to generation.
Subjective culture	Psychological features, assumptions, values, and needs, often expressed nonverbally or implicitly.
Intercultural skillset	The skills necessary to identify potential areas of misunderstanding and increase one's repertoire of behavior appropriately. Examples include knowing how to navigate and understand different styles of language, communication, behavior, and values.
Intercultural sensitivity	The ability to experience cultural difference. This ability is modeled in the Developmental Model of Intercultural Sensitivity as a range from ethnocentrism to ethnorelativism.
Ethnocentrism	The inability to experience reality differently than we were originally taught. When one's own culture (beliefs and behaviors) is "central to reality" and "just the way things are."
Ethnorelativism	The experience of one's own beliefs and behaviors as just one organization of reality among many viable possibilities. The ability to recognize that all behavior exists in cultural context.
Developmental Model of Intercultural Sensitivity (DMIS)	A framework, created Dr. Milton J. Bennett that explains how people experience and engage with cultural difference on a continuum of ethnocentrism and ethnorelativism. It has six stages that help describe an individual's ability to move past cultural biases, recognize and respect the differences of other cultures, and take steps to integrate among those cultures.

Required Materials

- PowerPoint slides and appropriate technology (optional)
- Flipchart and markers
- Handout 6.1.1 Developmental Model of Intercultural Sensitivity (DMIS) Stages of Experience (cut into strips according to each stage)
- Seats and nametags set up so that participants are arranged in their accountability groups

Pre-session Assignment:
- Participants should complete Handout 6.1.2 Circles of My Multicultural Self.
- "Intercultural Competence for Global Leadership" by Milton J. Bennett. https://www.idrinstitute.org/wp-content/uploads/2018/02/Global_ICC_IDRI.pdf

Session Outline

Session duration: 2 hours

Time Required		Description
20 minutes	Introduction	Introduce yourself and your background. Focus on the things in your experience that have made you passionate about this topic of global leadership and intercultural learning. Ask each participant to introduce themselves and share their statement from step four of the Circles of My Multicultural Self handout that they completed prior to the session. Lead an icebreaker that will help the cohort learn each other's names and become more comfortable with one another.
20 minutes	Framing	Cover the structure of the RGLP program. This includes explaining the research behind this program and the benefits of intercultural competence in the workplace. Explain why intercultural understanding is important. Describe the Learning Zone Model and its importance for participant learning.
10 minutes	Discussion	Give accountability groups three to five minutes to brainstorm the values, expectations, and desired behaviors they would like to set for the RGLP cohort. After small group discussion, create a list of values set by the cohort through participants' suggestions and reflections on a sheet of chart paper.
20 minutes	Framing	Introduce and define the rest of the key concepts.
35 minutes	Activity 1	Hand out the instructions and materials for the DMIS activity (Handout 6.1.1). The participants should be divided into six new groups and each assigned a stage from the DMIS. Each group must find something in the media (a video, image, news article, etc.) that represents the DMIS stage they have been assigned. They must brainstorm ideas for how to develop and move to the next DMIS stage and answer the following questions: *Where do you think your DMIS stage fits on the continuum? Is it more ethnocentric or ethnorelative?* After 15 minutes, ask each group to present the media clip or article they found and share the key points of their discussion.
15 minutes	Conclusion	Discuss participants thoughts, questions, or concerns about the DMIS. Ask participants to complete the session evaluation using your desired format. Close the session by thanking the participants.

Reflection Questions

- What did the media clips that were selected make you think about/feel?
- What do you think about the DMIS? Why is this important?
- What are some things you can do in your everyday life to move along the continuum and to encourage others to move along the continuum?
- Once you make it to the Integration stage, how do you stay there? Do you think there is a risk of going backward toward a more ethnocentric perspective?
- How can we use our understanding of DMIS in the future?
- How can we continue to understand and empathize with the differences of others while still maintaining a personal value system?

Supplemental Resources

Hernandez, F., & Kose, B. W. (2012). The developmental model of intercultural sensitivity: A tool for understanding principals' cultural competence. *Education and Urban Society*, *44*(4), 512–530. https://doi.org/10.1177/0013124510393336

Michael Paige, R., Jacobs-Cassuto, M., Yershova, Y. A., & DeJaeghere, J. (2003). Assessing intercultural sensitivity: An empirical analysis of the Hammer and Bennett intercultural development inventory. *International Journal of Intercultural Relations*, *27*(4), 467–486. https://doi.org/10.1016/S0147-1767(03)00034-8

Osgood, C. E. (1977). Objective indicators of subjective culture. *Annals of the New York Academy of Sciences*, *285*(1), 435–450. https://doi.org/10.1111/j.1749-6632.1977.tb29371.x

Senninger, T. (2000). *Abenteuer leiten-in Abenteuern lernen: Methodenset zur Planung ud Leitung kooperativer Lerngemeinschaften Für Taining und Teamentwicklung in Schule, Jugendarbeit und Betried.* [Leading adventures - learning adventures: a set of methods for planning and managing cooperative learning communities for training and team development in schools, youth work and companies]. Ökotopia-Verlag.

Participant Reflection

In this session, we talked a lot about the Developmental Model of Intercultural Sensitivity (DMIS). The model operates ranging from denial on the ethnocentric side to integration on the ethnorelative side. We were asked to identify our stages, explain why we were there, and why other people may be at the stages they are at. My group zeroed in on the ethnocentric stages and worked to provide justifications for each stage. Talking through these justifications helped me better understand the people in my life who fell into these categories. I feel like I have a better understanding of their perspectives. This session also provided me with tangible theory-based tools to address difficult conversations surrounding race, culture, and identity. Having these allow more analytical conversations to take place without minimizing any individuals' viewpoints because they lack the language necessary to discuss said issues.

RGLP Spring 2020

This session has been formatted and revised for consistency and clarity. The original session in the Rockefeller Global Leadership Program was facilitated by Leslie Wagner-Ould Ismail, reached at Leslie.R.Wagner-Ould.Ismail@dartmouth.edu.

Developmental Model of Intercultural Sensitivity (DMIS) Stages of Experience

Denial

People have not yet constructed the category of "cultural difference." To them, the world is completely their current experience of it, and alternatives to that experience are literally unimaginable. People of other cultures, insofar as they are perceived at all, seem less human, lacking the "real" feelings and thoughts of one's own kind. Cultural strangers exist as simpler forms in the environment to be tolerated, exploited, or eliminated as necessary. As a result, either cultural difference is not experienced at all or it is associated with a kind of undifferentiated other such as "foreigner" or "immigrant." At the Denial stage, the main issue to be resolved is the tendency to avoid noticing or confronting cultural difference.

Statements someone in Denial may make are as follows:

> **All big cities are the same:** *lots of buildings, too many cars, and McDonald's.*
> *I never experience culture shock.*
> *As long as we all speak the same language, there's no problem.*

Defense

People have become more adept at perceiving cultural difference. Exposure to media images of other cultures or casual contact may set the stage for this level of experience. Because one's own culture is still experienced as the only true reality, the existence of other cultures is threatening to that reality. To counter that threat, the world is organized into "us" and "them" associated with the denigration of "them" and the superiority of "us." People in the Defense stage tend to polarize any discussion of cultural difference, and jokes that denigrate other cultures are accepted as "normal." A variation on Defense is Reversal, in which an adopted culture is experienced as superior to the culture of one's primary socialization ("going native"). At the Defense stage, the main issue to be resolved is establishing commonality.

Statements someone in Defense may make are as follows:

> *What do you have against your own country?*
> *We could really teach these people a lot of stuff.*
> *You're either with us or against us.*

Minimization

The state in which elements of one's own cultural worldview are experienced as universal. People at Minimization expect similarities, and they may become insistent about correcting others' behavior to match their expectations. People in Minimization recognize cultural variation in institutions and customs (objective culture) and may be quite interested in those kinds of differences. However, they hold mightily to the idea that beneath these differences beats the heart of a person pretty much like them. Because they are still lacking cultural self-awareness, people in Minimization cannot see that their characterizations of similarity are usually based on their own culture. Particularly for people of dominant cultures, Minimization tends to mask recognition of their own culture (ethnicity) and the institutional privilege it affords its members. This stage is associated with various "Melting Pot" ideas, where a lot of emphasis may be placed on assimilation into the host culture. The main issue to be resolved is self-awareness.

Statements someone in Minimization may make are as follows:

Customs differ, of course, but when you really get to know them, they're pretty much like us.
It's a small world, after all!
If people are really honest, they'll recognize that some values are universal.

Acceptance

People have discovered their own cultural context, and therefore can accept the existence of different cultural contexts. They experience their own culture as just one of a number of equally complex worldviews. People in Acceptance are able to experience others as different from themselves, but equally human. They are adept at identifying how cultural differences in general operate in a wide range of human interactions. People in Acceptance may be curious about cultural differences and seek out information about the subjective cultural behavior and values of other groups. The experience of Acceptance is not the same as "agreement" of other cultural beliefs and behaviors. The main issue to be resolved is contextual relativism, or the ability to accept the relativity of values to cultural context, and thus to attain the potential to experience the world as organized by different values.

Statements someone in Acceptance may make are as follows:

As a person with German background, I am inclined to believe that…
I always try to research a new culture before I go there.
Sometimes it's confusing, knowing that values are different in various cultures. I want to be respectful, and still want to maintain my own core values.

Adaptation

People are able to shift their cultural frames of reference; that is, they are able to look at the world "through different eyes" and intentionally change their behavior to communicate more effectively in another culture. This is a conscious act, necessitating an awareness of one's own culture and a set of contrasts to the target culture. It is the ability to have a significant experience of a different culture without losing their own cultural worldviews. People in Adaptation can engage in intercultural empathy—the ability to take perspective or shift frame of reference vis-à-vis other cultures and are able to reorganize their perception of events so that it is more like the worldview of the target culture. The major issue to be resolved at Adaptation is that of authenticity. How is it possible to perceive and behave in culturally different ways and still "be yourself"?

Statements someone in Adaptation may make are as follows:

Let's imagine how a Muslim might react to…
To solve this dispute, I'm going to have to change my approach.
I greet people from my culture and people from the host culture somewhat differently to account for cultural differences in the way respect is communicated.

Integration

People extend their ability to perceive events within a cultural context to include their own definitions of identity. For these people, the process of shifting cultural perspective becomes a normal part of self, and so identity itself becomes a more fluid notion. People in Integration can move in and out of different cultural worldviews and are continually in the process of deciding what events in a variety of cultural contexts are intrinsic to who they are. They experience themselves as "in process," as opposed to having any set identity. The question "Who are you?" is likely to elicit a very long story, filled with examples of intercultural experience.

Statements someone in Integration may make are as follows:

My decision-making skills are enhanced by having multiple frames of reference.
Whatever the situation, I can usually look at it from a variety of cultural points of view.
Sometimes I don't feel like I fit anywhere.

Circles of My Multicultural Self

Description

This activity highlights the multiple dimensions of our identities. It addresses the importance of individuals self-defining their identities and challenging stereotypes.

Directions

> ➢ Place your name in the center circle of the structure below. Write an important aspect of your identity in each of the satellite circles, and an identifier or descriptor that you feel is important in defining your culture. This can include anything: Asian American, female, athlete, Taoist, or any descriptor with which you identify.
> ➢ Think about a time when you were especially proud to identify yourself with one of the descriptors used below.
> ➢ Think about a time when it was especially painful to be identified with one of your identifiers or descriptors.
> ➢ Name a stereotype associated with one of the groups with which you identify that is not consistent with who you are. Fill in the following sentence:

I am (a/an) _____ but I am NOT (a/an) _____.

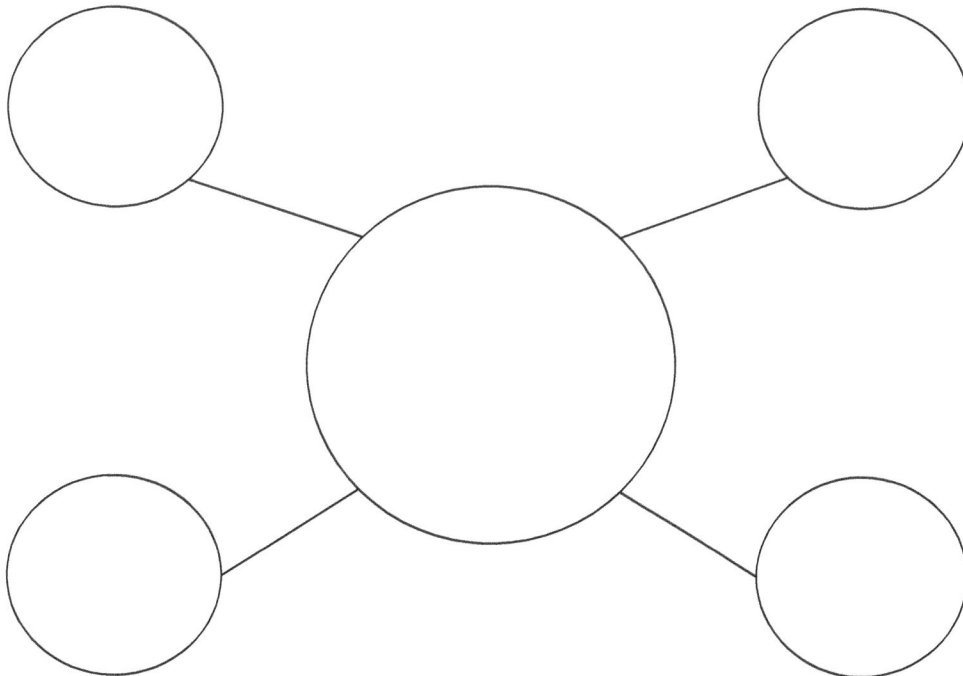

Note: Reprinted from *Circles of My Multicultural Self: Critical Multicultural Pavilion Awareness Activities* by P. C. Gorski, n.d., http://www.edchange.org/multicultural/activities/circlesofself.html. Copyright © 1995-2020 by Paul C. Gorski.

Session 6.2 Intercultural Conflict Style Inventory and Leadership

Session Description

In this session, the facilitator will discuss intercultural communication and conflict-resolution styles using the Intercultural Conflict Style (ICS) Inventory. Participants will use the ICS Inventory to gain self-awareness of their own communication and conflict-resolution style. Through the lens of their own experiences of intercultural communication, participants will reflect on their communication styles. Based on new information about other styles of communication, they will then problem-solve some past experiences. Participants will leave with an action plan for how they can use this information moving forward.

Leadership Competencies Addressed

Self-Knowledge
- Demonstrates realistic understanding of one's abilities

Principled Action
- Seeks appropriate and mutually beneficial solutions when conflict or controversy arises

Intercultural Mindset
- Understands, communicates with, and respectfully interacts with people across identities

---

Learning Objectives

Participants will do the following:
- Identify their communication and conflict resolution styles using the ICS Inventory
- Reflect on one good and one bad intercultural experience in their past, and analyze the experiences using the inventory
- Identify at least three action steps that are immediately relevant and applicable for improving their communication and conflict resolution style

Key Concepts and Definitions

Intercultural Conflict Style Inventory A tool that provides a descriptor of a person's preferred approach to communicate and conflict. This style is not hardwired, but it is the style one is most likely to use in a difficult situation. These styles are rooted in two separate spectrums: one's emotional restraint or emotional expressiveness, and one's indirect or direct style of communication." (ICS Inventory, n.d.)

Emotional restraint vs. emotional expressiveness	The two different patterns cultures use regarding the purpose of emotion in conflict. In an emotionally restrained style/culture, emotions are disguised and internalized, individuals are sensitive to the overall social harmony of an interaction and are thus more concerned with the feelings of the other party. Additionally, credibility and maturity are demonstrated through emotional control. In an emotionally expressive style/culture, emotions are externalized and overtly displayed as a means of emotional control. Additionally, credibility and trust are built upon the level of affective commitment (ICS Inventory, n.d).
Direct vs. indirect conflict style	The two different patterns cultures use when deciding the communication style to make use of during conflict. An indirect conflict style emphasizes the importance of social harmony, and thus sees this through with the usage of vague statements, third parties, and "talking around" disagreements and goals through discrete metaphors, analogies, and stories. The emphasis is on the listener to clear up disagreements. In a direct conflict style, meaning is derived from 'inside' the verbal message, and the message itself is explicit. Individuals are encouraged to voice out disagreements face-to-face and persuade each other. It is up to the speaker to clear up disagreements (ICS Inventory, n.d).

Required Materials

- Index card for each participant

Pre-session Assignment:
- Intercultural Conflict Style Inventory link for participants to complete the test: https://icsinventory.com/online-test. Participants will bring their test results to the session.

Session Outline

Session duration: 2 hours

Time Required		Description
10 minutes	Introduction	Using anecdotes, talk about the subject of intercultural communication. Describe why looking at intercultural conflict is important for becoming self-aware and understanding the concerns of others, as well as the implications for building a diverse community.

Time Required		Description
10 minutes	Activity 1	Ask participants to write on one side of an index card about a good intercultural communication experience. On the other side, ask them to write about a bad one. Divide participants into pairs. Each participant will share their positive experience and then their negative experience. When sharing the negative experiences, ask participants to focus on the facts, not their interpretations or reasoning for the events.
10 minutes	Framing	Explain the ICS Inventory and provide a broad overview of its purpose. Ask participants what their experience was in completing the ICS Inventory. Describe your own results and provide a story that highlights your intercultural communication preferences.
20 minutes	Activity 2	Divide participants into small groups of four or five. Ask participants to share their results with one another and describe a story that highlights their own preferences.
35 minutes	Discussion	As a large group, discuss the key takeaways from the stories that participants shared and what they need to be aware of to be successful communicators across cultures. Provide more information about the communication styles as provided in the ICS Inventory. Point out the proverbs from different countries. Discuss: *What do these proverbs indicate about the value of directness/ indirectness and emotional restraint/expressiveness in those cultures?* Using the ICS Inventory, demonstrate where certain cultural groups tend to fall on the quadrant of communication and conflict styles. Ask: *Do your styles align with the typical style of your country or culture? Are you surprised by or in disagreement over the communication and conflict style of any of these cultural groups?*
15 minutes	Activity 3	Ask participants to resolve conflicts noted on their index card with a new partner using the knowledge that they now have about cultural communication styles. Participants should identify which conflict resolution style the other party may have had and roleplay a resolution.
15 minutes	Reflection	Ask participants about their thoughts or concerns about the ICS Inventory. Ask participants to talk to a new partner about three things they have learned from the material as it specifically relates to them. Each participant should write down three to five action steps they will take moving forward to better

Time Required	Description
	handle communication and conflict resolution. Shift the reflection towards the large group and allow participants to share their ideas with each other.
5 minutes Conclusion	Ask participants to complete the session evaluation using your desired format. Close the session by thanking the participants.

Reflection Questions

- What steps can I take to be better at communication with individuals who have different intercultural communication styles?
- How will I use my knowledge of intercultural communication and conflict styles when interacting with people from different backgrounds?

Supplemental Resources

Batkhina, A. A. (2017). Intercultural conflict styles: Literature review. *Социальная Психология и Общество* [Social Psychology and Society], *8*(3), 45–62. https://doi.org/10.17759/sps.2017080305

Hammer, M. R. (2009). Solving problems and resolving conflict using the Intercultural Conflict Style model and inventory. In M. A. Moodian (Ed.), *Contemporary Leadership and Intercultural Competence: Exploring the Cross-Cultural Dynamics Within Organizations* (pp. 219–233). SAGE Publications. http://archive.org/details/contemporarylead0000unse_o6k9

ICS Inventory. (n.d.). *Intercultural Conflict Style® inventory: Online test*. Retrieved March 15, 2021, from https://icsinventory.com/online-test

Little, B. (2016, February). *Who are you, really? The puzzle of personality* [Video]. TED Conferences. https://www.ted.com/talks/brian_little_who_are_you_really_the_puzzle_of_personality

> ### Participant Reflection
>
> *I've always dealt with conflict directly. My conflict resolution style, discussion, reflects that. When there's a problem, I face it head-on and try to minimize intense expressions of emotion. Most of my friends don't deal with conflicts this way and I've always found it frustrating as I want to confront issues and get over them. This session helped me better understand other conflict styles and the reasoning behind them. It has helped me better tailor my expectations to the conflict styles of my friends and helped me grow into a better communicator.*
>
> **RGLP Spring 2020**

This session has been formatted and revised for consistency and clarity. The original session in the Rockefeller Global Leadership Program was facilitated by Sadhana Hall, reached at Sadhana.W.Hall@dartmouth.edu. The Intercultural Conflict Style (ICS) Inventory and ICS materials are trademarked and copyrighted by Mitchell R. Hammer Ph.D. (2020). For more information visit www.icsinventory.com

Session 6.3 Framing Global Leadership and Developing a Global Consciousness

Session Description

In this session, the facilitator will introduce the concept of Global Leadership to participants. This introduction serves as the basis for further exploration of how this concept relates to a participant's own leadership development in a global context. Participants will be asked to examine their own leadership development journey within the context of a global environment. Participants will reflect upon the values synonymous with global leadership.

Learning Objectives

Participants will do the following:
- Define key terms associated with global leadership: the Westphalian system, globalization, and "global leader" as a new category of leader in the global context
- Identify and analyze at least three skills and competencies necessary for a global leader and what it means to have a global mindset
- Describe and differentiate global leadership development strategies

Leadership Competencies Addressed

Self-Knowledge
- Continually explores and examines values and views
- Shows self-respect and respect for others

Intercultural Mindset
- Contextualizes social identities and experiences
- Actively engages in opportunities to expand worldview
- Applies intercultural knowledge and skills in local, national, and/or global contexts

Key Concepts and Definitions

The Westphalian System

A principle of international law that each state has sovereignty over its own territories and domestic affairs. A brief historical explanation: The Catholic Church, the predominant power in Europe, slowly lost power in the 1600s and kings filled in their place. The 30 Years' War began because of a land conflict as regional kings struggled to assert their territory. With the Treaty of Münster, the state principles of borders and sovereignty became standard. Over the next two centuries, nationalism arose as a way to garner support from the population in state-state conflict (Hickey, 2020).

Globalization	The process of economies, organizations, institutions, and businesses operating on an increasingly international scale. By Thomas Friedman's definition, globalization may be associated with three key stages: countries globalizing from 1400 to 1800 (Globalization 1.0), companies and/or multinationals globalizing from around 1800 to 2000 (Globalization 2.0), individuals and small groups of all nationalities globalizing themselves after 2000 (Globalization 3.0).
Global leader	The individuals within the current stage of globalization that do not fit the classification of international, national, or local leadership. The key skills of a global leader include intercultural-communication competence, leveraging diversity and inclusion, managing intercultural conflict, cultivating a global mindset, and effective teamwork in a cross-cultural context.
Global mindset	The capacity to combine an awareness of diverse cultures with an ability to integrate them into a new cultural map. This dual approach (awareness and integration) suggests a disposition to hold multiple perspectives within a single cultural map.
Contamination	Biased interpretations of another culture influenced by one's own cultural map.

Required Materials

- PowerPoint slides and appropriate technology (optional)
- Board and markers
- Space for break-out groups
- "Welcome to Albatros" simulation activity props

Session Outline

Session duration: 1 hour and 20 minutes

Time Required		Description
5 minutes	Introduction	Introduce yourself and provide historical or personal anecdotes of significant interactions between individuals with differing national and/or international identities.

Time Required		Description
35 minutes	Framing	Outline a brief history of the conflicts that eventually led to the current international system and the corresponding identities that national and world citizens hold. Draw a timeline on the board that begins in the 1600s and ends in the present. As you cover key concepts, mark them on the timeline.
		Explain the evolution of the Westphalian System of nation-states. Using roleplay or other discussion methods, explain the coinciding process of globalization and the changes in international systems throughout the three stages of globalization. Give some examples of globalizing systems, like trade, and ask participants for other examples. Finally, explain the concept of the 'global leader' as a new category of leader in the new global context. Discuss the skills of a "global leader"; the difference between global, international, national, and local leaders; and what it means to have a global mindset.
20 minutes	Activity	Explain to participants that the next activity is an anthropological simulation: half of participants will be "natives" or "islanders" of Albatros island (an imaginary place) and the other half of the group will be the "anthropologists" who have been granted the privilege of witnessing an important social ritual of the islanders. The anthropologists will be taking notes with the goal of understanding what type of society Albatros has and the islanders will follow the instructions of the ritual that you will have designed yourself. You can include props to suggest something about valuable island resources, give specific roles to specific people to suggest social hierarchies, etc. Allow the islanders time to look over the directions and prepare for the ritual.
		Make sure that the anthropologists are out of earshot. After the roleplay, the will share what they observed and their hypotheses. The islanders will then share what was really going on. Explain the concept of contamination and ask participants to identify their biases. The Albatros simulation is based on that of Donald Batchelder and Elisabeth Warner (*Beyond Experience: The experimental approach to cross-cultural education*, Experiment Press, 1977).

Time Required	Description	
15 minutes	Reflection	Based on the discussion of key concepts and the Albatros simulation, lead a group reflection about the implicit and explicit values of global leadership.
5 minutes	Conclusion	Ask participants to complete the session evaluation using your desired format. Close the session by thanking the participants.

Reflection Questions

- How has the evolution of the concept of state sovereignty changed international systems? How is this evolution connected to the advent of Globalization 3.0?
- How are recent developments in technology, communication, transportation, and economic interdependence reshaping the perception of national identity in a global environment?
- Describe the tensions between isolationism and interdependence in a global environment. How do some leaders contribute to these tensions? How can global leaders bridge the gap between the two sides?
- What is the connection between global leadership and cross-cultural communication?

Supplemental Resources

Participant Reflection

I learned how important it is to be aware of how your own cultural map can "contaminate" your interpretation of different cultural situations. Placing culture within the context of the long durée of human civilization also helps me appreciate that my own viewpoints are the culminations of thousands of years of history. It takes a lot of work to actively decolonize our minds. Furthermore, there is not innocent action or behavior; everything we do is rooted in a greater global process that is constantly affecting us whether we are aware of it or not. The cross-cultural activity allowed me to directly see my own biases and proclivities and how they may advantage or disadvantage other people.

RGLP Fall 2019

Batchelder, D. & Warner, E. G. (Eds). (1977). *Beyond experience: The experiential approach to cross-cultural education.* Experiment Press.

Gray, K. W., & Kalyalya, K. (2016). Overcoming statism from within: The international criminal court and the Westphalian system. *Critical Horizons, 17*(1), 53–65. https://doi.org/10.1080/14409917.2016.1117813

Hickey, W. (2020). *The sovereignty game: Neo-colonialism and the Westphalian system.* Palgrave Macmillan.

Kim, Y. (2013, October). *Business not as usual: The key to success for Korean global leaders* [Video]. TED Conferences. https://www.ted.com/talks/yeonhee_kim_business_not_as_usual_the_key_to_success_for_korean_global_leaders

TED. (2014, February 19). *What it takes to be a great leader | Roselinde Torres* [Video]. YouTube. https://www.youtube.com/watch?v=aUYSDEYdmzw&feature=youtu.be&ab_channel=TED

This session has been formatted and revised for consistency and clarity. The original session in the Rockefeller Global Leadership Program was facilitated by Gama Perruci, reached at perrucig@marietta.edu.

Session 6.4 Examining Values and Customs Through a Multicultural Lens

Session Description

In this session, the facilitator will introduce participants to the art of Brazilian dance, kickboxing, singing, and drumming. This is the first experiential session of the program and was led by an expert in Brazilian culture. It is designed to help participants unpack subjective and objective culture and addresses these questions: What are the values and customs in another's cultural practices and arts? What does the experience and practice of this culture further tell you about the values and customs of the culture itself? Those looking to recreate this session are encouraged to dive deep into any culture that is not their own through those that are willing to teach others about their valued culture. Participants will experience, for some, a new shared cultural experience, and unpack and process the experience both collectively as a group and in pairs.

Leadership Competencies Addressed
Self-Knowledge • Continually explores and examines values and views • Shows self-respect and respect for others • Moves beyond self-imposed limitations **Intercultural Mindset** • Contextualizes social identities and experiences • Actively engages in opportunities to expand worldview

Note: Given the complexity of this session, the original facilitator invites other capoeira instructors looking to adapt the session to reach out to him (f.fuacapoeira@gmail.com). It is his hope that all future facilitators, regardless of cultural background, have a thorough understanding of self, culture, and oppression.

Learning Objectives

Participants will do the following:
• Practice capoeira, a dance form specific to an art and culture from Brazil
• Describe the significance of capoeira to Brazilian culture
• Identify emotional reactions to experiencing a situation outside their comfort zone
• Examine and reflect on the implications for working in a culture different from their own

Key Concepts and Definitions

Risk-taking	Exploring a new form of movement.
Empowerment	Increasing comfort in dancing/performing/vocalization.
Creativity	Discovering new moves and rhythmic patterns in capoeira.

Required Materials

- Enough space to form a large circle and allow for side-to-side movement
- Lyrics printed for participants
- Traditional Brazilian instruments
- Paper and writing utensils

Note: This session focuses on capoeira and Brazilian culture, but if there is another culture about which you have expertise, you can adapt the session to it.

Session Outline

Session duration: 2 hours

Time Required		Description
10 minutes	Introduction	Introduce yourself and provide a brief background of the history of capoeira.
15 minutes	Framing	Begin by outlining how in the U.S., white culture is the dominant culture, and to be a minority in professional settings often requires adhering to white culture. Emphasize how understanding another culture requires being "under" it and learning what the different rules of that culture are to successfully abide by it. Demonstrate some of the main elements of capoeira while introducing the differences between the culture, where the dance form originates from, and the dominant culture within the area of the program.
25 minutes	Activity 1: Exploring Axé	Before participants begin, lead them through a breathing exercise. Ask participants to stand and take deep breaths. On the outbreath, first ask participants to hum. Then, ask participants to hum open-mouthed on the out-breath. Begin to teach the song using the printed lyrics for reference. Add the use of instruments and instruct participants how to make traditional beat patterns. Slowly begin adding all the pieces together and encourage participants to move past their inhibitions using the concept of Axé.
		Keep playing the instruments and repeating the song until everyone is enthusiastically participating. Invite participants to switch roles between rounds.

Time Required		Description
30 minutes	Activity 2: Forró	Divide participants into groups. Half will lead and half will follow. Instruct participants through the basics of the dance form, showing first the lead parts and then the parts in which they follow. Allow participants to switch partners often and encourage them to get close, as the main goal is to foster a better understanding of physical language/interactions between different genders.
	Capoeira	Spread participants around the room. Teach the basics of ginga and some variation, some defenses, and attacks. Put together a small sequence in which students can play around with concepts such as aggression or violence and understand these human characteristics without judgment. Ask students to answer the chorus of songs while playing with their partner.
20 minutes	Reflection	Discuss how formal culture is the seat of unconscious instincts, and that emotional actions are rooted in cultural behavior. Encourage participants to write a paragraph about a time before they were nine years old when an adult had a reaction to their behavior that made them feel uncomfortable, afraid, or embarrassed. Ask them to identify what it was that they did wrong, whether that is defined by themselves or society. Share an example from your own experience to begin. After the reflection, lead a discussion on formal culture and shedding the instinctual behavior it carries. Emphasize that without reflecting and seeing one's unconscious actions that typically arise out of awareness, the formal cultural cycle continues onto the next generation.
10 minutes	Discussion	Ask participants to think of a recent situation where they did something they are not happy about as a result of social pressure. This will be framed as an example of "examining our inner oppressor." Start with your own example. Rather than writing this one, participants will be encouraged to share.

Time Required		Description
10 minutes	Conclusion	Divide participants into pairs to discuss the following general reflection questions about the session: *What happened? What took place? What do you think about what happened? How do you feel about what happened?* Allow for pairs to share their thoughts on the session with the large group. Ask participants to complete the session evaluation using your desired format. Close the session by thanking the participants.

Reflection Questions

- Was your experience of capoeira like anyone else's in the group?
- Was your interpretation of the experience like anyone else's?

Supplemental Resources

Assunção, M. R. (2005). *Capoeira: The history of an Afro-Brazilian martial art*. Taylor & Francis Group. http://ebookcentral.proquest. com/lib/dartmouth-ebooks/detail. action?docID=183149

Bourrelle, J. S. (2016, September). *Learn a new culture* [Video]. TEDxArendal. https://www.ted. com/talks/julien_s_bourrelle_learn_a_ new_culture

TEDx Talks. (2014, July 22). *Cultural difference in business | Valerie Hoeks | TEDxHaarlem* [Video]. YouTube. https://www.youtube. com/watch?v=VMwjscSCcf0&ab_channel=TEDxTalks

Participant Reflection

This session allowed me to practice an intercultural experience in a physically and intellectually challenging environment. I am so grateful for Fua's expertise and his genuine love for sharing beautiful Brazilian culture. By actively participating in a new and foreign activity, I was forced to leave my comfort zone and actively find ways to adapt into a new setting. Although it was not a perfect transition, my process of immersing myself in Capoeira allowed me to physically partake in a new environment. This session taught me to not be afraid to fail and fail fast and jump in instead of being safe on the sidelines.

RGLP Winter 2019

This session has been formatted and revised for consistency and clarity. The original session in the Rockefeller Global Leadership Program was facilitated by Fuá Nascimento, reached at f.fuacapoeira@gmail.com.

Session 6.5 Cultural Intelligence— Strengthening Your Intercultural-Global Toolkit

Session Description

In this session, the facilitator will outline the key concepts related to global citizenship, such as empathy, dexterity, cultural intelligence, and other intercultural-global competencies. Participants will identify their current intercultural-global skills and those they need to possess to successfully navigate as future global leaders and citizens.

Learning Objectives

Participants will do the following:
- Identify and discuss two examples of global empathy in different cultural contexts
- List and define intercultural-global and cosmopolitan competencies
- Define the concepts of global dexterity and cultural intelligence
- Create and own a Cultural Intelligence (CQ) action plan

Key Concepts and Definitions

Leadership Competencies Addressed

Self-Knowledge
- Demonstrates realistic understanding of one's abilities

Intercultural Mindset
- Actively engages in opportunities to expand worldview
- Applies intercultural knowledge and skills in local, national, and/or global contexts

Effective Reasoning
- Integrates multiple types of information to effectively solve problems or address issues

Management
- Develops and implements a plan for goal attainment

Global empathy	Having the ability to understand, accept, and interact with individuals from all different backgrounds, regardless of race, nationality, language, religion, skin color, sex, etc.
Global dexterity	Being able to adapt one's behavior across cultures. Author Andy Molinsky (2013) describes "global dexterity" as a skill which reflects the ability to "adapt while feeling comfortable" and overcoming emotional and psychological challenges one may feel.
Cultural Intelligence (CQ)	According to David Livermore (2011), cultural intelligence is "the capability to function effectively in a variety of cultural contexts." Livermore assesses CQ by measuring four capabilities: drive, knowledge, strategy, and action.

Intercultural-global competencies	Self-awareness, ability to communicate and behave appropriately in intercultural situations based on specific attitudes, intercultural knowledge, skills, and reflection (Esterhuizen & Kirkpatrick, 2015); open-mindedness, risk-taking, attentiveness to diversity, global awareness, historical perspective, collaboration across cultures, and intercultural capability (Global Competence Associates, 2018).
Cosmopolitan competencies	Cosmopolitanism ("citizen of the world") refers to a "set of skills, outlooks, and practices which become necessary tools for individuals as they cross boundaries between the familiar and unfamiliar" (Skrbiš, 2014). The competencies are global languages/digital literacy, cultural diversity, global mindset & diversity, aesthetic capital & arts, sustainability & global challenges, mobility & adaptability, and innovation & entrepreneurship.
Design thinking	A human-centered approach that encourages organizations to focus on the people they're creating for, which leads to better products, services, and internal processes. When you sit down to create a solution for a business need, the first step is to identify the human need behind it.

Required Materials

- PowerPoint slides and appropriate technology (optional)
- Handout 6.5.1 Intercultural-Global Competencies printed for each participant
- Four poster papers, each titled with one scenario from Activity 1, and space for each group to write their ideas
- Markers

Session Outline

Session duration: 1 hour and 50 minutes

Time Required		Description
5 minutes	Introduction	Introduce yourself and your background, focusing on your global experiences and/or identity. Pass out Handout 6.5.1.
20 minutes	Activity 1	Define *global empathy*. In small groups of three or four, ask participants to think about different scenarios they would experience on a trip to a foreign country. In order to successfully navigate the following scenarios, the small groups are being asked to consider how the people who live there might think, feel, or act. The scenarios are as follows:

Time Required		Description
		communicating in a foreign language; ordering from a menu written in a different language; using public transportation in a different country; and asking for directions from someone who cannot speak English. Each group will have three minutes to list their ideas on the scenario poster. After the three minutes, rotate the posters among the groups and repeat until every group has written their ideas on each poster. At the end of the activity, ask each group to compare the commonalities and differences between the posters.
20 minutes	Activity 2	Define *global dexterity*. Explain that each accountability group will now practice global dexterity through role-play. Each group will think of a potential cultural challenge, such as making introductions, navigating dining etiquette, or choosing attire, and act out the event as it would occur with a person lacking global dexterity. Participants will reflect on what makes them feel in their comfort zone and mark the zone of appropriateness for each dimension of the global dexterity chart (see Handout 6.5.1). Then, each group will role-play the ideal interaction. Reflect with the large group on how participants felt when they had to change their "normal" behavior and whether they felt they could be successful at this in real life. If not, why? What can they work on?
15 minutes	Discussion	Define *cultural intelligence* (CQ). Ask participants to complete a CQ self-assessment to assess their strengths and weaknesses and develop action steps to address those weaknesses (see Handout 6.5.1). For example, if one scored low in knowledge, they could plan to read more international news on a regular basis.
15 minutes	Activity 3	Define *cosmopolitan competencies* and introduce the event-planning activity from Handout 6.5.1. Each small group will have 15 minutes to brainstorm an event that addresses a cosmopolitan theme. They will need to identify how their event addresses the theme, come up with a goal that fits some of the cosmopolitan competencies, write three learning objectives for participants, and estimate a budget. Ask each group to present their cosmopolitan event proposal.

Time Required		Description
20 minutes	Activity 4	Introduce *design-thinking*. Ask small groups to apply the design-thinking approach to this prompt: *Imagine a student traveling abroad to a country they have never been in before. Try to put yourself in their shoes and imagine their persona. Ask yourself: Whom are we empathizing with? What do they need to do? What do they see? What do they say? What do they do? What do they hear? What do they think and feel?* Through this approach, each group can identify the intercultural-global competencies that their "persona" would possess.
15 minutes	Conclusion	Review the key concepts and main takeaways from the session's activities. Ask participants to complete the session evaluation using your desired format. Close the session by thanking the participants.

Reflection Questions

- What does it mean to be a global worker and a true citizen of the world today?
- What is my level of confidence and motivation in the intercultural-global competencies I currently possess?
- What intercultural-global competencies do I need to include in my global toolkit and how do I plan to develop these?
- How can I train my mind to become more comfortable navigating uncomfortable cultural situations?

Participant Reflection

I rely on skills gained through this session in my work today as an undergraduate advisor. In this session, my group and I created an alternate persona and worked to explain how their background shaped them into the person they are. We focused on their competencies, their fears, frustrations, and more. Today, when dealing with residents, I work to understand them through these traits. I've grown into a better communicator and empathizer.

RGLP Spring 2020

Supplemental Resources

Adler, G. (2019). *Empathy beyond US borders: The challenges of transnational civic engagement.* Cambridge University Press.

Bachen, C. M., Hernández-Ramos, P. F., & Raphael, C. (2012). Simulating REAL LIVES: Promoting global empathy and interest in learning through simulation games. *Simulation & Gaming, 43*(4), 437–460. https://doi.org/10.1177/1046878111432108

Brandeis International Business School. (2016, July 14). *The basics of global dexterity with Prof. Andy Molinsky* [Video]. YouTube. https://www.youtube.com/watch?v=d18nnbAajek&ab_channel=BrandeisInternationalBusinessSchool

d.school Public Library. (2021). *Tools for taking action.* Stanford d.School. https://dschool.stanford.edu/resources

Esterhuizen, P., & Kirkpatrick, M. K. (2015). Intercultural–Global competencies for the 21st century and beyond. *The Journal of Continuing Education in Nursing, 46*(5), 209–214. https://doi.org/10.3928/01484834-20150420-01

Gentry, W., Weber, T., & Sadri, G. (2011). *Empathy in the workplace: A tool for effective leadership.* [White paper]. Center for Creative Leadership. https://cclinnovation.org/wp-content/uploads/2020/03/empathyintheworkplace.pdf

Global Competence Associates. (2018). *Global Competence Model*™. https://globallycompetent.com/global-competence-model/

Livermore, D. (2011). CQ: The missing ingredient for global collaboration. *MWorld: American Management Association, 10*(3), 41–44.

Martin, J. N., & Nakayama, T. K. (2015). Reconsidering intercultural (communication) competence in the workplace: A dialectical approach. *Language and Intercultural Communication, 15*(1), 13–28. https://doi.org/10.1080/14708477.2014.985303

Molinsky, A. (2013). *Global dexterity: How to adapt your behavior across cultures without losing yourself in the process.* Harvard Business Review Press.

Skrbiš, Z. (2014). *Coming to terms with cosmopolitanism, global citizenship, & global competence* [White paper]. International Education Association of Australia. https://www.ieaa.org.au/documents/item/294

Taylor, S. (2013). Globally-minded students: defining, measuring and developing intercultural sensitivity. *International Schools Journal, 33*(1), 65-75.

This session has been formatted and revised for consistency and clarity. The original session in the Rockefeller Global Leadership Program was facilitated by Sophia Koustas, reached at s.koustas@snhu.edu.

Intercultural-Global Competencies

Dexterity Activity (Role-play)

Global dexterity | Being able to adapt one's behavior across cultures. Author Andy Molinsky (2013) describes *global dexterity* as a skill that reflects the ability to "adapt while feeling comfortable" in overcoming emotional and psychological challenges one may feel.

DIRECTIONS: Role-play a potential cultural challenge that would require you to exercise global dexterity, like introductions, dining etiquette, or wearing proper attire. Think about how the situation could go poorly and also how it could go well! Use the chart below to help you consider the dimensions of global dexterity and the zone of appropriateness for each situation.

Dimensions	Zone of Appropriateness						
	Low-level			Mid-level		High-level	
Directness	1	2	3	4	5	6	7
Enthusiasm	1	2	3	4	5	6	7
Formality	1	2	3	4	5	6	7
Assertiveness	1	2	3	4	5	6	7
Self-promotion	1	2	3	4	5	6	7
Personal disclosure	1	2	3	4	5	6	7

DIRECTIONS: After your role-play, place your performance on the adaptation matrix considering your level of success and authenticity (Molinsky, 2013).

Adaptation Matrix

Do I feel authentic performing this behavior?

Can I perform the behavior successfully?		Yes	No
	Yes	**Comfort Zone** Authentic + Competent +	**Authenticity Challenge** Authentic - Competent +
	No	**Ability Challenge** Authentic + Competent -	**Double Challenge** Authentic - Competent -

Reflection Questions: What do I need to work on? Where do I want to see myself performing authentically and successfully?

How do you train your mind to become more comfortable and able to navigate uncomfortable cultural situations?

Cultural Intelligence (CQ) Self-Evaluation and Action Plan

Cultural intelligence (CQ) | According to David Livermore (2011), *cultural intelligence* is "the capability to function effectively in a variety of cultural contexts." Livermore assesses CQ by measuring four capabilities: drive, knowledge, strategy, and action.

Step 1: Assess your CQ (Livermore, 2011)

Quick Self-Assessment—Cultural intelligence includes the following capabilities. Identify which ones you're good at and which ones need improvement.

For each area, circle the number that best describes how you function in your leadership role (**1** being "this statement does not describe me" and **5** meaning "this statement describes me perfectly").

CQ DRIVE	1	2	3	4	5

I am very interested in other cultures and I enjoy meeting people who have different cultural backgrounds. I am confident I can work in different cultures and that I can adapt to different parts of the world.

CQ KNOWLEDGE	1	2	3	4	5

I generally understand other cultures and cultural values. I know about the basic ways cultures are similar and different.

CQ STRATEGY	1	2	3	4	5

I plan carefully before I meet with someone who is from a different cultural background. After one of these experiences, I reflect carefully and try to make sense of the interaction.

CQ ACTION	1	2	3	4	5

I change my behavior to make others more comfortable when I interact with people who are from different cultural backgrounds. I modify the way I speak and act when I am in cross-cultural settings.

This is simply meant to get you started in thinking about the four capabilities of CQ. Access to the full CQ Self-Assessment comes with purchase of the physical book, *The Cultural Intelligence Difference* (AMACOM 2011). Or visit www.culturalQ.com to learn about all the assessments available.

Step 2: Create a personal development plan (for example: I will learn a new language, etc.)

I will _____.

Reflection Question: How does CQ apply when I need to collaborate with someone from a different cultural background?

Cosmopolitan Competencies Event Design

Cosmopolitan competencies/Cosmopolitanism ("citizen of the world") | refers to a "set of skills, outlooks, and practices that become necessary tools for individuals as they cross boundaries between the familiar and unfamiliar (Skrbiš, 2014). Competencies/themes include the following: global languages & digital literacy, cultural diversity, global mindset & diversity, aesthetic capital & arts, sustainability and global challenges, mobility & adaptability, innovation & entrepreneurship.

DIRECTIONS: Design an event that will build cosmopolitan competencies for its attendees.

Cosmopolitan theme: • Global languages & digital literacy • Cultural diversity • Global mindset & diversity • Aesthetic capital & arts • Sustainability & global challenges • Mobility & adaptability • Innovation & entrepreneurship	**Budget:**
Goal:	**Learning Objectives:** • • •
When:	**Where:**
Who:	**Why:**
What:	**How:**

Reflection Question: What does it mean to be a global worker and a true citizen of the world today?

Identify Intercultural-Global Competencies Using a Design Thinking Approach

Design thinking has a human-centered core. It encourages organizations to focus on the people they're creating for, which leads to better products, services, and internal processes. When you sit down to create a solution for a business need, the first question should always be, *What's the human need behind it?*

Exercise: **A DAY IN THE LIFE**

Imagine a person traveling abroad to a country they have never visited before. Your team will assume the role of that traveler and spend the next 20 minutes acting from their point of view and interacting with the contexts and people that they would encounter daily. Develop a list of common themes that arise throughout your "day in the life." Relate this list of actions, reactions, and experiences to the list of intercultural-global competencies below.

Intercultural-Global Competencies

Esterhuizen & Kirkpatrick, 2015

- self-awareness
- ability to communicate and behave appropriately in intercultural situations based on specific attitudes
- intercultural knowledge, skills, and reflection

Global Competence Model, 2014

- open-mindedness
- risk-taking
- attentiveness to diversity
- global awareness
- historical perspective
- collaboration across cultures, and intercultural capability

Reflection Questions:

What's challenging about walking in someone else's shoes? What ways might you practice empathy in your daily life?

What is your level of confidence and motivation in the intercultural-global competencies you currently possess?

What intercultural-global competencies do you need to include in your global toolkit and how do you plan to develop these?

Session 6.6 Refugees and Immigrants—Stories of Oppression, Resilience, and Hope

Session Description

In this session, the facilitator will help participants strengthen their intercultural mindset, reflect on their own assumptions about immigration to the U.S., and understand the differences between immigrants and refugees. Participants will hear the unique stories of three people who have resettled locally: two refugees who escaped dire life circumstances in their home countries and an immigrant who came for other reasons. Participants will learn not only about realities of displaced persons across the globe but also about the policies and programs for immigrant resettlement close to home. Participants will discuss the significance of international migration in the context of global leadership and the tools necessary to make positive and impactful change for displaced peoples.

Leadership Competencies Addressed

Self-Knowledge
- Continually explores and examines values and views
- Understands social identities of self and others

Intercultural Mindset
- Contextualizes social identities and experiences
- Understands, communicates with, and respectfully interacts with people across identities
- Actively engages in opportunities to expand worldview

Learning Objectives

Participants will do the following:
- Examine the cultural, ethnic, and religious diversity of New Hampshire and the unique and distinctive experiences of refugees and immigrants coming to the U.S.
- Reflect on their values, views, and beliefs following the panelists' discussion of their experiences
- Explain how diversity helps foster an intercultural mindset, why this is important in the context of leadership, and how it can facilitate positive change for immigrant and refugee populations in the United States and abroad

Key Concepts and Definitions

Reasons for emigrating	Uniting with family; work; fleeing war, genocide; education; climate destruction.

Refugee	A person fleeing persecution, threats, violence, or genocide. Generally, they come to the U.S. through the United Nations High Commissioner for Refugees after a rigorous vetting process that considers their contributions and benefits to the local community.
Immigrant	Any person relocating to a country where they do not have citizenship. These people are not necessarily facing the adversity that would qualify them as a refugee and so there is a wider range of reasons for having entered the country. All refugees are immigrants but not all immigrants are refugees.

Required Materials

- PowerPoint slides and appropriate technology (optional)
- Table(s) should be set up in a hollow square with a table at the front for a panel of three guest speakers.
- Name cards at seats

Pre-session Assignment:

- Bhagirath Khatiwada. 2018. Can a government define happiness? TEDx Talk. (https://www.youtube.com/watch?v=yOOZL8nZ-Vw)
- UNHCR-USA. 2020. 1 per cent of humanity displaced: UNHCR Global Trends report. (https://www.unhcr.org/en-us/news/press/2020/6/5ee9db2e4/1-cent-humanity-displaced-unhcr-global-trends-report.html)

Session Outline

Session duration: 1 hour and 50 minutes

Time Required		Description
20 minutes	Introduction	Introduce yourself and your panelists, preferably a mix of both immigrants and refugees from the local area. Define refugee and immigrant and note the similarities and differences. Talk about the reality of immigration in your region, state, or city. Provide statistics, outline the resettlement processes for both refugees and immigrants, and use photographs to appreciate the diversity of these populations and build empathy with participants.

Time Required		Description
70 minutes	Discussion	Turn to the panelists. Each will take 10–15 minutes to tell their story. They should discuss what life was like in their home countries and why they decided to leave, the immigration process, both the good and the bad experiences settling into a new life, and, ultimately, how they will or how they have found their place within their community. After each of them has shared their stories, ask them to speak about the importance of including cultural diversity in all levels of leadership. Invite participants to share their thoughts and engage with the panelists through questions or comments.
15 minutes	Reflection	Ask the participants for the common themes that they identified in the stories, what challenges the panelists faced, and what they learned from those challenges. Some themes may be language barriers, transportation (difficulties in getting driver's licenses, affording a vehicle), lack of support system, healthcare, prejudice, etc. Ask participants to think of what they can do in their own communities to welcome people from other countries. Encourage participants to think about and discuss the immigration system in the U.S. and their possible role in it as future leaders.
5 minutes	Conclusion	Ask participants to complete the session evaluation using your desired format. Close the session by thanking the panelists and participants.

Reflection Questions

- Why is it important for refugees and immigrants to tell their story?
- What do immigrants and refugees contribute to our communities?
- What challenges do immigrants and refugees face when coming to the US?
- Why is RGLP offering this session? What does it have to do with leadership?
- How did this session make you feel? Did anything you heard or learned today come as a surprise?
- Do you think the immigration system in the U.S. needs to be reformed? If yes, how so? If no, why not?
- We've talked a lot about the experience of immigrants and refugees in America. How do you think it is the same or different when talking about immigration and refugees in a global context?
- What can we learn about American attitudes toward immigrants from the experiences of immigrants themselves?

Participant Reflection

I think generally the narratives of immigrants and refugees that I am exposed to are spun by those that are neither of the two. Hearing their stories and learning about their challenges—before life in the States and after—drastically changed my perspective. Moving away from reading or studying something in the classroom to actively engaging with a policy reality through people taught me to appreciate the humanity that exists within different processes in our system. This session pushed me to pursue more human-facing work that had direct impacts.

RGLP Winter 2020

Supplemental Resources

Berti, B., & Borgman, E. (2016, June). *What does it mean to be a refugee?* [Video]. TED Conferences. https://www.ted.com/talks/benedetta_berti_and_evelien_borgman_what_does_it_mean_to_be_a_refugee_feb_2018

Gundling, E., Caldwell, C., & Cvitkovich, K. (2015). Global mindset: Beyond culture. In *Leading across new borders: How to succeed as the center shifts* (pp. 50–71). John Wiley & Sons, Incorporated. https://doi.org/10.1002/9781119176312.ch03

UNHCR, the UN Refugee Agency. (2019, February 21). *What is the difference between a migrant and a refugee?* [Video]. https://www.youtube.com/watch?v=3e08v5GN__s&ab_channel=UNHCR%2CtheUNRefugeeAgency

This session has been formatted and revised for consistency and clarity. The original session in the Rockefeller Global Leadership Program was facilitated by Becky Field, reached at Fieldworkphotos@gmail.com.

Session 6.7 Inconspicuous Culture— Understanding "Other" by Developing "Self"

Session Description

In this session, the facilitator will examine ethnocentrism and cultural relativism as it applies to concepts of race and ethnicity. Participants will look at the different lenses of privilege to see that there are differences within cultures, ethnicities, and people. Participants will confront stereotypes, address potential bias, and work as a class to develop a definition of culture. This session will engage participants through self-reflection in three steps as a method to learn the basics of "being comfortable being uncomfortable" and examine how this cultural competency applies to leadership.

Learning Objectives

Participants will do the following:
- Identify at least three elements that combine to define their personal culture
- Identify at least three values that inform the way they shape their attitudes and beliefs
- Collectively define privilege, culture, and ethnocentrism

Leadership Competencies Addressed

Collaboration
- Acknowledges and listens to different voices when making decisions and taking action

Principled Action
- Identifies and commits to appropriate ethical framework

Intercultural Mindset
- Contextualizes social identities and experiences
- Understands, communicates with, and respectfully interacts with people across identities
- Actively engages in opportunities to expand worldview

Key Concepts and Definitions

Worldview	Defined by Janet Helms (1990) as "cognitive templates that people use to organize information about themselves, other people and institutions." One's worldview influences their perspective and interpretations of other people. If one uses only one's own worldview, they can be missing out on an important part of being a leader.
Legacies	Historical events so powerful their ripple effects continue to have an impact today.

Layers	All the obvious and not so obvious individual characteristics that make you distinctively who you are.
The Johari Window	A 2x2 grid delineating parts of ourselves (see Handout 6.7.1). It is important to acknowledge each of these spots. For example, acknowledging blind spots requires taking feedback from others. The unknown spot is something that is not known to anyone, but just because it is not known doesn't mean it has no effect on behavior.

Required Materials

- PowerPoint slides and appropriate technology (optional)
- TedTalk by Zachary Wood, "Why it's worth listening to people you disagree with." This video is available on the TED website (www.ted.com).

Pre-session Assignment:

- http://www.whiteprivilegeconference.com/resources/05-The-Complexity-of-Identity-Beverly-Tatum.pdf

Session Outline

Session duration: 1 hour and 45 minutes

Time Required		Description
5 minutes	Introduction	Introduce yourself and your background. Outline the session and its objectives.
25 minutes	Discussion	Ask participants how leaders can make sure multiple perspectives are presented "at the table." Discuss how being aware of one's own values and identity is important for leadership. In pairs, ask participants to answer these questions: *Who am I? What are my values? What is my life's purpose?* Ask participants to share in the large group what it was like to answer these questions. Encourage participants to think about how they can develop skills and use their learning to be in service of their personal mission and to help create the type of world they want to live in.

Time Required		Description
20 minutes	Framing	Introduce the key terms. Use imaginative and thought-provoking visuals and analogies to initiate discussion. For example, use the commonly seen visual of three individuals standing by a fence, watching baseball to depict the differences between equality and equity. This creative imagery simplifies the concepts of equity and equality and evokes other insights of these concepts. Give examples of events that have had very different impacts for different groups of people, depending on their worldview and lens. Encourage participants to share current examples. Use these examples as the basis for a collective conversation to define privilege, culture, and ethnocentrism with the cohort.
20 minutes	Discussion	With new partners, participants will discuss their worldview and lens. Ask: *How can you be aware of your worldview and make sure it does not keep you from understanding multiple perspectives? How can you develop an understanding of the multiple perspectives of the people you are leading? How might this impact your leadership behavior?* In the large group, discuss whether there are perspectives that "should" be excluded and who gets to decide them and how.
20 minutes	Activity	Play the TedTalk "Why it is worth listening to people we disagree with," by Zachary Williams. As participants watch, they will be asked to think about what they agree and disagree with and think about how his worldview led to this perspective. After the video, ask participants to share their thoughts.
15 minutes	Conclusion	Share closing thoughts for participants to consider as they grow as leaders, specifically having interculturalism as a goal. Ask participants to complete the session evaluation using your desired format. Close the session by thanking the participants.

Reflection Questions

- What can I do in my day-to-day life to be more comfortable being uncomfortable?
- What scares me most about _____?
- How committed am I to changing my thinking and ultimately my behavior when talking about people I don't like with friends?
- How does this apply to leadership in an organization?

Supplemental Resources

Astobiza, A. M. (2017). ¿Qué es cultura en la «economía de la cultura»? Definiendo la cultura para crear modelos mensurables en economía cultural [What is culture in «cultural economy»? Defining culture to create measurable models in cultural economy]. *Arbor: Ciencia, Pensamiento y Cultura, 193*(783), 1–10. https://doi.org/10.3989/arbor.2017.783n1007

Darnell, R. (2009). Part 4: The human in culture: Anthropological approaches to human nature, cultural relativism and ethnocentrism. *Anthropologica, 51*(1), 187–194.

Participant Reflection

Dottie taught us that being a good leader requires self-awareness, and that self-awareness requires awareness of culture—both my own and others. Identifying my privileges is the best place to start in leading others. People can only work toward a unified goal once they have recognized where differences and inequalities lie.

RGLP Winter 2019

TEDx Talks. (2017, June 2). *Your culture is not better than mine | Angela Zhou | TEDxUSC* [Video]. YouTube. https://www.youtube.com/watch?v=qnNpFYVaXIc&ab_channel=TEDxTalks

This session has been formatted and revised for consistency and clarity. The original session in the Rockefeller Global Leadership Program was facilitated by Dottie Morris, reached at dmorris@keene.edu.

The Johari Window Model

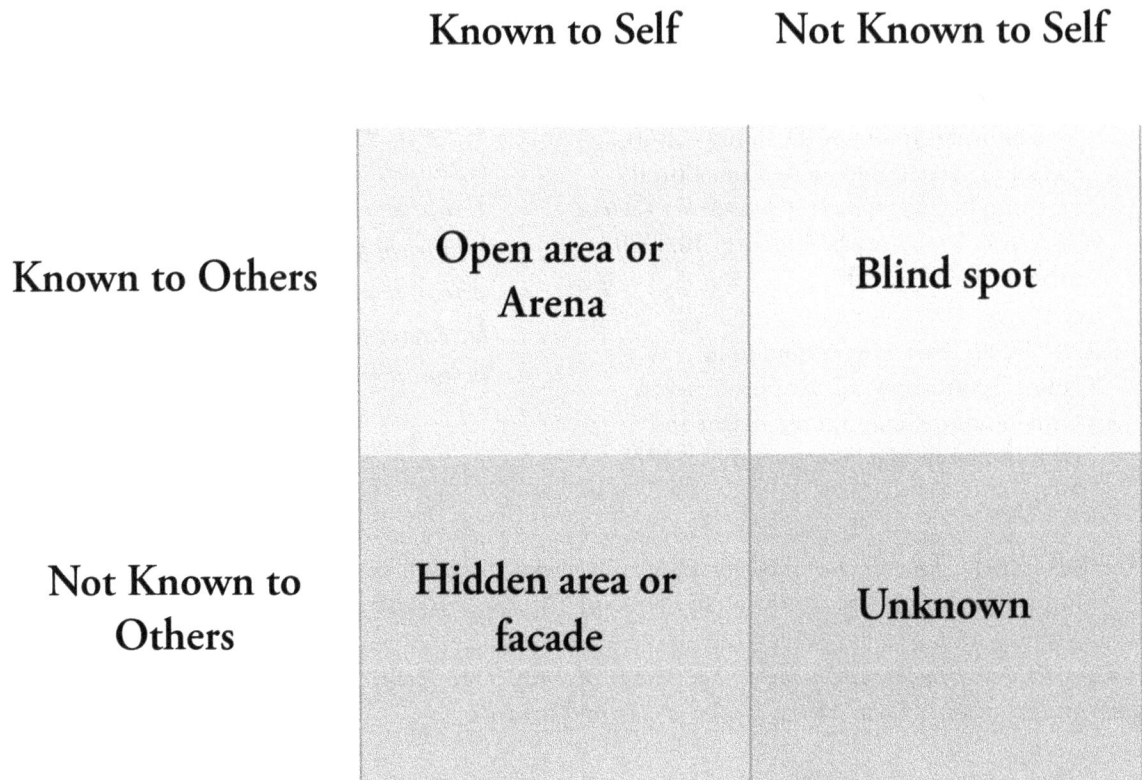

	Known to Self	Not Known to Self
Known to Others	Open area or Arena	Blind spot
Not Known to Others	Hidden area or facade	Unknown

Note: Adapted from *The Johari Window Model* by CommunicationTheory.Org, 2019, https://www. communicationtheory.org/the-johari-window-model/

Session 6.8 Conclusion—What Next?

Session Description

During this final session, participants will reflect on their experiences in RGLP through participant presentations, personal reflection, and group discussion.

Learning Objectives

Participants will do the following:
- Deliver a reflective presentation on lessons learned and key takeaways from the program
- Identify at least two markers of their personal intercultural development over the course of the program
- Determine and identify three ways the global leadership views, values, and skills developed in RGLP can be applied in their future

Leadership Competencies Addressed

Effective Reasoning
- Develops personal reflective practice

Intercultural Mindset
- Contextualizes social identities and experiences
- Actively engages in opportunities to expand worldview
- Applies intercultural knowledge and skills in local, national, and/or global contexts

Self-Knowledge
- Understands social identities of self and others

Key Concepts and Definitions

Ensure that previous key concepts and definitions are reviewed in this overall program reflection.

Required Materials

- PowerPoint slides and appropriate technology (optional)

Session Outline

Session duration: 2 hours

Time Required	Description	
60 minutes	Presentations	Give participants time to work in their groups to finish preparing and practicing for their final presentations about an issue at the local, national, or international level, and their recommendations for addressing it. Each group gives their final 5–8-minute presentation and answers questions from the audience afterward. Be prepared to highlight key learnings from the presentations and tie them to key concepts and definitions from previous sessions.

Time Required		Description
20 minutes	Reflection	Ask participants to turn to their accountability groups to discuss the following reflection questions about their experiential trip: *Did any of these experiences make you uncomfortable? Why? What did you do to deal with it? What was your favorite activity? Did you learn anything that challenged a conception you had? How will you use what you learned from this weekend experience in the future?* After small group discussion, come back to the large group to share observations.
25 minutes	Activity	Review Milton Bennett's Developmental Model of Intercultural Sensitivity discussed in the program orientation session. In their accountability groups, participants will answer these questions: *Which stage were you in at the beginning of the term? Do you think you are still in the same stage? Why or why not? How have your intercultural mindset, skillset, and sensitivity developed since the beginning of the term? How can you apply lessons learned in this program in your future?* Ask participants to share their significant reflections with the cohort.
15 minutes	Conclusion	Wrap up the session and program with closing remarks about what you hope participants will take away from their participation in the program. Ask participants to complete the program evaluation using your desired format. Close the program by thanking the participants.

Reflection Questions

- How can I apply lessons I learned in RGLP in the future?
- How can I continue to develop my intercultural mindset, skillset, and sensitivity?

Participant Reflection

Looking back at the DMIS model at the end of the program was so enlightening. Not only did I see how I progressed into another stage through what I learned, but I also realized how much more I understood about intercultural experience and what it means to me. I realized my own shortcomings and my own preconceived notions of identity and culture that I would not have seen outside of a theoretical framework. RGLP challenged me to push myself and grow in areas we don't often think of—empathy, cultural understanding, and sensitivity. It has reframed the way in which I approach and interact with others, respecting people and their individualities for who they are and the setting they are in.

RGLP Winter 2019

Supplemental Resources

Mertler, D. C. (2018, October). *Personal empowerment through reflection and learning* [Video]. TEDxLakelandUniversity. https://www.ted.com/talks/dr_craig_mertler_personal_empowerment_through_reflection_and_learning

Talks at Google. (2017, August 28). *Inclusion: Diversity, the new workplace & the will to change | Jennifer Brown | Talks at Google*. YouTube. https://www.youtube.com/watch?v=06-Js35QwPY&feature=youtu.be&ab_channel=TalksatGoogle

TrainingMag.Com. (2014). Striving for global leadership. *Training Magazine, 41*(3), 30–31. https://trainingmag.com/sites/default/files/trg0511-AMA-Leadership-Surv.pdf

This session has been formatted and revised for consistency and clarity. The original session in the Rockefeller Global Leadership Program was facilitated by Leslie Wagner, reached at Leslie.R.Wagner-Ould.Ismail@dartmouth.edu,.

RGLP Program Officer Reflection

by Leslie Wagner-Ould Ismail

As someone whose love for other cultures and languages led to years of teaching English to people from all over the world and helping them adapt to life in the United States, I have so much passion for the Rockefeller Global Leadership Program (RGLP). This program gives me the opportunity to lead college students, many of them from diverse backgrounds themselves, through a series of sessions that open their minds to the effects of culture on everything we think, say, and do and encourages them to think about how they will handle future interactions with diverse individuals.

One of the main objectives I want participants to take away from their participation in RGLP is the ability to face differences with curiosity and an open mind, rather than jumping to judgment and negative conclusions. I'll be the first to admit that this takes continuous effort and commitment, but once it becomes part of your thought process, it can truly make a difference in the way you view, interact, and communicate with others.

It's so rewarding to see the transformation that takes place in RGLP participants in just nine short weeks! It took me years to develop this mindset and the vocabulary to talk about it. Through deep reflection and activities, participants begin to identify elements of their own culture that they had not previously thought about while simultaneously becoming aware of the vast array of cultural differences that can easily lead to miscommunications in personal, academic, and professional settings. They go from seeing their way of thinking and doing as the "right way" to thinking of their way as only one option among a variety of ways.

I saw this mindset in action during an experiential weekend trip to Boston at the end of the Winter 2020 term. This trip serves as a culminating experience for RGLP participants and allows them to apply the things they have learned and discussed over the course of the term. One of the objectives of the program, particularly the trip, is the development of ambiguity tolerance. Participants have no prior knowledge of the activities and events planned. In fact, they aren't even given an itinerary until they are on the bus en route to their destination, and the itinerary is purposely as vague as possible! Furthermore, the activities and events are chosen with the objective of taking participants out of their comfort zone and provoking thoughtful discussion. During this particular trip, we toured a mosque and witnessed a Friday prayer, sampled new cuisine at an African restaurant, and attended a comedy show with Arab-American comedians. The entire trip was wonderful and memorable, but one event in particular stands out.

On our first night in Boston, we saw the film *We Are Little Zombies* as part of the Museum of Modern Art's Japanese film festival. I knew very little about the film beforehand and had no idea what to expect. It was like nothing I had ever seen before. If I remember correctly, when asked what I thought of the movie after it ended, I described it as "wild." I was nervous throughout the film because I couldn't read the participants' reactions and was afraid they were not enjoying it, but I was so wrong! That film sparked more discussion than I ever could have imagined. Some loved it and others hated it, but everyone talked about it nonstop the entire way back to the hotel. The discussion continued sporadically throughout the rest of the trip and even at our session later that week. The participants were eager to talk about how different cultures view themes in the movie such as death and parenting and also what they observed about the Japanese culture in the film. The absolute best part was how careful they were not to stereotype an entire country and culture by what they had seen in one film or to describe the things they saw as good or bad just because they were different. It was this experience that showed me how much growth had occurred over the course of the term.

The conversations and topics covered in RGLP are not always easy and require introspection and vulnerability. It is truly moving to see how quickly participants from all different backgrounds get out of their comfort zone and open up to people they've just met. They learn to listen to each other's perspectives and engage in dialogue instead of debating whether something is right or wrong. The best part is they are having fun while doing it! When the COVID-19 pandemic forced us to offer the program remotely, I was worried that this sense of cohort connection and willingness to demonstrate vulnerability would suffer, but to my surprise, it was even stronger. RGLP brings together a group of people who are willing to have difficult conversations and engage with diverse perspectives.

If you want to adopt a program such as RGLP, this sense of community is vital. Participants must be given ample opportunities to engage with each other and interact in small groups. When we are offering the program in person, this is accomplished through accountability groups and dinner discussions. Participants are assigned to small groups at the beginning of the term, and they eat dinner and have reflective discussions together during the first half hour of each session. After the dinner portion has ended, participants often move around and are assigned other partners or small groups for the remainder of the session. This ensures that they get to know everyone in the cohort, while also having an assigned group that they can contact if they miss a session. Although the setup of a remote session is somewhat different, the opportunities to engage with each other are very similar. Zoom breakout rooms are used liberally to allow students ample opportunities to get to know all members of a cohort. Accountability groups can still be used for activities at the beginning of the session and final projects. Whole group sharing activities are also particularly useful in a remote session. For example, during the most recent RGLP term, I asked students to choose a virtual background of a place they have been to or want to go to, and we all took turns explaining why we chose our picture.

Another tip for facilitating a program like RGLP is to model the transparency and openness that you want to see in participants. It is unfair to ask program participants to do things that the program leader is unwilling to do! I always try to share stories and examples from my experiences and be open about my mistakes and weaknesses. By doing this, we are communicating with participants that it is okay for them to talk about their own weaknesses.

My final words of advice for developing such a program are to utilize and take advantage of the diversity and resources available to you to enrich students' experience. Despite being in a somewhat rural and homogenous area of the country, we bring in diverse guest speakers from only an hour or two away, which minimizes the cost of speaker travel. Offering sessions remotely is also a great way to bring in guest speakers from all over the country without a huge expense. In addition to diversity of guest speakers, diversity within the cohort should be utilized to its full advantage. Differences such as race, ethnicity, religion, gender, political beliefs, and socioeconomic status can all be discussed and used to advance program goals. Students learn that differences exist even between people who look alike. Finally, I have found that some of the most meaningful conversations come from tying current events into the program objectives. This allows participants to apply the things they are learning and discussing and makes learning more meaningful.

7 | Rockefeller Leadership Fellows Program (RLF)

Watch your thoughts, they become your words; watch your words, they become your actions; watch your actions, they become your habits; watch your habits, they become your character; watch your character, it becomes your destiny.

—Lao Tzu

The Rockefeller Leadership Fellows Program (RLF) is a standalone program that spans a full academic year. Designed for students in their final year of undergraduate experience, RLF provides participants with a space for reflection, resources to develop personal leadership philosophies, and practical leadership skills. The program also addresses the needs of participants who are preparing to enter the workforce. While they may have had work experience in the past, these participants are beginning to establish their position in their work and in society. The program is also suitable for those who are new, existing, or emerging leaders. It could easily be adapted for mid-level managers and senior leaders in all fields of endeavor. As with other programs described in this book, use your creative energy to offer the program in its entirety or select those sessions that are relevant to your needs.

Program Goal

To provide participants a space to reflect on their leadership skills and experiences, as well as those of their peers and mentors, in preparation for leadership challenges after graduation and to articulate a leadership philosophy.

Program Prerequisites

None

Program Participation

RLF is intentional in its selection of participants. A unique feature of the program is that the current participants select their successors. In so doing, they learn about the importance of incorporating diversity within the cohort as well as the inclusion of underrepresented groups. For example, since the 2014–2015 academic year, RLF has served participants representing 42 different fields of study, ranging from the humanities to STEM and the arts. The five most popular majors for RLF participants are, in descending order: government, economics, history, geography, and anthropology. Table 7.1 presents the top 10 majors among RLF participants since 2014.

Table 7.1

Ten Most Popular Majors for RLF Participants 2014–2020

Major	Number of Participants
Government	47
Economics	30
History	11
Geography	6
Anthropology	6
Engineering	6
Biology	5
Computer Science	5
Psychology	5
Environmental Studies	5

This program attracts more female than male participants; 57% of the students who completed RLF since 2014 identified as female. In addition, RLF attracts a high percentage of international students. Historically, 14.4% of RLF participants have been international students who collectively represent 40 different countries. In this way, RLF leverages the advantages of diverse majors and perspectives that can be drawn upon from all parts of campus and different parts of the world.

The enrollment and participation in this year-long program need to be viewed differently from other programs that are one term long. Very few students drop out of the program because of the prestige it has on campus and because students feel that their time is well spent in RLF. This being said, there are a few who do choose to leave the program. These students were unable to commit to the year-long requirements of the program; or the program content did not resonate with them; or their interests aligned with other opportunities on campus.

It is not an option for participants in this program to miss a session. Program completion is defined as completing all assignments and completing makeup assignments for sessions missed. At the application stage, learners are informed that they can "miss" a session physically if they have scheduled exams conflicting with the program meeting time, job interviews, illness, or extenuating circumstances. These requirements are emphasized during the program's orientation. They are also discussed with the individual and the cohort when participants use a reason for missing a session other than the ones listed here. This sense of discipline develops a culture within the program cohort. In part due to the ability to make up missed sessions, there has been very little attrition in RLF as can be seen in Figure 7.1.

Figure 7.1 shows that the number of students who completed RLF has remained largely consistent from the 2014-2015 cohort to the 2019-2020 cohort. The number of students who completed the program each year varied from 18 in the 2019-2020 cohort to 26 in the 2016-2017 cohort.

Figure 7.1

RLF Participant and Completion Data Since 2014

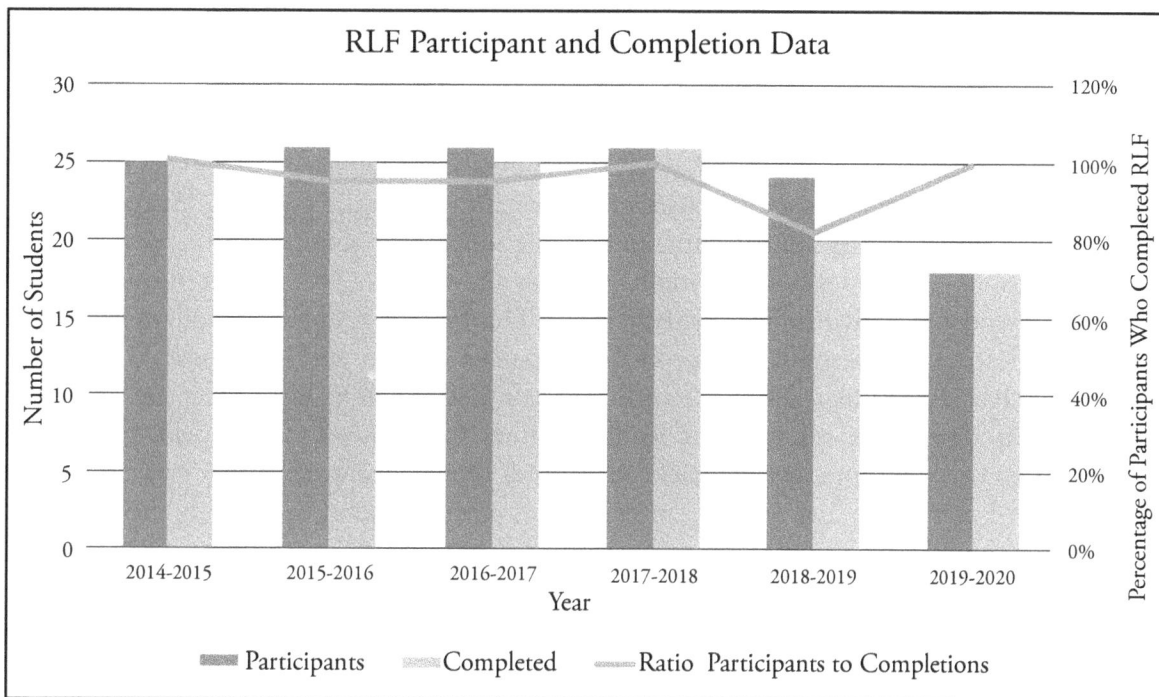

Key Program Elements

> Establishing accountability partners or groups
> Developing an understanding of management and leadership theories and principles, with the aim of creating self-awareness, becoming effective team members, and understanding organizational theories and behaviors
> Retreats designed to enable participants to build relationships and discover together their own views related to management and leadership
> Emerging from the program with a concrete leadership philosophy and a leadership presence, as well as the advanced public speaking skills to present them
> Current program participants select their successors

Program Description

In this program, participants reflect on their own leadership journeys as well as the leadership experiences of their peers and speakers. Some key themes emphasized in the program are reflective practices; awareness of one's strengths and weaknesses; enhanced communication skills, including framing difficult conversations; team dynamics and teamwork; organizational behavior, development, and growth; change management; and developing and articulating a leadership philosophy. These themes are explored through workshops, team-building exercises, dinner discussions, and speaker lectures. Each activity challenges participants to view leadership at a personal, organizational, and societal level, and to reflect on how they can improve their effectiveness as leaders in each setting.

The program consists of 25 or fewer participants in order to facilitate a close-knit cohort. At the beginning of the program, participants are paired with one to three other participants as accountability partners or groups who hold each other accountable for personal and professional goals. Accountability partners or pairs can be formed randomly or based on interest in learning more about some aspect of leadership. Each participant is also provided with a journal to develop their own leadership philosophy and record reflections throughout the program. At the beginning of the first and second terms, participants participate in full-day retreats. In the first retreat, in addition to various speaker sessions, the main goal is to allow the cohort to bond through informal conversations and fun activities like a talent show. The second retreat has additional bonding activities, a guest speaker session, and a panel or program alumni who speak with the cohort in small groups. Participants sign up to give a presentation on a leadership concept at one session during the year. They receive immediate feedback from their peers and meet with the program facilitator to go over presentation feedback. As a result of this exercise, the program touches on many aspects of leadership and, in one sense, engages participants in co-creating the curriculum by complementing topics covered by guest speakers, described below.

Throughout each term, the cohort meets weekly for a dinner discussion, a participant presentation, and speaker event. At the end of each weekly meeting, the cohort provides feedback for the guest speaker and has 30 minutes of "free" time. In the past, cohorts have used their time to plan organization-wide initiatives, discuss personal leadership challenges and philosophies, and bond as a group.

In the final term of the program, participants focus on recruiting the following year's cohort and plan the marketing, interviews, and selection from start to finish. This is considered by program alumni to be the strongest feature of this program because they have knowledge about the applicants; they ensure diverse representation; and they leave the program stronger with each passing year. Last but not the least, they practice concepts and skills learned in the program.

Key Leadership Competencies

The key competencies the program focuses on are self-awareness, collaboration, management, and self-knowledge. The program encourages participants to listen to different voices when making decisions and capitalize on these differences when working in a team. The program also emphasizes personal realization and moving beyond self-imposed limitations. Self-awareness, ability to work in teams, and working within organizations to achieve societal good are the aims of the program.

Possible Adaptations

In addition to higher education, the content is also applicable to nonprofit organizations, for-profit organizations, and government institutions. The program is suitable for those who are in management and leadership positions or aspire to be a manager and a leader.

➢ Many of the discussions related to the content in the program can be offered through a "lunch and learn" in which attendees select materials and discuss applicability to their work environment. It is important to end such discussions with concrete action steps.

➢ Identify your audience and their needs. Research what is known or not known about these needs.

➢ Use the Eight Pillars of Program Design to develop your concept.

➢ Make sure the content you cover matches the experience and maturity level of your audience. Create a structure within which you will sequence the content.

➢ Think about an "accountability partner" system and how it might work.

➢ If resources permit, consider surveys about knowledge, attitudes, and practice. Have a group discussion about the results.

➢ Set up a public presentation program to help colleagues build presentation skills and help participants build their leadership presence.

➢ Help your team to develop a personal development plan based on the content covered.

Session 7.1 Introduction—Perspectives on Leadership

Session Description

In this session, the facilitator will discuss perspectives on leadership. Specifically, the facilitator will cover the Learning Zone Model, the difference between dialogue and debate, practical listening skills, and the skills necessary to create a leadership presence. Participants will discuss their cohort culture and establish group norms and etiquette for the program.

Learning Objectives

Participants will do the following:
- Describe the Learning Zone Model
- Identify at least two differences between debate and dialogue and the implication of the differences in leadership
- Develop group norms
- Practice listening skills and identify at least three characteristics that create a leadership presence

Leadership Competencies Addressed
Collaboration • Builds and maintains partnerships based on shared purpose • Acknowledges and listens to different voices when making decisions and taking action **_Effective Communication_** • Exhibits effective listening skills

Key Concepts and Definitions

Learning Zone Model	This model helps demonstrate how to create learning situations. Each person has a Comfort Zone, Learning Zone, and a Panic Zone. The Comfort Zone contains things that are familiar; in the comfort zone, one does not take any risks. The Learning Zone is just outside the Comfort Zone and is where we can explore and grow. The Panic Zone lies beyond the Learning Zone where learning is inhibited by fear. We should aim to be in our Learning Zone.
Dialogue vs. debate	Dialogue is a collaborative process where knowledge is shared in order for participants to reach a common understanding together. Debate is an oppositional process where participants try to win and protect their own thoughts and knowledge. Each one has a place and it is important to understand when and how to use it.

| *Creating a leadership presence* | Creating a leadership presence includes the abilities to lead a room and be present, to assume a leadership role, to connect with others, to express your own thoughts, to listen to others, and to reflect on yourself. |

Required Materials

- PowerPoint slides and appropriate technology (optional)
- Journals for each participant

Session Outline

Session duration: 1 hour and 40 minutes

Time Required		Description
30 minutes	Introduction	Discuss the focus of the RLF program (examining self, team, and oneself in the context of an organization for societal good). Briefly review the structure of the RLF program and sessions. Discuss how this will require participants to always be in their learning zone by describing the Learning Zone Model. Discuss expectations of the program and these concepts: an intellectually supportive environment; a leadership presence; and the difference between dialogue and debate.
10 minutes	Activity 1	Hand out journals to participants. Invite participants to "create" a book cover for their journals that depicts their leadership philosophy. Ask participants to include a title and list themselves as the author on their journal cover. The back cover of each journal should include a picture and a bio of the journal owner. Throughout the term, participants will enter their reflections from each session. At the end of the term, each participant will select two others to write observations about them in their journal. At some point in the program, for example during the winter retreat, participants will select some of their reflections to exhibit to each other.
30 minutes	Activity 2	Explain the importance of listening as a leader, whether it is during a debate or while engaging in dialogue. Introduce the exercise, which is designed to make participants aware of their listening skills. Divide the participants into groups of three. Ask each participant to discuss an issue they care about and explain why it matters to the other two in the group.

Time Required		Description
		While one participant presents information for two minutes, the other two listen to the information and also observe the participant's "leadership presence." The others take turns presenting their information in a similar way. After each person completes individual presentations, end this segment by requesting each group to discuss how to develop a leadership presence and what people need to do to listen authentically. At the end of the discussion, ask participants to individually write down two or three things they can do to improve their leadership presence and their listening skills.
15 minutes	Discussion	Discuss the differences between dialogue and debate and how these communication approaches impact learning. Ask participants to select the one they identify most with and why. Ask participants to connect the discussion to leadership. If the participants identify with debate, ask them how this affects people's perceptions of them as leaders. If the participants identify with dialogue, ask them what motivates them to pursue dialogue. Discuss with participants when they think dialogue or debate should or should not be used and the impact of using dialogue or debate on the learning environment in the program. Develop group norms for the program.
15 minutes	Conclusion	Summarize key discussion points during the session and invite participants to complete their first journal entry. Ask participants if they have any further questions. Ask participants to complete the session evaluation using your desired format. Close the session by thanking the participants.

Reflection Questions

- To what extent am I in the Learning Zone?
- To what extent do I practice effective listening?
- Is my style typically to debate issues with someone or have a dialog with someone about an issue being discussed? How might I incorporate inclusivity regardless of my style?

Participant Reflection

When times get tough, I find myself wanting to fix it all. Often, this is not feasible and I create an unnecessary amount of heartache for myself. In this session, Sadhana recommended we focus on our circles of influence and control. Everything outside of these circles is "gravity." We cannot change it, so it is not worth worrying about. This lesson has been integral to my work as a consultant where I must work within many constraints and in ambiguous situations. I have excelled by concentrating my efforts on my circles of influence and control.

RLF 2019-20

Supplemental Resources

Cremin, H., Thomas, G., & Vincett, K. (2003). Learning zones: An evaluation of three models for improving learning through teacher/teaching assistant teamwork. *Support for Learning, 18*(4), 154–161. https://doi.org/10.1046/j.0268-2141.2003.00301.x

Støre, J. G. (2011, November). *In defense of dialogue* [Video]. TEDxRC2. https://www.ted.com/talks/jonas_gahr_store_in_defense_of_dialogue

Tkalcevich, S. (2015). *The self-made program leader: Taking charge in matrix organizations.* Auerbach Publications. https://doi.org/10.1201/b18804

This session has been formatted and revised for consistency and clarity. The original session in the Rockefeller Leadership Fellows Program was facilitated by Sadhana Hall, reached at Sadhana.W.Hall@dartmouth.edu.

Session 7.2 From Theory to Action— Leadership Theories From 19th Century to Contemporary Times

Session Description

In this session, the facilitator will present a range of leadership theories from a variety of contexts throughout history. Participants will explore these theories together to answer this question: How can we optimize leadership behaviors and actions? In the early 19th century, leadership was thought to be more trait- and personality-based, suggesting that leadership was not something learned but innate. Today, leadership theory is not based on the leader as a person but on what the leader does. By exploring the evolution of leadership theories, participants can shape their own leadership philosophies based upon situations and needs.

Leadership Competencies Addressed
Self-Knowledge   • Continually explores and examines values and views   **Effective Reasoning**   • Develops personal reflective practice   **Principled Action**   • Identifies and commits to appropriate ethical framework

Learning Objectives

Participants will do the following:
- Define what a theory is and identify three key components that make a theory credible
- Compare and contrast early theories of leadership to contemporary theories of leadership and identify the strengths and weaknesses of those theories
- Apply principles of leadership theories to their own leadership philosophy to bring an evidence-based approach to their leadership

Key Concepts and Definitions

Antecedents	Precursors to what someone does or how someone acts, the circumstances and factors that influence behavior.
Behaviors	How one acts or conducts themselves, sometimes due to stimuli or circumstance.
Consequences	The outcomes of one's behaviors, result of action or conditions.

Great Man Theory	The belief that leaders are born, not made. Fate or providence determines who becomes a leader.
Trait Theory of Leadership	The belief that personality traits influence who emerges as a leader and how effective that leader is.
Authentic Leadership	A leadership style that emphasizes building the leader's legitimacy through honest relationships with followers, that values their input, and is built on an ethical foundation.
Transformational Leadership	A way of leadership in which the leader works with teams to identify needed change, creating a vision to guide the change through inspiration and executing the change in tandem with committed members of a group.
Servant Leadership	A leadership style in which the goal of the leader is to serve others and share power.

Required Materials

- PowerPoint slides and appropriate technology (optional)
- Whiteboard or flipchart and markers
- Paper and writing utensils for participants

Pre-session Assignment:

- Mango, E. (2018). Rethinking leadership theories. *Open Journal of Leadership, 7,* 57–88.

Session Outline

Session duration: 1 hour and 10 minutes

Time Required		Description
5 minutes	Introduction	Introduce yourself and share the learning objectives and outcomes for the session.
10 minutes	Activity	Divide participants into small groups of three or four. In their small groups, ask participants to draw a picture of what their leadership style or philosophy looks like in action and explain the picture they drew. In a larger group discussion, each group member should be prepared to talk about the personal behaviors or characteristics depicted in their pictures.

Time Required		Description
10 minutes	Discussion	In the large group, ask participants to share common themes from their pictures. Ask participants: *What makes leaders great? What is it about these individuals? Who are they or what do they do?* Create a list of the responses as participants share. When enough ideas have been generated, ask participants to categorize the answers as actions or as personal traits. The group may conclude that both actions and personal traits define leaders, and neither one nor the other is the defining feature.
25 minutes	Framing	Divide participants into small groups of three or four. In their small groups, give participants three minutes to define what a theory is, how theories are used, and/or what theories do. In the large group, ask participants to share their discussions. Explain the "ABCs": antecedents, behaviors, and consequences. Give examples that illustrate how a good theory provides a behavioral framework that predicts ABCs. Discuss why and how theories lose their credibility or become outdated. Ask participants to think of examples of theories that were widely accepted but would be refuted today.
		Transition to a slideshow providing an overview of leadership theories from the 19th century to contemporary times. Some theories you may wish to discuss are Great Man Theory, Trait Theory, Leader Member Exchange Theory, Servant Leadership Theory, Transformational Leadership Theory, and Authentic Leadership Theory. There are many others that may resonate with you that you would like to discuss with participants. For each theory outlined, ask participants to discuss the ABCs associated with that leadership approach. Explain how this analysis can provide an evidence-based approach to shaping leadership behaviors intentionally.
10 minutes	Discussion	Divide participants into small groups of three or four. Ask the small groups to discuss which leadership theory or style best fits their goals as a leader. Then ask participants to answer these questions: *How does that theory integrate with their philosophy? What leaders do they know that best exemplify that style of leadership? Can you think of leaders that exemplify each theory of leadership? What are the pros and cons of each style of leadership?*

Time Required		Description
10 minutes	Conclusion	In the large group, invite participants to share any final thoughts from their small group discussions. Share an example, with either a video interview or article, that demonstrates what aligning actions with values looks like in real life. Ask participants to complete the session evaluation using your desired format. Close the session by thanking participants.

Reflection Questions

- What theories of leadership do I find to be ineffective for my needs and why?
- What theory of leadership is most attractive to me and why?
- According to my theory of choice, what purposeful behavioral changes do I need to make in my leadership to get the subordinate outcomes that I need for successful task accomplishment?

Supplemental Resources

Rüzgar, N. (2019). Leadership traits of Suleiman the Magnificent, in terms of "Great Man" theory. *Journal of Ottoman Legacy Studies*, 6(15). https://doi.org/10.17822/omad.2019.128

Wyatt, M., & Silvester, J. (2018). Do voters get it right? A test of the ascription-actuality trait theory of leadership with political elites. *The Leadership Quarterly*, 29(5), 609–621. https://doi.org/10.1016/j.leaqua.2018.02.001

Yasir, M., & Mohamad, N. A. (2016). Ethics and morality: Comparing ethical leadership with servant, authentic and transformational leadership Styles. *International Review of Management and Marketing*, 6(4S), 310–316.

Participant Reflection

We explored the origins of various leadership philosophies and their evolution. By being exposed to various theories and understanding their strengths and weaknesses, we can cherry-pick the facets that best align with our personalities and weave together a multitude of philosophies. In addition, we can better understand how our peers and superiors define leadership and adapt to their styles. This has been particularly important when working on intergenerational teams. I am able to tailor my approach to meet the leadership styles of my superiors and peers.

RLF 2019-20

This session has been formatted and revised for consistency. The original session in the Rockefeller Leadership Fellows Program was facilitated by Stephen Gonzalez, reached at Stephen.P.Gonzalez@dartmouth.edu.

Session 7.3. Facilitative Leadership— Blending Individual Styles to Achieve Common Goals

Session Description

In this session, the facilitator will explore various strategies for becoming successful facilitative leaders. Effective leadership of teams must honor individual styles and voices while simultaneously moving the group toward its collective goals and products.

Learning Objectives

Participants will do the following:
- Examine various leadership styles and learn to identify their characteristics
- Identify their personal leadership style and explore how their leadership style plays into team dynamics
- Apply new knowledge on leadership styles and team dynamics to the Rockefeller Leadership Fellows recruitment process

Leadership Competencies Addressed

Collaboration
- Fosters a welcoming and inclusive environment

Self-Knowledge
- Understands social identities of self and others
- Shows self-respect and respect for others

Effective Reasoning
- Develops personal reflective practice

Key Concepts and Definitions

Self-awareness	Having a deep understanding of your leadership style in relation to others will help you to collaborate effectively and lead diverse teams.
Communication	Self-awareness of your leadership style will give you the ability to communicate effectively with people who have very different styles from yours.
Conflict management	Many conflicts emerge when there is a clash of leadership styles. It is important to identify conflicts before they happen.
The Leadership Compass	The Leadership Compass has four directions, which represents the unique ways in which leaders approach work (see Handout 7.3.1).

Required Materials

- PowerPoint slides and appropriate technology (optional)
- Poster-size paper
- Markers
- Handout 7.3.1 Leadership Compass Styles

Session Outline

Session duration: 1 hour and 15 minutes

Time Required		Description
10 minutes	Introduction	Introduce the importance of facilitative leadership and identifying leadership styles. Ask participants for anecdotes on personal leadership styles and conflicts in management.
20 minutes	Framing	Explain the Leadership Compass and how it applies to leadership styles. Pass out Handout 7.3.1 to participants. Ask participants to review the Leadership Compass handouts for more specific information on the four types of leadership styles. Provide anecdotes on each leadership style and guide participants in identifying their personal leadership style. Ask participants to identify their most preferred leadership style.
25 minutes	Activity	Divide participants into four groups based on their preferred leadership style. Provide each group with a large sheet of paper and markers. In their leadership style groups, participants share why they identified with their leadership style. Participants write the reasons identify with their leadership style and other pertinent discussion points on their large sheet of paper. In their leadership style groups, participants discuss which leadership style would be the most difficult to work with for their leadership style. Participants brainstorm together and write on their papers reasons for why the style would be difficult to work with. Participants also write ideas for how to work more effectively together with other leadership styles.
15 minutes	Discussion	Ask participants to come back to the larger group and engage in a large group discussion. Ask participants from each leadership style group to share what is written on their papers and what they discussed in their groups. Brainstorm with participants how to overcome conflicts with different leadership styles.

Time Required		Description
5 minutes	Conclusion	Summarize participants' reflections and the topics covered in the session. Ask participants to complete the session evaluation using your desired format. Close the session by thanking the participants.

Reflection Questions

- What are the characteristics of your leadership style?
- What are ways you can effectively work with others who have leadership styles different from yours?

Supplemental Resources

De Vries, R. E., Bakker-Pieper, A., & Oostenveld, W. (2010). Leadership = communication? The relations of leaders' communication styles with leadership styles, knowledge sharing and leadership outcomes. *Journal of Business & Psychology, 25*(3), 367–380. https://doi.org/10.1007/s10869-009-9140-2

Lau, D. C., & Murnighan, J. K. (1998). Demographic diversity and faultlines: The compositional dynamics of organizational groups. *The Academy of Management Review, 23*(2), 325–340. https://doi.org/10.2307/259377

Participant Reflection

Whenever I join a new team, I reflect back on this session and try to identify which direction each team members points on the leadership compass. North—action-oriented; East—visionary; South—empathetic; and West— analytical. By identifying the individual styles of my team members, I can align the way I communicate and work with them to fit their preferences. Moreover, I can take advantage of their strengths and create a strong, diverse team. I face South East, but I can just as easily work with similar leaders as I can with North Wests by understanding their work style.

RLF 2019-20

John, K., Northcraft, G., & Neale, M. (1999). Why differences make a difference: A field study of diversity, conflict, and performance in workgroups. *Administrative Science Quarterly, 44*(4), 741-763. doi:10.2307/2667054

Raines, C., & Ewing, L. (2006). *The art of connecting: How to overcome differences, build rapport, and communicate effectively with anyone.* AMACOM. http://ebookcentral.proquest.com/lib/dartmouth-ebooks/detail.action?docID=1638694

The DO Lectures. (2010). *Gerd Leonhard | The journey from egosystem to ecosystem* [Video]. DO Wales 2010. https://thedolectures.com/blogs/talks/gerd-leonhard-the-journey-from-egosystem-to-ecosystem?_pos=10&_sid=2954b98aa&_ss=r

This session has been formatted and revised for consistency and clarity. The original session in the Rockefeller Leadership Fellows Program was facilitated by Jay Davis, reached at Jay.T.Davis@Dartmouth.edu.

Leadership Compass Styles

North

Strengths
- Assertive, active, decisive
- Likes to be in control
- Quick to act, sense of urgency
- Courageous, enjoys the challenge
- Likes variety
- Likes to be in a position of leadership
- "Just do it," "I'll do it," "What is stopping us?"

Possible problems with this style
- Gets defensive, may be argumentative
- May push for decisions too soon
- May take too many risks
- Have trouble giving up control or delegating to others
- May be seen as egomaniac

South

Strengths
- Trusting, innocent approach to others
- Willingness to believe and accept others
- Allows others to feel important and involved as decisions are made
- Sees emotions and intuitions as truth
- Supportive, nurturing, warm
- Relational, relationships come first
- "Let's do what's right," "We want to be fair"

Possible problems with this style
- May have trouble saying no to requests
- Internalizes difficulty and assumes blame
- May be taken advantage of
- Immersed in present, may lose track of time
- May have difficulty dealing with anger
- May avoid confrontations

East

Strengths
- Visionary, sees big picture
- Idea-oriented, forward looking
- Insight into mission and purpose
- Likes to explore
- Strongly spiritual
- "Endless possibilities," "We have options"

Possible problems with this style
- May lose focus on task
- Poor follow-through
- Can develop a reputation for lack of dependability
- May be very enthusiastic in the beginning and then lose interest over time
- May be seen as flaky

West

Strengths
- Will weigh all sides of the issue
- Uses data and analysis to make decisions
- Seen as very practical and reliable
- Follows procedures
- Careful, introspective, self-analytical
- "We must look at this objectively"

Possible problems with this style
- Can become stubborn
- May be resistant to change
- Not open to emotional arguments
- May be seen as withdrawn or cold

Note: Reprinted from *Youth Led Tech Leadership Compass Day 1* by Smart Chicago Collaborative, 2015, https://www.slideshare.net/smartchicago/youth-led-tech-leadership-compass-day-1.

Session 7.4 Myers-Briggs Type Indicator® (MBTI®) Assessment—Using Your Strengths for Effective Professional Communication

Session Description

In this session, the facilitator will explore how self-evaluation can help participants to communicate effectively in the workplace. First, participants will learn about general psychological communication preferences. Participants will then dissect their own communication strengths and areas of needed growth using the results of the MBTI® assessment completed prior to the session. Participants will utilize their strengths in oral communication to speak in clear, cohesive and concise manners that recognize their audience and their situations. Participants will discuss and practice active listening skills as both a speaker and listener. Finally, participants will learn how to use their strengths and their teammates' strengths to work most effectively in a workplace.

Leadership Competencies Addressed

Effective Reasoning
- Develops personal reflective practice

Self-Knowledge
- Continually explores and examines values and views
- Understands social identities of self and others
- Seeks opportunities for continued growth

Learning Objectives

Participants will do the following:
- Demonstrate knowledge of the different Myers-Briggs Communication Types and the characteristics of all 16 combinations
- Identify at least two personal strengths and at least two personal areas of growth related to their MBTI type and professional communication style
- Integrate at least one strength and at least one area of growth into their journal reflections

Key Concepts and Definitions

Extraversion/ introversion	Where one focuses one's attention. Extraversion means focusing attention on the outer world of people and things. Introversion means focusing attention on the inner world of ideas and impressions.

Sensing/intuition	The way one takes in information. Sensing means taking in information through the five senses, with a focus on the here and now. Intuition means taking in information by seeing patterns and the big picture, with a focus on future possibilities.
Thinking/feeling	The way one makes decisions. Thinking means making decisions mostly on the basis of logic and objective analysis. Feeling means making decisions mostly on the basis of values and subjective, people-centered concerns.
Judging/ perceiving	How one deals with the world. Judging means taking a planned and organized approach to life and often liking to have things settled. Perceiving means taking a flexible spontaneous approach to life and preferring to keep options open.

The Myers & Briggs Foundation. (n.d.). *MBTI® Basics.* My MBTI® Personality Type. Retrieved January 5, 2021, from https://www.myersbriggs.org/my-mbti-personality-type/mbti-basics/.

Required Materials

- PowerPoint slides and appropriate technology (optional)
- One name tag for each of the 16 personality types

Pre-session Assignment:
- Complete the MBTI assessment.

Session Outline

Session duration: 1 hour and 30 minutes

Time Required		Description
20 minutes	Introduction	Introduce the importance of learning communication styles of our own and others in the workplace. Explain how the Myers-Briggs assessment can help identify communication styles and preferences. Provide anecdote of own MBTI personality type and explanation of own MBTI personality type. Provide anecdote of MBTI personality types that are more difficult to work with based on your own type and anecdote of overcoming these communication differences.

Time Required		Description
10 minutes	Framing	Explain the four categories of the personality type and corresponding two preferences for each: extraversion/ introversion, sensing/intuition, thinking/feeling, judging/ perceiving. Point out key characteristics of each preference during explanation.
30 minutes	Activity	Place the 16 name tags for each MBTI personality type in a circle on the ground. Ask participants to stand behind the name tag for their personality type. For each MBTI personality type, first explain the features most commonly associated with the personality type to participants who identify with that personality type. Explain to participants who identify with that personality type the strengths and areas of growth that often characterize the personality type. Ask participants if they agree with the assessment of their personality type and the associated characteristics. Explain why or why not.
15 minutes	Discussion	Ask participants to share specific examples relating to their personality type. Share examples about working with different personality types. Ask participants to share their own examples about working with other personality types. Draw connections between the different personality types. Ask participants to draw connections to other personality types.
10 minutes	Debrief	Summarize the MBTI personality types and the discussion from today's session. Emphasize the importance of identifying personality types and how they relate to communication and effective relationships in the workplace.
5 minutes	Conclusion	Ask participants if they have any questions. Ask participants to complete the session evaluation using your desired format. Close the session by thanking the participants.

Reflection Questions

- What are my strengths based on my MBTI results?
- What areas do I need to improve in to better communicate in a professional setting based on my MBTI results?
- How can I use what I learned from my strengths and areas of improvement to accomplish the goals of my personal leadership challenge?

Participant Reflection

ENFJ—these letters initially didn't mean much to me but now they help me appreciate my personality, decision-making preferences, and communication style. In addition to helping me understand myself better, this session helped me understand how to more effectively communicate and collaborate with a diverse range of workstyles. Myers-Briggs has given me a toolkit to identify different personalities and understand their individual strengths and areas of improvement. This has helped me leverage my strengths to work with a diverse range of personalities in work and personal environments.

RLF 2019-20

Supplemental Resources

Storm, S. (2015, August 2). How each Myers-Briggs® type reacts to stress (and how to help!). *Psychology Junkie*. https://www.psychologyjunkie.com/2015/08/02/how-each-mbti-type-reacts-to-stress-and-how-to-help/

The Myers & Briggs Foundation. (n.d.). *Understanding MBTI® type dynamics*. Retrieved February 8, 2021, from https://www.myersbriggs.org/my-mbti-personality-type/understanding-mbti-type-dynamics/

Truity. (2019, June 21). *Myers & Briggs' 16 personality types*. https://www.truity.com/page/16-personality-types-myers-briggs

This session has been formatted and revised for consistency and clarity. The original session in the Rockefeller Leadership Fellows Program was facilitated by Jennifer Sargent, reached at jennifer.sargent@dartmouth.edu. It requires the facilitator to be MBTI® Certified.

Information about the MBTI® Instrument and Certification training is available from The Myers-Briggs Company at www.themyersbriggs.com. MBTI, Myers-Briggs, and Myers-Briggs Type Indicator are trademarks or registered trademarks of The Myers & Briggs Foundation in the United States and other countries.

Session 7.5 Designing Your Life

Session Description

In this session, the facilitator will lead an interactive, hands-on workshop based on the one of most popular courses at Stanford University. Participants will explore the creative problem-solving methodology of Design Thinking and consider how it can be applied to questions about their academic, personal, and vocational journeys.

Learning Objectives

Participants will do the following:
- Identify at least three characteristics of being "stuck" in their own experience
- Practice generating different alternatives when posed with a question or dilemma
- Envision several concrete (equally plausible) life trajectories through an individual exercise

---

Leadership Competencies Addressed

Self-Knowledge
- Moves beyond self-imposed limitations
- Practices self-compassion, friendliness, ease with self, and vulnerability

Management
- Develops and implements a plan for goal attainment

Effective Reasoning
- Employs creative thinking in problem solving
- Develops personal reflective practice

Key Concepts and Definitions

Design Thinking An interdisciplinary creative problem-solving methodology rooted in empathy for the end-user, divergent idea generation, and iterative experimentation.

Conceptual Blockbusting In his book, *Conceptual Blockbusting*, James Adams applies interdisciplinary insights into overcoming the key blocks (perceptual, emotional, cultural, environmental, intellectual, and expressive) that make us feel "stuck" when we are trying to think of new ideas. Often, looking at a problem from unconventional perspectives redefines the problem's constraints and new creative solutions emerge. This rule of thumb applies to thinking individually, in teams, and in organizations.

Required Materials

- PowerPoint slides and appropriate technology (optional)
- Handout 7.5.1 30 Circles Challenge

- "Odyssey Plans" handout for each participant (https://schoolofdesignthinking.echos.cc/wp-content/uploads/2018/01/DYL-Odyssey-Planning-Worksheet-v21.jpg) or blank paper
- Writing utensils

Session Outline

Session duration: 1 hour and 30 minutes

Time Required		Description
15 minutes	Introduction	Introduce the subject of Design Thinking. Explain how this way of thinking is applicable to multiple facets of life.
15 minutes	Activity 1	Pass out Handout 7.5.1 to each participant. Tell the participants they have three minutes to turn the circles into a recognizable object (such as a smiley face). After the activity is over, ask participants about their experience doing this. Explain how this drawing and idea-generation exercise re-creates the experience of getting "stuck" and forces participants to examine the self-imposed constraints under which they are operating.
15 minutes	Discussion	Building upon the "30 Circles" exercise and a short introduction of the main concepts in the book *Conceptual Blockbusting* by James Adams, ask participants to turn to small groups of four or five to engage in conversation about instances where they get stuck (academically, professionally, and personally), and how they can get unstuck. After the small-group discussions are over, bring participants back into the larger group. Ask participants to share what they discussed in their small groups, listing the specific methods and techniques they've discussed for getting unstuck.
20 minutes	Activity 2	Pass out the "Odyssey Plans" worksheet to each participant. Ask participants to envision three different trajectories for the next three years of their life. Give participants 10 minutes to fill out the three 3-year timelines on their worksheet. Participants may draw their own timelines as well. Ask participants to get into pairs to share their timelines with each other.
15 minutes	Reflection	Combine pairs into groups of four or six. Ask participants to reflect in their larger groups about the exercise and what they are learning through it. After a few minutes, bring participants back to the large group. Ask participants to share what they discussed.

Time Required		Description
10 minutes	Conclusion	Conclude the session with last thoughts about how designing your life is related to leadership. Explain how good leadership starts with knowing yourself and how designing your life is a good way to practice and enhance self-knowledge through the design mindset of building empathy for the end-user—future you! Ask participants if they have any questions. Ask participants to complete the session evaluation using your desired format. Close the session by thanking the participants.

Reflection Questions

- Which of the constraints under which I'm operating are externally imposed and which are self-imposed?
- How can I notice when I get "stuck" and how can I get "unstuck"?
- What are some different life trajectories that I can envision, and what does this act of envisioning teach me?

Supplemental Resources

Adams, J. L. (2001). *Conceptual blockbusting: A guide to better ideas* (4th ed.). Perseus Pub.

Burnett, B., & Evans, D. (2016). *Designing your life: How to build a well-lived, joyful life* (Illustrated ed.). Knopf.

Eurich, T. (2017, November). *Increase your self-awareness with one simple fix* [Video]. TEDxMileHigh. https://www.ted.com/talks/tasha_eurich_increase_your_self_awareness_with_one_simple_fix

Participant Reflection

During this session, we were given 30 empty circles and instructed to draw something different in each of them within a short amount of time. It was much harder than it sounds! Most of us created unnecessary rules for ourselves that limited our creativity and performance. Korsunskiy encouraged us to be aware of the "schemas" we are applying and when we may be artificially limiting our options. When I face roadblocks at work, I try to remember the circles activity. I force myself to pause, identify what are the true needs and limits, and then think outside of the box.

MLDP Spring 2020

This session has been formatted and revised for consistency and clarity. The original session in the Rockefeller Leadership Fellows Program was facilitated by Eugene Korsunskiy, reached at eugene.korsunskiy@dartmouth.edu.

30 Circles Challenge

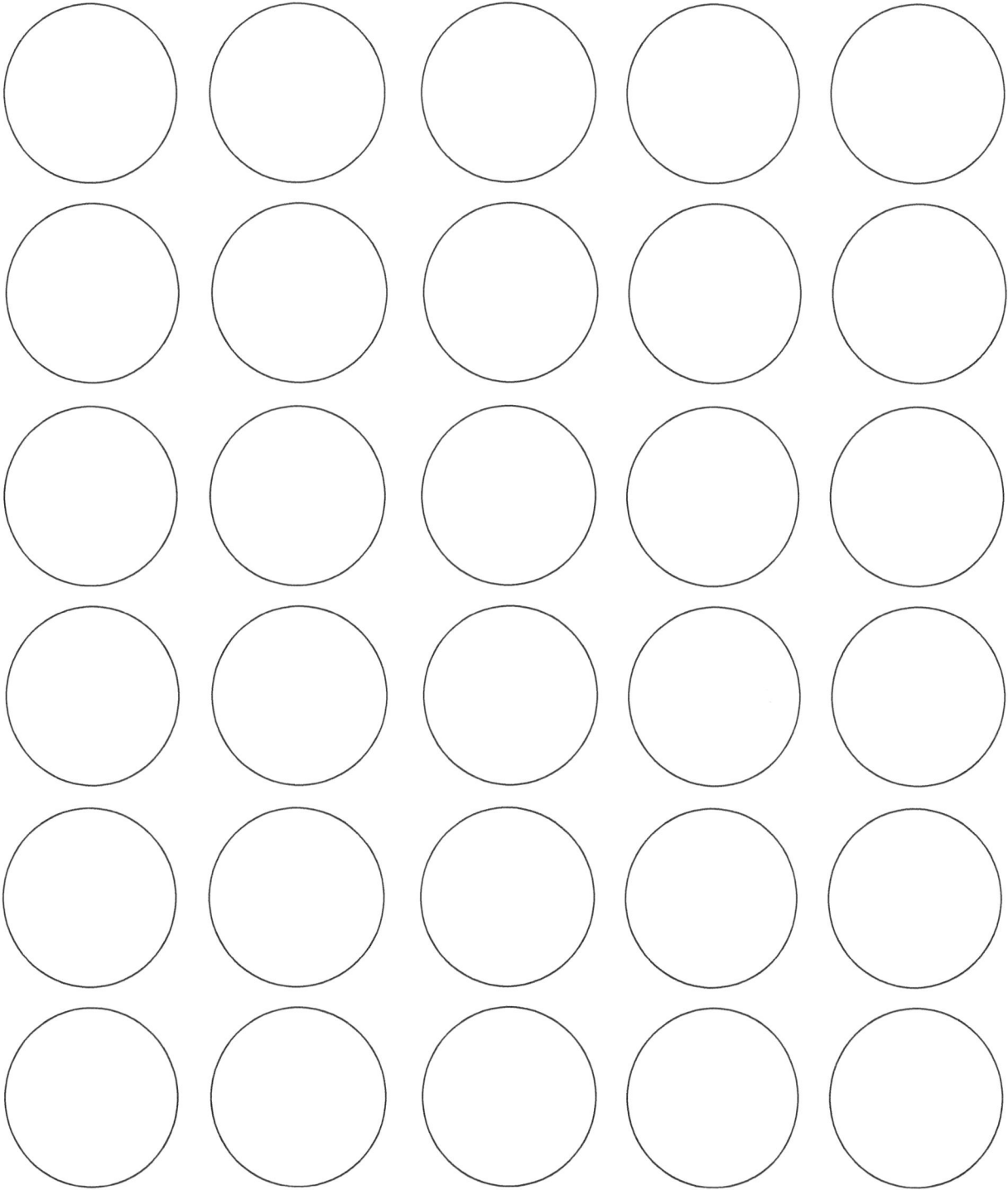

Note: Reprinted from *30 Circles Challenge: Creative Icebreaker Activity* by sgrizzlebgca, 2018, https://clubexperience.blog/2018/03/29/30-circles-challenge-creative-icebreaker-activity-with-free-download/

Session 7.6 Telling Your Story—Connecting to Others Through Personal Narrative and Vulnerability

Session Description

In this session, the facilitator will challenge participants through a series of improvisational comedy games and theatrical performance techniques. Participants will learn to tell their stories through three distinct but related competencies: 1) expressing vulnerability by participating in activities outside of their comfort zones, 2) exploring the art of personal narrative, and 3) using theatrical performance and public speaking techniques to express individual stories to a broader audience. The aim of the session will be to help participants not only learn *what* personal narrative to focus on in creating their "brand"/social image, but also discover *how* they can best tell an effective personal narrative.

Leadership Competencies Addressed

Self-Knowledge
- Moves beyond self-imposed limitations
- Practices self-compassion, friendliness, ease with self, and vulnerability

Effective Communication
- Writes and speaks after reflection
- Clearly articulates ideas in a written and spoken form
- Influences others through writing, speaking, or artistic expression

Learning Objectives

Participants will do the following:
- Practice vulnerability through a series of improvisational comedy games
- Gain experience drafting their personal narrative through storytelling techniques
- Practice personal narrative storytelling while using theatre performance techniques

Key Concepts and Definitions

Personal narrative	A storytelling technique in which the presenter connects details of their own lives to a illustrate a broader theme or social issue as a means of connecting with an audience.
Creativity/risk-taking	The two phrases are intertwined. The session will challenge non-performers to behave creatively and take risks by stepping out of their comfort zones into the world of performance.

Self-expression   Beyond sheer creativity, the session will focus on the concept of self-expression as a means to help participants fully translate their self-perception into a digestible story for the audience; self-expression in this case will focus on the translation of personal ideas into universal themes.

Required Materials

- PowerPoint slides and appropriate technology (optional)
- Pens and paper for all participants
- Room large enough for all participants to move around/stand in a circle.

Session Outline

Session duration: 1 hour and 35 minutes

Time Required		Description
25 minutes	Introduction	Lead a theatrical warm-up designed to help participants feel loose and present. Help participants overcome their fear of appearing "foolish" in order to enhance their personal expression. Introduce how theater and public speaking techniques can help grow vulnerability and lead to effective self-expression when telling personal narrative stories. Lead participants in improvisational games that focus on presence of mind.
20 minutes	Framing	Describe and define a personal narrative. Include real-life examples of personal narratives, such as clips from an NPR podcast in which world leaders discuss their fears and vulnerabilities or State of the Union Address presentation videos with personal narrative moments.
25 minutes	Activity	Explain that participants will now take some time to reflect on a personal narrative they would like to share. Hand out pieces of paper and pens to participants. Ask participants to individually brainstorm and write a one-minute personal narrative example.
15 minutes	Presentation	Bring participants back to the larger group after they finish writing their narratives. Ask for volunteers to present their personal narratives. Provide feedback on their personal narratives and presentation. Ask the audience for feedback on the presentation as well.

Time Required		Description
10 minutes	Conclusion	Ask participants why storytelling can be transformative for managers and leaders. Ask participants to complete the session evaluation using your desired format. Close the session by thanking the participants.

Reflection Questions

- What broader story am I trying to tell about myself?
- What are some strategic stories from my life that serve as examples to better tell that story?
- What are some areas for improvement in my presentation of said story?

Supplemental Resources

Gundling, E., Hogan, T., & Cvitkovich, K. (2011). *What is global leadership?: 10 key behaviors that define great global leaders* (Illustrated ed.). Nicholas Brealey Publishing.

Participant Reflection

Luke's background in theater brought a fresh take on leadership. He drew parallels of the storytelling found in theater with the strategic vulnerability that great leaders, such as Obama, use. Sharing my own personal narrative and hearing the personal narratives of those in the cohort deepened our connection and respect for one another. I learned to see our vulnerabilities as assets in leadership rather than weaknesses.

RLF 2019-20

TEDx Talks. (2018a, March 20). *The science of storytelling | Will Storr | TEDxManchester* [Video]. YouTube. https://www.youtube.com/watch?v=P2CVIGuRg4E&ab_channel=TEDxTalks

TEDx Talks. (2018b, August 30). *The power in effective data storytelling | Malavica Sridhar | TEDxUIUC* [Video]. YouTube. https://www.youtube.com/watch?v=0e52QfQngrM&ab_channel=TEDxTalks

This session has been formatted and revised for consistency and clarity. The original session in the Rockefeller Leadership Fellows Program was facilitated by Lucas Katler, reached at luke.katler@gmail.com.

Session 7.7 Leading in a Noisy World— How Intentional Solitude Can Help You Be a More Effective and Resilient Leader

Session Description

In this session, the facilitator will illustrate new ways of leading in a world that is increasingly noisy, interconnected, and complex. Participants will explore the connection between intentional doses of solitude and being an effective and resilient leader in the digital age. The facilitator will define solitude and explain how it provides the space for leaders to cultivate inner clarity, creativity, moral courage, emotional balance, and deeper connection to self and others. Participants will discover how solitude frees leaders to act and respond more intentionally rather than being reactive. The session will focus on exploring simple individual and interpersonal practices for integrating solitude and mindfulness into participants' life and work.

Leadership Competencies Addressed

Principled Action
- Demonstrates congruence between actions and values

Effective Communication
- Exhibits effective listening skills

Effective Reasoning
- Develops personal reflective practice

Self-Knowledge
- Continually explores and examines values and views
- Practices self-compassion, friendliness, ease with self, and vulnerability

Learning Objectives

Participants will do the following:
- Reflect on the connection between intentional solitude and mindfulness and being an effective and resilient leader by drawing on personal experiences
- Explore at least five individual and interpersonal practices and tools to embed intentional doses of solitude and mindfulness into their work and life
- Identify and commit to one to three actions for embedding intentional solitude and mindfulness into their work and life

Key Concepts and Definitions

Solitude	Intentionally being with yourself for periods of time free from the input of other minds (instant messages, emails, news, podcasts, social media, etc.)
Silence	Silence is not an absence of sound but an absence of noise.
Mindfulness	Intentionally being aware of the present moment without judgment.

| *Resilience* | Expanding our capacity to be with and adapt amidst challenging experiences. |
| *Inner guide* | Inner intelligence or inner wisdom. |

Required Materials

- PowerPoint slides and appropriate technology (optional)

Pre-session Assignment:
- Deresiewicz, W. (2010) *Solitude and Leadership: if you want others to follow, learn to be alone with your thoughts.* The American Scholar
- Lightman, A. (2018) *Why we owe it to ourselves to spend quiet time alone everyday.* https://ideas.ted.com/why-we-owe-it-to-ourselves-to-spend-quiet-time-alone-every-day/ retrieved 8/29/20

Session Outline

Session duration: 1 hour and 40 minutes

Time Required		Description
20 minutes	Introduction	Lead the participants through a mindful breathing exercise to help them ground themselves and set the tone for the session. Introduce yourself and the session objectives. Explain the connection between intentional solitude and being an effective and resilient leader in the digital age.
10 minutes	Framing	Encourage participants to take five minutes for self-reflection. Invite participants to reflect on the inner and outer noise and distractions they experience as well as the current role of solitude and silence in their lives. Pair up participants to share their reflections with a partner. Afterwards, invite participants to share what they explored with their partners in the larger group. Highlight overall themes that emerged.
12 minutes	Activity 1	Ask participants to think of a current leadership challenge and frame a "How might I …?" question that could help them think of possibilities for addressing the challenge. Invite participants to write that question at the top of a blank page and free-write whatever comes to mind for the next eight minutes without judging or overthinking. Then invite participants to reread what they have written and notice how it makes them feel. Afterwards, invite participants to share any insights or challenges from the activity with the group.

Time Required		Description
25 minutes	Discussion	Introduce deep listening and asking open, honest questions to help open or expand someone's thinking about a challenge, options, or possibilities and connect with their inner guide. Pair up participants and ask them to assign a Partner A and a Partner B. Partner A shares a current challenge they are facing (2 min). Then Partner B asks Partner A open, honest questions (6 min) and jots down phrases of what Partner A shares. At the end, Partner B mirrors back what they heard Partner A share, repeating the phrases they captured (2 min). Then the partners thank each other and switch roles. Afterwards, invite participants to share what they learned from the activity with the larger group.
8 minutes	Activity 2	Acknowledge that the previous exercise may have brought up some difficult emotions and that we all face difficulty in our lives. Self-compassion can help us be more resilient and kinder to ourselves as we navigate life's challenges. Invite participants into a guided practice to cultivate self-compassion in the face of a current challenge. Afterwards, invite anyone who would like to share about their experience with the practice with the larger group.
10 minutes	Discussion	Explain the importance of integrating simple daily practices for being effective and resilient as a leader. Introduce examples of simple daily practices, including mindfulness practice, journaling, going for a walk in solitude, setting an intention at the start of the day or before meetings, being mindful of technology and smartphone use, single-tasking, integrating purposeful pauses throughout the day (e.g., when checking email, opening a door, making tea), and practicing awareness of breath and body exercises during meetings, before big decisions, or in the midst of conflict. Invite participants to share examples of daily practices they currently implement or want to cultivate.
10 minutes	Conclusion	Invite participants to identify one to three concrete actions/ practices for embedding solitude into their work and life over the next month. Invite participants to share these actions/ practices with their accountability partner and discuss how they'd like to check in and support each other. Ask participants to complete the session evaluation using your desired format. Close the session by thanking the participants.

Reflection Questions

- How am I embedding intentional solitude and mindfulness into my life and work?
- How do I know I'm tuning into my inner guide among all the other voices and noises that play within and without? How do I act on these insights?
- How does deep listening and asking open, honest questions of others affect the quality of my interactions and how I'm able to support others?

Supplemental Resources

Brown, B. (2017). *Braving the wilderness: The quest for true belonging and the courage to stand alone* (1st ed.). Random House.

Cain, S. (2013). *Quiet: The power of introverts in a world that can't stop talking.* Crown.

Kethledge, R. M., Erwin, M. S., & Collins, J. (2017). *Lead yourself first: Inspiring leadership through solitude.* Bloomsbury USA.

Newport, C. (2016). *Deep work* (1st ed.). Grand Central Publishing.

Newport, C. (2019). *Digital minimalism: Choosing a focused life in a noisy world.* Portfolio.

This session has been formatted and revised for consistency and clarity. The original session in the Rockefeller Leadership Fellows Program was facilitated by Sarah-Marie Hopf, reached at shopf@thrivingquiet.com.

Participant Reflection

It is more important than ever to take time for self-reflection in a world in which we are constantly bombarded by digital notifications and distractions. This "noise" can fuel our insecurities, create unhealthy escape mechanisms, and lead to a state of exhaustion. To combat our noise, Hopf emphasized the importance of integrating simple daily practices such as mindfulness, journaling, and integrating purposeful pauses. When it feels like I am pulled in different directions at work and leaders can make everything feel urgent all the time, these practices have been incredibly beneficial. Taking as little as 30 seconds to focus on my breathing before a client call or high-stress situation has made a world of difference for my mental and emotional health.

RLF 2019-20

Session 7.8 Leadership Paradigm—The Good and the Bad

Session Description

In this session, the facilitator will guide learners toward understanding their own individual view about leadership: what it is, what it means, and how they get there. Through a series of art activities and organic conversations, participants will discuss how their individual understanding of leadership influences their ability to work in teams and how to overcome leadership challenges, such as working across generations. Participants will reference their individual leadership philosophies, which they drafted at the start of the Rockefeller Leadership Fellows Program. This session will provide participants the opportunity to reflect on the concept of the leadership paradigm on an individual level. Using a storytelling method, participants will be introduced to real-world leadership challenges that provide them the opportunity to better understand how to use their individual leadership philosophy to impact change.

Leadership Competencies Addressed

Effective Reasoning
- Develops personal reflective practice

Intercultural Mindset
- Contextualizes social identities and experiences

Self-knowledge
- Continually explores and examines values and views
- Seeks opportunities for continued growth

Principled Action
- Demonstrates personal responsibility

Learning Objectives

Participants will do the following:
- List five of their individual leadership skills and abilities based upon their individual leadership philosophy
- Increase their knowledge of leadership theories and concepts, including the leadership paradigm, and be able to identify at least two new leadership theories and concepts they can actively apply
- Develop two ways to apply their individual leadership philosophy within teams and organizations for social impact and change

Key Concepts and Definitions

Leadership paradigm   A way of looking or thinking about issues. We all have a personal leadership paradigm, the model that we use to help us make decisions based on our personal beliefs and values.

Required Materials

- Blank piece of paper and writing utensil for each participant

Session Outline

Session duration: 1 hour and 15 minutes

Time Required		Description
5 minutes	Introduction	Introduce yourself and provide an overview of the session.
10 minutes	Activity 1	Hand out papers and pens to the participants. Introduce the art activity, geared towards challenging participants' preconceived notions. Ask participants to draw several items, for example, a television. For the example of the television, ask participants how many of them drew the television with antennas. Point out how even though modern televisions do not have antennas today, many participants gravitated towards drawing that image. Continue this explanation for several drawings. Explain how this activity shows the mental prints we have about different aspects of the world. Preface the rest of the session by introducing the idea that things are not always what we expect them to be or how we expect them to happen.
30 minutes	Framing	Through a series of anecdotes and life experiences, talk about your journey and your story. Emphasize the times when things did not go as expected, that you had dreamed of something but ended up doing something else. Draw out examples that emphasize the role of diversity, inclusivity, and respect in your life. Define what a leadership paradigm is. Using personal anecdotes, explain how a leadership paradigm has impacted your own life when facing real-world leadership challenges.
15 minutes	Discussion	Ask participants to discuss what they would do when faced with various real-world leadership challenges. Ask participants to reflect on their personal leadership paradigm and how they approach leadership challenges with the group.
10 minutes	Debrief	Summarize the topics covered and the main points of the discussions.

Time Required		Description
5 minutes	Conclusion	End the session with Q&A time. Ask participants to complete the session evaluation using your desired format. Close the session by thanking the participants.

Reflection Questions

- How can I use my leadership skills and abilities to create systems of change (e.g., becoming more civically engaged)?
- What can I do to shift my leadership paradigm?

Supplemental Resources

Benson, D. (2015). Creating your personal leadership philosophy. *Physician Leadership Journal, 2*(6), 64–66.

Dudley, D. (2010, September). *Everyday leadership* [Video]. TEDxToronto. https://www.ted.com/talks/drew_dudley_everyday_leadership

Figliuolo, M. (2011). *One piece of paper: The simple approach to powerful, personal leadership* (1ˢᵗ ed.). Jossey-Bass.

Participant Reflection

Dr. Matthews began the session by asking us to draw common objects such as a television. It was amazing how similar our drawings looked—all televisions with antennas! This activity highlighted the prevalence of stereotypes. We are frequently putting people into boxes and being put into boxes. When trying to establish a pilot program between his university and a Connecticut prison, Dr. Matthews had to overcome many stereotypes. His story and the drawing activity remind me to be an open-minded and inclusive leader. Things are not always what we expect them to be.

RLF 2019-20

This session has been formatted and revised for consistency and clarity. The original session in the Rockefeller Leadership Fellows Program was facilitated by Lowell Chris Matthews, reached at l.matthews@snhu.edu.

Session 7.9 Practitioner Panel—Advice from Community Leaders and Managers

Session Description

In this session, participants will hear the personal leadership and management stories from three practitioners in New Hampshire and Vermont. Each panelist will highlight their career trajectory, what management and leadership means to them and why, and the defining moments in their career. Each panelist will describe their background and career path, things they did not do well and learned from, what it means to be a leader, and advice on how to be a good leader no matter where you are in an organization. Panelists may talk about their view of the mission of their respective organizations, intergenerational communication, and overcoming management and leadership challenges.

Leadership Competencies Addressed

Effective Reasoning
- Develops personal reflective practice

Self-knowledge
- Continually explores and examines values and views
- Takes appropriate action toward potential benefits despite possible failure

Learning Objectives

Participants will do the following:
- Identify at least two leadership trends and defining moments for each panelist that helped them decide which path to take in their careers
- Reflect on what it means to be a leader regardless of where they are in an organization's hierarchy
- Learn and identify one to three techniques for overcoming management and leadership challenges

Key Concepts and Definitions

Management   "Doing things right."

Leadership   "Doing the right thing."

Required Materials

- PowerPoint slides and appropriate technology (optional)
- Name cards for panelists and participants

Session Outline

Session duration: 1 hour and 15 minutes

Time Required		Description
15 minutes	Introduction	Introduce panelists and allow them to share their leadership stories, with five minutes per panelist. Ask them to emphasize how they navigated their career and the defining moments along the way. Divide participants into three groups. Assign one panelist to each group.
45 minutes	Discussion	Give the panelists 15 minutes for Q&A with each group. Panelists will rotate through the groups until they have spoken to every group.
15 minutes	Conclusion	Bring the participants and panelists back to the large group. Conclude the session by asking participants if they have any final questions. Ask participants to complete the session evaluation using your desired format. Close the session by thanking the participants and panelists.

Reflection Questions

- What should I consider when choosing my career path?
- What are three or four things that will help me become a good leader?
- How can I be a good leader despite where I am in the organization?

Participant Reflection

It was amazing to hear from so many perspectives stemming from experiences in legislature, public education, and engineering, all in one night. One piece of advice that stuck out to me from this night was "Management is doing things right. Leadership is doing the right thing." Hearing their unique leadership journeys affirmed that there is no one correct path to becoming an effective leader. We each have our own strengths and we are all leaders in our own spheres of influence.

RLF 2019-200

This session has been formatted and revised for consistency and clarity. The original session in the Rockefeller Leadership Fellows Program was facilitated by local practitioners living and practicing in the states of Vermont and New Hampshire.

Session 7.10 The Art of Difficult Conversations—What Is the Right Thing to Say and Do as a Leader?

Session Description

In this session, the facilitator will explore the challenges of having difficult conversations as a leader. Participants will discuss what makes these conversations difficult and why. The session will also touch on ethical dilemmas in the workplace and the resulting difficult conversations that need to take place. Finally, the session will address ways to make communication effective—whether personal or professional—and explore the use of the "best appropriate" mode of communication when faced with a variety of difficult situations.

Learning Objectives

Participants will do the following:

- Describe at least three components that make a personal or a professional conversation difficult versus what makes a conversation crucial, based on the summer reading books
- Demonstrate and analyze how to engage in an effective conversation in a variety of situations using role plays
- Identify one or two skills of effective conversations to apply to real life situations

Key Concepts and Definitions

Crucial conversations	Conversations between at least two parties where there are differing opinions and needs or wants, high stakes, and strong emotions.
Difficult conversations	Conversations that involve a personal or professional issue between two people. They can be split into three distinct categories: conversations concerning who is right, intentions, and blame; conversations concerning feelings; or conversations concerning identities.

Leadership Competencies Addressed

Principled Action
- Seeks appropriate and mutually beneficial solutions when conflict or controversy arises

Effective Communication
- Acknowledges and appropriately communicates in situations with divergent opinions and values

Effective Reasoning
- Develops personal reflective practice

Different working styles (EWNS)	"East" is the approach of looking at the bigger picture. "West" describes those that are detail oriented. "North" is an action-oriented approach, and "South" is concerned with feelings and processes. There is a tendency to favor one working style in most people, but this is flexible depending on the situation.
Tuckman stages of team formation	The stages are forming, storming, norming, performing, and adjourning. **Forming** is the stage when team members are still getting to know each other and may be anxious when beginning to work together. **Storming** is the phase where team members may face conflict in working with each other due to working styles, roles within the teams, or doubt surrounding overall objectives. After storming, **norming** comes next, where team members begin to resolve differences and appreciate each other's' strengths. **Performing** is the stage where team members are able to work hard to achieve their mutual goal. Finally, **adjourning** is the last phase where teams that are not permanent may disband.
Ladder of inference	A model of the thinking process we use in order to make sense of situations and go from information to decision to action. The rungs of the ladder are reality and facts, selected reality, interpreted reality, assumptions, conclusions, beliefs, and actions. We start with facing reality and facts, then experiencing them selectively based on our prior beliefs and experiences. We interpret and apply existing assumptions, and we draw conclusions based on our interpretations and assumptions. We develop beliefs based on our conclusions and take actions based on what we believe in.

Required Materials

- PowerPoint slides and appropriate technology (optional)
- Handout 7.10.1 Commonalities Between Crucial Conversations and Difficult Conversations
- Handout 7.10.2 Scenarios for Role-plays (optional)

Pre-session Assignment:

- Stone, D., Patton, B., Heen, S., & Fisher, R. (1999). *Difficult conversations: How to discuss what matters most*. Penguin Books.
- Patterson, K., Grenny, J., & Switzler, A. (2012). *Crucial conversations: Tools for talking when stakes are high* (2nd ed.). McGraw-Hill.

Session Outline

Session duration: 1 hour and 20 minutes

Time Required		Description
5 minutes	Introduction	Introduce the session objectives as well as the situations in which difficult conversations can arise through examples and anecdotes.
15 minutes	Discussion	Ask participants what they think the differences between "crucial" and "difficult" conversations are. Pass out Handout 7.10.1 and engage in discussion with the participants about these differences.
10 minutes	Framing	Introduce and discuss communication skills with the participants, including EWNS styles and Tuckman stages.
20 minutes	Activity	Divide participants into small groups of four or five participants. In their small groups, participants first reflect independently on the real-life difficult conversation scenarios they have faced or currently face and then share with their group. Afterwards, each participant will role play their real-life difficult conversation scenario with their group. Alternatively, you may provide some scenarios for groups to role play (see Handout 7.10.2). Participants continue to practice their role playing.
15 minutes	Debrief	Call back the participants to the larger group. Ask each small group to perform the roleplay scenarios they have practiced in front of the larger group. Ask participants to observe how participants are handling difficult conversations in each scenario.
15 minutes	Conclusion	Discuss the role-play scenario performances with the participants. Summarize the findings and discussions of the session and end with final thoughts about implications for management and leadership. Ask participants to write one or two actions they will take to become effective communicators. Ask participants to complete the session evaluation using your desired format. Close the session by thanking the participants.

Reflection Questions

- Am I a good communicator? Why or why not? What is my biggest challenge in this realm?
- What are three or four situations in which I could have affected the outcome differently as a result of this session?
- Moving forward, what are three or four things I will do differently when faced with the prospect of a difficult conversation?

Supplemental Resources

Coleman, P. T., Deutsch, M., & Marcus, E. C. (Eds.). (2014). *The handbook of conflict resolution: Theory and practice* (3rd ed.). John Wiley & Sons, Incorporated. http://ebookcentral. proquest.com/lib/dartmouth-ebooks/detail. action?docID=1643662

Headlee, C. (2015, May). *10 ways to have a better conversation* [Video]. TEDxCreativeCoast. https://www.ted.com/talks/celeste_headlee_10_ways_to_have_a_better_conversation

Patterson, K., Grenny, J., McMillan, R., & Switzler, A. (2012). *Crucial conversations: Tools for talking when stakes are high* (2nd ed.). McGraw-Hill.

Stone, D., Heen, S., & Patton, B. (2010). *Difficult conversations: How to discuss what matters most.* Penguin.

Taylor, S. (2018). *The art of handling difficult conversation.* Independently published.

Tuckman, B. W., & Jensen, M. A. C. (1977). Stages of small-group development revisited. *Group & Organization Studies, 2*(4), 419–427.

Participant Reflection

Prior to this session, difficult conversations terrified me, and I would do everything in my power to avoid them. This session helped me appreciate the common patterns across difficult conversations and develop strategies to tactfully approach them. One of the most important takeaways was to always come to conversations with curiosity and to assume positive intent. By trying to understand why a person is acting a certain way, we can find points of similarity and overcome implicit biases. I now feel comfortable handling difficult conversations and focus on understanding the other person's perspective.

RLF 2019-20

This session has been formatted and revised for consistency and clarity. The original session in the Rockefeller Leadership Fellows Program was facilitated by Roshini Pinto-Powell, reached at Roshini.Pinto-Powell@dartmouth.edu.

Commonalities Between Crucial Conversations and Difficult Conversations

Purpose for talking: Both stress the importance of having a good purpose for both people, lest the conversation go awry.

Difficult	*Crucial*
Assessing overall purpose is extremely important. If you wish to change the other person, to vent at them, or to only half-heartedly engage, it is best to rethink doing the conversation. If you wish to learn their perspective, express your own views and feelings, or to problem-solve collaboratively, you have a good purpose and will have a good conversation.	*Mutual Purpose* is a *safety condition*, or a factor that must be present for people to engage fully in a conversation. The *Mutual Purpose* condition fails when the other person believes you have a bad motive in holding the conversation. If you have one of the "bad" purposes mentioned in the book, for example, the other person is likely to catch on and will become defensive or start accusing. To create *Mutual Purpose*, it is important to ask, "Do others believe I care about their goals, and do they trust my motives?"

Solving the problem: Both say that partnering to explore solutions is important so that the conversation is two-sided.

Difficult	*Crucial*
Step three of engaging in a difficult conversation ("Create a Learning Conversation") is to invite the other person to *jointly* explore solutions with you, emphasizing the joint aspect so it comes across as a team effort.	Sometimes, a conversation becomes a debate because the two parties indeed have different purposes in mind. So, you must *Create a Mutual Purpose* to move toward a common goal. The acronym CRIB helps here: **C**ommit to seeking mutual purpose, **R**ecognize the purpose behind the strategy, **I**nvent a mutual purpose, and **B**rainstorm new strategies.

Intention errors: Intentions are often judged mistakenly by the feelings a person had in response, which is not indicative of the other person's actual intentions.

Difficult	*Crucial*
One error that disrupts talking about the event that happened is the *Intention Invention*, which is the idea that you are sure of the other person's malicious intentions. But you are not as right as you think; people often mistakenly attribute how they *feel* about the actions to what the person intended.	*Clever stories* are stories that people tell themselves about a situation that justifies their own behavior; these stories are not necessarily accurate. One common story is the *Villain story* that over-exaggerates the bad qualities and malicious intent of the other person.

Our simplified thinking: Denial of our own role is a common response to a situation because the alternative is to have an identity crisis due to distorted thinking.

Difficult	*Crucial*
Identity conversations are another facet of the difficult conversation, a facet concerning the anxiety you feel when the conversation or event threatens a core identity of yours. This happens through "all-or-nothing" thinking, which is a binary way of thinking that assumes you must not have any contradicting qualities or actions. When you are faced with contradictory evidence, you either deny it to protect your identity or exaggerate its role because it is so antithetical to your identity. Denial lets us cling to our identities because we have left absolutely zero room for negative feedback.	*Clever stories* justify our current behavior and let us disconnect from current results. One reason for clever stories is to disconnect from the results because the other option is to accept the evidence and become overwhelmed because of all-or-nothing thinking.

Nuance and our own role: Situations are always more complex than they seem, and it is imperative to acknowledge and point to this complexity and how both people have added to it.

Difficult	*Crucial*
Rather than centering a conversation around *blame*, it is important to think in terms of a *contribution system*. A contribution system's goal is understanding—understanding how both people contributed to the current issue or dynamic.	To avoid stories that assign 100% blame (the Villain story) or 100% innocence (the Victim story), a necessary question is, "Am I pretending not to notice my role in the problem?" Such a question adds nuance and complexity and allows a fuller conversation to happen.

Role of feelings: Feelings are important but also must be handled carefully, without judging or accusing.

Difficult	*Crucial*
The *Feelings conversation* is a facet of a difficult conversation and cannot be avoided should the conversation go successfully. It is important to express feelings so that both sides can understand each other and move forward. It is also important, however, to express feelings *without judgment*: without accusations, insults, or rants. To figure out your feelings, you should dig deeper into the labels you are applying to the person or situation. What feelings are being covered up by accusations and judgments?	Feelings are important here as well. However, the *stories behind feelings* should be shared before the feelings themselves. And even before you share the stories, you should share the actual evidence you have that made you draw that conclusion. You must work backwards to get a read on all the important details: from your behavior, to the feelings behind that behavior, to the stories behind that feeling, to the evidence behind that story. Then, you should share it in the opposite direction so others understand your thought process and are not caught off guard. Share the facts first, then the stories, then your feelings. Just as in *Difficult Conversation*, dig past the behavior to get to the feelings and then objectively share the evidence you found, without judgments or accusations.

Handling a conversation neutrally: Objectivity, inviting collaboration, walking through and trying out each side's conclusions or stories

Difficult	*Crucial*
The way the authors recommend starting a conversation is a three-step process: (1) mention the topic in a neutral, third-party way, (2) mention that you and the other person might have disagreements on the issue, and (3) invite them to jointly explore solutions with you. These steps are important because they emphasize a more objective middle ground rather than emotionally charged sides, and stick to facts rather than feelings or accusations.	An important part of the conversation is to STATE your path; the most relevant steps are **S**hare your evidence, **A**sk for others' paths, and **E**ncourage testing. Sharing your evidence means sticking to facts first; asking for others' paths acknowledges that you are not necessarily correct and the other person may disagree; and encouraging testing is a form of jointly exploring the solutions or conclusions you each may have.

Note: Summaries of *Difficult Conversations: How to Discuss What Matters Most* by D. Stone, B. M. Patton, & S. Heen, 1999, Penguin Books; and *Crucial Conversations: Tools for Talking When Stakes Are High* by K. Patterson, J. Grenny, R. McMillan & A. Switzler, 2012, McGraw-Hill.

Scenarios for Role Plays

Scenario 1: Dysfunctional Team

A team project represents the capstone for this Econ course. At the beginning of the term, teams were *randomly assigned by the professor.* The project consists of a business plan and presentation of the recommendations included in that plan. The plan needs to be at least 3,500 words long (not including exhibits, attachments, or other calculations and supporting information). An Executive Summary memo is also expected. All members must participate in the 20-minute presentation.

Each member of the team will earn the SAME GRADE for the assignment. This is your second meeting—the first time all three of you are present with the goal of dividing up the work for this project.

Team Member A–Jordan

You love when a course has a capstone project like this rather than a final exam. You love working and studying with others and really get energized by group work. In your opinion, working on and developing something like a business plan is so much more valuable than writing an exam because you generate an actual end product. You like practicing your presentation skills and like the creative process of putting together a slideshow. You like to jump on any project planning process as soon as possible. You are not a procrastinator at all.

You were the first to establish a group text, and Ann said she could come, but then didn't show to the first meeting! Chris, who has yet to respond to any of your email communications, did however show up for the first meeting but had little to say during the brainstorming process. You've had other classes with Chris but don't know him well. Anytime he's called on by the professor he knows the answer and rumor has it his GPA is a 4.0.

Team Member B– Ann

Wow, did you overcommit this term. You are taking three classes, auditing one, and participating in a pilot leadership program at Tuck. In addition, you are captain of the club tennis team. You're trying to juggle everything but at the moment are struggling a bit in keeping up. You appreciate the fact that Jordan has taken the lead on the group project. You don't know Chris but have heard he is an Econ whiz. You're secretly hoping that between Jordan, who seems to be an eager organizer, and Chris, you'll be able to coast a bit on this project, but you're obviously not going to let the others know that.

You said you would be there but blew off the first group meeting because you got an email from your Tuck mentor asking to meet at the same time. That seemed the more important of the two commitments. You're somewhat of a procrastinator and think you do your best work when you are under a deadline crunch. Jordan thinks the group should already have an outline for the plan, but there are still four weeks before this project is due! He needs to relax.

Team Member C—
Chris

You hate when a course has a teamwork capstone project rather than a final exam. What a colossal waste of time! You could have the business plan written yourself in the amount of time spent just trying to find a time when everyone can meet! You did not respond to the email about the first meeting, but you did show up. Turned out Ann did not show, despite saying she could come. It drives you nuts, so you just stay out of it all.

You've always preferred to conduct research on your own and to study alone and, when left to do so, you produce excellent work and usually ace most exams. To top it off you also absolutely loath public speaking and feel like its gives naturally outgoing people (which you are not) an unfair advantage. Jordan seems to have taken on the role of group leader, which you resent. You're actually working with an Econ prof at the moment on some research that would make for excellent material for this plan; however, it pains you to think about letting the others in on your research results. You'd love it if they'd just let you write the plan, and then they can present it, but of course that won't happen.

Observer

Jordan, Ann, and Chris are part of this team.
Jordan is the self-appointed leader/organizer who loves this kind of "project" work and is trying to organize the team.
Ann is an overcommitted student who is a bit of a procrastinator and hoping to coast on this project.
Chris is a brilliant introvert who dislikes this kind of project and wishes he could do the whole thing himself.

Notice the communication skills and non-verbal cues displayed by each. Do they try to form a "pool of shared meaning"?
Did you notice commanding, consulting, or reaching consensus? By which person?
Can you identify these segments as they happen? Jot down a few sentences that reflect these conversations:
• The "What Happened"?
• The Feelings conversation?
• The identity conversation?

Scenario 2: Your Boss Is Coasting While You Do All the Work

(Turns Out to Be True)

Employee Your days start early and end late. You haven't worked less than a 10–hour day since you started over two years ago. Your job is to conduct research and analyze trends in the industry. You have excellent technical skills and want to demonstrate these to your boss. However, he never seems interested in looking at your work. He is more than happy for you to work hard. In fact, he has made comments that junior employees are expected to put in long hours and not to expect a lot of thanks for it.

Your boss is a very engaging guy and seems to have a huge network of friends. He frequently invites you into his office or along for lunches but tends to cut you off if you try to share any of the more technical aspects of the current projects you're working on. You also suspect that half of the time he doesn't really grasp the technical part of the work and is relying on how things were done in the industry 10 or more years ago when he offers advice. You have several ideas on how to improve the two projects you are currently working on, but it's going to take a lot of support and buy-in from senior management to get going in that direction. You doubt your boss has the interest in exerting any additional effort for either of these projects.

Boss You killed yourself for over two decades in this business, and now you really feel like you have earned the right to take it easy. You've always been a people-person and playing office politics has always come easy for you. You made all the right connections early in your career. You still put in 8-hour days (counting lunch) and make yourself available to staff, but they work for you and not the other way around. Your career has taught you, it's about who you know, not necessarily what you know. You like having junior employees around to shoot the breeze with, but they need to remember their place, as you did years ago. You're happy to discuss projects and offer advice and you consider yourself very astute at spotting an error in someone's logic or project early on. Once a project is underway, however, it's better not to make changes. You get especially annoyed when direct reports start going on and on about new technology and expect you to be interested in looking over one of their spreadsheets in detail, or to actually log onto the shared drive to access their latest graph or model. Their job is to brief you, *brief* being the key word. The days of sweating over every little detail are over. You did your time in the trenches; now it's time to enjoy the fruits of their labor.

Observer Role Note words used and behaviors of the participants doing the role play. Discuss with participants and the larger group what you observed.

Scenario #3: Your Boss Coasting While You Do All the Work

(Turns Out to Be False)

Employee Your days start early and end late. Your job is to analyze trends, conduct research, crunch numbers, write copy, etc. You try to crank out the work for your boss as fast as possible, but she still never seems to be satisfied with the data you provide her. You are very careful not to make mistakes, but she always responds to your work with more questions and requests more research, more data, etc. You're trying to give her what she is asking for, but she never seems particularly enthusiastic about your work and she never seems to have time to offer you any feedback.

Your boss on the other hand arrives to the office a full two hours after you do. Once there, she immediately goes into what seems like back-to-back meetings. Sometimes these meetings are in your department, which means she's at least still available for questions, but more often than not, she's not even in the building. You can only imagine she's taking long lunches and probably running personal errands because there never seems to be any work or business generated from all of these hours out of the office. Of course, you're never invited along—which makes you all the more suspicious and frustrated, because if it is work related, you really want to meet more people in the business. You don't mind working hard but only if you're learning more about the business and gaining more responsibility, not just taking on more tasks.

Boss Your days start early and end late. Several years ago, when you assumed a greater management role, you found that the only way you could get some guaranteed uninterrupted time was early in the morning at your home office. You got permission to do this from your boss but under the strict instructions that you shouldn't advertise this arrangement. He's not keen on "working from home" and doesn't want it to become a trend. You had to work very hard to earn his respect and you don't plan to ever violate his trust. You spend these two hours very productively. In fact, you consider them sometimes the best two hours of your day. When you arrive to work, you feel prepared and are able to give your undivided attention in meetings, which seems to start the minute you arrive. Additionally, your boss has asked you to take on a project (called Project X) that for no, is under the radar. It is taking more and more of your time and at some point, you're really going to need help executing it.

You were hoping to mentor your newest employee, but the reality is you just don't have a lot of extra time now with this new project on top of everything else. You're not naturally a very trusting person. You've noticed that he tends to rush through the tasks assigned to him. His work is good, he doesn't make mistakes, but he only gives you exactly what you ask for. What you would really like, however, is for him to start asking better questions of himself or, even better, reading your mind because, really, you just don't have the time to get him up to speed. He also seems really chatty and social. You do not have time for small talk. You're happy he's making friends in the organization, but you worry how discreet he is. At some point you're going to need to bring him in on Project X, but you fear that he won't appreciate the necessity for discretion.

Observer Role	Note words used and behaviors of the participants doing the role play. Discuss with participants and the larger group what you observed.

Session 7.11 Developing Identities and Capacity to Engage in Leadership for Social Justice

Session Description

In this session, the facilitator will focus on a crucial goal of leadership education: to develop participants' capacity to address complex societal problems in inclusive communities. Participants will engage in personal storytelling, develop a shared definition of leadership for social justice, and situate themselves in a continuum of social justice work. By the end of the session, participants will be prepared to engage in learning and leading toward a more just society.

Learning Objectives

Participants will do the following:
- Define leadership through a social justice lens
- Situate themselves within the leader activist identity continuum
- Identify three next steps for continued development and leadership projects that align with social justice goals through the development of a Theory of Change model

Leadership Competencies Addressed

Collaboration
- Facilitates collective action toward common goals

Intercultural Mindset:
- Understands, communicates with, and respectfully interacts with people across identities

Self-Knowledge
- Continually explores and examines values and views

Principled Action
- Bases actions on thoughtful consideration of their impact and consequences

Key Concepts and Definitions

Transformative leadership	Leadership practices that build equity, social justice, and quality of life by expanding access and opportunity, respecting diversity, serving the long-term interests of society, strengthening democracy, and reframing worldviews to develop new solutions and systems (Bruce et al., 2019).
Social change leadership	An approach to systemic change motivated by the recognition of the realities of systemic inequality and vision of human well-being and justice (Ospina et al., 2012).
Social justice work	Enacting commitment to work through both process and goal towards a society where all persons have access and opportunity in an equitable manner.

Leader activist identity continuum	A continuum of being a learner, advocate, ally, and activist or organizer relating to social justice work (Bruce et al., 2019).
Theory of Change	A conceptual model that articulates the linkages between strategies and hoped-for outcomes that support a mission or vision for achieving social impact.

Required Materials

- PowerPoint slides and appropriate technology (optional)
- Handout 7.11.1 Theory of Change—Action Planning Tool

Pre-session Assignment:

- Kliewer, B. W., & Priest, K. L. (2017). Why civic leadership for social justice? *eJournal of Public Affairs, 6*(1), 1–10. doi: 10.21768/ejopa.v6i1.164

Session Outline

Session duration: 1 hour and 25 minutes

Time Required		Description
20 minutes	Introduction	Introduce yourself, your story, and what you care about. Ask participants to also share about who they are and what they care about. Notice and summarize common stories within the room. Identify and explain the need for a lens of equity and justice.
20 minutes	Discussion	Begin a discussion on social justice leadership. Ask participants what social justice means and listen to their responses. Provide examples of social justice. Ask participants what leadership perspectives support social justice goals. Ask participants how they can develop as a social justice leader. Listen to their answers and facilitate a discussion between participants.
35 minutes	Activity	Introduce the leader-activist identity continuum. Ask participants to situate themselves across the continuum of being a learner, advocate, ally, and activist/organizer. Share examples of each identity. Identify examples of actions demonstrated by each identity. Describe a Theory of Change tool and its application to service projects. Using Handout 7.11.1, ask participants to think of a project that may address an issue in their domain and identify its strategies, outcomes, and impacts. Apply a social justice lens by applying the Theory of Change to the project.

Time Required		Description
10 minutes	Conclusion	Summarize the processes discussed in the session: development along the leader activist identity continuum and projects built on the Theory of Change model. Ask participants to identify next steps for continued development on the identity continuum, as well as next steps for projects they are working on as leaders. Everyone should share one idea with a partner or the entire group. Ask participants to complete the session evaluation using your desired format. Close the session by thanking the participants.

Reflection Questions

- What motivates my leadership?
- How can I continue to increase my understanding of social justice in the work of leadership and stretch my comfort zone of social justice work?
- How do my service-project strategies and outcomes support broader social justice goals?

Supplemental Resources

Bruce, J. A., & McKee, K. E. (Eds.). (2020). *Transformative leadership in action: Allyship, advocacy & activism.* Emerald Group Publishing.

Bruce, J., McKee, K., Morgan-Fleming, J., & Warner, W. (2019). The Oaks Leadership Scholars Program: Transformative leadership in action. *International Journal of Teaching and Learning in Higher Education, 31*(3), 536–546

Participant Reflection

Dr. Priest began the session by suggesting that many of the issues plaguing society today—like climate change and poverty—are the results of failed leadership. It's not that the technology, or ideas, or structures do not exist to tackle such issues—it's that today's leaders are vulnerable to crippling shortcomings like greed, selfishness, and more. Leadership for social justice requires virtues like reliability, transparency, and commitment. Each day, we have the opportunity to either be a learner, ally, advocate, or activist and must live by these virtues.

RLF 2019-20

Fraser, N. (1996, May). *Social justice in the age of identity politics: Redistribution, recognition, and participation* [Lecture]. The Tanner Lectures on Human Values, Stanford University. https://tannerlectures. utah.edu/_documents/a-to-z/f/Fraser98.pdf

Goldman Schuyler, K., Baugher, J. E., & Jironet, K. (Eds.). (2016). *Creative social change: Leadership for a healthy world* (1st ed.). Emerald Group Publishing Limited.

Opsina. S.M., Foldy, E.G., El Hadidy, W., Dodge, J., Hoffman-Pinilla, A. & Su, C. (2012). Social change leadership as relational leadership. In M. Uhl-Bien & S. M. Ospina (Eds.), *Advancing relational leadership: A dialogue among perspectives* (pp. 203–225). Information Age Publishing.

Uitermark, J., & Nicholls, W. (2017). Planning for social justice: Strategies, dilemmas, tradeoffs: *Planning Theory, 16*(1). https://doi.org/10.1177/1473095215599027

This session has been formatted and revised for consistency and clarity. The original session in the Rockefeller Leadership Fellows Program was facilitated by Kerry Priest, reached at kerryp@ksu.edu.

Handout 7.11.1 Theory of Change— Action Planning Tool

As you begin to develop action plans, consider a simple "theory of change"— *strategies lead to outcomes lead to impact.* This is sometimes also referred to as a "logic model" in organizational or community planning.

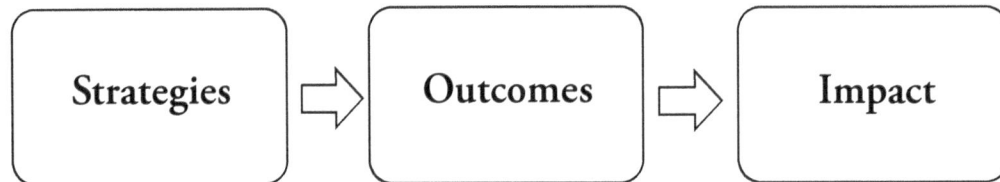

```
┌──────────────┐      ┌──────────────┐      ┌──────────────┐
│              │      │              │      │              │
│  Strategies  │ ⇨    │   Outcomes   │ ⇨    │    Impact    │
│              │      │              │      │              │
└──────────────┘      └──────────────┘      └──────────────┘
```

Developing a Theory of Change

Start with the end in mind—the "why" of the work and then move towards the "how."

1. **Impact**: What is the big picture vision you have for our campus/community? This is your WHY.

2. Based on the data and learning you have done so far, what are your **outcomes or goals** (the outcomes you hope to achieve)? Outcomes are short-term wins but are not an end in themselves. Accomplishing outcomes also builds capacity for long-term change. Outcomes may be **individual** (What kind of change or learning or growth do we need in ourselves?), **group-level** (What kind of changes do we need in our group and how we operate?), and **inter-group/community level** (What kind of changes do we want to see more broadly among people and groups in our community system?).

3. Strategies are the **tasks, actions, steps** you plan to actually take to reach your goals. This is the *who, what, when, where* and *how* of the work. It's important that every strategy directly supports an outcome. Strategies should *engage others* and create opportunities for participation, learning, and growth at varying levels of engagement.

Strategy	Outcomes	Impact
The **specific activities** and/or events you undertake to carry out the work	The **changes** that you expect to occur among individuals, families, communities, organizations, or systems as a result of your work	Sizeable, lasting, positive, long-term aspirational **vision** or **goal**

Strategy	Outcomes	Impact
• What resources/assets are available? Who can we partner with/how can we mobilize people and resources that already exist? What resources do we need to create? • What are specific actions we need to take to make progress toward our goals? • Are we creating opportunities to engage as learners, allies, advocates, and/or activists? • Who will do what? • What is our timeline? • How will we hold each other accountable?	• What change is needed (based on data or other sources)? • What are the short-term changes we are trying to make or progress on (this semester)? • Are we focused on individual capacity building, organizational capacity building, interorganizational capacity building, or all of these?	• What is our hope or vision, our aspiration for our community?
Example 1: *Attend or watch Workshop on Asking for Help or Reducing Stigmas*	Example 1: *Increase personal capacity of self/ class as peer-advocates for mental health*	Example 1: *Every member of the university community feels welcome, safe, supported, cared about, and included.*

References

Ganz, M. (2014). *Organizing: People, power, change.* Leading Change Network. https://commonslibrary.org/wp-content/uploads/Organizers_Handbook.pdf

Kansas Health Foundation. (2017). *Guiding your organization with a theory of change: Strategies, outcomes and impact* (pp. 1–75). https://kansashealth.org/wp-content/uploads/2017/04/ORS-Impact-TOC-Session-KHF-Learning-Conference-EXTERNAL-3-23-2017.pdf

Opsina. S. M., Foldy, E. G., El Hadidy, W., Dodge, J., Hoffman-Pinilla, A. & Su, C. (2012). Social change leadership as relational leadership. In M. Uhl-Bien & S. M. Ospina (Eds.), *Advancing relational leadership: A dialogue among perspectives* (pp. 203–225). Information Age Publishing.

Session 7.12 "Naked" Leadership

Session Description

In this session, the facilitator leads an exploration of the inner work that is necessary to be a leader. Participants will discuss whether leadership is all about accumulation of knowledge, skills, and contacts or if there is also a simultaneous, somewhat paradoxical, stripping away that is crucial to being a leader. The facilitator will also introduce the concept of spirituality to leadership.

Learning Objectives

Participants will do the following:
- Articulate one to three ways they are armored up and one to three ways they can strip down and understand what it means to be a "naked leader"
- Identify the inner processes of leadership development according to key spiritual teachers
- Explore what "stripping down" looks like as leaders and come up with three ways they can further strip down as leaders

Leadership Competencies Addressed

Intercultural Mindset
- Actively engages in opportunities to expand worldview

Effective Communication
- Exhibits effective listening skills

Self-Knowledge
- Seeks opportunities for continued growth
- Practices self-compassion, friendliness, ease with self, and vulnerability

Principled Action
- Demonstrates congruence between actions and values

Key Concepts and Definitions

"Stripping down"	Liberating oneself from all the layers of duties and social status that the society puts on us.
"Naked leader"	One who is able to be free from societal and inner pressure caused by various statuses in society.
Spirituality	According to *Sounds True* founder Tami Simon, "the word *spiritual* points to a dimension of our experience that can never be seen under a magnifying glass or measured or explained or proven. It is the ultimate mystery. It is that dimension of our experience that fills us with inexplicable love and calls us to give beyond reason. It can't be nailed down because it is infinite; it can't be defined because it is dynamic and ever-changing" (Simon, 2016).

"Spirituality is recognizing and celebrating that we are all inextricably connected to each other by a power greater than all of us, and that our connection to that power and to one another is grounded in love and compassion. Practicing spirituality brings a sense of perspective, meaning, and purpose to our lives" (Brown, 2010).

Religion	"[Religion is] a system of symbols (creed, code, cultus) by means of which people (a community) orient themselves in the world with reference to both ordinary and extraordinary powers, meanings, and values" (Albanese, 2012).
Faith	In the Christian New Testament, the Greek word translated for "faith" is *pistus*, which can also mean trust. Faith is trusting in something that cannot be proven with scientific fact. Faith is mysterious. Hence the phrase "a leap of faith." Faith is trusting in something enough to orient one's life by that faith.
Mindfulness	Vietnamese Buddhist monk and author, Thich Nhat Hanh states, "I define mindfulness as the practice of being fully present and alive, body and mind united. Mindfulness is the energy that helps us to know what is going on in the present moment."
Joy and happiness	Happiness is based on what is happening around us. Joy is based on what is happening within us.

Required Materials

- PowerPoint slides and appropriate technology (optional)

Pre-Session Assignment:

- Each participant should write down their top 10 content-related takeaways from the RLF program so far. They should also write down the top 10 takeaways that they have learned about themselves so far in this program.
- Participants should do the "Observing Anew" exercise at least once by following this prompt: *Really take the time to observe something that you normally don't even think twice about doing or seeing (e.g., drinking a cup of coffee, brushing your teeth, washing your hair, looking at a tree you pass every day on your way to class). This time, pay close attention to what you are doing or observing and jot it down.*

Session Outline

Session duration: 1 hour and 25 minutes

Time Required		Description
10 minutes	Introduction	Introduce the session by explaining the concepts of "naked leadership" and "stripping down." Lead the participants in a mindfulness meditation exercise to set the tone and focus for the session.
20 minutes	Framing	Refer to the "Observing Anew" exercise participants completed prior to the session. Ask participants to share their thoughts and reflections on the exercise. Shift participants' focus to their top 10 takeaways list they created prior to the session. Ask participants to share what they wrote in their lists. Ask participants what they learned through writing their lists.
10 minutes	Discussion	Explore with participants the rich wisdom that spirituality and mindfulness can add to the topic of "naked leadership." Give an expansive understanding of spirituality/religion in order that most participants can connect. Ask participants to offer examples of their own connection to spirituality/religion/faith/mindfulness as well as examples they see in spiritual leaders that they look up to—first in pairs and then with the whole group. Explore commonalities and differences.
25 minutes	Activity 1	Divide participants into groups of three. In their groups of three, participants will practice the skill of listening to understand and not to refute. Ask each participant to speak for five minutes on a topic of their choosing to the other participants in the group. Ask the listening participants to reflect on and repeat what they heard. Rotate through until each participant has had a chance to speak once and listen twice. Call participants back to the larger group.
10 minutes	Activity 2	With all participants back in the larger group, explore the role of joy as a foundational aspect to leadership through a game "Coffee Pot." In the game, ask one participant to think of an activity that they do. Then have the group try to guess that activity by asking questions of the person, substituting "coffee pot" for the activity. For example, "Can you 'coffee pot' outside? etc. The group continues to ask questions until someone figures out the activity. Explain the importance of joy as an element of "naked leadership."

Time Required		Description
10 minutes	Conclusion	Briefly recap key concepts. Discuss with the participants what they have learned in today's session about what it means to be a "naked leader." End the session by asking the participants to identify what inner work they are interested in exploring about themselves, what they want to start doing more intentionally, and what they want to stop. Ask participants to complete the session evaluation using your desired format. Close the session by thanking the participants.

Reflection Questions

- What inner work am I interested in exploring about myself?
- What do I want to start doing more intentionally as a result of this session?
- What do I want to stop doing as a result of this session?

Supplemental Resources

Albanese, C. L. (2012). *America: Religions and religion.* Cengage Learning.

Brown, B. (2010). *The gifts of imperfection: Let go of who you think you're supposed to be and embrace who you are* (1st ed.). Hazelden Publishing.

(Jody) Fry, L. W., & Egel, E. (2017). Spiritual leadership. *Graziadio Business Review, 20(3).* https://gbr.pepperdine.edu/2017/12/spiritual-leadership/

Gieseke, A. R. (2014). *The relationship between spiritual intelligence, mindfulness, and transformational leadership among public higher education leaders* (Publication No. 3617784) [Doctoral dissertation, Northeastern University]. ProQuest Dissertations & Theses Global.

Panico, C. R. (2013). Naked leadership: Lead to win hearts and minds. *Business & Professional Ethics Journal, 32*(3/4), 259–270. https://www.pdcnet.org/bpej/content/bpej_2013_0032_0003_0119_0130

Simon, T. (2016, April 10). *Standing for the spiritual, in a secular world* [Audio podcast]. https://resources.soundstrue.com/podcast/standing-for-the-spiritual-in-a-secular-world/

Participant Reflection

Throughout the session, Vogele highlighted the importance of inner work, reflection, and savoring the present moment. To be an effective leader you must lead from within. The more leadership positions and responsibilities you accumulate, the more vital this inner work—mindfulness, reflection, and spirituality—becomes. As a group, we participated in a guided meditation from Thich Nhat Hanh's The Blooming of a Lotus. This has become one of my favorite mindfulness activities and I regularly do it during the workweek.

RLF 2019-20

This session has been formatted and revised for consistency and clarity. The original session in the Rockefeller Leadership Fellows Program was facilitated by Nancy Vogele, reached at nvogele@gmail.com.

Session 7.13 Leading Creative Collaborations

Session Description

In this session, the facilitator will explore lessons from design thinking in order to help participants learn to lead creative problem solving in group settings. Participants will engage in a series of discussions, group exercises, and a problem identification exercise on improving community.

Learning Objectives

Participants will do the following:
- Examine lessons from design thinking, in particular the necessity for creative collaboration in problem solving
- Explore the process of creative collaboration through a problem identification exercise on improving community in small groups

Leadership Competencies Addressed

Collaboration
- Acknowledges and listens to different voices when making decisions and taking action
- Fosters a welcoming and inclusive environment

Self-knowledge
- Takes appropriate action toward potential benefits despite possible failure

Effective Reasoning
- Employs creative thinking in problem solving

Management
- Develops appropriate strategies for effective teamwork

Key Concepts and Definitions

Design thinking   A critical tool for effective problem identification, team process, and idea generation. Defined as the combination of knowledge, skills, cognitive processes, and attitudes relevant in design, design thinking helps create effective solutions. It focuses on idea generation from the ground up: exploring the status quo and evaluating problems before jumping into the solution generation.

Creative collaboration   This allows for a group of people to create an inclusive and judgment-free space that allows for ideation to take place.

Required Materials

PowerPoint slides and appropriate technology (optional)

Pre-session Assignment:

- Ed Catmull, HBR 9/2008. How Pixar Fosters Collaborative Creativity (https://hbr.org/2008/09/how-pixar-fosters-collective-creativity)
- Cracking the Code of Sustained Collaboration (https://hbr.org/2019/11/cracking-the-code-of-sustained-collaboration)
- Kelley, T. (2016). The Perfect Brainstorm. In *The art of innovation* (pp. 53-66). Profile Books.

Session Outline

Session duration: 1 hour and 30 minutes

Time Required		Description
10 minutes	Introduction	Introduce design thinking to participants. Use anecdotes and examples when explaining design thinking. Give the example of the GE Engineer, Doug Dietz, who designed an MRI scanner for kids with the design thinking framework.
30 minutes	Framing	Explain the various design thinking lessons and strategies that can be employed while problem solving. Introduce the idea of creative collaboration and corresponding examples.
20 minutes	Activity	Divide participants into groups of four. Participants will brainstorm solutions to improving community in their social circles. Each group goes through the problem identification exercise, using strategies they learned during the presentation.
10 minutes	Debrief	Call participants back to the larger group. Ask each group to explain their creative collaboration process and the solutions they came up with.
10 minutes	Reflection	Summarize the previous exercise and what participants have accomplished and explored in their groups. Ask participants to share what they learned and observed through this exercise.
10 minutes	Conclusion	Ask participants if they have any further questions and discuss implications of design thinking for management and leadership. Ask participants to complete the session evaluation using your desired format. Close the session by thanking the participants.

Reflection Questions

- How do we address the most vital issues of today's reality while living in the illusion of normalcy?
- What are tools and strategies from design thinking you can apply to problem solving?

Supplemental Resources

Kelley, T., & Kelley, D. (2013). *Creative confidence: Unleashing the creative potential within us all.* Currency.

Kelley, T., & Kelley, D. (2012, December 1). Reclaim your creative confidence. *Harvard Business Review, 90*(12), 115–118. https://hbr.org/2012/12/reclaim-your-creative-confidence

Liedtka, J. (2011). Learning to use design thinking tools for successful innovation. *Strategy & Leadership, 39*(5), 13–19. https://doi.org/10.1108/10878571111161480

Lorenzo, R. (2017, October). *How diversity makes teams more innovative* [Video]. TED Conferences. https://www.ted.com/talks/rocio_lorenzo_how_diversity_makes_teams_more_innovative

Mugadza, G., & Marcus, R. (2019). A systems thinking and design thinking approach to leadership. *Expert Journal of Business and Management, 7*(1), 1–10.

Pokras, S. (1994). *Team problem solving* (M. Crisp & F. Lundy Ruvolo, Eds.). Course Technology Crisp. https://ebookcentral.proquest.com/lib/dartmouth-ebooks/detail.action?docID=3116989 (Original work published 1989)

This session has been formatted and revised for consistency and clarity. The original session in the Rockefeller Leadership Fellows Program was facilitated by Peter Robbie, reached at peter.robbie@dartmouth.edu.

Participant Reflection

In a creative economy, it is critical that leaders facilitate creative collaboration and apply design thinking. This requires observing a situation, defining the problem, and using creative ideation. It is far easier to tone down an idea than to pump up an idea, so Professor Robbie encouraged us to think outside the box and think big. In the workforce, it can be easy to get tied down with constraints and this piece of advice has helped me keep my creative juices flowing.

RLF 2019-20

Session 7.14 Activism and Institutional Change—Tools for People-Powered Policymaking

Session Description

In this session, the facilitator will focus on previous work with those who have served as agents for change. While referencing multiple examples in which political leaders have fulfilled their campaign promises, participants will learn how to galvanize public support to achieve sustainable institutional change. Participants will examine a case study that challenges them to analyze the policy-making process from multiple perspectives and the role of social mobilization within that process.

Learning Objectives

Participants will do the following:
* Identify and understand three different tactics needed to make change both inside and outside institutions
* Assess two personal leadership situations to see whether they call for larger social mobilization or behind-the-scenes negotiation
* Gain a better understanding of their own preferred leadership style

Leadership Competencies Addressed

Effective Communication
* Acknowledges and appropriately communicates in situations with divergent opinions and values

Intercultural Mindset
* Contextualizes social identities and experiences

Effective Reasoning
* Integrates multiple types of information to effectively solve problems or address issues

Principled Action
* Bases actions on thoughtful consideration of their impact and consequences

Self-Knowledge
* Continually explores and examines values and views

Key Concepts and Definitions

Social mobilization   A process that raises awareness and motivates people to demand change or a particular development. It is mostly used by social movements in grassroots groups, governments and political organizations to achieve a particular goal, and in most cases, the process of social mobilization takes place in large gatherings, such as processions, demonstrations, marches, and mass meetings.

Policy-making process	Public policy refers to the actions taken by the government—its decisions that are intended to solve problems and improve the quality of life for its citizens. A policy established and carried out by the government goes through several stages from inception to conclusion, including agenda building, formulation, adoption, and implementation.
Marshall Ganz Public Narrative	How the story of self, the story of now, leads to a story of us which is used as a communication tool to galvanize support during the public policy-making process.

Required Materials

- PowerPoint slides and appropriate technology (optional)
- Handout 7.14.1 Role-play Worksheet

Pre-session Assignment:

- Participants should read a government study/report on a selected issue (e.g., Cannabis legalization, reproductive rights, etc.) of your choice. Include two or three examples of differing views on the issue in your preparations.

Session Outline

Session duration: 1 hour and 15 minutes

Time Required		Description
10 minutes	Introduction	Introduce yourself and your story. Focus on past experiences working with those who are agents of change and your work in social movements and making institutional changes.
15 minutes	Framing	Explain social mobilization and the policy-making process to participants. Define the key concepts and use examples to bring them to life.
10 minutes	Discussion	Describe a political leader's campaign promise for effecting reform in a chosen issue (healthcare, education, environment, poverty, etc.). Introduce and analyze the different stakeholders involved in the chosen case situation with participants.
20 minutes	Activity	Give out Handout 7.14.1 and divide participants into groups of three or four to work on the case study. Ask participants to assume different roles in their group, such as a small business owner, researcher, student. Each participant will analyze the information given in the case study based on their role.

Time Required		Description
		Afterwards, participants will present and explain whether they support the law or not according to their role within their groups. Each group will roleplay a discussion of the law and come to a consensus as a group.
15 minutes	Debrief	Call participants back to the larger group. Ask each group what the consensus they came to was and the reasoning behind their decision. Ask each group to share what occurred during their discussions.
5 minutes	Conclusion	Review key points and takeaways from the session. Ask participants if they have any further questions. Ask participants to complete the session evaluation using your desired format. Close the session by thanking participants.

Reflection Questions

- What am I most inclined to be engaged in: social mobilization or internal negotiation?
- When faced with particular problems that need to be solved, what kind of style suits the current context? Can this problem be solved quietly with internal players or does it need a larger public presence to pressure for change?
- How can I be more inclusive in making sure diverse voices are included in the decision-making process?

Supplemental Resources

Cannan, J. (2016). A (Mostly) Legislative history of the Defend Trade Secrets Act of 2016. *Law Library Journal, 109*(3), 363–386. https://doi.org/10.2139/ssrn.2775390

Participant Reflection

Shasti's own personal experience along with the interactive activity highlighted the importance of working with various, often conflicting, perspectives and gaining their support when creating change. While acting during our roleplay activity, I analyzed my own needs and truly listened to the needs of others in their roles. My reflections from the activity and Shasti's stories brought to life how difficult it is to reach a consensus yet how crucial that is to move a decision forward. Even today, this is a skill that I am actively working to improve on.

RLF 2019-20

Mahoney, J., & Thelen, K. Ann. (2010). *Explaining institutional change: Ambiguity, agency, and power.* Cambridge University Press.

Ryan, J. (2016). Strategic activism, educational leadership and social justice. *International Journal of Leadership in Education*, *19*(1), 87-100. https://doi.org/10.1080/13603124.2015.1096077

Ryan, J., & Tuters, S. (2017). Picking a hill to die on: Discreet activism, leadership and social justice in education. *Journal of Educational Administration*, 55(5), 569–588. https://doi.org/10.1108/JEA-07-2016-0075

The DO Lectures. (2015). *Steve Jennings | What matters, what's possible, and what's important: Entrepreneur amping up human potential* [Video]. DO Wales 2015. https://thedolectures.com/blogs/talks/steve-jennings-what-matters-whats-possible-and-whats-important?_pos=5&_sid=1fd2b87e8&_ss=r

This session has been formatted and revised for consistency and clarity. The original session was facilitated in the Rockefeller Leadership Fellows Program by Shasti Conrad, reached at shasti.conrad@gmail.com.

Role Play Worksheet

Situation

Cannabis legalization is a multifaceted issue; representatives across the U.S. are tasked with assessing the varying layers and perspectives on the matter. In New Hampshire, a cannabis legalization bill, HB 481, passed in the House, but its companion senate bill was delayed till January 2020. You are advising State Senator Martha Hennessy, NH Senate District 5, on whether or not to support legalizing cannabis in New Hampshire. As stated earlier, there are many components and positions to consider. The American Civil Liberties Union, a commission studying legalizing and regulating cannabis in NH, and The Police Foundation have, respectively, published reports highlighting the impacts, consequences, and benefits of legalizing adult-use cannabis.

Roles

> **Role A—Owner of a small-scale dispensary:** Your job is to bring forward the views of small and medium enterprises in the cannabis industry. Some of what you will be responsible for is representing business owners who have wanted to legitimize their businesses and participate in the cannabis industry, as well as utilize the same services (e.g., banking) available to businesses in other industries.

> **Role B—Marijuana policy project (research person):** Your job is to help advance policy proposals, utilizing key indicators and research to address the growing questions and concerns over legalizing cannabis.

> **Role C—Law enforcement officer:** Your job is to present law enforcement's unique viewpoints on this issue.

> **Role D—Constituent:** You are a constituent in NH. You can create your own story.

Individual Assessment: Your Role

Use this space to brainstorm the objectives and desired outcomes for your role.

Group Work:

Strategize: Write down each person's objective.

A

B

C

D

Action Plan: What is your combined plan for getting your solution passed?

Session 7.15 Leadership in Civil Society— Social Capital Building

Session Description

In this session, the facilitator will discuss the interrelationships among three political and social concepts: civil society, social capital, and leadership. Participants will explore a variety of factors that have hastened the decline in social capital in American society and will assess the challenges facing civil society leaders in communities across the nation. Participants will have a firm understanding of the nature of followership, civil society, and social capital. By the end of the session, participants will identify the qualities that best serve civil society leaders in creating and maintaining social networks and utilizing such networks for the common good.

Learning Objectives

Participants will do the following:
- Identify three unique characteristics of nonprofit leaders
- Assess the state of civil society in their social spheres
- Identify five opportunities and challenges in nonprofit leadership

Leadership Competencies Addressed

Collaboration
- Facilitates collective action toward common goals

Management
- Develops appropriate strategies for capitalizing on human talent
- Evaluates efficacy of current course(s) of action
- Identifies structure and culture of organization

Effective Reasoning
- Integrates multiple types of information to effectively solve problems or address issues

Key Concepts and Definitions

Civil society	The social and political space between the citizens and the state; organizations and networks in a society that are independent of the state/government.
Social capital	Institutions, relationships, and norms that shape the quality and quantity of a society's social infractions. The three dimensions of social capital are social networks, trust and reciprocity, and shared norms and values. Social capital can be conceptualized as acting in two ways: bonding and bridging.
Bonding	A term for the way that social capital is utilized to strengthen connections between homogenous groups.

Bridging	A term for the way that social capital is utilized to strengthen connections between heterogeneous groups.
Nonprofit/ Voluntary sector leadership	The capacity to mobilize and sustain multiple key relationships toward a common purpose.
Followership	The active participation of an individual in the pursuit of a common goal.

Required Materials

- PowerPoint slides and appropriate technology (optional)
- Poster-sized sticky-notes
- Markers

Pre-session Assignment:

- Shaiko, R. G. (2013, June 9). Admissions is just part of the diversity puzzle. *The Chronicle of Higher Education.* https://www.chronicle.com/article/admissions-is-just-part-of-the-diversity-puzzle/
- Bruni, F. (2015, December 12). The lie about college diversity. *The New York Times.* https://www.nytimes.com/2015/12/13/opinion/sunday/the-lie-about-college-diversity.html

Session Outline

Session duration: 1 hour and 30 minutes

Time Required		Description
20 minutes	Introduction	Introduce and explain civil society and social capital. Encourage participants to provide examples from both in the broader society and within their own social spaces.
20 minutes	Framing	Discuss leadership in civil society. Ask participants, what does it take to be an effective leader in civil society? Define nonprofit/ voluntary sector leadership. It is important to talk about followership as a complementary component of leadership, especially in the nonprofit and voluntary sectors.
15 minutes	Discussion	Ask participants to consider examples of social capital building in their social spheres. Encourage examples across various areas of life, from work to leisure to community. Discuss what leadership within these contexts looks like.

Time Required		Description
5 minutes	Framing	Define and distinguish bonding and bridging.
15 minutes	Activity	Divide participants into two groups, each with poster paper for recording their responses. Ask the groups to assess the abilities of civil society leaders in their social spheres to build social capital through bonding and bridging. Ask participants to consider how "bridged and bonded" their experiences are and to provide examples of each. Ask participants how many of their peers they "know." Have participants as a group decide what "knowing" their peers means.
10 minutes	Discussion	Bring the groups back together. Have participants report on their group's average of the estimated peers they feel they "know" within their social spheres. Have one participant from each group share the examples of bridging and bonding.
5 minutes	Conclusion	Conclude with your thoughts about social capital and the role it plays in building strong communities. Read the reflection questions for participants' consideration. Address any thoughts and remarks. Ask participants to complete the session evaluation using your desired format. Close the session by thanking the participants.

Reflection Questions

- Do I have required characteristics and inclinations to be a leader in a nonprofit sector?
- What are some examples of bridging and bonding experiences in my life? How could these experiences be improved?

Participant Reflection

I really enjoyed the opportunity to dissect campus and evaluate which organizations focused on bonding, which focused on bridging, and which focused on both. We realized that most organizations prioritized bonding over bridging. It could be easy to stay within your safety zone as "birds of a feather flock together" in bonding organizations. The bridging organizations were crucial for widespread social change. This session has helped me be more self-aware of my social capital and the networks I am involved in.

RLF 2019-20

Supplemental Resources

Bruni, F. (2015, December 12). The lie about college diversity. *The New York Times.* https://www.nytimes.com/2015/12/13/opinion/sunday/the-lie-about-college-diversity.html.

Putnam, R. D. (2000). *Bowling alone: The collapse and revival of American community.* Simon & Schuster.

Putnam, R. D., & Feldstein, L. (2003). *Better together: Restoring the American community.* Simon & Schuster.

Shaiko, R. G. (2013, June 9). Admissions is just part of the diversity puzzle. *The Chronicle of Higher Education.* https://www.chronicle.com/article/admissions-is-just-part-of-the-diversity-puzzle/

This session has been formatted and revised for consistency and clarity. The original session was facilitated in the Rockefeller Leadership Fellows Program by Ronald G. Shaiko, reached at ronald.g.shaiko@dartmouth.edu.

Session 7.16 Leading in an Intergenerational Work Environment

Session Description

In this session, the facilitator will address intergenerational differences and why they matter for the workplace and beyond. As emerging leaders, participants will be required to navigate multiple generations, experiences, perceptions, and beliefs about what leadership should look, feel, and sound like, all the while building their own presence, brand, and voice as leaders. Participants will role-play scenarios to learn to navigate areas of tension and reflect on how to apply the session to their current and future leadership. Participants will leave the session with a commitment to themselves and their leadership potential.

Learning Objectives

Participants will do the following:
- Provide three examples of leadership within self, groups, and systems that are required for transformational change
- Analyze three scenarios for how to navigate intergenerational work environments
- Commit to a change based on their reflections of what is required to thrive as leaders in diverse and intergenerational work environments

Key Concepts and Definitions

Transformational leadership	This leadership style acknowledges that change in people, policies, and practices requires change within self, change within groups/teams, and change within systems/organizations.
Intergenerational work environment	Differences in the work environment can be examined through the broader framework of generational identities, such as Gen X and Millennials. Generational differences may explain the multiplicity of working styles across lines of difference in race, socioeconomic status, background, and experience.

Leadership Competencies Addressed

Self-Knowledge
- Understands social identities of self and others
- Shows self-respect and respect for others

Effective Communication
- Acknowledges and appropriately communicates in situations with divergent opinions and values

Intercultural Mindset
- Understands, communicates with, and respectfully interacts with people across identities

| *Leadership presence* | The set of individual and collective actions one takes to shift the current reality. It is built (or diminished) through strong communication, resilience, and elegance in the face of conflict and meaningful relationships. |

Required Materials

- PowerPoint slides and appropriate technology (optional)
- Chart paper and markers

Pre-session Assignment:

- Haidt, J., and Lukianoff, G. (2015, September). The coddling of the American mind. *The Atlantic.* https://www.theatlantic.com/magazine/archive/2015/09/the-coddling-of-the-american-mind/399356/

Session Outline

Session duration: 1 hour and 35 minutes

Time Required		Description
10 minutes	Introduction	Introduce yourself and your background. Ask participants what they are most nervous or excited about in joining the workforce. Remind participants that it is always helpful to hear what others are thinking and feeling.
10 minutes	Framing	Remind participants that leadership is not about one's position, but about the individual and collective choices one makes to change reality. Define transformational leadership. Acknowledge as a leader navigating new environments and desiring to make long-lasting change in the status quo, one must always think through self, groups, and systems.
10 minutes	Discussion	Introduce participants to the areas of tension in the workplace that are often the result of generational differences in approaches to work but are extremely important for one's leadership presence. The areas are communication, navigating conflict, and building meaningful relationships.
30 minutes	Activity	Introduce the next activity and divide participants into groups of three or four. Present the groups with the following scenarios, featuring persons A and B. Scenario 1 is an email exchange in which there are, for example, poor communication skills, poor etiquette, or late responses.

Time Required		Description
		Scenario 2 is a difficult conversation: person A is giving feedback to a colleague across lines of difference—generation, race, or experience. Scenario 3 focuses on challenges to building meaningful relationships. Between each scenario, participants should record what their initial reactions were, how they would feel in either position, and what their perception are of the employer of their employees and their leadership. Ask participants to rewrite the scenarios.
20 minutes	Debrief	In the large group, ask participants how they rewrote the scenarios and why they considered the things they did. Ask participants what comes to mind when they consider how they might approach new relationships, conflicts, and communication as emerging leaders. Notice and discuss key trends in their responses and connect them back to the key concepts. Conclude the discussion with three key takeaways: to acknowledge the limitations of one's perspective—be curious, ask questions, and always seek to understand; to acknowledge that the impact of words and actions matters more than intent; and to understand and be aware of oneself and their relation to others—examine such things as the importance of identity, values, experiences, and orientations.
10 minutes	Reflection	Remind participants that they are all currently leaders and that they are currently navigating multiple relationships. Instruct participants to think of a recent moment in which they have engaged with a coworker, peer, professor, or boss and their communication was in some way off, their relationship was rocky, or they had to have a courageous conversation. Ask participants to consider how they would approach the situation differently. Have participants commit to doing something differently moving forward. Have three participants share their reflections with the group.
5 minutes	Conclusion	Conclude by making the point that regardless of age, social identity markers, or engagement with others, committing to work on one's self and potential growth is the first key to leadership success. Ask participants to complete the session evaluation using your desired format. Close the session by thanking the participants.

Reflection Questions

- What cues and perspectives of others younger or older than I might I be missing?
- Am I aware of the impact of my choices/decisions/words on others?
- In a difficult situation, do I think about how I am perceived by others? Did the impact match my original intention?
- Am I the leader that I want to be and am I showing up that way?

Supplemental Resources

Gottlieb, L. (2019, September). *How changing your story can change your life* [Video]. TED@ DuPont. https://www.ted.com/talks/lori_gottlieb_how_changing_your_story_can_change_your_life

Haidt, J., and Lukianoff, G. (2015, September). The coddling of the American mind. *The Atlantic.* https://www.theatlantic.com/magazine/archive/2015/09/the-coddling-of-the-american-mind/399356/

Lukianoff, G., & Haidt, J. (2019). *The coddling of the American mind: How good intentions and bad ideas are setting up a generation for failure.* Penguin Books.

Stillman, D., & Stillman, J. (2017). *Gen Z @ work: How the next generation is transforming the workplace.* Harper Business.

Twenge, J. M. (2017). *iGen: Why today's super-connected kids are growing up less rebellious, more tolerant, less happy— and completely unprepared for adulthood—and what that means for the rest of us.* Simon & Schuster.

This session has been formatted and revised for consistency and clarity. The original session was facilitated in the Rockefeller Leadership Fellows Program by Jessica Guthrie, reached at jessica.guthrie@gmail.com.

Participant Reflection

The activities were highly effective in showing the importance of being self-aware when communicating with colleagues, especially in an intergenerational workforce. Poor etiquette, a late response, or a terse reply can have long-term consequences. The case studies helped me understand that we are constantly being judged by how we present ourselves. We must do our best to understand the background of who we are working with to be effective communicators. I try to step into the other person's shoes and evaluate how I may be coming across to my peers and superiors.

RLF 2019-20

Session 7.17 The Art of Telling People What They Don't Want to Hear

Session Description

In this session, the facilitator will highlight the gap between the intellectual understanding of policies and the public perception of those same policies. Participants will gain an understanding of how people process policies and political messages. Participants will discuss how messaging, including language, images, etc., influences public perception of everything from products to policies, and how reframing can change the way people think about policies.

Learning Objectives

Participants will do the following:
- Recognize at least three differences between policy and persuasion
- Understand the power of language, imagery, and anecdotes, with three examples
- Recognize and use strategic communication in a group activity

Leadership Competencies Addressed

Collaboration
- Facilitates collective action toward common goals

Effective Communication
- Clearly articulates ideas in a written and spoken form
- Influences others through writing, speaking, or artistic expression

Effective Reasoning
- Employs critical thinking in problem solving

Management
- Develops and implements a plan for goal attainment

Key Concepts and Definitions

Framing   A technique employed by using deliberately chosen language to make listeners feel a particular way about something.

Wonks   A term for policy experts, researchers, and individuals who are interested in and knowledgeable about public policy.

Hacks   A term for politicians who implement policies and are skilled at communicating and connecting.

Required Materials

- PowerPoint slides and appropriate technology (optional)
- Video segment starting at 39:00

○   PBS Frontline. (2005). *The Persuaders* [Video]. https://www.filmsforaction.org/watch/
      frontline-the-persuaders-2005/

Pre-session Assignment:
•   Wheelan, C. (April 2007). Working paper no. 46: Wonks and hacks: How public policy
    programs can narrow the gap between good policy and good politics. *University of Chicago,
    Harris School of Public Policy*; Reed, B. (2004, March 1).
•   Bush's war against wonks. *Washington Monthly*. https://washingtonmonthly.com/2004/03/01/
    bushs-war-against-wonks/

Session Outline

Session duration: 1 hour and 25 minutes

Time Required		Description
5 minutes	Introduction	Explain how the different values and narrow interests of people make persuasion a critical tool for getting others to take action alongside a certain idea. Discuss examples of figures in politics who have successfully connected with people, even those they disagree with. Define and explain *wonks* and *hacks*.
10 minutes	Activity 1	Play the video segment from Frontline video on Frank Lutz. Start the clip at 39:00. Identify the strategies he used to change public opinion through messaging (e.g., changing the "Estate Tax" to the "Death Tax"). Define *framing* and conclude that Frank Lutz has had a lasting impact on the use of framing to shape and change public opinion.
30 minutes	Discussion	Ask participants for examples of instances in which language and framing influence public opinion (e.g., not "Pro-Abortion" or "Anti-Abortion," but "Pro-Life" and "Pro-Choice") and discuss. Discuss how people sometimes like "what's in the package," but not the "package" (e.g., some Republicans like what's included in Obamacare but not the name "Obamacare"). Ask for examples and discuss aspirational language used by figures like MLK or in movements like "Marriage Equality," where equality highlights one's aspirations. Conclude that framing is an essential tool for policy wonks as it enables them to further their policy ideas.

Time Required		Description
30 minutes	Activity 2	Divide participants into groups of four around the room. Each group will write a policy focusing on the language around specific policy examples. Each group will focus on the pro or con side of two issues; for example, the four groups may be pro-carbon tax, anti-carbon tax; pro-hard liquor ban, anti-hard liquor ban. Give participants time to work in their groups on a strategy to frame their argument to push their cause. Ask each group to choose a representative to present their ideas for reframing their given tax in order to either increase or decrease its appeal. Let each group present.
10 minutes	Conclusion	Reflect as a group on the process of experimenting with language to influence public opinion. Conclude with the implications of using this skill when faced with contentious issues. Ask participants to complete the session evaluation using your desired format. Close the session by thanking the participants.

Reflection Questions

- How can I use the material covered to be a better communicator at my institution around contentious and sensitive issues?
- As a leader, what strategies will you take to deal with contentious issues and what do you need to be aware of?

Supplemental Resources

Bakir, V., Herring, E., Miller, D., & Robinson, P. (2019). Organized persuasive communication: A new conceptual framework for research on public relations, propaganda and promotional culture. *Critical Sociology*, *45*(3), 311–328. https://doi.org/10.1177/0896920518764586

Brown, B. (2018). *Dare to lead: Brave work. Tough conversations. Whole hearts.* Random House.

Participant Reflection

Professor Wheelan's session increased my awareness of the role language plays in our everyday lives. I learned to choose words based on my audience's values as my words are what frame the situation. I realized a simple way of improving my communication was being more critical of my choice of words because of their power to alter my audience's perception. This revelation has made me more conscious in everyday life, from how politicians present issues to the public to how I interact with my colleagues at work.

RLF 2019-20

Egnal, B. (2016). *Leading through language: Choosing words that influence and inspire* (1st ed.). Wiley.

Greenberger, L. (2013). *What to say when things get tough: Business communication strategies for winning people over when they're angry, worried and suspicious of everything you say* (1st ed.). McGraw-Hill Education.

Harvard Business Review (2011). *Communicating effectively.* Harvard Business Review Press.

Patterson, K., Grenny, J., McMillan, R., & Switzler, A. (2012). *Crucial conversations tools for talking when stakes are high* (2nd ed.). McGraw-Hill Education.

This session has been formatted and revised for consistency and clarity. The original session in the Rockefeller Leadership Fellows Program was facilitated by Charles Wheelan, reached at charles.j.wheelan@dartmouth.edu.

Session 7.18 Don't Go It Alone—Effective Delegation and Empowerment for Leaders

Session Description

In this session, the facilitator will discuss the role of delegation and empowerment in effective leadership. Participants will analyze their own experiences with delegation, as well as the experiences of others through case analysis, and talk about best practices for delegating effectively. By the end of the session, participants will be equipped with strategies and practices that not only enable them to manage their time most effectively but also get the best performance out of those that they lead.

Learning Objectives

Leadership Competencies Addressed
Collaboration
• Acknowledges and listens to different voices when making decisions and taking action
• Facilitates collective action toward common goals
Management
• Develops appropriate strategies for capitalizing on human talent
• Prepares for leadership transition

Participants will do the following:
• Assess their current level of delegation within their leadership role
• Identify (1) what else could be delegated to others, (2) how it should be delegated using the EPO Model, and (3) to whom it should be delegated
• Describe action steps they will take to incorporate their improved delegation capabilities

Key Concepts and Definitions

Spiral of Despair   This describes the process employees go through when they feel ignored or underutilized. First, one might have hope and feel engaged and energized. Then, one might despair and feel frustration and confusion. Next, one is in a state of apathy and feels indifferent and alienated. Lastly, one is angry and feels frustration, and then worthlessness. This often leads to absenteeism.

Delegation   A shift in decision-making authority from one level of hierarchy to another. Responsibility, authority, and accountability are prerequisites for delegation. Responsibility means setting clear expectations about the assignment and results. Authority is demonstrated by giving appropriate power to make decisions. Accountability is willingness to accept responsibility for something that goes well or fails.

| *EPO Model* | EPO stands for effort, performance, and outcome. E → P: If I put in effort, will I succeed?; P → O: If I perform, will I get rewarded?; O: Do I value the outcome? |

Required Materials

- PowerPoint slides and appropriate technology (optional)
- Scrap paper
- Handout 7.18.1 Tangram Activity materials and instructions prepared for participants
- Additional space for half of the students to work in for Tangram activity

Pre-session Assignment:
- Oncken, W., Jr., & Wass, D. L. (1999). Management time: Who's got the monkey? *Harvard Business Review*, *77*, 178–189.

Session Outline

Session duration: 1 hour and 45 minutes

Time Required		Description
5 minutes	Introduction	Introduce yourself and provide instructions for the Tangram activity (Handout 7.18.1). Hand out small pieces of paper that tell participants what organization they are in (A or B) and their role (management or production). Instruct participants to join their respective groups. Separate the management teams into different rooms. Give the production teams their briefing information and explain that they will join their management team in 20 minutes.
40 minutes	Activity	Once the management teams are in their rooms, give them briefing information that tells them that they have 25 minutes to plan how the production team will assemble the "product." During this time, if the production team has questions or notes for the management team, deliver these messages to the management team. If the management team is prepared to call in the production team before the 20 minutes is up, they may. If not, call in the production team after 20 minutes. The final five minutes must be used for instruction before production begins. Once production begins, each team starts a timer. Management can watch but cannot speak or help with production. Once the product is complete, the team should stop their timer. Both teams work until production is complete. Log times.

Time Required	Description	
10 minutes	Reflection	Have groups come back together to discuss the activity and how they can learn from it. Share the production times for each team and go over the process each team went through. For example, how long did the management team take to call in the production team? What were the members of the production team feeling? What were the group dynamics between members of the management team? Emphasize the importance of communicating with production early and helping them construct their own blueprint. Conclude this discussion with talking about the importance of communicating information in a timely way so that program management, administration, and financial considerations or operations can operate smoothly. This is another way of building transparency as a leader.
25 minutes	Framing	Explain that most managers (in Tangram and real life) overestimate their ability to solve the problem on their own without input. Describe the "Spiral of Despair." Ask participants to define delegation before providing them with a definition. Describe delegation and the prerequisites of delegation. Lead a discussion of what delegation is *not*. Go over examples of why people do not delegate and ask participants to raise their hands if they have ever said these statements: *It will be quicker if I do it myself. I don't trust anyone else to do it correctly.* Explain that it is a critical leadership competency to be able to delegate; at some point in a career, one stops doing the work themselves.
20 minutes	Discussion	Have participants write down on a piece of paper the things that (a) they do better than anyone else, and (b) the things that are critical for the organization. Ask them to make a list of tasks they've done for an organization they are involved in over the last week. Now ask them to put an asterisk next to any of the tasks that fit into categories (a) and (b). Explain that anything that they didn't put an asterisk next to is something they should delegate to someone else.

Give participants the EPO model for thinking about delegating. To demonstrate the model, hold up a dollar and say: *The first person to come take this dollar from my hand gets to keep it.* Once a participant gets the dollar, discuss why others didn't go for the dollar. |

Time Required		Description
		Conclude by saying that EPO is in the eye of the beholder. Provide a summary of how to delegate: 1. Clearly define the task (P), 2. Pick the person with the necessary skills (E → P), 3. Provide resources and coaching (E → P), 4. Explain the value of the assignment to you and the organization (P → O).
5 minutes	Conclusion	Answer final questions from the participants. Ask for key takeaways and for participants to create an action plan to practice delegation in the next week. Ask participants to complete the session evaluation using your desired format. Close the session by thanking the participants.

Reflection Questions

- What are the tasks that (a) I do better than anyone else, and (b) are critical for my organization?
- What is currently on my to-do list that doesn't meet the above criteria?
- What obstacles stand in the way of me delegating these lower priority items to others? How can these obstacles be overcome?

Supplemental Resources

Clayton, M. (2014). *Business express: Delegating effectively: Develop a simple and practical process for delegating successfully*. Pearson Education.

Goleman, D. (2017). *Leadership that gets results*. Harvard Business Press.

Harvard Business Essentials (2005). *Time management: Increase your personal productivity and effectiveness*. Harvard Business School Press.

Thomas, G. (2015). *The gift of time: How delegation can give you space to succeed*. John Wiley & Sons.

Wujec, T. (2010, February). *Build a tower, build a team* [Video]. TED Conferences. https://www.ted.com/talks/tom_wujec_build_a_tower_build_a_team

Participant Reflection

Many leaders are prone to under-delegating and take on extra "monkeys," work that is better left to another colleague. We discussed the most common personal justifications used to avoid delegating work and why delegating was important and necessary for effective management. Dr. Fragale asked us to list all the tasks we do as least as well as anyone else and are critical to an organization and which tasks we had done in the past month. Anything on the first list but not the second was fair game for delegation. This thought activity has helped me identify tasks that I can delegate at work.

RLF 2019-20

This session has been formatted and revised for consistency and clarity. The original session in the Rockefeller Leadership Fellows Program was facilitated by Alison Fragale, reached at afragale@unc.edu.

Handout 7.18.1 Tangram Activity

INSTRUCTIONS: Cut out as many boxes from the role sheet as there are participants. Have participants draw their roles randomly and organize in their management and production teams.

Management and Production Team Roles

Management A	Management A	Management A	Management A
Management A	Management A	Management A	Management A
Management B	Management B	Management B	Management B
Management B	Management B	Management B	Management B
Production A	Production A	Production A	Production A
Production A	Production A	Production A	Production A
Production B	Production B	Production B	Production B
Production B	Production B	Production B	Production B

INSTRUCTIONS: Print enough tangram puzzles for each management team to have two, one cut into pieces and laid out and the other whole.

Tangram Figure

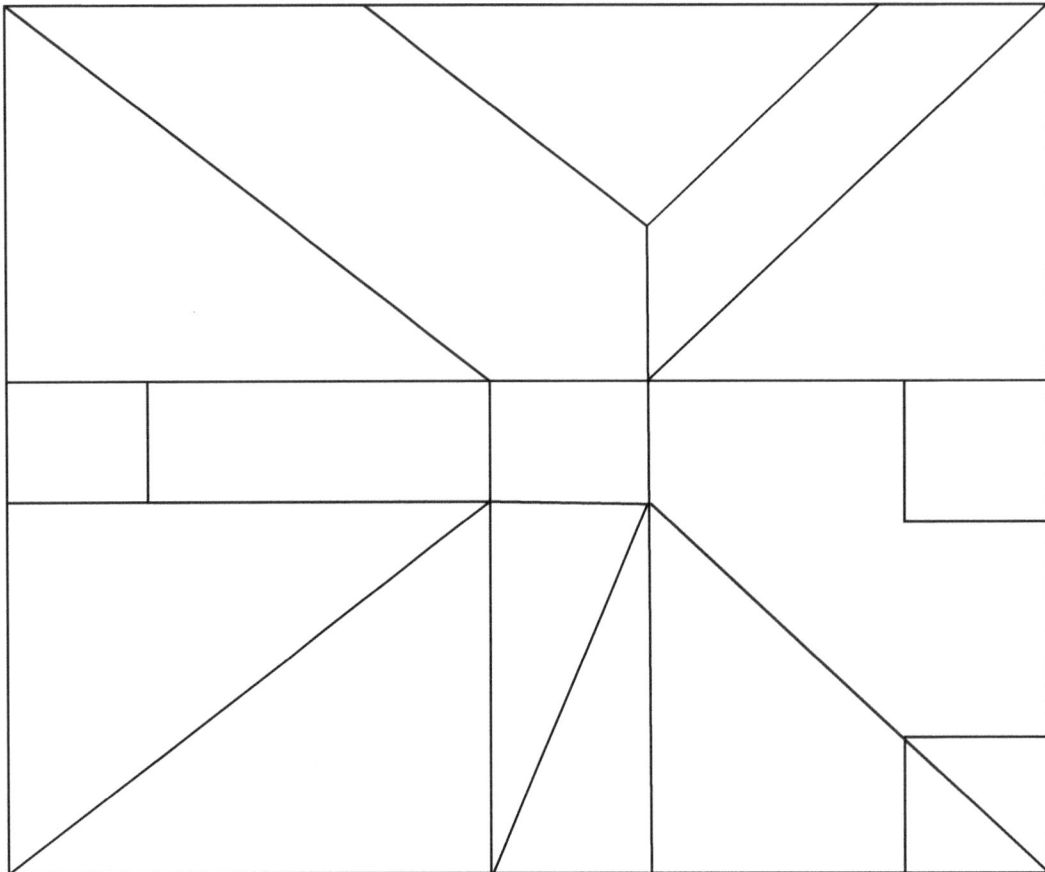

INSTRUCTIONS: Handout the briefing information to the management and production teams.

Briefing Information for Management Team

The table in front of you represents the "factory floor" and you are the management team of your organization, competing against the other organizations to see who can be "first to market" (once the plants all open) with their product. In other words, the first organization to produce their product accurately wins. The pieces on the table are the parts for your firm's product. When your production team properly assembles all of the pieces on the table, those pieces will form your firm's "product"—a large square containing an empty place in the middle. A schematic diagram of your firm's product (the assembled puzzle) has been provided to you.

YOUR TASK

- Plan how to instruct your production team to assemble your firm›s «product.»
- **_Your plant opens for production in 25 minutes._** You may call the production team and begin instructing them at any time during the next 20 minutes. The union contract requires that management give the production team **_at least 5 minutes of instruction before the plant opens for production._**
- **MEMBERS OF THE MANAGEMENT TEAM (I.E., YOU) MAY NOT TOUCH THE PIECES AT ANY TIME!** This is a union-shop. Only the production team can touch the pieces.
- Do not attempt to assemble the pieces into the product. That is the production team's job. See Point 3.
- Do not mark on the pieces. Management is not allowed to touch the pieces. See Point 3.
- Do not move the pieces. Management is not allowed to touch the pieces. See Point 3.
- **GIVE ALL INSTRUCTIONS TO THE PRODUCTION TEAM ONLY IN WORDS (WRITTEN OR SPOKEN).** You may not show the product diagram to the production team. You may not draw a picture of the product, either on paper or in the air with gestures.
- **THE PRODUCTION TEAM CANNOT TOUCH THE PIECES UNTIL THE PLANT IS OPEN FOR PRODUCTION (in 25 minutes).**
- After the signal is given that production can begin, management (i.e., you) is **NOT ALLOWED TO GIVE ANY FURTHER INSTRUCTION.** Stand back and observe.
- When the production team begins to assemble the puzzle, one member of your team should **time them** and record the time in minutes and seconds to give to the facilitator.

Briefing Information for Production Team

Your production team will have the responsibility of carrying out a task according to the instructions given you by your management team. Your task will begin 25 minutes from now. Your management team may call you in to give you your instructions any time during the next 20 minutes. If they do not summon you during the next 20 minutes, you should report to them at the end of the 20 minutes. You may send notes to the management team and they may send notes in reply. The facilitator will be happy to courier notes for you.

Once you have begun the task, your management team will not be allowed to give you any further instruction.

Session 7.19 How to Frame Three Hard Cases—Abortion, Same-Sex Marriage, and Affirmative Action

Session Description

In this session, the facilitator outlines debates over abortion, same sex marriage, and affirmative action. Participants will review the ethical and conceptual principles that are appropriate in framing these dilemmas in order to lead to genuine engagement rather than stalemate. They will explore these issues by considering how courts have approached these cases. By the end of the session, participants will find that the language of rights does not structure these debates in a constructive fashion and that as leaders, they can do better to avoid such language.

Learning Objectives

Participants will do the following:
- Identify the rights on both sides of the three debates on issues of same sex marriage, abortion, and affirmative action by reading excerpts from court cases
- Reframe these debates into "a conversation about reasons" instead of "a fight about rights"
- Reflect on two ways to avoid the language of rights in order to create a space for conversation when talking about controversial issues

Leadership Competencies Addressed

Self-Knowledge
- Continually explores and examines values and views
- Understands social identities of self and others

Effective Communication
- Acknowledges and appropriately communicates in situations with divergent opinions and values

Effective Reasoning
- Employs critical thinking in problem solving
- Employs creative thinking in problem solving

Key Concepts and Definitions

A fight about rights	This describes how people debate controversial issues such as same sex marriage, abortion, and affirmative action in the language of "rights," which ends the conversation or closes the debate.
A conversation about reasons	This describes a way to frame controversial issues that opens up a space for conversation and uses questions to ask for reasons.

Required Materials

* White board with markers
* Printed copies of the reading

Pre-session Assignment:

* Bedi, S. (2020). How to Frame Three Hard Cases: Abortion, Same Sex Marriage, and Affirmative Action. 1–19. Dartmouth College.

Session Outline

Session duration: 1 hour and 10 minutes

Time Required		Description
5 minutes	Introduction	Introduce the topics of gay marriage, abortion, and affirmative action to be discussed.
25 minutes	Activity	Divide participants into three groups, each to consider one of the three issues: same sex marriage, abortion, and affirmative action. Distribute the corresponding readings to each group to have them look over as they consider the following questions: *What are rights? How is same sex marriage/abortion/affirmative action often a fight about rights? How do opposing sides convey the issue as a fight about rights? What rights are they fighting for?* As groups discuss, circulate the room, spending time with each group and engaging in discussion with them. Ask them to share what they have come up with.
30 minutes	Discussion	Come back together and have a participant from each group share their answers to the discussion questions. Discuss the impact of evoking rights in a discussion: When people claim their argument is about *rights*, it effectively ends the discussion by polarizing the parties involved and closing off debate. Discuss how we can turn conversations about rights into conversations about reasons. Have participants discuss reasons for both sides of each issue (e.g., "What are the reasons for limiting marriage just to opposite sex couples?"). Ask participants how talking about issues in the language of *reasons* instead of *rights* opens up a conversation.

Time Required		Description
		Examples of guiding questions: • On the topic of abortion: Why is it important for Alabama to ban abortion even in the case of rape? … To save innocent lives…. But does Alabama force others to save innocent lives when they see a stranger in grave danger? … No… Why are only pregnant women forced to save innocent lives and sustain that life for nine months? *What are the reasons?* Why are these women not compensated for doing so? What are the obligations the man has under the law to sustain this life? • On the topic of affirmative action: Why is it important for elite colleges and universities to engage in affirmative action on the basis of race? Why is it important for elite colleges and universities to engage in affirmative action on the basis of legacy status? How does preferring applicants whose parents graduated from the college or university advance an elite university's mission?
10 minutes	Conclusion	Discuss how conversations can be reframed for each of the issues: in regard to same sex marriage, a conversation about whether society should only appeal to religious reasons to limit liberty; in regard to abortion, a conversation about how far society should go in forcing individuals to save and sustain an innocent life; in regard to affirmative action, a conversation about the mission of a university and how universities can best advance that mission in its application process. Reflect with participants on other difficult conversations they have or would like to have and encourage them to maintain a focus on reasons rather than rights in the future. Conclude the session by explaining why this is important to leadership. Ask participants to complete the session evaluation using your desired format. Close the session by thanking the participants.

Reflection Questions

• How are gay marriage, abortion, and affirmative action often a fight about rights?
• As a leader, how can I create a space for conversation instead of a fight about rights?

Participant Reflection

This session allowed me to take a step back from certain social "dilemmas" such as abortion, same-sex marriage, and affirmative actions and dissect the cases through understanding the power of language and emotion. This session allowed me to see how the use of framing exploits the strategic resonance of language, so that people process the substance of an idea as emotionally positive or emotionally negative. Moving forward, I will be able to recognize the influence of framing in our daily lives and remind myself that it is essential to question why people feel a certain way about certain topics.

RLF 2020-21

Supplemental Resources

Bedi, S. (2009). *Rejecting rights.* Cambridge University Press.

Bedi, S. (2013). *Beyond race, sex, and sexual orientation: Legal equality without identity.* Cambridge University Press.

Lusk, A., & Weinberg, A. (1994). Discussing controversial topics in the classroom: Creating a context for learning: Interpersonal and interactional aspects of teaching. *Teaching Sociology, 22*(4), 301–308. https://doi.org/10.2307/1318922

This session has been formatted and revised for consistency and clarity. The original session in the Rockefeller Leadership Fellows Program was facilitated by Sonu Bedi, reached at sonu.s.bedi@dartmouth.edu.

Session 7.20 Business, Strategy, Society, and Leadership

Session Description

In this session, the facilitator introduces the concept of business strategy and leadership in the context of a controversial social issue: same sex marriage. Participants will understand the interconnections and applicability of this session to the nonprofit and government sectors. By the end of the session, participants will have practice with a framework for developing business strategy and addressing crises.

Learning Objectives

Participants will do the following:
- Understand the definition of strategy and put it in their own words
- Examine the SWOT framework for developing strategy
- Apply the framework to a case study in a controversial context

Leadership Competencies Addressed

Intercultural Mindset
- Contextualizes social identities and experiences

Management
- Develops and implements a plan for goal attainment
- Manages multiple priorities

Effective Reasoning
- Employs critical thinking in problem solving
- Integrates multiple types of information to effectively solve problems or address issues

Key Concepts and Definitions

Crisis	A situation in which you need to make a decision without knowing all the information, often time-bound and unexpected.
Business strategy	A plan that is meant to achieve a certain goal or objective of the business. Leaders developing a business strategy consider company/organizational mission and goals, core values, consumers, brand, history, competition, resources, core competencies, and the market.
SWOT analysis	A framework that examines strengths, weaknesses, opportunities, and threats to help gauge the risks of any business strategy.

Required Materials

• Whiteboard

Pre-session Assignment:

• Create or find a case study that will present participants with an opportunity to practice business strategy and avoid crisis within a company or organization, fictional or otherwise. The casecenter.org is a valuable resource.

Session Outline

Session duration: 1 hour and 15 minutes

Time Required		Description
5 minutes	Introduction	Introduce the topic and why it's important for management and leadership. Use this time to introduce your experiences to the participants.
5 minutes	Framing	Ask if participants have prior knowledge or experience with strategy development. Ask participants to define *strategy* and discuss the goal setting and planning aspects of strategy. Ask participants to describe the difference between a strategy and a tactic: tactics don't have meaning or substance unless they are informed by a goal. Ask participants to define the term *crisis*. Provide a definition of crisis. Ask participants, based on what they have just learned, what it means for a company to develop a strategic framework? What must companies consider when developing a strategy? Define business strategy.
25 minutes	Discussion	Introduce the SWOT analysis framework. Ask participants to keep this framework in mind as they discuss the case study. Provide details of the marketplace and industry of the organizational case study (revenue, growth, users, etc.). Go through the four elements of SWOT for the chosen organization based on the case study summary.
30 minutes	Activity	Tell the group to imagine that you are the CEO of this organization. Divide participants into small groups of three or four to discuss how they might advise you to handle this crisis. After 15 minutes of discussion, a representative from each group will have five minutes to advise you. Ask clarifying questions of the representatives as they share so as to challenge them to elaborate on their thoughts and their reasoning, as they would in front of a real CEO.

Time Required		Description
10 minutes	Conclusion	Wrap-up the conversation and answer any questions from the participants. Ask participants to complete the session evaluation using your desired format. Close the session by thanking the participants.

Reflection Questions

- What is the "right" decision for the CEO? Why?
- How might the strategy frameworks help me personally?
- What implications does this have for the nonprofit and government sector?

Supplemental Resources

Neal, A., & Sonsino, D. (2012). *Developing a leadership strategy* (1st ed.). American Society for Training & Development.

Payne, K. (2017). e*Harmony Harvard Business case* [Thesis]. https://shareok.org/bitstream/handle/11244/317249/oksd_payne_HT_2017.pdf?sequence=1&isAllowed=y

Piskorski, M. J., Halaburda, H., & Smith, T. (2008). e*Harmony* (No. 709424-PDF-ENG). Harvard Business School. https://hbsp.harvard.edu/product/709424-PDF-ENG

Participant Reflection

The session was authentic and tangible because we were working with a real-life scenario. I vividly remember the role play activity where our group representatives met with the CEO. We learned actionable skills, such as the SWOT analysis, as well as soft skills, including knowing how to confront the unknowns and uncertainties in our lives, like the personality of those you will need to meet and work with. This experience has equipped me with the skills and confidence to be flexible when thinking strategically and dealing with the uncertainties of work and daily life.

RLF 2019-20

This session has been formatted and revised for consistency and clarity. The original session in the Rockefeller Leadership Fellows Program was facilitated by Curt Welling, reached at wellingcurt@gmail.com.

Session 7.21 Intrapreneurship—Becoming a Change Agent Within Your Organization

Session Description

In this session, the facilitator will introduce the concept of intrapreneurship. Participants will explore organizational structure and their role within it, looking for ways to make a positive impact. Specifically, participants will discuss effective ways to communicate with their supervisor and colleagues, increase their technical competency, strengthen their situational awareness and ability to understand context, and light a fire in their heart to match the mission of the organization.

Learning Objectives

Participants will do the following:
- Identify two ways they can become an agent of change within their organizations
- Identify two techniques for mobilizing people within their organization at all levels (horizontally, diagonally, etc.)

Leadership Competencies Addressed

Collaboration
- Builds and maintains partnerships based on shared purpose

Self-Knowledge
- Understands social identities of self and others

Effective Reasoning
- Employs critical thinking in problem solving
- Employs creative thinking in problem solving

Management
- Develops appropriate strategies for capitalizing on human talent

Key Concepts and Definitions

Entrepreneurship	Strategic change that increases the market value of a product or service through its resources or with the resources themselves.
Intrapreneur	An individual or leader who promotes innovation inside their organization.
Everett's Innovation Adoption Curve	"This is the mental process through which an individual (or other decision-making unit) passes from first knowledge of an innovation to forming an attitude toward the innovation; then to a decision to adopt or reject it; then to implementation of the new idea; and finally to confirmation of the decision to adopt the innovation." The diffusion of innovation curve highlights five types of people: innovators, early adopters (of ideas or products), the early majority, the late majority, and laggards (or skeptics). The early majority determine what will be "mainstream." The late majority join only after iterations that make the product or innovation more ubiquitous.

| *Formal and informal leadership* | Formal leaders are designated leaders with certain privileges and have the authority to take actions that informal leaders don't, like management responsibilities such as goal setting, hiring, and policy making. Informal leaders are people who are not officially titled as leaders but inspire and motivate their peers. Typically, they have excellent communication skills, are technically competent, and know how things work within the organization. They know how to get things done. |

Required Materials

• PowerPoint slides and appropriate technology (optional)

Session Outline

Session duration: 1 hour and 30 minutes

Time Required		Description
10 minutes	Introduction	Provide an overview of the session and expected outcomes for the session. Understanding organizational structure and roles within it are extremely important for identifying ways to make a positive change.
40 minutes	Discussion	Ask participants to think of an entrepreneur and the qualities of that person. Discuss entrepreneurs in the context of entrepreneurship, then connect that definition to the topic of intrapreneurship. Define intrapreneur and talk about how they are unique to other change agents in an organization, as well as how entrepreneurial traits can be used in other contexts, such as within an organization. Brainstorm and discuss with participants how intrapreneurs act in their organization. Present and explain Everett's Innovation Adoption Curve with input from participants.
20 minutes	Activity	Divide participants into groups of three or four and give them the task of making a plan to scale their program to 1000 participants. Ask them what they would do to inspire that change. After 15 minutes, ask a representative from each group to share their ideas.

Time Required		Description
15 minutes	Reflection	Discuss the role of formal and informal leadership within an organization and how to identify these individuals. Ask participants to think about examples of people in their organizations that embody leadership but do not necessarily have a formal title. Discuss with participants the characteristics that these people have that make them informal leaders.
5 minutes	Conclusion	As a group, discuss the reflection questions. Invite participants to ask any questions. Ask participants to complete the session evaluation using your desired format. Close the session by thanking the participants.

Reflection Questions

- How do you anchor yourself in such a way that you are laying the foundations for solid management and leadership?
- What are organizations made of and how do we as intrapreneurs address these concepts?
- When you face challenging situations in your organization, how will you respond?

Supplemental Resources

Blanka, C. (2019). An individual-level perspective on intrapreneurship: A review and ways forward. *Review of Managerial Science, 13*(5), 919–961. https://doi.org/10.1007/s11846-018-0277-0

McGrath, C., & Zell, D. (2001). The future of innovation diffusion research and its implications for management: A conversation with Everett Rogers. *Journal of Management Inquiry, 10*(4), 386–391. https://doi.org/10.1177/1056492601104012

Pielstick, C. D. (2000). Formal vs. informal leading: A comparative analysis. *Journal of Leadership Studies, 7*(3), 99–114. https://doi.org/10.1177/107179190000700307

Participant Reflection

We began the session by brainstorming entrepreneurs and the qualities we admired most about them. Innovation, risk-taking, self-driven, confidence were among the most common qualities listed. These traits were not unique to startups and could also be applied within organizations as intrapreneurs. Intrapreneurship requires both formal and informal leaders in order to create widespread support for change. Everett's innovation adoption curve highlighted the importance of focusing efforts on convincing the "early majority" of the value of change. The "late majority" would quickly follow and the "laggards" weren't worth worrying about. This session has encouraged me to seek opportunities for improvement and innovation despite working at a large corporation.

RLF 2019-20

Tuominen, K. & Ahola, T. (2011). *Intrapreneurship excellence criteria: Self-Assessment workbook: 37 probing questions and contrasting pairs of examples: How to identify intrapreneurial ways of thinking and acting?* Benchmarking Ltd.

White, L., Currie, G., & Lockett, A. (2016). Pluralized leadership in complex organizations: Exploring the cross network effects between formal and informal leadership relations. *The Leadership Quarterly*, *27*(2), 280–297. https://doi.org/10.1016/j.leaqua.2016.01.004

This session has been formatted and revised for consistency and clarity. The original session was facilitated in the Rockefeller Leadership Fellows Program by Joshua Marcuse, reached at jmarcuse@gmail.com.

Session 7.22 Building Your Credibility as a Leader Through the Quality of Your Work

Session Description

In this session, the facilitator addresses the emphasis in leadership literature on change and change management and challenges participants to consider how they can become agents for change within their organizations even as new hires. Leaders must have a creative vision for how to move their organizations forward, which includes identifying strategic change opportunities and readying their organizations to make those moves. But how do new employees create the credibility needed for the organization to trust their vision for change especially if their organization is in crisis? The facilitator suggests that one can build this credibility through the quality of work. That quality is a function of alignment with an organization's core values. By the end of the session, participants will know how they can build their credibility to contribute to and lead change efforts.

Leadership Competencies Addressed
Collaboration • Facilitates collective action toward common goals **Management** • Identifies structure and culture of organization **Self-Knowledge** • Demonstrates realistic understanding of one's abilities • Seeks opportunities for continued growth

Learning Objectives

Participants will do the following:
- Identify and discern how an organization's core values define product quality
- Demonstrate how to assess problems and create change through the lens of an organization's core values and definition of quality
- Develop awareness on how to translate the core values of an organization and their definition of product quality into professional credibility

Key Concepts and Definitions

Quality   The totality of features and characteristics of a product or service that bears its ability to satisfy stated or implied needs.

Credibility The work produced is what was promised, the work was produced with integrity, and the outcome of the work is reliable.

Organizational   Deeply ingrained principles that define all of an organization's actions.
core values

Required Materials

- PowerPoint slides and appropriate technology (optional)
- For each case group, a flipchart/easel and markers or notetaking materials

Pre-session Assignment:
- Srinivasan, A., & Kurey, B. (2014, April 1). Creating a culture of quality. *Harvard Business Review, April 2014.* https://hbr.org/2014/04/creating-a-culture-of-quality;
- Lencioni, P. M. (2002, July 1). Make your values mean something. *Harvard Business Review, July 2002.* https://hbr.org/2002/07/make-your-values-mean-something;
- Molinsky, A., & Newfield, J. (2017, Oct. 6) How to gain credibility when you have little experience *Harvard Business Review, October 2017.* https://hbr.org/2017/10/how-to-gain-credibility-when-you-have-little-experience
- Each of the participant groups will have one set of case documents on an organization, each from different sectors (private, nonprofit, business, etc.). Refer to Handout 7.22.1 to develop the handouts for this session. The first document should be provided to participants in advance of the session.

Session Outline

Session duration: 1 hour and 25 minutes

Time Required		Description
15 minutes	Introduction	Define and discuss quality, credibility, and organizational core values. Ask participants what it means for an organization to have core values. Ask participants how an organization defines quality. Discuss possible quality metrics.
20 minutes	Activity 1	Divide the participants into smaller groups of five to six. Groups should be based on the organization they read about prior to the session (see Handout 7.22.1). Each group will discuss and report out on the following: what they can discern about the organization's core values; what they can discern about the organization's product line; given 1 and 2, what they can discern about how the organization would define quality; given 1, 2, and 3, reflect on how you would demonstrate quality in your work to build your personal credibility as a new employee. Groups should take notes (on flip charts or paper) and should select a representative to report out.

Time Required		Description
10 minutes	Discussion	Lead a discussion based on organization-specific definitions of quality you have identified. From the first group exercise, ask participants how quality manifests differently depending on organizational values. Compare across cases.
20 minutes	Activity 2	In the same small groups, hand out the document for the second exercise which is based on an organizational change problem for the same organization they had previously assessed. Develop this change problem based on a real problem encountered by the organization (as reported in the news, a company's annual report, or case material from, for example *Harvard Business Review*). Given what they now know about their organization's values and definition of quality, ask participants to discuss and report out on (1) ideas for the change strategies that will be most effective for their organization and (2) why they believe these strategies will be most effective. At the end of 20 minutes, ask one participant from each group to share their findings.
10 minutes	Discussion	Ask participants to consider the extent to which the change strategies they identified as being potentially effective align with their organization's core values and would be viewed as enhancing quality. Facilitate discussion, especially around potential misalignment.
10 minutes	Conclusion	Pose the following reflection questions in the context of participants' employment: *What does demonstrating quality work look like for you now? How can you demonstrate through your work that you understand your organization's core values? If you have a change proposal, how can you pitch it to demonstrate its consistency with organizational core values and that it will enhance quality? What steps can you take in your work to ensure your organization will believe you?* Ask participants to complete the session evaluation using your desired format. Close the session by thanking the participants.

Reflection Questions

- How do I go about identifying my organization's core values, and how do I demonstrate them in the conduct of my work to build my personal credibility?
- How does my organization define quality, and what is the link between quality and core values?
- Are the changes I want to propose in my organization consistent with core values and would they enhance quality?

Participant Reflection

We were asked to deeply reflect on the connection between integrity and quality, how it is implicitly present in our and companies' values. Through this session, I learned the importance of the credibility I can gain from my diligence as that can lead to larger responsibilities and leadership in my career. When I began my first job after college, I experienced these lessons first-hand. After my first few months, I received positive feedback from my coworkers about my diligence. They immediately took notice of my attention to detail and the amount of effort I placed in my work, even in small tasks.

RLF 2019-20

Supplemental Resources

Jolles, R., & Tracy, B. (2018). *Why people don't believe you: Building credibility from the inside out* (1ˢᵗ ed.). Berrett-Koehler Publishers.

Kouzes, J. M., & Posner, B. Z. (1993). *Credibility* (Vol. 11). Jossey-Bass.

Oh, J., Cho, D., & Lim, D. H. (2018). Authentic leadership and work engagement: The mediating effect of practicing core values. *Leadership & Organization Development Journal, 39*(2), 276–290. http://dx.doi.org.dartmouth.idm.oclc.org/10.1108/LODJ-02-2016-0030

This session has been formatted and revised for consistency and clarity. The original session was facilitated in the Rockefeller Leadership Fellows Program by Allison Bawden, reached bawdena@gao.gov.

Generic Case Assignment

For each case, the instructor should pick an organization (public, nonprofit, or government sectors) that would be well known to participants. This organization should have identifiable core values based on publicly available documents and should have experienced a publicly reported challenge or crisis.

For the end of exercise 1 (using Case Document #1), the instructor should be prepared with answers to the part 3 questions that can be used as discussion prompts or to compare and contrast participants' answers across cases.

For the end of exercise 2 (using Case Document #2), the instructor should be prepared with answers to the part 3 questions that can be used as discussion prompts. In addition, the instructor should inform participants of the *actual resolution* of the crisis and draw comparisons with what participants recommended.

Case Document #1

The instructor should develop the first case document, provided in advance to participants, preferably by taking excerpts from publicly available sources. Sources could include an organization's website, annual reports, strategic plans, vision/mission statements, press releases, SEC filings, news articles, or corporate profiles. In addition, the instructor can use job search websites such as Glassdoor. This first document should create a position description for an entry-level employee at the organization.

PART 1: Organizational description. This should include enough information that the participant group can reasonably determine (1) the organization's core values and (2) the organization's products/services. It should also include enough information that the participant group, based on 1 and 2, can brainstorm about how the organization would define product quality given its values.

PART 2: Entry-level position description. This can be based on real information or can be developed by the instructor for demonstration purposes. Participants should be able to easily connect the position description to the organization's products/services and should have some information about how success in the position will be evaluated.

PART 3: Questions. The instructor should include the following discussion prompts for participants to cover (the same prompts for all cases).

> - What are this organization's core values?
> - What kind of work does this organization do/what does it produce/what services does it provide?
> - How do you think this organization defines quality?
> - From what you've read and any preexisting knowledge you may have of this organization, to what extent do you believe this organization's core values and definition of quality are in alignment?

> ➤ Based on the entry-level position description, what does "quality work" look like, and what would characterize your work for it to be viewed as credible?

Case Document #2

The instructor should develop the second case document, provided to participants at the start of exercise 2, preferably by taking excerpts from publicly available sources. The same sources described in Case Document #1 apply. This document should be short enough (limited to a single page) that students can quickly read it and participate in exercise 2. It should (a) challenge the organization's core values/credibility/quality, (b) require development of a change strategy, and (c) include the new employee in the development of that strategy.

PART 1: Event description. This should include a short description of the "crisis" event. This will include enough background to characterize the problem and factually explain what occurred.

PART 2: Change management challenge. This section should create a scenario for the participant group in their role as the new employee described in case #1, to participate in a team assigned to address the crisis.

PART 3: Questions. The instructor should include the following discussion prompts for participants to cover (the same prompts for all cases).

> ➤ Can you envision an approach to this situation that addresses the crisis, is consistent with the organization's core values, and would enhance the organization's product quality?
> ➤ What would you have had to have demonstrated in your work to be included on the change management team?
> ➤ Why would your organization's executives trust the recommendations made by the change management team?

Session 7.23 The Psychology of Change

Session Description

In this session, the facilitator will explain the "psychology of change" through leadership practices that address resistance in individuals, in others, and in organizational settings. Participants will learn about the many reasons why people resist change. Harvard Business School professor Rosabeth Moss Kanter identifies several: loss of control, excess uncertainty, unease with surprise, concerns about competence, more work, loss of face, ripple effects, past resentments, and fears that the change threatens one's way of doing things. Physician Dr. Mark Jaben, who researches the science behind resistance to change, notes that resistance is the judgment made by the brain that the proposal for change threatens what people are currently doing. Practically, resistance comes in the form of emotions or behaviors meant to impede change.

Leadership Competencies Addressed

Collaboration
- Facilitates collective action toward common goals
- Encourages, supports, and recognizes the contributions of others

Management
- Develops appropriate strategies for effective teamwork
- Identifies structure and culture of organization

Self-Knowledge
- Takes appropriate action towards potential benefits despite possible failure

Learning Objectives

Participants will do the following:
- Identify at least three adaptive barriers to change
- Explore and understand the psychological experience of change
- Introduce and explain the psychology of change framework
- Practice asking open, honest questions to elicit and understand people's feelings on change

Key Concepts and Definitions

Psychology of change	Psychology is the study of the mind and human behavior, especially as a function of awareness, feeling, or motivation. Change is to cause to be different or to transform. Put together, the "psychology of change" is the science and art of human behavior as related to transformation.
Technical change	A type of change where an expert has a clear solution to a problem and can work quickly through the problem.

Adaptive change	A type of change where stakeholders have to experiment to make progress and where working through the change requires learning.
Diffusion of Innovations Theory	There is a particular way in which people accept change. It is outlined in the Diffusion of Innovation theory by E.M. Rogers. In this theory he suggests that people react to change in several ways, some experiencing more resistance than others.
Emotional Change Curve	This model developed by Elizabeth Kubler Ross illustrates how people adjust to organizational change and it describes four stages.
Agency	The ability of an individual or group to choose to act with purpose. This breaks into two components: power (acting with purpose) and courage (having the emotional resources to choose to act).
Open, honest questions	An open, honest question is one where you are engaging others with different lived experiences and are seeking to demonstrate real listening and to gain understanding. In service of outcomes, these have objectives and plans that fully include and reflect all stakeholders, particularly traditionally marginalized people.

Required Materials

- PowerPoint slides and appropriate technology (optional)
- Open, honest questions handout (refer to Handout 5.6.2 in Chapter 5)

Pre-session Assignment:

- Hilton K, Anderson A (2018). IHI Psychology of Change Framework to Advance and Sustain Improvement. Boston, Massachusetts: Institute for Healthcare Improvement. (Available at ihi.org)

Session Outline

Session duration: 1 hour and 25 minutes

Time Required		Description
5 minutes	Introduction	Present the objectives, emphasizing that they will be exploring the psychological experience of change and the Psychology of Change framework, practicing open, honest questions to elicit and understand people's feelings on change. Invite participants to ask and answer questions throughout the session.

Time Required		Description
15 minutes	Discussion	In pairs, participants identify the changes that they have experienced in the past couple of months and how they have managed the change. After seven minutes, bring participants back to the large group. Ask participants to report their discussions. Share your personal experience regarding change and how you have experienced it. The objective is to enable participants to reflect on their own psychological experience of change.
30 minutes	Framing	Define technical and adaptive change by drawing on the participant examples from the earlier discussion. Identify other examples of adaptive barriers to change experienced in leadership roles, including lack of buy-in, confusing strategies, too much change at once, maintaining motivation, or inhibiting environments. Ask participants to discuss how they have responded to how others experience change as leaders.
		Ask participants to discuss why change matters and explain why it matters. Introduce the mindsets involved in change by explaining the diffusion of innovation curve. Introduce and explain the transition and emotions curve. Ask participants to discuss how they would map their psychological responses to a relevant experience of change over time in their lives.
		Introduce mindset shifts in dealing with our own and others' resistance. Describe how resistance can be good and how to work with resistance. Explain how to get people to do what they want to do instead of telling people what to do.
		Define the psychology of change and agency. Discuss how to activate people's agency. Provide an overview of the IHI Psychology of Change Framework. Focus on the strategy of co-producing an authentic relationship.
		Introduce the idea of asking open, honest questions. Define and explain the purpose of an open, honest question. Show how asking open, honest questions requires an open, honest mindset. Provide examples of open, honest questions.

Time Required		Description
20 minutes	Activity	In pairs, participants practice asking open, honest questions. Each participant will listen to their partner share their experience of a difficult and ongoing change they have had to encounter, what they are doing effectively, and how they can build from their strengths. After their partners are finished talking, participants will ask several open, honest questions. Then the participants will switch roles, sharing and asking questions.
10 minutes	Reflection	Ask participants to share what they noticed in asking open, honest questions. Ask participants to also share why they think open, honest questions are important in their work as a leader and what is difficult about the practice. Ask participants to discuss what stood out in the activity. Ask participants to share with the group their reflections during their pair activity.
5 minutes	Conclusion	Ask participants if they have any further questions. Provide additional resources for participants. Ask participants to evaluate the session using your desired format. Close the session by thanking the participants.

Reflection Questions

- Where do I encounter resistance to change in myself, in others and, going forward, in my organization?
- How can I activate my own and others' agency to move from feelings of resistance toward exploration and commitment?

Participant Reflection

This session felt very timely as we were facing significant changes with remote learning in response to the COVID-19 pandemic. Hilton emphasized the importance of "adaptive changes," changes that require learning and experimentation. We must overcome resistance to change by helping others understand why they want to change and make others feel invested in the change. A strategy Hilton suggested was exploring how others feel and why they are hesitant to change. At work, I am constantly trying to develop identify opportunities to improve the way organizations work. Applying Hilton's strategy has made it much easier to create organizational change.

RLF 2019–20

Supplemental Resources

Cohen, G. L., & Sherman, D. K. (2014). The psychology of change: Self-Affirmation and social psychological intervention. *Annual review of psychology, 65,* 333–371. https://doi.org/10.1146/annurev-psych-010213-115137

Dweck, C. S. (2007). *Mindset: The new psychology of success* (Illustrated ed.). Ballantine Books. (Original work published 2006)

Elizabeth Kübler Ross Foundation. (n.d.). *Kübler-Ross Change Curve®.* Retrieved March 13, 2021, from https://www.ekrfoundation.org/5-stages-of-grief/change-curve/

Graban, M., & Jaben, M. (2016, June 28). *Webinar recording: The science behind resistance to change.* KaiNexus. https://www.kainexus.com/continuous-improvement/webinars/the-science-behind-resistance-to-change/thanks

Institute for Healthcare Improvement. (2018). *IHI Psychology of Change Online Course.* http://www.ihi.org/education/WebTraining/Webinars/psychology-of-change/Pages/default.aspx?utm_source=IHI_Marketing&utm_medium=IHI_Expedition_Psych&utm_campaign=2020_Spring_Psych&utm_content=Redirect?utm_source=IHI_blog&utm_medium=how_to_make_change_happen&utm_campaign=2018_expeditions

Kanter, R. M. (2003, June). Leadership and the psychology of turnarounds. *Harvard Business Review, June 2003.* https://hbr.org/2003/06/leadership-and-the-psychology-of-turnarounds

Palmer, P. J. (2007). *The courage to teach: Exploring the inner landscape of a teacher's life* (10th anniversary). Jossey-Bass.

Rogers, E. M. (2003). *Diffusion of innovations* (5th ed.) Free Press.

This session has been formatted and revised for consistency and clarity. The original session was facilitated virtually in the Rockefeller Leadership Fellows Program by Kate Hilton, reached at kate.b.hilton@gmail.com.

Session 7.24 A Conversation with a Prominent Leader

Session Description

In this session, the facilitator will interview a prominent leader. Participants will watch and reflect upon the recorded conversation. The conversation, which consists of questions submitted by the participants themselves, deals with themes of personal leadership, managing stakeholders, and advice for the participants. Participants will discuss what resonated with them and use the conversation as a springboard for writing short, one-line versions of their own leadership philosophies.

Learning Objectives

Participants will do the following:
- Use the recorded conversation as a tool to reflect upon their own leadership philosophies and experiences
- Create a leadership one-liner by condensing their leadership philosophy into one or two lines

Leadership Competencies Addressed

Collaboration
- Acknowledges and listens to different voices when making decisions and taking action

Effective Communication
- Acknowledges and appropriately communicates in situations with divergent opinions and values

Effective Reasoning
- Develops personal reflective practice

Self-Knowledge
- Continually explores and examines values and views

Key Concepts and Definitions

Leadership philosophy   At the start of the program, participants are asked to write a statement of their leadership philosophy. Over the course of the program, they update their philosophy and their thinking according to new insights they are gaining. At the end of the program, they condense their personal leadership philosophy into one or two lines.

Required Materials

- Recording capability

Session Outline

Session duration: 1 hour and 30 minutes

Time Required		Description
45 minutes	Discussion	Prior to the session, record your conversation with your interviewee. Use the questions submitted by the participants prior to the conversation. Additionally, ask the speaker to provide advice for the participants as they graduate or enter the workforce. Request the speaker to reflect on something they wish they heard when they were in the position of the participants. Ask the speaker to explain such things as how they manage various, competing stakeholders and provide advice for working with multiple stakeholders; what their leadership philosophy is; how they stay level-headed and calm when under pressure; a reflection on the mistakes they have made in their career. End the conversation by asking the speaker to share final thoughts about their experience as a leader. Send the link to the recording to participants at the beginning of the session. Ask participants to review the recorded conversation. Discuss what struck them about the conversation and how they can apply it to their own situations.
10 minutes	Reflection	Ask participants to individually work on updating their personal leadership philosophies.
20 minutes	Activity	Divide participants into groups of three or four to discuss the conversation. Ask participants to focus on what struck them as they watched the conversation and what resonated with them regarding their own personal leadership philosophies. Then, participants will each work on condensing their leadership philosophy into a short "one-liner" with help from their group members.
10 minutes	Debrief	Ask one representative from each group to report back to the whole cohort with a summary of what the group discussed. Then, ask each participant to share their leadership one-liners.
5 minutes	Conclusion	Ask participants to share any final thoughts. Ask participants to complete the session evaluation using your desired format. Close the session by thanking the participants.

Reflection Questions

- How have I grown in my leadership capacities in the past few years?
- How can I use the advice in the conversation to guide me as I prepare to continue developing my leadership skills and competencies?
- How has my leadership philosophy changed and developed since the beginning of this program?

Participant Reflection

With only a few weeks left until graduation, the conversation with President Hanlon was bittersweet. President Hanlon emphasized that the next few years of our lives would require a lot of hard work and dedication. It was highly likely that we wouldn't be in our dream jobs, but we would learn something new about ourselves and each step would help us towards achieving our goals. This has been very helpful advice in my first job out of college. I am constantly trying to compete with myself and do a little bit better or learn something new to be the best version of myself.

RLF 2019-20

This session has been formatted and revised for consistency and clarity. The original session in the Rockefeller Leadership Fellows Program was facilitated virtually by Sadhana Hall, reached at Sadhana.W.Hall@dartmouth.edu, and Leslie Wagner-Ould Ismail, reached at Leslie.R.Wagner-Ould.Ismail@dartmouth.edu.

RLF Program Officer Reflection

by Leslie Wagner-Ould Ismail

My initial reaction to the Rockefeller Leadership Fellows (RLF) program upon joining the Rockefeller Center in December 2019 was a strong desire to go back in time to my undergraduate years and participate in something similar. As I attended session after session and interacted with participants and guest speakers throughout the winter and spring terms, I wondered how my past academic, career, and personal experiences might have been different, had I been a part of such a program in my senior year. Fortunately, it is never too late to learn, and the truly amazing thing about my first year as the program officer for the RLF Program is that, in addition to witnessing the growth of the fellows, I am learning alongside them.

I have been with the program for less than a year, yet I already recognize how transformational it can be for participants who put in the time and effort. They develop amazing self-awareness and skills to work more effectively with others and within organizations. They experience tremendous growth and are able to apply their learning to their current leadership positions and relationships. RLF alumni return year after year to talk to the current fellows about how RLF impacted their career trajectory upon leaving Dartmouth. All of these things make working with the RLF program rewarding, but most importantly I love being a part of a program that aims to develop compassionate, ethical leaders who can lead from ahead or behind and who strive to achieve good. This viewpoint of leadership is refreshing and reassuring, especially in our current times during which leadership appears polarizing, selfish, and transactional.

One of my most memorable experiences from this past year was the RLF Winter Retreat in January 2020. It was a half-day retreat on a frigid Friday afternoon and evening during the second week back after winter break. The fellows attended a session on intergenerational communication led by alumna Jessica G from the class of 2010, enjoyed each other's company during a cocktail hour and dinner, and bonded with a salsa dancing lesson. These events were educational and fun, but it was what came next that stands out to me almost a year later. Four Dartmouth alumni who had participated in past years of RLF ranging from the classes of 2002 to 2016 traveled back to campus to join the current class of fellows for an alumni panel at the retreat. They came from different majors, backgrounds, and career fields but were all confident, well spoken, and eager to share their experiences and advice with their successors. Moreover, they all spoke fondly of RLF and gave examples of the impact it had on their experiences post-Dartmouth. I could tell the current fellows were completely engaged by the way they leaned towards the guests, asked countless questions, and stuck around to talk after the retreat ended. They were eager to learn what to expect in interviews and in their first jobs. For many of the fellows, this alumni panel was a validating experience that confirmed the effectiveness of RLF and renewed their commitment to the program. The RLF program produces leaders who are ready to go out in the world and make a difference. This strong alumni network and their commitment to the RLF program and its mission years later is one of the most special things about the program and also one if its greatest strengths.

With that being said, my first piece of advice for starting or developing a program similar to RLF is to bring in diverse speakers. Participants come from all different majors and backgrounds and will end up in different careers, so it is important for them to engage with speakers from various sectors. The Rockefeller Center also demonstrates value for diversity and inclusion by intentionally inviting speakers from different backgrounds. Another strategy that has been successful for RLF is to bring in alumni to lead sessions or participate in panel discussions. Participants love to hear about the career trajectories of professionals who were in their shoes not too long ago, and they appreciate the opportunity to practice networking skills. Sessions led by alumni are particularly meaningful for RLF participants.

Another important piece of advice for creating a program such as RLF is to be intentional about modeling what you are teaching program participants. This is another thing I love about working for the Rockefeller Center. I have been able to practice many of the lessons learned in RLF as I reflect on my own programs, work with my team to accomplish group objectives, and contribute to the overall mission of the organization. Students who participate in programs such as RLF can see that we practice what we preach. There is no shortage of examples from within the Rockefeller Center that can be given to support session topics.

One last suggestion for developing a program like RLF is to be intentional in the selection of the cohort and community-building. RLF has a unique recruitment process that is run by the participants themselves. They market the program to rising seniors across campus with the hopes of attracting applicants from all different majors and backgrounds. This ensures that multiple perspectives are brought to the table and prepares participants for their future careers and experiences, which will undoubtedly require interaction with diverse individuals. Once the new cohort is selected, much emphasis is placed on building cohort cohesion. Fellows are assigned accountability partners or groups that they meet with regularly, and team building takes place at fall and winter retreats and at the beginning and end of some sessions. This sense of community creates a comfort level that encourages fellows to be open with one another, which in turn leads to group cohesion and a better learning environment.

When I joined the Rockefeller Center as the program officer for the Rockefeller Global Leadership Program (RGLP) and the Rockefeller Leadership Fellows Program (RLF), I felt much more confident about my role and ability to contribute to RGLP than to RLF. I was new to leadership education and did not know what to expect from RLF or if I would be able to contribute anything to the program beyond planning and logistical support. Now, going into my second year of RLF, I feel much more confident in my own leadership abilities, and I can honestly say that I have experienced tremendous professional and personal growth as a result of my involvement with RLF and the Rockefeller Center as a whole.

My initial reaction when I first started learning about RLF and my feelings at the conclusion of the academic year were the same: I wish I had participated in something similar as an undergraduate. The aim of RLF is to develop participants' leadership skills by focusing on self-awareness, working as a team, and working within an organization. It aims to develop compassionate, ethical leaders who can lead from ahead or behind and who strive to achieve good. The idea is that leadership happens at all levels.

The main way the program accomplishes its objectives is with guest speakers who lead sessions that allow participants to reflect on a variety of topics related to leadership. Participants apply these lessons to their current leadership positions and relationships on campus and think about how they will play out after graduation. I was so impressed by the participants' ability to deeply reflect on their strengths and weaknesses and their strong motivation to improve themselves. I loved seeing them engage with the speakers and the content, and experience so much growth, and I was excited by the growth that I was experiencing as well.

I found myself enthralled with the guest speakers' sessions! The topics were as relevant to me as they were to the participants. I learned concrete strategies to delegate more effectively, to foster dialogue instead of debate, and to be a leader even when not in a position of leadership. I have started developing vocabulary for many of the leadership skills that I learned indirectly. I know that this will make me a more effective leadership educator and team member, and I feel motivated to continue learning. I am excited about continuing to learn from the speakers and participants in the years ahead.

One of the amazing parts of being a staff member at the Rockefeller Center is that the staff is intentional about modeling what we teach program participants. Because of this, I have been able to practice many of the lessons learned in RLF as I reflect on my own programs, work with my team to accomplish group objectives, and contribute to the overall mission of the organization. Students who participate in programs such as RLF can see that we practice what we preach. There is no shortage of examples from within the Rockefeller Center that can be given to support session topics.

One of the last sessions of the academic year focused on the psychology of change. This topic was especially relevant this year as we all adapted to a remote teaching and learning environment amid a global pandemic. I feel lucky to be a part of a team that handled this change so seamlessly and who modeled flexibility, adaptability, and positivity for program participants. As we prepare to begin a new academic year remotely, Sadhana Hall and I are implementing a variety of changes to the RLF program that were inspired by the remote spring term. We are excited to offer RLF asynchronously for the first time, opening it up to participants who have time conflicts or who are off campus.

I conclude this reflection by reiterating that it is important to bring in diverse speakers—if you are creating a program like RLF. Participants come from all different majors and backgrounds and will end up in different careers, so it is important for them to engage with speakers from various sectors. Another strategy is to engage alumni to lead sessions or participate in panel discussions. Participants love to hear about the career trajectories of professionals who were in their shoes not too long ago, and they appreciate the opportunity to practice networking skills. Sessions led by alumni are particularly meaningful for RLF participants. I cannot emphasize enough the importance of selecting your participants intentionally and prioritizing community building as a strategy. The recruitment process is one way in which students 'own' their program and establish bonds among themselves and invest in its future. This sense of community creates a comfort level that encourages fellows to be open with one another, which in turn leads to group cohesion and a better learning environment.

8 | Ideas for Online Learning

If you want to teach people a new way of thinking,
don't bother trying to teach them. Instead, give them a tool,
the use of which will lead to new ways of thinking.

— R. Buckminster Fuller

Communication technology is at a point now where online education has become a reality and we are headed toward widespread online leadership education. This thought was expressed by a colleague when we were discussing issues related to online education. I agreed with him. The trends to move to online learning and working remotely had already begun to gather momentum. COVID-19 simply accelerated that pace, which led to changing the way we deliver programs. If we look further, it is also changing how we provide care and manage or lead organizations. I do acknowledge that not everyone has the luxury of working from home and there are essential workers who are still offering programming in person. It also remains the case with healthcare workers and other essential workers who continue to provide services.

This chapter provides an account of how my colleagues and I adapted our programs and have moved to online programming because of COVID-19. Like many other colleagues, we had a short turnaround time to move our in-person program to online programs, and we were forced to see ourselves and our leadership programs in a new light. We were required to dig deep down within ourselves and draw upon our sense of creativity and our determination that we would offer the programs virtually. Flexibility and the ability to adapt to the new or the unexpected were the vital traits of leadership that we all relied upon then and continue to rely upon now. We also had to work hard to learn various technologies to adapt our in-person programs to a virtual format.

Though we shifted all our leadership offerings to online platforms, the co-curricular programming continued to follow Kolb's Experiential Cycle of Learning and the Learning Zone Model. There was no time to research, study, and come to conclusions about what a virtual format would look like; we simply did the best we could, just as everyone does and needs to do in times of emergency. Until the spring term of 2020 concluded, we were not able to reflect on the relevance of the Seven Pillars of Design, on which our Rocky programs are based. Despite this, the strength of the Seven Pillars of Program Design carried us through that time of ambiguity and change. Subsequent review of literature on online learning revealed that we were merging the Community of Inquiry (CoI) Model with Kolb's Experiential Cycle of Learning without even being aware of it.[1] The new insights we developed resulted in the articulation of the eighth pillar, **participant**

learning and empowerment, described in the introduction of this book. Participant learning and empowerment is not new to us, but it certainly deserves its own pillar.

This chapter is devoted to facilitating effective teaching and learning in a virtual format. Before I begin, I want to acknowledge that although some of us are newcomers to the world of online learning, it has existed for a long time. Now speaking from the recent experiences of teaching an online course and working with the Rockefeller team members to adapt our programs to a virtual format, I recognize how much more there is to learn about online teaching. The Rockefeller Center mainly offered opportunities for synchronous learning, which happens in real time with participants and facilitators interacting with one other. Asynchronous learning, by contrast, takes place without real-time interaction. There are many hybrid learning models which are a blend of both asynchronous and synchronous online learning for our team to explore. Our sudden need to determine how to convert our live programming to synchronous virtual programming was immediate. We were able to also incorporate asynchronous instruction. Now that we have seen the success and the flexibility in our asynchronous programming, we plan to offer more of these learning experiences in the future.

So, what are my thoughts about these two ways of offering learning experiences to participants? Plan for synchronous sessions, asynchronous sessions, or a combination of the two, using the Eight Pillars of Program Design.

Some educators believe that in-person courses and programs are more effective than online learning formats. Through this recent experience of moving to virtual programming, I believe the fundamental pillars of program design are the same and that the two formats are simply different in style, not substance. In a virtual format, we need to carry over our learning from in-person programming on the innovative practices in delivering content, engaging learners, and creating a space in which our participants can have control and agency over their own learning. While human contact and connection in-person are wonderful, we can "reach out" through our screens and make authentic connections with each other. As facilitators of online learning, we need to be willing to share our authentic selves and organize content in such a way that it not only strikes the imagination of our learners but, at the same time, inspires them to take control of their own learning. We can also create community and cohesion so that we, as well as the participants, feel supported and build lifelong friendships and relationships.

Recall that we discussed the Eight Pillars of Program Design in detail in Chapter 2. These were Intentionality, Structure, Theoretical Grounding, Rigor, Community, Reflection, Assessment and Evaluation, and Participant Learning and Empowerment. In this chapter, I will review how these pillars might or might not work in a virtual format. The chapter also includes practical tips for facilitating and helping others to facilitate in an online environment, some technological considerations, and a few concluding thoughts.

How One Might Move to a Virtual Format

Earlier, I mentioned that transitioning from an in-person format is a matter of change in style, not in substance. Once the flurry of program implementation ended, I took a moment to review the existing seven pillars of design upon which our programs were originally built and discovered they were naturally applicable to a virtual format. I also discovered that we needed to have an eighth pillar. This is an account of how the eight pillars were addressed or not addressed by the transition to a virtual format.

Eight Pillars of Program Design in a Virtual Format

Although I mention the Eight Pillars of Program Design as separate and distinct categories again in this chapter, they are interrelated, build upon each other, and inform each other. If you adopt this framework, please take the time to notice how they influence each other.

Intentionality: Incorporating intentionality within the virtual sessions meant we had to consider the additional implications of what it meant for students to not be on campus and instead learning from home. Once again, participants and their needs rose to the top of our concerns. We recognized that in addition to adjusting to a virtual format, some students, as well as presenters, faced additional constraints not normally found in an in-person session. These included such things as poor-quality internet, differences in time zones, and distractions found from working at home. Crafting a program that addressed these considerations was critical. We needed to acknowledge these difficulties and demonstrate flexibility at the beginning of the program in order to make participants comfortable. For example, we encouraged participants (registered in the program) with poor internet connection to return to the session(s) without worrying about being disruptive to others. Another action taken was to allow the option to keep their cameras off while attending the program. This allowed participants who felt uncomfortable about their surroundings being visible to participate freely without feeling embarrassed or violated.

What conclusions can we draw from this sense of discomfort? On the one hand, it is important to have an understanding that when having their camera on, students are allowing us into their homes, into their space. For a variety of reasons, they may not be feeling comfortable having us there. At other times, we may not feel comfortable being there and seeing what we see on their cameras. On the other hand, there are other faculty members who feel that keeping the camera on promotes engagement and mitigates multi-tasking. This is a challenge all of us face and I believe that there is no right or wrong answer because it is context-specific.

There are other considerations while offering programs online. Program staff were forced to very quickly consider that participants were often looking at a brightly lit screen for hours at a time, engaging in Zoom call after Zoom call. Giving everyone stretch breaks or quiet time to contemplate an idea away from the screen was a way to address this. It was done frequently throughout the programs offered by the Rockefeller Center. Additionally, through a virtual medium, understanding how to address the communication styles of introverts and extroverts in the room rose again to the top of our concerns—being inclusive to both was critical. Reflective activities off-screen also drew introverts into the program as it gave them time to think and rest from the screen as well.

Uma A., class of 2023, reflected on her time with the Center's Civic Skills Training Program that was offered virtually for the first time. Here is an insight into how an introvert developed confidence:

> One CST lesson that stands out to me is… [the speaker's] public speaking session. As a naturally introverted person, I have struggled with expressing myself to others. When [the speaker] told us that public speaking is every time that we speak, it resonated with me because I often felt the same nervousness while speaking in class, to peers, or on Zoom as I do when formally addressing a crowd. [The speaker's] lesson, like each CST lesson, provided practical advice on how we could improve our professional skill set. In the case of public speaking, [the speaker's] advice on reminding yourself of what you want to improve right before speaking not only helped me develop professionally but also personally. I am so grateful for this lesson as my ability to speak confidently and assertively has allowed me to contribute to workshop discussions among staff of varying levels of seniority, to ask clarifying questions whenever I needed, and to express my ideas and passions more effectively. I appreciate all of the professional and personal growth that my First-Year Fellows experience has sparked in me, and I look forward to pursuing more opportunities through Rocky throughout my remaining time at Dartmouth.

Structure: Establishing structure in a virtual context meant addressing additional nuances. We were fortunate to have a wealth of tools and platforms at our disposal. Structure calls to mind the "who, why, what, when, where, and how," and we used these questions to guide our technology selections and implementation. When we looked at who was planning to participate in the programs, not surprisingly, we noticed that in two programs (Management and Leadership Development Program and the Rockefeller Global Leadership Program), participant enrollment dropped because many opted to do the program in the future. The Rockefeller Leadership Fellows Program did not suffer much because only two formal sessions were left in the spring term as a continuation of the year-long commitment, and they went very well. The facilitator for one of the sessions was very experienced with online teaching. For the other session, we invited participants to submit questions and used these questions to interview a guest speaker. We then provided the recording of the interview to the participants. They reviewed the recording before the session and we used the planned session time to discuss the speaker's views on management and leadership, what participants had learned, and how the learning from this session applied to them.

Turning back to our own experience in implementing online programs, expectations of enrolled participants made us not only learn how to use online tools but also work hard to make interactive sessions meet participant expectations.

Our programs needed to be housed in a platform that would allow an open, easy channel of communication with participants and that would host additional program materials such as submitted pre-work assignments. For Civic Skills Training (CST), we recognized that Unified Communication and Collaboration platforms were being widely adopted in response to remote work because they enable users to work together in one space. For example, we opted to house the Civic Skills Training Program in Microsoft Teams to help students become accustomed to this type of collaboration platform, commonly used in professional environments before their fellowships. Through the instant message feature, we could post announcements and reminders, and engage in quick chats. Canvas and Google Classroom were used for other programs to reach similar results.

Our programs also needed a synchronous component for the sessions. At the time we went online, we opted to use Zoom because of the various features such as polls, chat sessions, and breakout rooms this platform offers. All these features offered ways of both adding variety to these sessions while addressing different goals. More recently, many other video chat platforms have advanced to offer similar or the same capabilities that may be suitable for a particular context and allow users to consider other options as well.

The most significant change in this pillar was in how facilitators worked with us to prepare for their sessions. They, too, wrestled with ideas and with technology and worked hard to retain the interactive nature of their sessions. I attended discussions with the facilitators and learned that a majority were unfamiliar with remote teaching and learning. Those who were familiar willingly shared their expertise and advice. It was an honor to belong to such a committed group of educators, scholars, and practitioners who helped the Rockefeller Center maintain its dedication to deliver virtual programming.

The Session Proposal Form (Handout 2.5 in Chapter 2) we typically use to design our in-person programs was the most helpful tool in conversations with all the facilitators. Conversations focused on whether the learning objectives would remain the same; how key concepts and definitions and corresponding activities would need to be adapted; what reflection activities would work; and how the session would flow. Prior to the actual sessions, we also introduced practice sessions for speakers who were not comfortable with technology. These practice sessions also helped staff to assist the facilitators because they were aware of when and how to help with technology tools. This was additional work for speakers and program officers, but they did it willingly. I believe that this approach not only made the session implementation rigorous, but it also gave facilitators a chance to develop their comfort with implementing their sessions. It was marvelous to see how helpful and patient participants were when some aspect of technology did not work as well as planned.

In some cases, the speaker was able to use all of Zoom tools on hand to deliver the content. Table 8.1 is an example of how Kate Hilton, a Rockefeller Leadership Fellows Program facilitator, adapted her in-person session to a virtual format using a few tools (e.g., chat function and breakout rooms). While this was "new" at the time, the main point is that there are so many tools that can be used to make a session lively and mimic an in-person experience. Table 8.1 uses a part of her session proposal form to show how she adapted her in-person session to a virtual format.

Table 8.1

In-person Session Versus Its Adaptation to a Virtual Format

Time Required	In-Person Description	Virtual Description
5 minutes	**Introduction** Present the objectives, emphasizing that they will be exploring the psychological experience of change, psychology of change framework, and practice of using open, honest questions to elicit and understand people's feelings on change. **Invite participants to ask and answer questions throughout the session.**	**Introduction** Present the objectives, emphasizing that they will be exploring the psychological experience of change, psychology of change framework, and practice of using open, honest questions to elicit and understand people's feelings on change. **Invite participants to use the chat function to ask and answer questions throughout the session.**
15 minutes	**Discussion** In pairs, participants identify the changes that they have experienced in the past couple of months and how they have managed the change. After 7 minutes, bring participants back to the large group. **Ask participants to report their discussions.** Share your personal experience regarding change and how you have experienced it. The objective is to enable participants to reflect on their own psychological experience of change.	**Discussion** **Using breakout rooms**, put the participants into pairs. In pairs, participants identify the changes that they have experienced in the current pandemic and how they have managed the change. After 7 minutes, bring participants back to the large group. **Ask participants to type what they discussed using the chat function. Choose one participant to read out the responses in the chat. Call on other participants to share their experiences verbally by unmuting themselves.** Share your personal experience regarding change in the pandemic. The objective is to enable participants to reflect on their own psychological experience of change.

In this comparison of the first 20 minutes of her session, notice how Hilton in the introduction encouraged the participants to use the chat function. By doing this, she accomplished two things: She clarified her expectation of how participants will participate in the virtual setting, and she introduced the specific tool (chat function) they could use to ask questions and give answers. In the next activity, the discussion in pairs was now shifted to a discussion in pairs in a breakout room, which allowed participants the opportunity to express thoughts in a private setting. She then created the space for everyone (introverts and extroverts) to use the chat session and share their feelings. She took it to another step by asking participants to verbally express their thoughts by "unmuting" themselves. Hilton then established a personal connection with participants by sharing her own experience. She brought this personal experience to life by sharing pictures of her family pre- and post-COVID-19.

In other cases, creativity was needed in changing how to present content that seemed, at first, impossible to adapt. Perhaps Fuá Nascimento's session in the Rockefeller Global Leadership Program is the best example of how to address the same learning objectives while accommodating the lack of in-person interaction. Nascimento's in-person session brings forth a lively discussion on intercultural difference using physical activities such as dancing and singing. He teaches participants *Capoeira*, which is a Brazilian martial art that combines elements of dance, acrobatics, and music. These activities often make participants uncomfortable at first because of the general unfamiliarity for some students from the U.S. or other cultures of singing in groups and the physical proximity the dance form requires. In addition to the unfamiliarity and the proximity, it also is the very act of letting go—physically, mentally, and emotionally that push participants to be uncomfortable and thus enter the Learning Zone.

In the virtual format, physical closeness was not an option. So, in the virtual adaptation, Nascimento started with a solo performance, which the participants replicated via practicing in front of their own cameras. Further, Nascimento did an excellent job of developing prompts that enabled difficult discussions in breakout rooms about customs and cultural practices that influence individuals and societies. He visited each breakout room while these discussions were taking place.

Nascimento also created space for personal writing and reflection. All these activities made the participants uncomfortable at first, but we could see them becoming more comfortable as the session progressed. The in-person and virtual sessions were necessarily different but met the same objectives. In Table 8.2 is a comparison of evaluations for his in-person and virtual sessions. You can see that participants gave similar feedback despite the difference in format.

Table 8.2

Evaluations of In-person Versus Virtual Session

In-Person Session Comments	Virtual Session Comments
• How to lean into being uncomfortable. • It pushed me out of my comfort zone. • I loved how uncomfortable it was in the beginning and how comfortable it became. Also, the physical activity was a fun way to focus. • Loved the engagement and enthusiasm! • Good chance to get close with the cohort. • Learned a lot more about Brazilian culture.	• He did great on getting us to relax and open up. • It was very engaging, and I liked the physicality of it. I also liked that it really pushed me outside of my comfort zone. • I like that he forced us to be physically involved. • I liked his energy. • I really enjoyed how he got everyone to tell stories about themselves and shed their armor.

I have highlighted the positive comments in Table 8.2. Constructive comments for Nascimento's session mirror what we often observe in the virtual format of delivering content: Limit screen time by shortening a session to "essential-to-know" information and include "good-to-know" information in handouts and required readings, TED Talks, etc.; accept that participants will process their sense of discomfort in different ways, and some will be more uncomfortable than others; understand that not everyone will be comfortable sharing their background in their home.

Theoretical Grounding: Kolb's Cycle of Learning and the Learning Zone Model have for a long time guided us to offer vibrant programs that strike the imagination of facilitators and participants. As we enter into virtual learning, we have had a chance to review their applicability. Much to our joy and satisfaction, we are still able to provide our participants with concrete experiences through which they can analyze, observe, and explain these experiences and apply the learning to their own reality. Our remote programs have endeavored to keep participants in their Learning Zone. Being uncomfortable with new knowledge is a prerequisite to true learning. The biggest area for improvement is to find additional ways to gauge participant responses, because it is hard to see reactions to content that were visible to us in our in-person programming.

Virtual learning and teaching have opened the door for educators and program managers to examine theories and documented best practices for online learning, and it opens the door to facilitators for countless opportunities. Some of them are referenced in this part of the book and support our personal experiences as newcomers to the world of online learning.

The Community of Inquiry (CoI) Model merits attention as we learn more and become better at delivering online programs in our foreseeable future. The CoI Model has three elements (see Handout 8.1).[2] It aims to create an understanding of cognitive and social processes in eLearning environments. The cognitive element of the model focuses on participant interaction with content: the way in which it is delivered by educators and the ways in which it is received and processed by participants. The social element in the model defines the type of engagement and interaction between participants, as well as the interaction between participants and educators. The third element of the CoI Model is the teaching presence:

> …to establish a teaching presence, an instructor must attend to the design and organization of the learning experiences; the design and facilitation of communication and interactive activities occurring between and among students, students and the instructor, and students and the content; and share content/ discipline knowledge and expertise through direct instruction.[3]

In thinking about all three elements I have referenced here and, in our effort, to make virtual programs even more responsive to participant needs, I believe we need to pay closest attention to the social element.

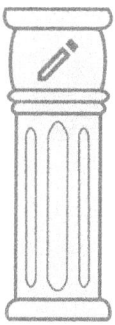

Rigor: Few of us ever feel like we have all the facts, information, and training necessary to feel prepared to implement a change, particularly if it requires us to make a sudden change. The short turnaround from in-person to virtual programming did not give us the time to research and study the theory and best practices in online learning. We did the best we could. We used crowdsourcing of information amongst ourselves as a team, consulted with other facilitators who were familiar with the programming, and taught ourselves the "essential-to-know" information related to online programming. In retrospect, we learned that the theories and practices that guide our programs still applied. The incorporation of technology and the remote program experience were new. Most of our time was spent in learning how to use it and deploy it as best as we could. We learned many lessons along the way. Perhaps the biggest takeaway for me from this experience was how the need as well as the willingness to adapt kept me in a learning mindset. It also created excitement within me and that generated a positive learning environment for me.

Community: Developing community happens in several ways. The Center's team responsible for implementing co-curricular programs is already a strong unit that is dedicated to implementing meaningful programs. The transition to virtual teaching and learning, however, added another angle to further strengthen our teamwork and community spirit. All of us became engaged disciples in learning how to use Zoom. Tutorials and regular discussions about what works and what does not work permeated our weekly staff meetings. Reading about online learning became a priority, and staff shared timely articles they had read with one another. This built a technology-focused learning community amongst us where we freely shared information and helped each other.

The next challenge was to consider how to build a sense of community in which participants feel supported by each other. I have observed that participant empowerment and growth are multiplied when participants feel that they are part of a community that shares successes and challenges. Everyone is faced with the challenge of trying to establish community in a virtual environment where members are geographically scattered. This said, it is important to create an intellectually supportive environment that is rigorous, encourages discussions and diversity of thoughts and is inclusive and respectful. To support this environment, we gave participants tools to help with team building, while also giving them the main responsibility for building a community in which they take pride. For example, participants in the First-Year Fellows Program were encouraged to create their own GroupMe, a messaging app where users can send group or private messages from their computer or phone using Wi-Fi. This way, they were invited to take control and ownership over their cohort connection. While we would offer community-building within the time all of us were together, outside of that, they had to put in the time. We made that very clear at the start of the program, we expected them to not only create a GroupMe, but also set up a time to meet virtually on weekends as well. I think that played a part in them becoming a cohort again and gave them an opportunity to get to know each other better.

We learned that assigning group projects is another way to build connections. For example, the First-Year Fellows Program divided participants into smaller self-selected groups to complete a project. As is normal, the groups went through the Tuckman's stages of group development.[4] But not being together physically did not deter them from completing the project. They were given deliberately vague guidelines for the project. We checked in with them and were mindful about not solving all their problems or answering all the questions they had. They simply had to struggle and come up with their own project parameters, the process they would use to complete the project, and the way they would deliver their findings in a paper and a presentation. We saw that participants rose to the challenge and not only completed the projects on time but also had unique insights to share. They also reported that they had become "close" and had established friendships they thought would last beyond the program.

Finally, organizing virtual lunch and dinner meetings and virtual games built a connection between program staff and participants in the First-Year Fellows Program. At the time of this writing, it has been over a month since the program formally ended and participants still reach out to me and the program officer with questions or concerns or even just to say hello.

Reflection: Reflection in the virtual format space looked different than it did before, but there were still multiple avenues to explore. In many of the sessions of the program, the chat function was used extensively as one way to provide additional opportunities to reflect among all the participants, which resulted in including those who preferred writing to speaking. Surveys that were sent after the session using Google forms were another tool used to invite participant reflection.

Another way to invite reflection on the content were check-ins with participants, as was done by the program officer responsible for the First-Year Fellows Program. The pre-COVID iteration of the program had only a mid-term check-in with the fellows housed together in Washington, D.C. during their fellowships with alumni mentors. The virtual program, by contrast, now had planned virtual check-ins with fellows throughout their fellowships—individually and in groups. These check-ins helped the program officer to discuss with participants not only how they were applying the content they had learned during the program thus far but also what new skills they were gaining and how they were doing physically and emotionally. As O'Shaughnessy

(2020) says, "Students are more open to learning when they are emotionally and physically regulated, feel connected to others, and have opportunities for meaningful engagement.... Survey your students often on what they need to feel engaged and connected."[5]

Assessment and Evaluation: Of the Eight Pillars, we found that Assessment and Evaluation largely carried over in the transition to virtual programs. The tools that the Rockefeller Center used to conduct participant evaluations were already online, so little changed in terms of resources. Additional evaluations became necessary to determine how the Rockefeller Center was best meeting the challenges of virtual instruction. The program staff asked questions related to participant reactions to virtual learning, structure of sessions, and tools used (polls, breakout rooms, chat) during the sessions. Evaluation, then, expanded its scope to include the tools the Center had at its disposal during its virtual programs.

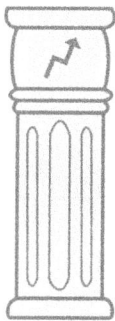

Participant Learning and Empowerment: In-person programs offer the opportunity to observe participants during their learning in a different way. As a facilitator, you think about something they say during a session, notice something that strikes their imagination, and even notice changes in their non-verbal communication. A chance meeting in the corridors where a hurried conversation takes place is yet another way in which you become aware of something in the session that resonated or did not resonate with them. So, how does this work for a remote environment? It places enormous responsibility on the facilitators to connect with participants. However, it is possible; it just takes more time and requires patience. I mentioned the frequent check-ins incorporated into the First-Year Fellows Program earlier. Another example is the Personal Leadership Challenge exercise, in which the program officer for the Management and Leadership Development Program meets with every single participant to discuss the challenge and provide coaching.

These examples create opportunities for building relationships with participants and empowering them to become actively engaged in their own learning. Empowerment, then, becomes an interdependent practice where facilitators encourage participants to chart their own paths both within the sessions and beyond them. I acknowledge that such approaches as the one-on-one check-in and the Personal Leadership Challenge take time and may not seem feasible for institutions that face staffing constraints, have less resources, or have a large number of participants. In such cases, group reflections can save time, or finding a participant or participants who can take the lead and get credit for organizing participant reflection groups might serve as an adaptation to approaches I have described. In all my years of working with communities and now in an academic setting, I have observed that there are always community members or students who are inspired and energized to take an opportunity to lead and give back.

Several examples of how we were able to get participants to become responsible for their own learning are shared in this part of the book. The Civic Skills Training Program described in Chapter 4 encouraged participants to develop a "virtual presence." In the first session, we discussed with participants their "virtual presence" based on our observations and a screenshot taken during the session. Participants observed such things as someone looking engaged, someone looking disengaged, or presumably engaged in another activity. Some looked bored while others looked distracted. Some simply looked unhappy. The discussion then progressed to how all these observations could have an unintentional impact on how a person is judged because of their virtual presence. It finally evolved into video log assignments (vlogging activities) where participants themselves identified their goals for developing a virtual presence, a few of which are quoted here:

> One thing that I want to focus on is smiling fully. I know that when I smile, after a while it becomes a little weaker and less convincing, so always working on maintaining that full smile! I also really liked the strategy mentioned by one of the groups of pinning the person you are addressing near the camera, so even if you are looking at their image, it appears as though you are making eye contact.
>
> —John K., class of 2023

> I will make sure to incorporate more smiling into my talking as well as my listening. I will also work to keep eye contact with the camera and try not to look off screen to gather or recall thoughts.
>
> — Paridhi K., class of 2023

> Although it may seem trivial, the First-Year Fellows Program taught me the importance of maintaining a strong Zoom presence. Whether it be fixing my posture, maintaining eye contact, or always having a smile on my face, these small fixes have made a massive difference in the interactions I have with my co-workers. I have also become more cognizant of people who have a "bad" Zoom presence. For example, some of the other interns I work with tend to look at their phones or browse the internet during our meetings. Although I hope I wouldn't have made those mistakes, I am very thankful to have learned these lessons before my program started.
>
> — Sienna H., class of 2023

Participants were assigned other vlogging prompts subsequently, asking them to reflect upon how they were managing their time, attention, work processes, communication, and expectations during CST and their summer fellowships. They were asked to record videos of themselves discussing elements of the preparatory course and what they expect from their remote fellowship work. Vlogging activities have helped participants to develop their virtual presence by practicing actions such as maintaining eye contact with the camera lens, presenting with engaging nonverbals, and managing their environment with, for example, a clean background, decent lighting, etc.

Finally, understanding information that has stayed with participants after they have completed the program is helpful in evaluating a virtual program. Sienna H., class of 2023, shared these insights with me after she completed the First-Year Fellows Program:

> Imposter syndrome is real, but you are not alone. Don't wait for your co-workers to reach out to you. If you want to build relationships, take on the responsibility of creating them. FYF provides you with an internship. You are in charge of making

it a meaningful and valuable experience from there. People generally want to help you. You just need to reach out. Positivity is often contagious and reciprocated.

And finally... the advice that I have received from FYF reminds me of Maya Angelou's quote: "People will forget what you said, people will forget what you did, but people will never forget how you made them feel."

Practical Tips for Facilitating and Helping Others to Facilitate

In this part of the book, I focus entirely on tips for those who are using their talents to design and facilitate eLearning experiences. So much of this has been learned through experience, and I refer to many authors who have provided wisdom through their writings.

Mindset: Most of us did not choose to work from home. It just happened and took us by surprise. Many of us have not had the time to truly reflect on the impact of COVID-19 in our personal lives. By all accounts, this situation may not change soon. So, we need to adopt a "growth mindset," as Carol Dweck (2007/2006) would say.[6] We also need to develop our own personal strategy to bring out the entrepreneur within us. I have found that creating a systematic personal and professional development plan and carving out a set amount of time in a week, month, or any defined period helps immensely. If you are a manager, help your team to do this as well. It takes a toll to navigate uncertainty and ambiguity, but telling yourself, "I don't know, but I'll figure it out" can be of immense comfort.

Self-Care: These are difficult times for all of us. One time or another, my colleagues and I have complained about Zoom fatigue and have preferred to just talk on a phone. It is important to acknowledge this fatigue and, at the same time, develop plans to address it. Quick breaks, deep breaths, meditation, taking short walks, using a standing desk, drinking lots of water, journaling, and spending time with family and people you care for are a few simple ways that help combat this fatigue. Since we need to support others, we need to take care of ourselves to be in the best physical, mental, and emotional state. So, "secure your own safety belt first," as Krause (2020a) would say.[7]

Participants are able to sense when you are stressed or overwhelmed even during an online learning experience. O'Shaughnessy (2020) notes, "Struggling to find files, links, or browser tabs can cause your stress level to rise, which students will feel and mirror. Close any programs that you won't be using and print out your agenda so that you don't need to frantically search for it on your screen." She further invites facilitators to share their reasons for feeling stressed with participants, as it only serves to humanize the facilitator-participant relationship.[8]

Involve Participants: Different ways of empowering participants and building community have been described earlier in this part of the book. This observation from Stachowiak (2019) strikes me:

> The role of a teacher is more than presenting concepts and having students present those same ideas back to us at some future time. By having students engage with

each other in classes, the richness of the interactions increases, and the learning deepens. Make student-to-student interaction more personable by making it easy for them to engage with each other, rethinking discussion boards, and using video for conversations.[9]

Another interesting way to engage participants in their own learning is to ask them to articulate their own objectives for the program.[10] You can then analyze themes from those responses and include the student-generated learning objectives in your session plans.

Deal with Participant Discomfort: I described the high points of Fuá Nascimento's session under "Structure" in this part of the book. We also received constructive comments for his session and these comments mirror what we often observe in the virtual format of delivering content. This is an important lesson from this session. We must accept that if we want participants to be in the Learning Zone, they will process their sense of discomfort in different ways, and some will be more uncomfortable than others. Help participants reach their Comfort Zone about information that makes them uncomfortable. This may mean additional time spent with the participants, but every minute is worth it! Understand that not everyone will be comfortable in sharing their background in their home and that standing up to practice in a session that requires physical moves needs to be accommodated in other creative ways.

Support Participants: Encourage participants and support them to carry momentum forward. Holding an attitude of accountability also means understanding the challenges participants face and, at the same time, creating a space for building relationships. A facilitator received this message shortly after the last session in one of the programs offered by the Center:

> Thank you so much for everything this summer! It's crazy to think we still haven't met in person yet, and I'm looking forward to the day I can finally see you in real life. Your constant support, wonderful stories, and general presence have been a massive help, comfort, and joy throughout the FYF program. You always make me smile on our Zoom calls, and I'm genuinely looking forward to getting to know you better over the next few years. Thanks again for everything.

This participant hopefully realizes how uplifting such a message has been for the concerned facilitator as well! Krause (2020b) describes the impact on relations as the necessary catalyst for learning: "The number one focus is connection. Participants need to feel connected to you as a facilitator of the learning. Online learning is most effective when everyone belongs. It hinges on relational trust, and your job, in part, is to keep the foundation on safety and inclusion."[11]

Use Humor as a Tool: We also recognized how important it is to use humor as a tool and a way of helping everyone to relax. While including humor and not taking yourself too seriously are important for in-person sessions, creating space for it in a virtual setting really lightens the environment. I also think it makes the space open to learning, particularly because the barrier of traditional authority evaporates, and participants can personally relate to you.

Creative Engagement: Think creatively about ways of engaging participants (introverts versus extroverts), in addition to the methods you are comfortable with. It is important to be inclusive. Use chat sessions and other reflective activities. Short breaks help to alleviate the strains of extended screen time. Either give them a chat session with goals or give them a break in the middle. You could also give them an activity to think about for the following week. Also, consider group projects to build community as described earlier.

Invite Co-Creation: Participants' investment in design enhances their virtual experience. For example, throughout the process of redesigning the First-Year Fellows Program (FYF), we invited participants to help. The opportunity to network with alumni in the Washington D.C. area is a key benefit of FYF, and we did not want to lose that aspect of the program. However, we had difficulty imagining how networking might happen. With participants in the mix, we developed and piloted a networking session with session participants and former First-Year Fellows. Afterwards, fellows, past and present, provided us with constructive feedback, which in turn, allowed us to craft the official networking session with alumni.

This example above explains the idea of prototype testing. Chawla (2015) suggests including prototyping for developing a course, and I believe this advice also applies to developing a co-curricular program. He says:

> An additional benefit of prototype testing is that it will help you identify expert blind spots in your course. Learning scientists classify expert blind spot as the inability of some instructors to make accurate predictions about the difficulty level of new ideas as perceived by their learners. In other words, experts are sometimes unable to recall what it feels like to be a novice and are unaware of the difficulties a beginner experiences with their subject. Prototype testing the course in the design stage can help you identify such spots.[12]

Make Information Easily Accessible: Be clear about where information from your program can be located. "When students use a lot of cognitive resources just trying to figure out where to go to access readings, videos, discussions, or quizzes, they have little mental energy left for the content itself. Discouraged and/or irritated students are less likely to learn."[13] I have found this to be true even for myself. Taking the time to organize information and letting participants know where it can be found saves a lot of irritation in the long run.

Technology Considerations for Synchronous Sessions

How to use technology appropriately and effectively has been the largest area of growth for us. I hope this section helps you to think about how you are using technology to support your objectives and also sparks other ideas as well. While this has been written based on lessons learned in an academic setting, the lessons apply for meetings in any other organizational setting. Also, although I have described our experiences with Zoom here, please look for the same or similar features in the platform you are using.

Start Time: We have observed that it takes 2–3 minutes for everyone to get logged in and get settled. If starting a session at 1:00 pm with an end time of 2:00 pm, you will likely have to wait until 1:03 pm before getting started. Based on what we learned, all Rockefeller leadership programs are going to invite participants to arrive five minutes early for a prompt start time.

Communication Takes Longer: Always keep in mind that communication takes longer over a virtual platform, so sessions will extend in length. We don't have the in-person social cues to know if we should talk, ask a question, add on to an idea, etc. If a session normally takes you 1.5 hours, it will likely take 2 hours. Either cut or adjust content or extend time, although the latter is not advised. If your session exceeds 1.5 hours, build in a break from the screen or a group stretch. Build in some flexibility in your sessions and do not plan your session so tightly for the planned hour that it cannot accommodate any unexpected discussions that may take longer.

When you plan out your session, add another column for "technical directions" (for example, "screen share here," "have participants enter in the chat"). Incorporating such prompts into the lesson plan will help you estimate time.

Screen Time: Please limit screen time by shortening a session by focusing on "essential-to-know" information and include "good-to-know" information in handouts and required readings, TED Talks, etc.

Introductions: Have participants introduce themselves. This helps them feel like they are part of the session and not an observer. Getting them to unmute right off the bat lowers the perceived risk of unmuting later. However, call on them by name to save time and reduce anxiety. If there are too many participants, use breakout groups for introductions.

Seek Help: We learned that it is helpful for facilitators to focus on the content and delivery of the session but have assistance in running the technology aspect of the session. In our case, the program officers and student assistants helped to organize breakout rooms, the chat function, and polls. The practice sessions before the actual sessions helped the facilitator and those who were assisting with the technology component. But what can those in institutions with fewer resources do to incorporate this structure? As one option, consider how to use participants who are comfortable with technology and invite them to assist you with the session. They can be co-creators of the sessions with you, a process that could engage you and them alike in creating a vibrant session.

Screen Share: With Zoom specifically, it takes a minute to set up screen share. It can be difficult to navigate between screens during screen share. Practice becoming comfortable toggling between screens. Further, as the person using the screen-share function, you can see only four video pictures at a time. Others watching your screen can expand their gallery view to show more video feeds. If you are asking a question, your participants can't see each other to get social cues and will not answer (or ask a question of their own). Have them raise their hands virtually or use the chat. Finally, if you want to share a video with its audio, there is a box you need to check that says, "share computer audio." Do not mute yourself when you are screen-sharing with audio! This will also mute the audio you are playing for all the other attendees.

Learn to Use Breakout Rooms: When you divide participants into breakout rooms, you lose the ability to talk to them all at once to clarify instructions. This is different from facilitating a session in a classroom in which you have the advantage of interrupting discussions and clarifying instructions to the group. Therefore, it is essential to have clear written instructions accessible for participants when they are in their breakout rooms.

You can even have them record their answers into the same Google doc, as Minero (2020) describes of Tahmaseb, a teacher: "[He] divided his students into Zoom breakout rooms, had them 'record their answers on a shared Google doc' to a class-wide prompt, then had volunteers share out their responses to the whole class."[14] We have practiced several variations of this idea of using Google Docs in breakout groups and found that it works because it allows participants to discuss, record information, and share it with others efficiently and effectively. It also allows us as facilitators to keep a record of conversations that we can analyze later. To ensure clarity, test the instructions with someone before you use them in the session.

Breakout rooms mimic the in-person, small-group discussion format. In such a format, a facilitator could simply walk by and clarify questions or concerns the group had. Since this was not possible in a virtual format, breakout rooms provided the opportunity for participants to review the material they had just learned in a relaxed format without the presence of a facilitator. Participants could interact with each other to "dive deep" into the topics discussed during the session. In so doing, they were able to establish bonds that lasted throughout the program. The facilitator could also "drop in" virtually to see how discussions were progressing.

Breakout rooms are effective as we see in these observations from participants from the First-Year Fellows Program:

> I think the breakout rooms are the most effective way to do most ice breakers. As much as I want to get to know all of the fellows and program coordinators, it takes a lot of time to share even a small amount of information if each person is sharing one at a time. By doing random breakout rooms, we can interact with others more meaningfully and (eventually) get time with everyone.
> — Isabella D., class of 2023

> I really enjoyed the breakout rooms because I was able to be relaxed and have meaningful conversations with a small group of people.
> — Natasha R., class of 2023

> I really enjoyed the breakout rooms; it was neat getting to know some of my classmates better and I think the smaller group setting was conducive to deeper, easier discussions.
> — Joshua F., class of 2023

Security: If you are running the sessions, or being assisted by someone else, have a conversation about making the session as secure as possible. We learned the need to understand the importance of being alert about security features for our guests and participants the hard way. It took only one unpleasant "Zoom bombing" incident in one of our programs to pay even closer attention to security considerations.

Choosing Technology: When deciding on what technology tool or platform you're going to use for your virtual program, it's important to consider your audience in the decision. What is their exposure and comfort with that tool or platform? Do they use it often like our participants used Zoom, for instance? Is it new to them, like our participants in the First-Year Fellows Program who used Microsoft Teams? If the platform is new to them, deeply consider if this is the right path for you. If you feel a tool or platform is right for you, develop some instructional videos, training, and reminders to facilitate the adoption process. Training is a must, even if you're working with Generation Z, the digital natives. Being familiar with technology does not make them experts in every tool or platform.

You and your learners can take advantage of external tools such as headphones, lights, external webcams, and other items you can think of to create a good working environment.

Becoming Comfortable with the Technology: Having access to technology does not equate to knowing how to use it. Our team devoted intentional time to practicing, prototyping, and iterating. We hosted practice sessions with speakers, relied on knowledge sharing, and created prototype Microsoft Teams and Google Classrooms. A team's willingness to explore and embrace technology leads to their ease with it. Use it to its fullest!

Being Kind to Yourself: Unprecedented times have created an unforeseen situation. Leadership must not only be about transmitting what you know, it must also be about admitting what you do not know. Virtual sessions ask all of us to embrace the uncertainty, and with speakers, doubly so, as they are confronting both the challenges of a new format and a way to fit their material into that format. So, learn about how you will adapt your course or program design, imagine how you will engage participants for maximum learning, and learn the technology yourself or get the support of others who can help you with implementing the technology component. Rest easy in the knowledge that mistakes will be made and are part of the learning curve. We made many mistakes while we were learning about technology and implementing it. We were surprised at how supportive our participants were and even more delighted when they stepped up to help us navigate a technological challenge.

Concluding Thoughts

The COVID-19 pandemic has devastated us in so many ways, but it has also provided us with an environment ripe with learning. If it had not happened, "business as usual" would have prevailed, and we would not have realized so many insights in such a short period of time. It has unleashed our latent creativity and fostered an environment in which both facilitators and learners shared an experience they are not likely to forget—now or ever. I was also surprised and energized with the connections my program officers and I built with our participants.

Personally, I was humbled with how much I learned in a short period of time and how much more there is to learn as I continue to explore the world of online learning. Please use the references at the end of this chapter to add to your knowledge and your toolkit.

One final note must be made about the opportunities for keeping morale high when it was difficult to foster relationships. A huge and lasting lesson I learned is that, as a manager, it is my responsibility to create and relish moments of joy for myself and for others, despite the unpredictability of our current situation. It is on me to reach out to people and address the isolation and loneliness when it begins to surface. We can create spaces in which our participants can enjoy each other's thoughts and company. I come back to the simple yet delightful breakout room as an example. We have demonstrated already how breakout rooms were important to generate more intimate connections in a time where loneliness ran high; as one participant stated, "I enjoyed having the ability to connect with peers during a time of such disconnect."

I want to share a realization from this experience of putting my thoughts about the transition to virtual learning into words for your consideration. When reading this chapter, a colleague was confused about what these terms (supporting participants, participant involvement, creative engagement, and co-creation) really meant. In her mind, they were either similar or the same. What I really want to convey is that there is something deeper happening. By supporting participants, we are giving and receiving emotional support to weather an extraordinary situation created by the pandemic with which none of us is familiar. By creating spaces for participant involvement, we are creating agency within participants to own the programs and own their own learning. When I refer to creative engagement, I am thinking about honing into facilitators' and participants' sense of creativity and innovation for engagement. The act of co-creation helps facilitators and participants develop an idea or product (e.g., the alumni networking session referenced earlier). All these interactions, used together in the implementation of programs, create energy and inspiration in participants and facilitators alike.

Notes

1. Garrison et al., 2000.
2. Garrison et al., 2000.
3. Dunlap et al., 2016, pp. 146.
4. ProjectPM., 2020.
5. O'Shaughnessy, 2020.
6. Dweck, 2006.
7. Krause, 2020a.
8. O'Shaughnessy, 2020.
9. Stachowiak, 2019.
10. Chawla, 2015.
11. Krause, 2020b.
12. Chawla, 2015.
13. Darby, 2019.
14. Minero, 2020.

References

Center for Teaching Support and Education. (2016, May). Community of inquiry. University of Toronto. https://teaching.utoronto.ca/wp-content/uploads/2016/05/Community-of-Inquiry.pdf.

Chawla, K. (2015, June 11). *6 Essential tips for planning an effective online course*. EdSurge. https://www.edsurge.com/news/2015-06-11-6-essential-tips-for-planning-an-effective-online-course

CoI Framework. (2015). https://coi.athabascau.ca/coi-model/

Darby, F. (2019, April 17). How to be a better online teacher. *Chronicle of Higher Education*. https://www.chronicle.com/article/how-to-be-a-better-online-teacher/

Dunlap, J. C., Verma, G., & Johnson, H. L. (2016). Presence+experience: A framework for the purposeful design of presence in online courses. *TechTrends*, *60*(2), 145–151. https://doi.org/10.1007/s11528-016-0029-4

Dweck, C. S. (2007). *Mindset: The new psychology of success* (Illustrated ed.). Ballantine Books. (Original work published 2006)

Gail, M. Ed. (2016). *Reflecting on service-learning in higher education: Contemporary issues and perspectives*. Lexington Books.

Garrison, D. R. (2007). Online community of inquiry review: Social, cognitive, and teaching presence issues. *Journal of Asynchronous Learning Networks*, *11*(1), 61–72. https://eric.ed.gov/?id=EJ842688

Garrison, D. R., Anderson, T., & Archer, W. (2000). Critical inquiry in a text-based environment: Computer conferencing in higher education. *The Internet and Higher Education*, *2*(2–3), 87–105. https://doi.org/10.1016/S1096-7516(00)00016-6

Gray, K. (2020, July 20). *5 apps to enhance distance learning*. Edutopia. https://www.edutopia.org/article/5-apps-enhance-distance-learning

Huang, W., Hurt, A., Richardson, J. C., Swan, K., & Caskurlu, S. (2018). *Community of inquiry framework*. Purdue Repository for Online Teaching and Learning. https://www.purdue.edu/innovativelearning/supporting-instruction/portal/files/4_Community_of_Inquiry_Framework.pdf

Krause, C. (2020a, April 15). *How to forge a strong community in an online classroom*. Edutopia. https://www.edutopia.org/article/how-forge-strong-community-online-classroom

Krause, C. (2020b, July 14). *Emotionally connected learning is possible online. Start with relationships.* EdSurge.   https://www.edsurge.com/news/2020-07-14-emotionally-connected-learning-is-possible-online-start-with-relationships

Lynch, J. (2016). *Teaching presence: Higher education services* [White paper]. 1–6. https://www.pearsoned.com/wp-content/uploads/INSTR6230_TeachingPresence_WP_f.pdf

Minero, E. (2020, June 12). *Distance learning FAQ: Solving teachers' and students' common problems.* Edutopia.   https://www.edutopia.org/article/distance-learning-faq-solving-teachers-and-students-common-problems

Morris, S. M. (2020, June 10). *Technology is not pedagogy.* SeanMichaelMorris.Com. https://www.seanmichaelmorris.com/technology-is-not-pedagogy/

O'Malley, S. (2017, July 26). *Ideas for building an online community.* Inside Higher Ed. https://www.insidehighered.com/digital-learning/article/2017/07/26/ideas-building-online-community

O'Shaughnessy, A. (2020, May 29). *Tips to create a warmer, more engaging online classroom.* Edutopia. https://www.edutopia.org/article/tips-create-warmer-more-engaging-online-classroom

ProjectPM. (2020, November 15). *5 Stages of a team development: Tuckman.* https://project.pm/team-development-tuckman/

Reed, M. (2020, May 13). Should showing faces be mandatory? *Confessions of a Community College Dean.* https://www.insidehighered.com/blogs/confessions-community-college-dean/should-showing-faces-be-mandatory

Stachowiak, B. (2019, January 9). *How can online instructors get students to talk to each other?* EdSurge. https://www.edsurge.com/news/2019-01-09-how-can-online-instructors-get-students-to-talk-to-each-other

Whitman, G. (2020, June 10). *How brain research helped retool our school schedule for remote learning.* EdSurge. https://www.edsurge.com/news/2020-06-10-how-brain-research-helped-retool-our-school-schedule-for-remote-learning.

Community of Inquiry Model

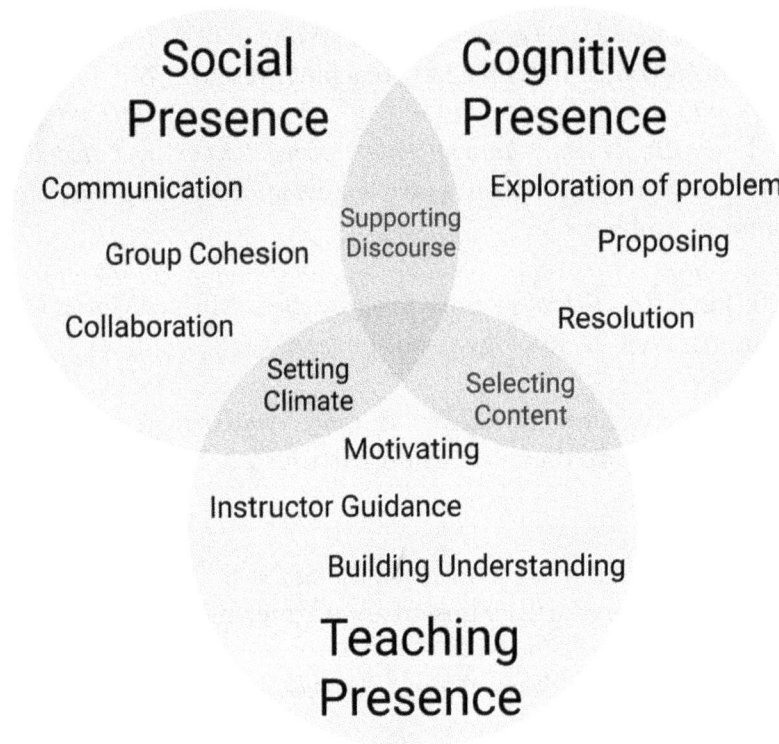

Social Presence
Communication
Group Cohesion
Collaboration

Cognitive Presence
Exploration of problem
Proposing
Resolution

Supporting Discourse

Setting Climate

Selecting Content

Motivating

Instructor Guidance

Building Understanding

Teaching Presence

Note: Adapted from "Critical Inquiry in a Text-Based Environment: Computer Conferencing in Higher Education" by D. R. Garrison, T. Anderson, & W. Archer, 2000, *The Internet and Higher Education 2*(2–3), p. 88. Copyright © 2000 by Elsevier Science Inc.

The Community of Inquiry Model (CoI), developed by D. Randy Garrison, Terry Anderson, and Walter Archer, and published in 2000, is in essence <u>a framework of the learning process as a constant interaction among three dimensions applicable for in-person and online environments.</u>

The *Social Presence* dimension considers the person's ability to project their personality with the aim of developing relationships and communicating in different environments. This is why experiences closely related to this element of the model are encouraging interactions with others and seeking opportunities to express personal views.

Equally important is the second dimension, *Cognitive Presence*, which revolves around the goal of making sense of oneself and the environment through consistent reflection. This dimension is closely related to experiencing and overcoming confusion or uncertainty, making connections, and integrating new ideas within one's thought process.

The third dimension, *Teaching Presence*, is built upon the concepts of facilitating social and cognitive processes with the aim of producing worthwhile and meaningful learning. Its key elements are all related to practices that educators implement, such as initiating discussions, proposing and defining ideas, and maintaining focus throughout verbal communication.

There are many practices that can amplify the benefits that each dimension brings to the learning process; however, within an online environment it might seem harder to apply all of them. Below is a list of activities that educators can engage in—even in virtual settings—to create a community of inquiry.

Social Presence

> Project the teaching persona through constant communication with the students.
> Provide opportunities for office hours as a way for interacting with students one-on-one.
> Rely on icebreakers and similar activities to encourage students to project their personalities in a less academic setting.
> Integrate sharing personal anecdotes as a part of weekly check-ins to encourage students to feel connected even when physically distanced. Encourage students to share related anecdotes, experiences, and beliefs in online discussions.

Cognitive Presence

> Pose open-ended questions as a tool to promote a variety of perspectives and deep thinking.
> Encourage peer-review as a process of providing feedback and acquiring a sense of confidence about one's impact on others.
> Rely on a diverse set of activities for the acquisition of the same set of skills to illustrate the multiple applications of concepts.
> Provide opportunities for experimentation and creative thinking utilizing online-based visualization platforms.

Teaching Presence

> Provide students with enough information on expectations.
> Spend sufficient time on resource-utilization and ensure that all students feel confident in working with online programs.
> Rely on visualization during class activities and text-based resources for out-of-class work to maintain attention and diversify the learning experience.

References

Centre for Teaching Support & Innovation. (2016). *Community of inquiry*. University of Toronto. https://teaching.utoronto.ca/wp-content/uploads/2016/05/Community-of-Inquiry.pdf

CoI Framework. (2015). https://coi.athabascau.ca/coi-model/

Garrison, D. R., Anderson, T., & Archer, W. (2000). Critical inquiry in a text-based environment: Computer conferencing in higher education model. *The Internet and Higher Education, 2*(2-3), 87–105.

Huang, W., Hurt, A., Richardson, J. C., Swan, K., & Caskurlu, S. (2020). Community of inquiry framework. *Purdue Repository for Online Teaching and Learning.* https://www.purdue.edu/innovativelearning/supporting-instruction/portal/files/4_Community_of_Inquiry_Framework.pdf

Handout created by Kristabel Konta, class of 2024

9 | Measuring Effectiveness and Impact

To acquire knowledge, one must study; but to acquire wisdom, one must observe.

— Marilyn vos Savant

Time is a like a slippery little eel: I try hard to catch it, it struggles with might, and then it successfully slips away. All I am left with are memories—many great and some that I choose to reflect on and reimagine! Every year is bittersweet. I welcome new participants in their first year of our programs. I see some often during their four years as they progress through the continuum of programs you just read about. In four short years, I say goodbye to those who graduate and move on to the next phase in their lives. I am in touch with many, and for the others that I am not in touch with, I wonder how they are and what they are doing.

I am grateful to the alumni with whom I have stayed in touch, for through them, I continuously learn. We have established lasting and meaningful relationships through these programs. It is a joyful experience to receive a wedding invitation or a picture of a newborn, and to hear about changes in their lives. They also play an important role in keeping me in touch with management and leadership issues they face in the workplace, and this allows me to think about the relevance of our programs. So, throughout this four-year cycle of entry, intervening years, and departure, I continue to think about the effectiveness of programs we implement and ask myself, "How can our team members measure program effectiveness and impact? How do participants and alumni measure the success and impact of these programs?"

Measuring program effectiveness and impact lies within the purview of my colleagues and my "circle of influence," as described by Covey (1989/2020).[1] By that, Covey simply means engaging with activities and responsibilities that we have control and influence over. We use the usual techniques of measuring participant learning, program content, structure, and process. We collect data and study reflections and come to conclusions about the strengths, weaknesses, effectiveness, and efficiency of these programs periodically and annually. We also observe how they address not only our organizational mission, but also the larger institutional mission. These approaches have often felt mechanical to me, yet they have played a significant role in how we continuously adopt, adapt, and adjust. These results are based on feedback we receive from our participants through our commitment to continuous quality improvement.

Previously, in Chapter 2, I outlined the steps we have used to a complete program design. As shown again in Figure 9.1, these steps include a *conceptualization stage* and a *development stage*, building the program on the foundation of the Eight Pillars of Program Design. Finally, I explained the *assessment stage* involves asking the key questions about this process using the tools required for the different levels. The rest of this chapter is devoted to assessment. It is important to emphasize, however, that it is merely the final one in a multi-step process in which the idea of reflection is related to all these stages.

Figure 9.1

Roadmap for Effective Program Conceptualization and Development

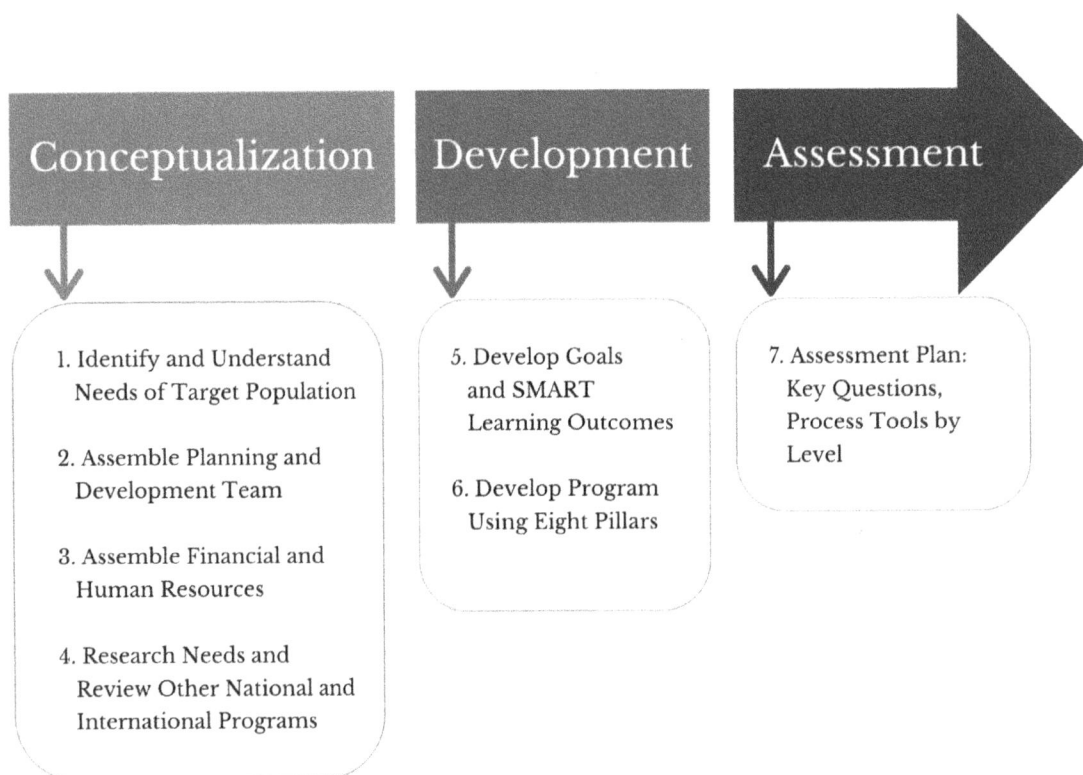

Note. Adapted from *Teaching Leadership: Bridging Theory and Practice* (p. 130) by G. Perruci & S. W. Hall, 2018, Edward Elgar Publishing. Copyright © 2018 by Gama Perruci and Sadhana Warty Hall.

A detailed chapter in *Teaching Leadership: Bridging Theory and Practice* is devoted to program assessment and evaluation. I provide the following definitions that apply to the discussion in this book as well. The Rockefeller Center Assessment Framework uses the following terms, definitions for which are provided below: impact, assessment, evaluation, efficiency, effectiveness, and learning outcomes. Multiple definitions exist for the terms listed. Therefore, it is useful to establish a common understanding of how they will be used in the discussion of the Rockefeller Center's particular assessment framework.[2]

Impact

This term encompasses our understanding of what success looks like upon completion of a program, and it is defined as a measurable change (ideally positive) in an outcome of interest. For example, at the participant level, an outcome of interest might be an improvement in the measure of the learner's self-awareness over the course of a program. At the center level, it might be an increase in participants compared to the previous year or an increase in the number of times competencies are reached within each of the seven categories addressed over the course of the program. At the institutional level, it may be measured as a change in the levels of financial support or recognition as a result of the program. While we always work toward positive outcomes, we acknowledge that impact can also capture unintended consequences or negative outcomes.

Assessment

Schuh and Upcraft (2001) define assessment as "any effort to gather, analyze, and interpret evidence which describes institutional, departmental, divisional, or agency effectiveness."[3] This definition aligns closely with how assessment is defined in this chapter. Assessment should be distinguished from research, which is defined as "any effort to gather evidence which guides theory by testing hypotheses."[4]

We define assessment as a systematic process of data collection and analysis that allows us to:

- ➢ Determine and measure student learning;
- ➢ Monitor the effectiveness and efficiency of programs;
- ➢ Articulate the achievement of program outcomes;
- ➢ State how programs meet organizational and institutional missions; and
- ➢ Determine long-term program impact among participants (current students and alumni).

Evaluation

Assessment and evaluation are often used interchangeably, but while assessment involves the effort to gather, analyze and interpret evidence, evaluation is the effort to use this assessment evidence to improve the effectiveness of programs. This definition is consistent with the work of other researchers who have explored this topic.[5] In the context of the framework presented, evaluation is an annual decision-making process derived from qualitative and quantitative assessments that promote program improvement, inclusion, and modification.

Efficiency and Effectiveness

Efficiency and effectiveness are equally important when assessing and evaluating programs.[6] Efficiency measures how well a program uses its human, material, and financial resources, while effectiveness refers to how well the organization and its programs align to meet the organizational mission along with program goals and learning outcomes.[7] By ensuring that programs are both efficient and effective, we can help to maximize their impact on our learners.

In this book, I also review briefly the cycle of program assessment through the framework we follow for co-curricular programs at the Rockefeller Center using the Management and Leadership Development Program as an example to explain it. In this cycle (see Figure 9.2), we seek to do the following: assess student learning; monitor and evaluate program development, design, and implementation; establish mechanisms for continuous quality improvement; and learn to articulate the impact of the program. In effect, this cycle is the way we at the Rockefeller Center determine whether we are "doing the right thing and doing things right."

Figure 9.2

Rockefeller Center Assessment Framework

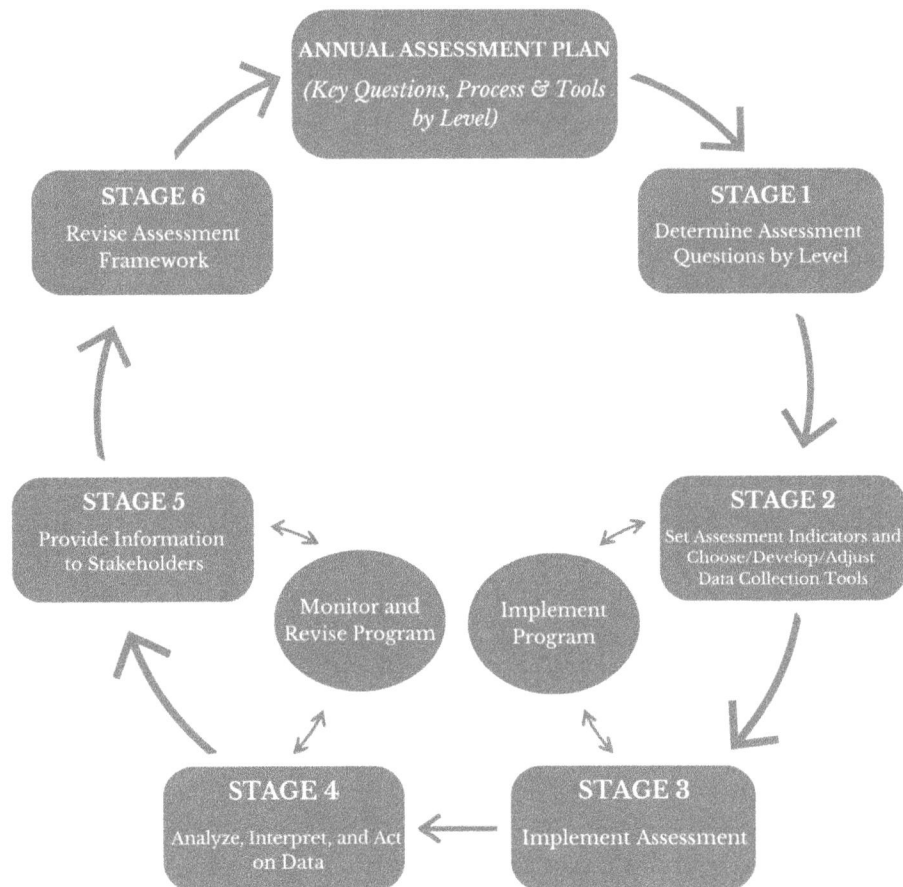

Note. Adapted from *Teaching Leadership: Bridging Theory and Practice* (p. 175) by G. Perruci & S. W. Hall, 2018, Edward Elgar Publishing. Copyright © 2018 by Gama Perruci and Sadhana Warty Hall.

As a beginning, we thought about key questions we wanted to ask at different levels (participant, organization, institution) to assess student learning, impact, efficiency, and effectiveness. This is in line with Anderson and Krathwohl's revised Bloom's Taxonomy (2001), which incorporates both the kind of knowledge to be learned (knowledge dimension) and the process used to learn (cognitive process).[8] The questions allow you to align objectives to assessment techniques.[9]

These were and are the questions on our minds when we think about assessment and evaluation. When you review your own program, you might have other questions; please make a note of them as you read along and follow the framework in Figure 9.2.

Measuring Impact: The framework is really focused on a conceptual cycle that helps us to implement our commitment to continuous quality improvement. We constantly think about the impact of our programs.[10] For example, how effective are alumni in their jobs as a result of participating in these programs? How do they remember them? What do they recall about specific sessions, and how have they been applying them to their work and to their lives?

Participant Level: What are participants learning, and does this learning relate to the objectives and competencies stated in the Session Proposal Form (Handout 2.5 in Chapter 2) by the speakers? How are participants using what they learned?[11]

Program Level: What are the strengths, weaknesses, opportunities, and constraints for program development, design, implementation, monitoring and evaluation? How is this seen by participants, facilitators, and program staff? What competencies are we addressing in each of the sessions? What gaps do we see in the competencies when we review sessions within a program? How might we address these gaps? Is it necessary to address all competencies within a program, or can we look at a continuum of programs and capture a picture of all leadership competencies we have identified?

Organization and Institutional Level: We have seen how co-curricular programs contribute to the participants' personal and professional growth. As shown in Table 1.1 in Chapter 1, data analysis indicates growth in participation in recent graduating classes, and over 25% of the students have participated in at least one term-long co-curricular program at the Center during their time at Dartmouth. Our aspirational goal continues to be to make these programs available and accessible to a majority of the student population. At the Center level, then, we ask specific questions that help us to understand how we can reach more participants and meet the mission of the organization, revisiting participant learning to do so. We also evaluate whether the programs meet or do not meet the budget allocated for them. Equally important, we pay attention to the mission of the institution and how we are in harmony with its aspirations.

Once we have the questions listed, we define the tools and processes we will use to gather information. As an example, I have chosen the Management and Leadership Development Program to explain how it uses the following methods at each level; I also provide the strengths and considerations for each tool.

Participant Level

Weekly Online Surveys Taken Immediately After the Session

This involves a quick qualitative assessment of activities, speaker and content on a scale of 1 to 5. It asks participants to list their top three takeaways and to indicate how they plan to use their new knowledge. The key is that the survey is quick and easily recordable. Because the survey takes place right after the session, we can capture an immediate response. We must consider, however, that participants are rushed at the end of a session and do the bare minimum because they may have other commitments. Since this survey captures an immediate response, participants may not have time to reflect on or digest information.

One example of information gleaned from these surveys is data on participant evaluations of speakers. This information is now collected for all our programs, but program officers have asked different questions over the years as they adapted and administered their programs. Because of this, we do not have complete or consistent speaker-level data for the First-Year Fellows, Rockefeller Global Leadership Program, or Rockefeller Leadership Fellows. We do, however, have consistent data for the Management and Leadership Development Program (MLDP).

Speaker ratings give us an indication of how learners are evaluating their performance. For example, the following data reflect speaker survey ratings for MLDP from the spring of 2018 through fall of 2019. We have consistent survey data for MLDP sessions going back multiple years. For this reason, we highlight MLDP data as an example of collecting speaker/session ratings from participants. This is an important piece of feedback that program officers and student assistants discuss in order to improve existing sessions. While you are using quantitative ratings, aspire to average ratings for your session between this range. In this instance, we used a scale of 1 to 5, with 5 being outstanding. We believe any score between 4 and 5 is a very good performance, and there is always room for improvement. This is the context on which we base our dialogue with speakers term after term, year after year. Figure 9.3 highlights speaker and session ratings for each term from Spring 2018 to Fall 2019.

Figure 9.3

MLDP Content, Activities, and Speaker Ratings by Session (Spring 2018 – Fall 2019)

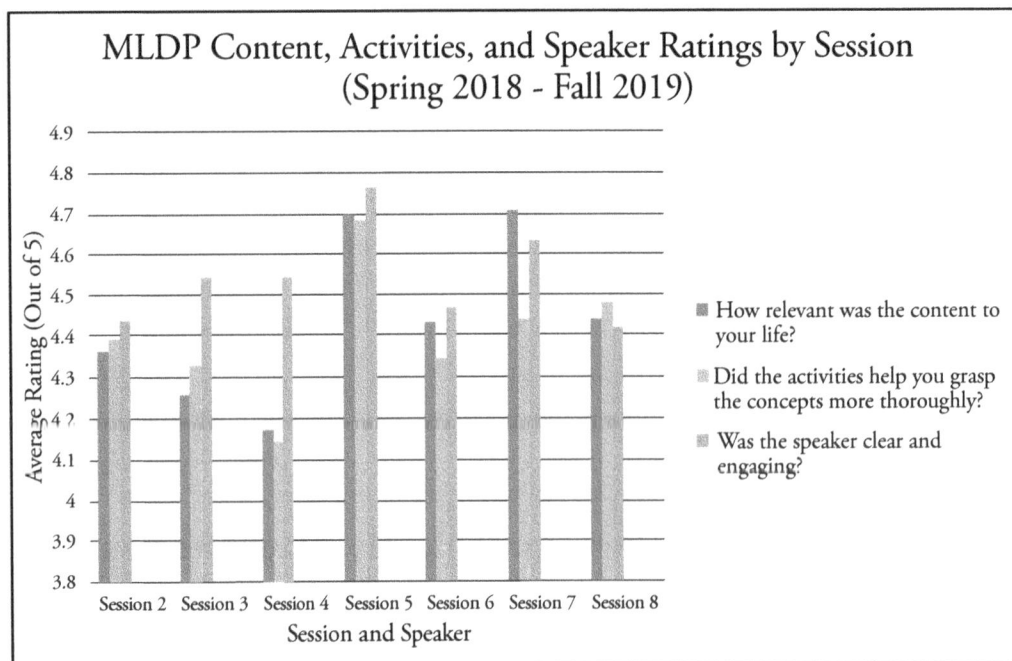

Learners consistently report high levels of satisfaction with speakers, content, and activities. During the selected period, for example, students reported 4.4/5 on relevance, 4.4/5 on activities, and 4.5/5 on speakers. Speaker ratings tend to be higher than relevance/activity scores; the exceptions to this are Sessions 6, 7, and 8. Data for session 1 and 9 are not included because they are introductory and reflection sessions and are not evaluated in the same way.

Weekly Reflections Due a Few Days After the Session

This weekly reflection gives a quantitative assessment of select activities and speaker content. It asks the participants to reflect on past events (recent or distant) and re-evaluate the situation they face based on new knowledge gained during the session. While participants do have the time to digest information and tend to be more thoughtful in their responses, the reflection questions focus on only one objective or a very narrow area rather than the entire session.

Student Assistants and Ambassadors

Student program assistants and ambassadors (students selected for program outreach and community building) in this program give unfiltered session feedback that may not have been written by program participants. It is a way to collect honest feedback, given to the program officer verbally through weekly or bi-weekly meetings. Ambassadors and student assistants may ask other students for their feedback verbally. We notice that the feedback received is filtered through the opinion or perception of the ambassadors and student assistants. It also appears to focus more on negative feedback. However, this process is very useful because it teaches ambassadors and assistants how to give feedback to the person managing the program, and it helps program officers and the deputy director consider positive and negative feedback. Due to the necessarily anonymous nature of this feedback, it becomes difficult to directly address these concerns with the individuals who voiced them in the first place. This can be a setback for program officers who would like more clarity from the participant who raised the concern.

Program Level

Session Proposal Forms

The outcome of conversations between speakers (or facilitators) and staff is realized in this foundational document, defining the content for each individual session. If this conversation had not taken place, there would be no session! We want speakers to be clear on the objectives of this session, and we want program officers to collectively define how this session fits into the overall objective of the program. Therefore, speakers and staff work closely to develop a session. The Session Proposal Form contains both speaker details and session details. Handout 2.5 in Chapter 2 is the template of the form we use to initiate conversations. It is important to follow the form during the facilitation of the session; at the end, it provides an opportunity for program officers to verify with the speaker whether the content followed the original discussion.

Session Proposal Forms are also useful in assessing whether the learning objectives fit in with the Center's mission. They serve as a tool for a conversation with the facilitator and help them to articulate key concepts and definitions. Forms also enable facilitators to learn how to stay within the allotted time for the session. They help the facilitator to think about how they will garner reflection on the session. We have learned it is important to build-in time to review the session proposal verification, and therefore suggest that it should happen during or directly after the sessions.

In the Introduction, we talked about how Kolb's Cycle of Learning was integral to the delivery of the session. The Session Proposal Form helps emphasize the need to ensure active engagement for participants to analyze, reflect, and apply the session content. Our experience tells us that 70% of the time, participants should be actively engaged in structured activities. About 30% of the time can be devoted to providing instructions and lectures. Please note, however, that this is just a guideline and that a different time allocation or format may be more effective for some sessions. For example, a compelling speaker may devote more than 30% of the allotted time to storytelling or a lecture.

Mapping Leadership Competencies

Figure 9.4 maps the leadership competencies across the sessions of the Management and Leadership Development Program (MLDP). This analysis is based on the seven categories of competencies the Center has adopted, as shown in Handout 1.1 in Chapter 1. The seven categories of competencies include the following: collaboration, effective communication, effective reasoning, management, self-knowledge, principled action, and intercultural mindset. As can be seen from Handout 1.1, competencies are addressed across categories, and the emphasis is on effective communication, self-knowledge, and management. Zooming out from one specific program, if we map out all the competencies addressed by all of our co-curricular programs, we can see our organizational emphasis at a glance.

Figure 9.4

MLDP Leadership Competencies (Fall 2019–Spring 2020)

Management & Leadership Development Program	Session 1	Session 2	Session 3	Session 4	Session 5	Session 6	Session 7	Session 8	Session 9	Session 10	
Competency	Kick-Off Frye	Communication Skyrme	Leader or Manager Perruci	Mindful Presence Chiu	Team Player Johnson	Relationships Hilton	Workplace Etiquette Bedford	Negotiating Garvey	Intergenerational Communication Hall	Off-Campus Session(s)	Total
Collaboration											**8**
Builds and maintains partnerships based on shared purpose						1					1
Acknowledges and listens to different voices when making decisions and taking action		1	1								2
Facilitates collective action toward common goals					1					1	2
Encourages, supports and recognizes the contributions of others				1						1	2
Fosters a welcoming and inclusive environment	1										1
Effective Communication											**12**
Writes and speaks after reflection											0
Clearly articulates ideas in a written and spoken form		1		1			1				3
Exhibits effective listening skills				1		1					2
Influences others through writing, speaking or artistic expression		1		1			1	1			4
Acknowledges and appropriately communicates in situations with divergent opinions and values								1	1	1	3
Effective Reasoning											**5**
Employs critical thinking in problem solving											0
Employs creative thinking in problem solving					1						1
Develops personal reflective practice	1		1						1	1	4
Engages in inquiry, analysis and follow-through											0
Integrates multiple types of information to effectively solve problems or address issues											0
Management											**6**
Develops and implements a plan for goal attainment	1										1
Develops appropriate strategies for capitalizing on human talent					1						1
Stewards and maximizes all resources						1					1
Manages multiple priorities											0
Prepares for leadership transition											0
Develops appropriate strategies for effective team work					1						1
Evaluates efficacy of current course(s) of action											0
Identifies structure and culture of organization										2	2
Demonstrates effective and appropriate use of technology											0
Demonstrates financial, task and resource management skills											0
Self-knowledge											**11**
Continually explores and examines values and views			1								1
Understands social identities of self and others			1			1			1	1	4
Demonstrates realistic understanding of one's abilities		1		1							2
Seeks opportunities for continued growth		1									1
Takes appropriate action towards potential benefits despite possible failure					1						1
Shows self-respect and respect for others	1										1
Moves beyond self-imposed limitations				1							1
Practices self-compassion, friendliness and ease with self, and vulnerability											0
Principled Action											**5**
Identifies and commits to appropriate ethical framework											0
Demonstrates congruence between actions and values					1						1
Demonstrates personal responsibility	1										1
Appropriately challenges the unethical behavior of individuals or groups							1				1
Bases actions on thoughtful consideration of their impact and consequences								1			1
Seeks appropriate and mutually beneficial solutions when conflict or controversy arises								1			1
Inter-Cultural Mindset											**6**
Contextualizes social identities and experiences										1	1
Understands, communicates with, and respectfully interacts with people across cultures							1		1	2	4
Actively engages in opportunities to expand world view			1								1
Applies inter-cultural knowledge and skills in local, national or global contexts											0

Figure 9.5 is a chart describing the leadership competencies addressed by all co-curricular programs at the Rockefeller Center. As shown in the chart, our center prioritizes programming that addresses self-knowledge, principled action, and management skills. In addition, we work hard to improve students' abilities to work effectively in teams through teaching effective communication, reasoning, and collaboration techniques.

Figure 9.5

Leadership Competencies Reflected Across all Co-Curricular Programs as of 2018

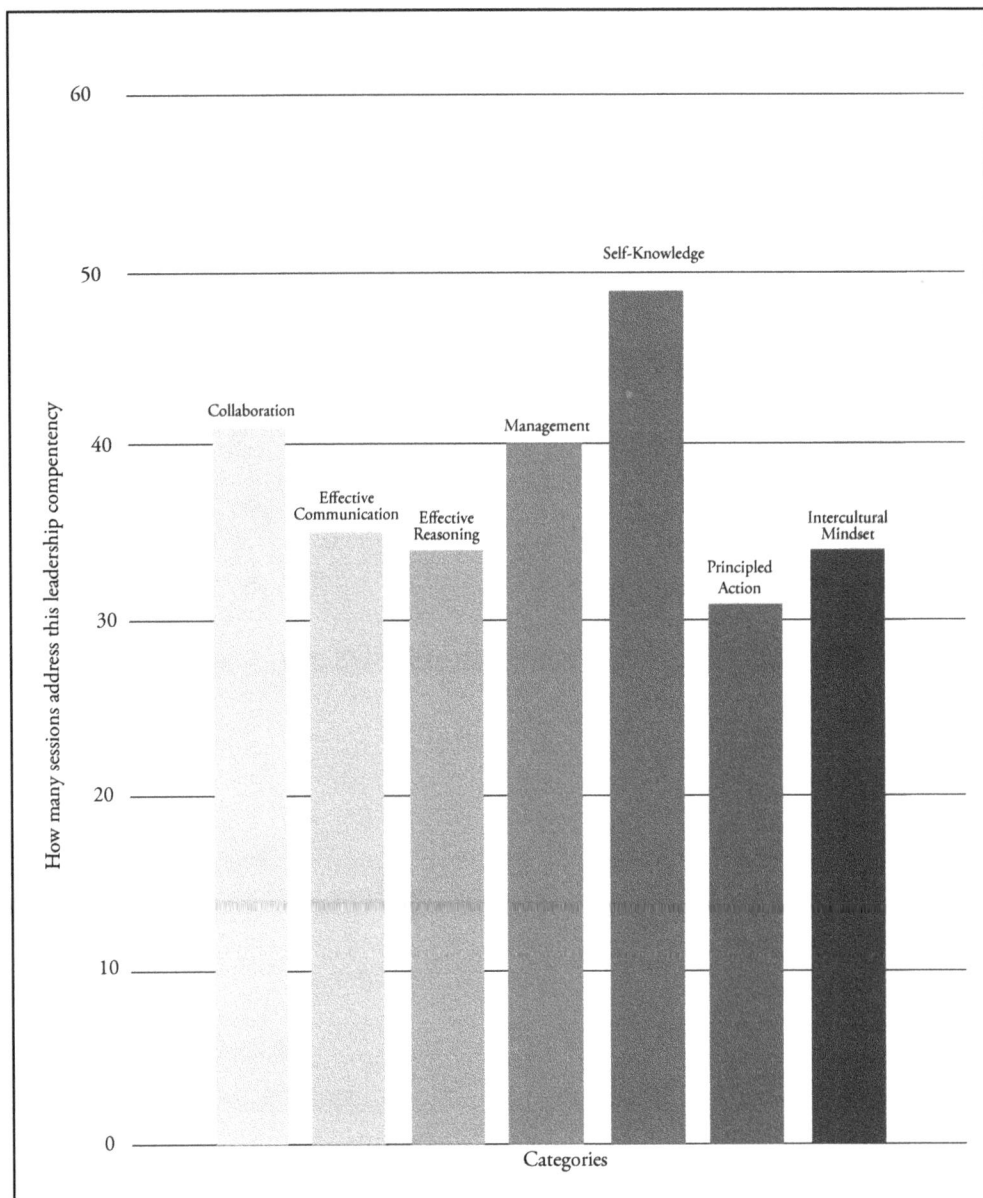

The competencies are not only identified in an initial discussion between the facilitator and program officer, but the co-curricular team also reviews each session proposal form as well. Any new additions have also been reviewed by the team. This has helped us to provide consistency in how we view competencies for each session across programs. Moreover, it also helps us to be rigorous and become aware of all sessions offered by the five programs as a team.

These competencies represent a broad umbrella in building our programs. Some stay within one narrow lane, while others spread out into multiple categories. The competencies addressed by the Rockefeller Center resulted from the higher institutional level process, a discussion of Dartmouth's competencies. This list of competencies is based on a review of the *Council for Advancement of Standards (CAS)*, *Learning Reconsidered*, and *Liberal Education and America's Promise (LEAP Standards)*.[12]

Strengths, Weaknesses, Opportunities, Constraints (SWOC) Analysis

The MLDP program team, consisting of the student program assistants and the program officer, do a SWOC analysis after the program ends. This process incorporates student assistant feedback. It is generated by targeted questions that get them to assess strengths, weaknesses, opportunities, and constraints the program faces. The result of this process is that we acquire promising ideas about ways to change the program. Student assistants participating also gain analytical skills to assess programs. When evaluating your own program, please consider organizing your process so that changes for the next iteration of the program are recorded, implemented, and evaluated. Please examine recommendations carefully; often it is not possible to accept all feedback. Instead, a facilitator should take the time to explain to participants why that suggestion was not feasible.

Personal Leadership Challenge (PLC) Pre- and Post-Program Reflections and Coaching Sessions

These two approaches generate a lot of information that program managers can use to become aware of participant learning and help participants to reflect deeply on personal leadership challenges they have identified in the beginning of the program. Through the coaching sessions, the program officer can discover where the students are in their development and make small adjustments to the program or offer supplemental information and support to meet their needs. The reflection asks students which sessions and program elements helped them achieve their personal leadership challenge. This approach is helpful in assessing relevance of program sessions at an individual participant level and identifying common trends. It also enables the program team to be nimble and adjust the program to suit participant needs. One point made by our program officer was that if participants did not start with a well-defined challenge, then the way to proceed was equally unclear. Coaching skills helped her work with participants to redefine or clarify their challenge. This turned out to be a rewarding, yet time-consuming, endeavor.

Speaker Feedback

Through a meeting with the speakers (one-on-one or as a group), we have collaborative conversations about program improvement and ways to tie the sessions together. This helps to make the program cohesive, rather than a series of workshops. Originally, when MLDP was first implemented, the inaugural speakers were so committed to developing this cohesion and further improving the program, that they made it a priority to meet as a group and discuss improvement. This is a wonderful technique because it builds on the collective wisdom of facilitators and makes the program stronger. It also creates an opportunity for building a community of practice and learning. The program has evolved due to the solid foundation that was established through these efforts. Today, program officers serve as the central hub of this process of increasing cohesion.

Center and Institution Level

Meeting Goals

Discussions about how programs are progressing take place with the senior management team, led by the Center's director. In these discussions, we review relevant data provided at least four times a year by the MLDP program officer, ensuring that it meets the program goals and mission of the Center. The goal is to determine whether the program is within the allocated budget and whether it meets the Center's mission. Once a year, we also review budget needs for the program. Budget allocation is based on whether we determine that the program should be "level-funded" or whether it needs an extra allocation of resources for the upcoming year.

The preceding sections covered the tools and methods we use to evaluate the Management and Leadership Development Program. Similar tools and methods are used in our other programs. We also map the competencies across programs to assess our overall focus and the competencies we support through our programming.

A major lesson I have learned from assessing and evaluating programs is not to underestimate your own power of observation! Participants often are adept at providing the kind of feedback and responses they think others would like to hear. For this reason, observation can be a powerful tool. What goes unsaid in formal evaluations becomes evident if you observe how engaged or disengaged participants are with the content when they are participating in a session. Even if they politely tell you that they enjoyed a particular session, please pay close attention to their non-verbal communication! It will tell you all you need to know.

Alumni and Impact of the Center's Programs

Throughout *Leadership Blueprints*, I have presented thoughts of alumni participating in the Center's program. Sustained relationships also provide insights. Many alumni of these programs and I have stayed connected—while they are in school and after they graduate. As they recount their stories, references to the Rockefeller Center's programs inevitably creep in, and we laugh and reminisce about our collective experiences—good and bad. But most importantly, they give back to the Center when we ask them to participate in helping us to educate and train current and future program participants.

Most recently, I was catching up with an alumna in a different country and a different time zone. We had not been in touch for a while, but as we chatted on Zoom, the time we have spent apart since she graduated disappeared and the distance between us seemed to melt away. I was thrilled by her account of how quickly she has moved up in her organization. It was also exciting to hear her spontaneously talk about how the leadership programs discussed in this book had transformed her, equipped her with management tools, and developed her leadership philosophy. Alumni have given back in so many ways. I am fortunate to be able to count on them for views on the field through their eyes, which makes it possible for me and our team to make our programs relevant. They also provide current participants with career advice, come back as speakers to our current programs, create internship opportunities for our current participants, and, most of all, provide a glimpse into the changes they underwent as a result of our programs.

At the end of this conversation, I was inspired to include what all of us educators have known all along: a powerful way to measure our organization's impact is to hear and observe what alumni have retained and say they value about our programs. What content has transformed them, stuck with them, and given them skills to be successful? No other voice, aside from their own, could be more powerful in answering these questions.

My first account comes from Invo from the class of 2016, where she double majored in economics and women, gender, and sexuality studies. At Dartmouth, in addition to the Rockefeller Center, Invo was involved with the Dartmouth African Students Association, Dartmouth Minorities in Business, and the John Sloan Dickey Center for International Understanding. She has been working in management consulting in East Africa since graduation and serves on the board of a prominent local NGO fighting for girls' rights in Tanzania:

> My Dartmouth career was a dual existence for me in many ways. I fit into many sections of the Dartmouth community, as an international student, a black student, and a female student in a university that only started accepting women in 1972. I was the president of the Dartmouth African Students Association, but I was also a member of a predominantly white sorority. I majored in economics, but I also majored in women and gender studies. I participated in protests on campus, but I also found myself wanting to focus on dialogue as a means of conflict resolution. And at the end of my college journey, I opted for a common career path for many Dartmouth students: management consulting. But I chose to pursue it in my home country, a developing country where my work largely focused on supporting public health and financial inclusion.

> In a span of four years, I have transitioned from being a young analyst to leading the culture transformation of my firm's East Africa regional practice. A few weeks ago, prior to writing this, a colleague asked me, "Are you sure you've only been working for four years?" after hearing me facilitate a virtual call for senior leadership as we worked from home during the COVID-19 pandemic. I repeated something to

him that I've said before, that I technically might have four years of experience in the workplace, but I would consider it eight. My professional development journey did not start when I landed my first job, it started as a freshman student at the Rockefeller Center.

To be fair, I have always been interested in leadership. Taking on the mantle, driving a cause when it meant something to me. But leadership is not an innate trait. It is a learned one. And truth be told, most of the experiences I have today were not necessarily because I had an Ivy League education, which is an immense privilege in and of itself, but it was because of the incremental lessons in leadership I was able to learn throughout my college experience at the Rockefeller Center.

I didn't just happen to be naturally able to facilitate senior leadership workshops for government agencies at the beginning of my career. I learned public speaking tips from the Civic Skills Training Program as a freshman that helped me learn how to position my body and voice to speak authoritatively, even though I was a 24-year-old speaking to a largely male audience above the age of 40. I'm not just "great at presentation skills," as my performance report indicates. I've been practicing my presentations since David Uejio presented a session on Design for the User Experience at the Management and Leadership Development Program. He was the one that taught me the role of storytelling in presenting information, long before I needed to develop reports for boards or senior teams.

Through the Rockefeller Center, I came into the workforce having already built a robust understanding of the tools needed from me to communicate and influence decisions, and these are not always lessons that are taught in the standard classroom. This is not to say the journey through these programs was easy.

In my junior year, I struggled with the idea of applying to become a Rockefeller Leadership Fellow. A year-long commitment to building my leadership skills amongst campus leaders like myself? I was filled with uncertainty, a lot of imposter syndrome, and a lack of confidence that I could commit to a year's worth of weekly leadership sessions, on top of classes and all my other activities. My first real lesson began here, when I started to understand the importance of showing up when you are afraid, when you are uncertain and sometimes when you are not sure if you're ready. Sharing this vulnerability was the beginning of one of the most important lessons of leadership for me and that was: showing up. I learned that real leadership only begins when you develop a personal responsibility to show up. With no additional credits, or measures to hold you accountable, the Rockefeller leadership programs were simply a personal test in whether you were able to show up and keep your word, regardless of your imposter syndrome, or the young collegiate dislike for responsibility.

So far, showing up has helped me become a member of my firm's first millennial board, a group of young professionals advising our Africa CEO on firm matters across the continent. It has pushed me to volunteer to develop and facilitate design thinking workshops for public health facilities as an analyst with no prior public health experience, and to accept my current role of driving an entire firm's culture transformation. I am also a board member of a Tanzanian NGO that has successfully spearheaded the fight to make child marriage illegal in Tanzania. None of this would be possible if I did not show up or keep my word. For me, this is where leadership begins, and I am grateful that Rocky taught me first.

My next narrative comes from Terra B-T, who is from the class of 2010, where she majored in Native American studies. At Dartmouth, in addition to the Rockefeller Center, Terra was involved with the Dartmouth Native American Student Organization. She is currently serving as a cabinet member of the Muscogee (Creek) Nation.

As a first-generation college student and one of the few in my family to ever leave the state of Oklahoma, Dartmouth offered new social, educational and experiential growth opportunities. While there, I decided to pursue history and relationships specifically, the intertwined relationship and history of Tribal Nations. As I grew into my major, I learned that I enjoyed studying the interplay of human connections, identifying levers that changed outcomes and weighing the benefits of one path versus another. I practiced relationship development as a student leader in the Native American Student Organization and with other interest-based student groups.

Interning at the Rockefeller Center provided both practical and theoretical professional development. My primary responsibility was to assist Center leadership in formulating, deploying, and evaluating the inaugural sessions of the Management and Leadership Development Program (MLDP). This opportunity also allowed me to participate in other Center academic and co-curricular programs. Looking back, I would equate the MLDP to a middle management professional development training series. It was focused on skill development that sophomores and juniors needed to move into on-campus leadership positions, internships, and post-Dartmouth jobs. Like much in the Dartmouth space, it was a crash course on the most important tools we would need to launch our lives from Hanover, New Hampshire.

There is one session that I still recall regularly in my life. Although the session details are fragmented, the training objectives remain clear. They included public speaking tips, storytelling, and the importance of a personal narrative. The speaker shared videos and transcripts of current public figures and historically famous orators but highlighted the personal life or connection that the speaker drew between themselves and listeners. The details used to illustrate a story calling on the senses of listeners, using narration that stirs raw emotions, asking the listener to step into the speaker's experience, and, finally, the delivery of an ask or call to action. She explained how these skills would be critical in job interviews, career searches and day-to-day interpersonal relations for Dartmouth undergraduates and newly minted alumni.

Since graduation, I have worked as a tribal advocate and policy analyst in Washington, D.C., a tribal nonprofit organization director, and, today, an appointed and confirmed cabinet member of the Muscogee (Creek) Nation. The session's focus on personal narrative and oration remains an undertone throughout my professional life and reminds me of specific traits to include in crafting a message that others will hear, feel, and act upon.

My final story is narrated by Mary S. from the class of 2017, where she majored in government with a minor in sociology. At Dartmouth, in addition to the Rockefeller Center, Mary competed in Dartmouth Track and Field as a heptathlete, served in leadership positions in her sorority, and held two part-time jobs. Despite being so busy, Mary still found the time to take part in several programs at the Rockefeller Center.

> At the time, I did not realize that the quality of training I was receiving at the Rockefeller Center was not only essential to my success in collegiate endeavors but also would become crucial to saving my "renewal" school in Harlem that was in danger of being shut down.

> After college, I joined Teach For America (TFA), where I was assigned to a public middle school as a math and science special education teacher. In all honesty, TFA's new teacher training was inadequate for the overwhelming obstacles I was about to face. Two days before the year began, I arrived at my new school to an empty classroom and a new teacher handbook. Although I had expected to simply lead kids in their learning, I quickly realized that I had to be a manager first. My inspiring words would be meaningless if there was no classroom in place—furniture needed to be set up, seat assignments created, classroom procedures designed, and, of course, lessons had to be made, as there was no curriculum. Later there would be leadership moments, like reinvigorating a crying girl in the stairwell who had been bullied about her hair and reminding her that the only reason others were bringing her down was because she stood so tall, full of kindness, hard work, and intelligence. MLDP taught us how these roles—manager and leader—are differentiated and when they are most applicable.

> As if managing my own classroom was not difficult enough, inspiring students with vastly different backgrounds was twice as hard. After assigning my first test, every student had failed. I announced this to the class, thinking they would be distraught by this news and determined to work harder, but one student said, "I don't care, we're dumb anyways." I was shocked by their response and realized I needed more than their failing grades and my encouraging attitude to motivate them to work harder. RGLP taught me about the intercultural continuum—how to understand and operate within other world paradigms, beyond just accepting different world views. With this in mind, I studied how my students had previously experienced school in order to convince them that school mattered and they were capable of achieving success.

Lastly, the lessons from RLF helped me navigate the adult relationships in the building. I had a fiercely driven principal and a divided school. Almost immediately, I used my understanding of the Myers Briggs test to read my principal. She was a hard T, or "thinker," meaning she put deliverables before emotions. Once I took notes on her management style, I was able to "manage-up," quickly earning her respect. Another example is when my principal made administrative decisions that seemed insulting to some teachers. I recalled RLF lessons on how organizational leaders have to balance multiple interests. As teachers, we sometimes forget all the entities principals work with—parents, students, teachers, superintendents, and local and state officials. However, I did see genuine pain in teachers who did not see eye to eye with her, so I listened, seeking to understand their frustrations. In attempts to build school community, I used dialogue instead of debate to try to build bridges and enable both sides to see each other's perspectives. By the end of my three years, colleagues from both sides would confide in me, and we were able to save the school together.

As I prepare to start my fourth year in teaching, I've realized how important "buy-in" is. If students do not feel like their teachers care about them, they will not truly learn. I see now that I first learned this at the Rockefeller Center. [My mentor at Rocky] was a leader who made you feel like you mattered and who took genuine interest in every student in her program. For this reason, I believe at the center of every successful leadership program is a leader who makes each participant feel empowered. Without a passionate and genuine leader, a leadership program is simply a blueprint.

I am sure you've also heard stories about how different programs have impacted your participants in unusual ways. An effective way to capture impact is to gather narratives from alumni regularly and systematically. In these three stories, we learned that participants have gained both hard and soft skills. They have learned the power of crafting an authentic message, speaking effectively, and balancing perspectives. All these skills point back to our original research and intention with these programs, which tied these mentioned skills to competencies that are needed to be successful. And, if as educators, we can help them carve the path to gaining wisdom, we have done the work to make their life fulfilling and meaningful. So, the past 15 years have created splendid opportunities for me to reflect on the stories of program effectiveness and impact.

This book started with my friend Katie's encouragement to turn "talk into action," and so I must return to this phrase at the conclusion of this chapter. Writing this chapter has made me think harder about what I can do to further strengthen our efforts at measuring effectiveness and impact. My preliminary thoughts are to include a systematic evaluation of the Eight Pillars, further collect quantitative data to measure effectiveness and impact, do studies and evaluations of individual components, and even invite colleagues to do an external evaluation of the programs. I also acknowledge to myself and to others that all these ideas will take time as well as human and financial resources. I recognize that actual implementation will depend on their feasibility. I hope this chapter inspires you to develop a system that works for you.

Although this book began with my desire to reflection upon and document the growth of the Rockefeller Center programs, what I realize now is that it is ever evolving in the minds and hearts of our future managers and leaders worldwide. Like a stone thrown into a pond, its ripple effects last far beyond our own individual programs.

Notes

1 Covey, 1989/2020.
2 Perruci & Hall, 2018.
3 Schuh & Upcraft, 2001.
4 Upcraft & Schuh, 1996.
5 Komives et al., 2011.
6 Chavan, 2009.
7 Komives et al., 2011.
8 Anderson et al., 2001.
9 Cruz, 2003.
10 Banner & Cannon, 1999.
11 Rabinowitz, 2020.
12 Council for the Advancement of Standards in Higher Education, n.d.; Keeling, 2004; Association of American Colleges & Universities, n.d.

References

Anderson, L., Krathwohl, D., Airasian, P., Cruikshank, K., Mayer, R., Pintrich, P., Raths, J., & Wittrock, M. (2001). *Taxonomy for learning, teaching, and assessing: A revision of Bloom's taxonomy of educational Objectives, abridged edition* (1ˢᵗ ed.). Addison-Wesley Longman.

Association of American Colleges & Universities. (n.d.). *Liberal Education and America's Promise (LEAP)*. Retrieved March 16, 2021, from https://www.aacu.org/leap

Banner, H. C., & Cannon, J. M. (1999). *The elements of learning.* Yale University Press.

Banta, T. W., Palomba, C. A., & Kinzie, J. (2014). *Assessment essentials: Planning, implementing, and improving assessment in higher education.* Jossey-Bass.

Baker, G. R., Jankowski N. A., Provezis, S., & Kinzie, J. (2012). *Using assessment results: Promising practices of institutions that do it well* [White paper]. National Institute for Learning Outcomes Assessment.

Bloom, B.S. (1956). *Taxonomy of educational objectives, Handbook I: The cognitive domain.* David McKay Co.

Chavan, M. (2009). The balanced scorecard: A new challenge. *Journal of Management Development, 28*(5), 393-406.

Council for the Advancement of Standards in Higher Education. (n.d.). *CAS Standards.* Retrieved March 15, 2021, from https://www.cas.edu/standards

Covey, S. R. (2020). *The 7 habits of highly effective people* (30ᵗʰ anniversary ed.). Simon & Schuster. (Original work published 1989)

Cruz, E. (2003). Bloom's revised taxonomy. In B. Hoffman (Ed.), *Encyclopedia of educational technology.* http://www.studentachievement.org/wp-content/uploads/Bloom_s-Revised-Taxomony.doc

Fulcher, K. H., Good, M. R., Coleman, C. M., & Smith, K. L. (2014, December). *A simple model for learning improvement: Weigh pig, feed pig, weigh pig.* (Occasional Paper No. 23). University of Illinois and Indiana University, National Institute for Learning Outcomes Assessment. https://files.eric.ed.gov/fulltext/ED555526.pdf

Jankowski N., & Slotnick R. (2015). The five essential roles of assessment practitioners. *Journal of Assessment of Assessment and Institutional Effectiveness, 5*(1), 78–100.

Keeling, R. P. (Ed.). (2004). *Learning reconsidered: A campus-wide focus on the student experience*. National Association of Student Personnel Administrators. https://www.naspa.org/images/uploads/main/Learning_Reconsidered_Report.pdf

Komives, S. R., Dugan, J. P., Owen, J. E., Slack, C., & Wagner, W. (2011). *The handbook for student leadership development*. John Wiley & Sons.

Perruci, G., & Hall, S. W. (2018). *Teaching leadership: Bridging theory and practice*. Edward Elgar Publishing.

Rabinowitz, P. (2020). *Maintaining quality performance: Obtaining and using feedback from participants. Community toolbox*. Center for Community Health and Development at the University of Kansas. https://ctb.ku.edu/en/table-of-contents/maintain/maintain-quality-performance/feedback-from-clients/main

Seemiller, C. (2013). *The student leadership competencies guidebook: Designing intentional leadership learning and development*. Jossey-Bass.

Schuh, J. H., Upcraft, M. L., & Associates (2001). *Assessment practice in student affairs: An applications manual*. Jossey-Bass.

Upcraft, M. L., & Schuh, J. H. (1996). *Assessment in student affairs: A guide for practitioners*. Jossey-Bass.

10 | Adopt, Adapt, Adjust: Your Turn!

I have learned that I still have a lot to learn.

—Maya Angelou

I was reminded by a thoughtful friend that, even with the knowledge in this book, it could be quite overwhelming to start or even revise a leadership program. Please recall that this book is based on over 15 years of experimentation, reflection, and action. I started with one program, revised it, and added small things to make it better and stronger. I chose to work with people who were committed to the idea of developing leadership programs and they gave me the support and courage I needed to progress with the development of the programs. Knowledge and practice grew, and, over time, we had a continuum of programs. They are ever evolving, and our team is continuously and enthusiastically grappling with them to make them better. Hopefully, participants in our programs embrace the idea of being lifelong learners, starting from the programs in which they participate and long after they graduate. To continually adopt, adapt, and adjust to new challenges and professional environments have become necessary today.

So, please use this book as a beginning to or a continuation of your process to develop your ideas and your programs. But what should you do if you don't have the resources that I was lucky enough to have to build these programs? Maybe start by creating a rationale for having such a program or programs. Start however and wherever you can with a small group of committed people who support your ideas and believe in them. Start with faith and determination to do something! Think about senior leaders in your organization, your colleagues, and peers who will support you in your endeavor. Start small and focus on the key concepts you want to cover and then gradually scale up your programming. Start with a standalone program or select sessions that meet the needs of your participants. Your enthusiasm and passion might lead to the institutional commitment that you richly deserve!

How might you scale up these programs? At the end of each overview of programs in this book, I have shared some ideas about how you might be able to do this. Please consider that online learning is a cost-effective way to share information to large audiences. You could also combine online learning with in-person sessions designed explicitly for deep reflection, networking, and community building. Although there can be issues of unequal access regarding the use of technology for teaching and learning, something is better than nothing.

We need leadership anywhere and everywhere, and you might just be the person to create the enthusiasm in others to take complex problems, wrestle with them, and work together to develop a common vision that leads to a vibrant program. Whether you are in government, civil society, or the corporate sector, we require leadership and change. Leadership begins with individuals acting together for a common cause. You don't need degrees in leadership; anyone can become a leader.

Through your examination of the past few chapters, I hope you agree with me that management and leadership can be learned and taught. Consider the order of the sessions within a program and how you will build knowledge—starting from simple concepts and ending with more complex ideas. Build in periodic synthesis of key concepts throughout the program and end strong with facilitating participants to reflect on their learning and plan steps they would like to take to grow personally and professionally as leaders.

I hope that this book has inspired you to find your own vision of how you might adopt, adapt, and adjust the management and leadership programs described in this book—regardless of your field of endeavor. The past chapters have covered program implementation considerations, program descriptions, and lessons from online learning, as well as ideas for assessing and evaluating leadership programs. Throughout the book, we have included reflections from speakers, program officers, current participants, and alumni to show you how enthusiastic program participants can be and how they continue to apply the principles and strategies they have learned.

> **Student Assistant Reflection**
>
> *My participation in various leadership programs has rarely allowed me to take a peek at their backbone. Rather than witnessing the final versions of the programs, I was now able to explore them at the stage of theoretical grounding which deepened my understanding of the value and purpose of teaching leadership.*
>
> **Kristabel K., class of 2024**

Even when coming up with the ideas to design or develop a leadership program, over time, I have fully embraced the idea of working with colleagues to develop the programs further. The notion of a program being "my program" has rightfully changed ownership to "our program." This really means that I have had to check my ego at the door and share with others the joy that comes from collectively creating a program. I now have come to believe that not only should the programs transform audiences for whom they are intended, but they should also be a transformative process for the program implementors, who, given the space to harness talent and creativity, make it a meaningful experience for both themselves and others.

This book is yet another example of how I have changed my philosophy of leadership and my approach toward developing programs. I began the project with a group of student research assistants. What I did not realize was that, unconsciously, I was thinking about not only the end project (the book in this case) but also the value to the student research assistants of being involved in the project. In a short period of time, an intellectually supportive environment had been created by ALL of us, in which everyone in the book project felt free to listen carefully, suggest new ideas or alternative approaches, rely on each other, and discuss, not argue. The result of this process has been this book in which all of us share collective pride. It is a labor of love and I hope you notice how student program assistant reflections in this chapter demonstrate their self-awareness and appreciation for working as a team toward a shared goal—which, in this case, is what you are reading now.

Leadership is a collective venture: There are times you need to lead and other times you need to follow. But a few things show up as a result of a good process: Anyone involved in the process is inspired and becomes more self-aware, understands how to work as a team member, and shares collective ownership and pride in a project, program, or product.

It's your turn now! I have developed this final chapter with the intent of creating space for you to think about your own personal and professional growth as a manager and a leader. The handouts at the end of this chapter are developed for you. They cover some key

> ### Student Assistant Reflection
>
> *By knowing our strengths and inclinations, our team was able to find strength in diversity, delegate roles effectively, and take risks that paid off. I found myself taking more creative liberties, relying more on my fellow student editors, and having greater appreciation for the work we did, together or apart.*
>
> **Elizabeth P., class of 2021**

concepts, explained previously, that are very important to me and that have transformed me as a person and professional interested in practicing good leadership. I use the handouts myself and continually rate myself. I record my thoughts as I consider each question. As a result of this exercise, I now have a list of things I have done well, things I need to think about, and a list of things to do.

Using the format for the handouts, you can create your own for other topics and build a systematic way to reflect and assess your progress. You might be wondering why I used an even-numbered Likert scale rather than the usual odd-numbered scales. I like to use even-numbered scales so that I can never be neutral on any issue I am evaluating.

Let's begin your process of reflection on the ideas contained in this book.

Eight Pillars of Program Design. As you may recall, Chapter 2 covers the Eight Pillars of Program Design. These pillars (Intentionality, Theoretical Grounding, Rigor, Structure, Reflection, Community, Assessment and Evaluation, and Participant Learning and

> ### Student Assistant Reflection
>
> *Both the content of this book and the process of creating it have taught me a tremendous amount about my own personal leadership style and how to work best as a team. This experience has not only helped me enhance my research and technical skills, but it has also allowed me to become a stronger leader, a clearer communicator, a more confident team member, and an experienced problem solver.*
>
> **Madeleine B., class of 2022**

Empowerment.) are at the heart of our programs at the Rockefeller Center and allow us to turn our experiences and creativity into personal and professional growth as leaders. If you implement these principles and reflect on them as you progress, you will discover what you are doing well and where there is room for growth in your own program development, design, and delivery. Handout 10.1 at the end of this chapter will help you document your reflections about them so far and give you space to document thoughts to make new or existing programs stronger.

Self-Awareness. Personal and professional awareness of strengths and weaknesses is critical. This awareness allows us to play to our strengths and develop plans to address our weaknesses. At the very least, we can surround ourselves with team members who have strengths where we have weaknesses. Becoming self-aware provides us with the opportunity to grow and learn. In this process, we can decide when to lead, when to manage, and when to follow others because they have the required talents to not only get a job done, but a job done well.

How might we identify our strengths and weaknesses? Consider using assessment tools (e.g., MBTI or Strengths Test) developed in your own country or elsewhere. Many people are skeptical about such tests because they are not sure about their validity and reliability. They often believe they are reductionist and lead to or reinforce stereotypes. Personally, I think they are useful because, whether I agree or disagree with the results, I find myself reflecting more deeply and coming to a realization of what I know or don't know about myself. This has set me on the path of continuous learning, which is so important in our rapidly changing times.

Asking others to share their perceptions of your strengths and weaknesses through a 360-evaluation is a practice that is gaining popularity. This tool uses results from self-evaluation and feedback from co-workers, colleagues, and subordinates on topics such as technical skills, interpersonal communication skills, and ability to lead or manage a team or an organization. I have found that this tool is useful for individuals open to feedback but often upsetting for others not good at receiving feedback. For this reason, it works best in a work environment built on trust, or an environment that is rebuilding itself based on trust. Handout 10.2 at the end of this chapter has questions that you could use to learn more about yourself and how you relate to your team.

Team Dynamics and Working Together. Let's dive deeper into team dynamics and some factors that lead to effective teamwork. When everything is going according to plan, we are able to identify the strengths and weaknesses of our team members and determine whether we are meeting the organization's mission. Even if we do not explicitly talk about individual working styles within our team, we know from experience that each person has a unique style that contributes to or affects the ability of a team to work together. Therefore, leadership and management cannot follow the idea "of one size fits all."[1]

Our role as managers, leaders, or followers is visible to others through our actions, and we strive to always maintain the morale of the team. It is our responsibility to support everyone, and we need to pay particular attention to those who have personal constraints and yet work very hard to meet their job responsibilities. This requires flexibility, empathy, and compassion. We are inspired to think about tools that will help us to see how tasks are being accomplished and how we, as a team, work together to meet our stated goals.

The true soul of a team, however, becomes visible in times of emergency. We are tested in our ability to work with uncertainty and ambiguity, and circumstances that require us to change our plans at a moment's notice. The demonstration of how we work together and support each other suddenly becomes much clearer. In such times, we get to observe the strengths and weaknesses of our team and its members in a new light. Also, our role in a leadership capacity (formal or informal) becomes even more visible to others.

Here is an example about how this worked for the Center's co-curricular team recently. Before COVID-19, we took pride in our work as a team and our ability to work together. The pandemic brought chaos and uncertainty in every program approach we had worked hard to establish for our in-person programs, and our team was forced to begin working remotely without prior notice. For many people across the world, I am sure this is a shared experience.

> **Student Assistant Reflection**
>
> *In addition to sitting in on countless sessions, as participants of these programs do, I had the privilege of engaging in the sort of teamwork, mentorship, and self-reflection that underpin every strong leadership program. Working so closely to get a project done on a tight timeline while coasts apart taught me a lot about clear communication and personal accountability.*
>
> **Caitlin D., class of 2022**

We adapted quickly and these adaptations maintained the integrity of the programs' rigor and organization. We helped each other through strengthening our organizational and technological skills. We worked with speakers to adapt their sessions for the new reality we were facing. We changed our meeting times to accommodate time zone differences. We talked about how we were feeling and used humor to get us through the sudden change in our lives. The term flew by and, before we knew it, programs had taken place on time, and we were thinking about how we might tweak our programs and what we needed to do better for the next iteration.

Survey results indicated that the programs exceeded the expectations of the participants who had initially expected to learn less from online learning. We are happy to see how the enrollments in the new cycle of program offerings have returned to pre-online enrollment numbers, suggesting that online programming is seen to be as valuable as in-person offerings. Today, our team continues to iterate in the spirit of continuous quality improvement, and we direct our efforts particularly toward building community. While there are many reasons for why we were able to react so quickly, I will share a few: Our foundation of previous experiences had created an environment open to innovation and learning; we trusted and relied on each other; and each person on the team knew that they could experiment without fear of reprisal. Finally, formal or informal leadership positions did not matter; what mattered most was getting the job done effectively and efficiently.

Staying in touch in different ways and for different reasons helps to create team cohesion. Given that we were adjusting to a remote work environment, we created an online tool that team members used to complete their weekly priorities. This online tool helped team members not only to keep track of priorities but also to understand what their priorities were in the first place, and this significantly reduced stress! For example, I had a project that I could not get to for four weeks in a row. That made me stop, pause, and ask myself, "Is this truly a priority or can I plan to do

> ### Student Assistant Reflection
>
> *When you are in a project group full of peers you trust, you trust not just them, but the quality of their work, their intelligence, and their decisions. That does not come immediately; building a dynamic where we each knew our strengths and pursued our sub-projects took time as we got to know each other.*
>
> **Dylan G., class of 2020**

this project later on in the year?" This moment of reflection enabled me to delay this project and removed the pressure I imposed on myself to complete it. Keeping this list on Google Sheets gave me an understanding about how the team was performing as a whole and who needed additional support in this period of transition. This "weekly priorities" tool worked better for some than others, but I have continued to encourage the team to use the tool, all the time realizing that sometimes, in formal leadership positions, we make decisions that may not be popular, but these are decisions we make for the larger purpose.

This experience taught me that, as managers, we should ask our team members to review their work and prioritize their tasks often and especially in times of emergency. Leadership as a process to support team and organizational growth takes on a new meaning because it is dynamic and helps us to address a changing environment by being more flexible. Another important consideration when we face uncertain times or environments is for us to make time to take care of ourselves and the others who rely on us. This requires emotional intelligence, flexibility, empathy, and compassion—for ourselves and for others.

We have continued to have weekly meetings and find that they work just as well online. In uncertain times, sticking to routine introduces a sense of normalcy in everyone's lives. Lastly, our team uses humor very effectively! This really lightens people's hearts and increases a sense of community and creates a strong network of support. Establishing a strong community of educators who deliver programming also inspires participants to create community and cohesion. Handout 10.3 at the end of the chapter covers a few questions for you to reflect on for building and supporting your team in all types of work conditions.

Organizational Development. Leadership development, education, and training are supported by strong organizational practices. In the words of Warren Bennis (2008), "leadership is the capacity to translate vision into reality."[2] As leaders and managers, we need to develop a vision—and a mission, strategies, and goals for reaching our vision. As we embark on this journey, we must model behaviors that we expect from our own employees and participants. All these concepts together must address the needs of the stakeholders. Finally, we need to be clear about our organizational culture, practice our values, and demonstrate our beliefs through our actions.

Strong and transparent administrative, program, management, and financial systems help us implement change efficiently, and we need to pay particular attention to succession planning in these systems and our programs. Further, as soon as we identify weaknesses or gaps, we should address them. I share two examples of gaps I came across as a result of writing this book. We have always been committed to gathering qualitative and quantitative information about the leadership programs described in this book. However, when I started looking at this information about our programs, I realized that as a result of staff turnover, while the information was available, it simply was not easily accessible because each person had used their own filing system to save this information. Recognizing this inconsistency, our program officers have worked together to standardize our filing systems related to the five programs.

We also learned the importance of adopting commonly used databases in an organization. So many new technologies and platforms are available today that it is a temptation to try them. We adopted a new and exciting database that was not used or supported by our institution. All went well until the database company went out of business. While we did have access to the data we had gathered, selecting a new database system meant that we needed to put a tremendous amount of effort into reorganizing the data. The positive aspect, however, is that the new database system will allow us to meet our current needs and will help us to gather information in a more efficient and timely manner. It is also supported by the institution, should we run into problems.

> **Student Assistant Reflection**
>
> *In sharing the Rockefeller Center's story through tables, charts, and graphs, I have gained an appreciation for the importance of data in complementing anecdotal narratives and a comfort level with large (and sometimes inconsistent) datasets. Our team's constant feedback and support gave me the permission to test new analyses and the confidence to propose different ways of visualizing data.*
>
> **Nathan P., class of 2022**

Building strong monitoring and evaluation systems cannot be emphasized enough. They enable us to define and measure the success and impact of our programs and open us up to new possibilities. Look for industry standards that have been developed for this purpose and use these to inform your systems. For example, the *ILA Guiding Questions, ILA Guiding Principles for Leadership Programs,* the *CAS Standards, Learning Reconsidered,* and the *ILEC Collaborative Priorities & Critical Considerations for Leadership Education* are a few resources we can use to develop content and measure impact and effectiveness of academic curricular and co-curricular leadership programs.[3]

I have often polled my teams about their vision of an ideal work culture and environment. Most people tell me that they thrive in a peaceful, effective, and efficient workplace and one that is filled with purpose and meaning. Our team members have written up our team values in a "Staff Values and Professional Etiquette" document and visit them when a new team member joins or at least once a year. Team etiquette is important to us and when we review the document periodically, we discuss what is going well and what we need to address. The greatest lesson I have learned from this exercise is that our team owns the document and models behaviors. This is noticed by our participants and our student assistants, who in turn, begin modeling the same behaviors.

Words matter and transparent communication systems lead to a healthy work environment. Ineffective communication systems, in contrast, create a dysfunctional workplace environment. Lack of transparency in communication systems is exacerbated by gossip in the workplace and this is why I have zero tolerance for it! If you are confronted with such a situation, it is useful to share your understanding of why gossip in a workplace is not acceptable and the negative impact it has on the team's culture, morale, trust in each other, productivity, and efficiency. Through coaching and being clear with your expectations, a discussion with employees should lead to a common understanding of the negative impact gossip has on teamwork and results. Through this shared understanding, we can begin to create practices that will reinforce the desired workplace culture. Regularly discussing why you have a zero tolerance for gossip is a reminder for managers and leaders as well as other team members about their own role in maintaining harmony and peace in the workplace

Conflicts between employees destroy the harmony of a workplace and, as managers and leaders we must deal with them as soon as we become aware of their existence. Being invested in a chain of action for conflict resolution helps employees to take clear next steps toward addressing and settling their conflicts. I suggest that we take a systems approach to communication and conflict in the workplace. Here is how it has worked for me in one instance: An employee who had a conflict with another employee was requested to have an open and honest conversation with the concerned individual. When the situation was unresolved, the employee discussed the matter with a mentor or a coach, who maintained confidentiality and helped the person come up with a plan to resolve the conflict. It continued to be a problem and soon became an issue that affected team morale. At that point, I had a difficult conversation with both employees, and we were fortunate to resolve the conflict.

Paying close attention to the personal and professional development of team members is invaluable for individuals, teams, and organizations. Not only does it create energy and enthusiasm, but it also keeps the organization keenly aware of the near and long-term changes on the horizon. For example, every person on our team makes an intentional effort to develop their personal and professional development plan. Complementing this is team learning about new ideas through reading books together and discussing them once a month. Another example is enrolling for a short course together and studying together. Perhaps you

> **Student Assistant Reflection**
>
> *I quickly realized that aside from my role as a designer, I had to be a flexible leader, an active listener, and an open collaborator. As a designer, I was challenged to create simple designs that communicated intricate concepts, and it enabled me to broaden my perspective and become a malleable creator.*
>
> **Gia K., class of 2022**

arc thinking that all this requires financial resources. But lack of financial resources should not be a deterrent. "Begin with the end in mind" as Covey says and develop the professional development objectives first.[4] Consider all the free courses and webinars that are available now and develop your own curriculum.

Many colleagues I have spoken to often tell me that there is not enough time in a day to pay attention to personal development or even allocate time for it. My experience has been that when you create space for personal development, it creates spaces for a different kind of energy and motivation to get the job done. For instance, staff who have articulated their personal and development needs have not only kept up with the responsibilities and performed well, but they also have carved out the time to keep up with their own professional development. A key for managers and leaders to supporting personal and professional development within an organization is to create a transparent system of accountability in which achievement of work objectives, staff development, and growth go hand in hand. Professional development plans should be co-created, taking into consideration individual employee and organizational aspirations. At times there may not appear to be a direct link between the employee's and the organization's professional development plans. In such cases, consider the employee's intellectual development and how their learning still improves skills that are transferable if they move on to other responsibilities or challenges.

Mentoring and coaching are gaining attention in leadership development, training and education. These two practices are essential for personal and professional growth and provide employees and participants with a framework that supports critical analysis of problems and, at the same time, improves communication skills. For example, training our minds to ask "open and honest questions" without judgment or practice active listening, which requires us to listen to understand and not to refute.[5]

Recognizing contributions of team members is critical to developing a vibrant work environment. While financial compensation is important, it is not the only thing that motivates employees within an organization to do their best work. Recognition for efforts, big or small, go a long way in inspiring colleagues to do their best. Our team, for instance, has created a space in our weekly meetings to thank and recognize colleagues. In the beginning, it seemed forced and unnatural, but now it is simply part of our team's culture to acknowledge one another for a job well done. For instance, when I think of *Leadership Blueprints*, it is an example of collaborative work that has been done tirelessly behind the scenes by student research assistants. Based on their academic schedules, some of them worked with me through the duration of this project while others joined at various times. I must confess that until I had asked them to reflect on their experiences, I did not realize how much they valued working on this book together. In their reflections, they are demonstrating how they view teamwork, self-awareness, and the achievement of common goals. Periodic reflections are yet another powerful tool in our toolkit as managers and leaders to glean practical wisdom and carry momentum from growth. Let's continuously recognize and appreciate the small and big contributions that move us toward our personal and collective aspirations. Handout 10.4 lists some of the questions that I use to think about our leadership programs and how they are supported through our organizational efforts.

You may have other questions that are not listed here, and I am delighted that you are thinking of them. Please take a moment to list them and, if you have time, please contact me at Teachingleadershipcooperative.com. I would love to hear from you: What do you think about *Leadership Blueprints*? What do you plan to do with the information you have learned? How do you plan to use it or how have you used it? How has it helped you to grow personally or professionally? How has it changed your ideas for leadership programming?

In *Leadership Blueprints*, I am simply giving space to thoughts and ideas that have evolved over time with the commitment and the hard work of my colleagues, session facilitators, and thought leaders in the fields of management and leadership. I cannot help but smile when I think about all the students who have enriched my life with their energy, enthusiasm, and genuine love.

I began with the thought that a good idea becomes a great idea with the input of many, and so I end with it. If you have an idea that will help to make the world better, please share it freely, joyfully, and with reckless abandon. I wish you all the best!

Notes

1. Politis, 2016, and Silverstein & West Duffy, 2016.
2. Bennis, 2008.
3. International Leadership Association, 2009; Council for the Advancement of Standards in Higher Education, n.d.; Keeling, 2004; Inter-association Leadership Education Collaborative, 2018.
4. Covey, 1989/2020.
5. Palmer, 2007.

References

Bennis, Warren G. (2008) Leadership is the capacity to translate vision into reality. *Journal of Property Management, 73*(5), 13.

Council for the Advancement of Standards in Higher Education. (n.d.). *CAS standards.* Retrieved March 15, 2021, from https://www.cas.edu/standards

Covey, S. R. (2020). *The 7 habits of highly effective people* (30th anniversary ed.). Simon & Schuster. (Original work published 1989)

Dugan, J. P., Turman, N. T., & Barnes, A. C. (2017). *Leadership theory: Facilitator's guide for cultivating critical perspectives* (1st ed.). Jossey-Bass.

George, B., McLean, A., & Craig, N. (2008). *Finding your true north: A personal guide* (1st ed.). Jossey-Bass.

Inter-association Leadership Education Collaborative. (2018). *Collaborative priorities & critical considerations for leadership education.* (2nd ed.). https://www.stu.edu/wp-content/uploads/sites/13/2020/09/ILEC-2018-draft3.pdf

International Leadership Association. (2009). *Guiding questions: Guidelines for leadership education programs* (pp. 216–227). International Leadership Association. http://www.ila-net.org/communities/LC/GuidingQuestionsFinal.pdf

Keeling, R. P. (Ed.). (2004). *Learning reconsidered: A campus-wide focus on the student experience.* National Association of Student Personnel Administrators. https://www.naspa.org/images/uploads/main/Learning_Reconsidered_Report.pdf

Kegan, R., & Lahey, L. L. (2009). *Immunity to change: How to overcome it and unlock potential in yourself and your organization.* Harvard Business Press.

Komives, S. R., Dugan, J. P., Owen, J. E., Slack, C., & Wagner, W. (2011). *The handbook for student leadership development.* John Wiley & Sons.

Kouzes J.M. & Posner, B.Z. (1993). *Credibility: How leaders gain and lose it, why people demand it.* Jossey-Bass.

Northouse, P. G. (2017). *Introduction to leadership: Concepts and practice* (4th ed.). SAGE Publications, Inc.

Parker J. Palmer (2004). *A Hidden Wholeness: The Journey Toward an Undivided Life.* Jossey-Bass

Palmer, P. J. (2007). *The courage to teach: Exploring the inner landscape of a teacher's life* (10th anniversary ed.). Jossey-Bass.

Perruci, G. & Hall, S. W. (2018) *Teaching leadership: Bridging theory and practice*. Edward Elgar Publishing.

Politis, D. (2016, March 29). This is how you revolutionize the way your team works together... and all it takes is 15 minutes. *LinkedIn*. https://www.linkedin.com/pulse/how-you-revolutionize-way-your-team-works-together-all-david-politis/

Seemiller, C. (2013). *The student leadership competencies guidebook: Designing intentional leadership learning and development*. John Wiley & Sons.

Silverstein, A., & West Duffy, W. (2019, February 26). Turns out emotions do belong in the workplace—Here's why. *IDEO*. https://www.ideo.com/blog/turns-out-emotions-do-belong-in-the-workplace-heres-why

Reflecting on the Eight Pillars of Program Design

Rate yourself on the questions below on a scale of 1 to 6 (1 being poor and 6 being excellent). Please add questions you feel are important and are not listed in this handout.

Question	Rating	Comments and Next Steps
1. Am I intentional about considering learners' background, age, diversity, and maturity when I start designing programs?		
2. Does the learning space I create foster an intellectually supportive environment? Do I have a strong understanding of the attitudes, beliefs, and values of my participants?		
3. Are my program designs based on research and theories? Are there other theories that can inform my research?		
4. How well am I or my speakers prepared to deliver and co-create content with participants?		
5. How well-organized are the logistics of my program?		
6. Have I created dedicated spaces for participant reflection?		
7. Are my programs creating a sense of community?		
8. Do I have a systematic assessment and evaluation system?		
9. Are participants satisfied with and empowered by the program?		
10. Are participants gaining knowledge about leadership theories, and developing and practicing skills and competencies as a result of participating in my program?		
11. How engaged are the participants in my program? Do participants recommend the program to their friends?		
12. Do I apply my emotional intelligence in the hard work of developing a program design?		
Your Questions:		

Self-Awareness & Understanding Your Team

Rate yourself on the questions below on a scale of 1 to 6 (1 being poor and 6 being excellent). Please add questions you feel are important and are not listed in this handout.

Question	Rating	Comments and Next Steps
1. What are my values? How congruent are they with my behaviors?		
2. What are my strengths? How do I use them? What else can I do to use my strengths?		
3. What are my weaknesses? How might I address them? What can I do differently to address them? How can I do things differently to address them?		
4. What is my working style? What makes me happy and what frustrates me?		
5. Do I believe in self-care? Why is it important? How well do I practice self-care? What stops me from taking care of myself? How do I define self-care?		
6. What are my identities and biases? How do they affect the way in which I work with others?		
7. How skilled am I at participating in difficult conversations? Do I actively listen even when I disagree? Why is this important for management and leadership?		
8. Do I have a fixed mindset or a growth mindset? Why is it important for me to have a growth mindset? What do I need to do to develop the habits of a lifelong learner?		
9. What are my immediate goals? What are my long-term goals? How do I allocate and manage my time toward achieving these goals?		
10. What are the working styles of my team? How do we resolve conflict?		
Your Questions:		

Team Dynamics and Work

Rate yourself on the questions below on a scale of 1 to 6 (1 being poor and 6 being excellent). Add questions you feel are important and are not listed in this handout.

Question	Rating	Comments and Next Steps
1. Do I demonstrate empathy, flexibility, and compassion toward my team members as well as myself?		
2. Am I fair and equitable in my approach toward my team members so that I am not creating a feeling that some are inside and others outside the circle?		
3. Are team norms and professional etiquette as a team revisited periodically? Do I know about the workstyles of my team members?		
4. What do I feel about gossip in the workplace and its impact on workplace culture, productivity, efficiency, and morale?		
5. Have I created space for team members to reflect on their priorities, strengths, and weaknesses? What they are doing well and where do they need to improve?		
6. Is there a system in place of regular check-ins with team members?		
7. Do I contribute to creating a sense of community? What else do I need to do to create a sense of community?		
8. Am I in my circle of influence and not in my circle of concern?		
9. Do I demonstrate empathy, flexibility, and compassion toward my team members as well as myself?		
Your Questions:		

Organizational Development

Rate yourself on the questions below on a scale of 1 to 6 (1 being poor and 6 being excellent). Please add questions you feel are important and are not listed in this handout.

	Question	Rating	Comments and Next Steps
1.	Does our organization consider the local, national, and global contexts within which our programs operate?		
2.	Do we have a clearly articulated vision, mission, goals, and strategies?		
3.	Are my programs aligned with my organization's and institution's mission?		
4.	Do we have strategies in place that embrace the idea of continuous quality improvement and a growth mindset that allows us to improve our productivity, efficiency, and impact?		
5.	Are our programs informed by relevant standards established for our industry?		
6.	Does our organizational culture demonstrate our organizational values?		
7.	Are we intentional in our efforts to address diversity, equity, and inclusion in our programs? Do we have systems in place to assess and test new and innovative approaches?		
8.	Do we have systems in place that enable us to identify problems and to plan, implement, monitor, and evaluate our programs, including how they measure success and address the organization's mission?		
9.	Have I created a system to document changes to align with changing environments we face?		
10.	Do I have systems that allow me to document successes and take action on challenges in issues related to program, administration, management, and finance?		

Question	Rating	Comments and Next Steps
11. Are the skills and talents of members of my team aligned well with their responsibilities? Does the organizational chart demonstrate that the people with right talents for the job are placed correctly within the organization?		
12. Do our team members feel respected and valued? Have we created psychological safety for employees that allows them to innovate freely and with an intent to support continuous quality improvement?		
13. Are employees and program participants mentored and coached?		
14. Are colleagues in the organization encouraged to develop a personal and professional growth plan?		

Your Questions:

Index

About the Author

Deputy Director, Nelson A. Rockefeller Center for Public Policy and the Social Sciences, Dartmouth College, USA

Sadhana Warty Hall's commitment as both a teacher and practitioner of leadership reflects a deep dedication to justice and empowerment both locally and globally. She has applied her experience in management and strategic thinking to community development in institutions ranging from New Hampshire and Vermont to Tuvalu, Armenia, and Bhutan. As the current Deputy Director of the Rockefeller Center for Public Policy at Dartmouth College, Hall manages operations and oversees the curricula of high-impact leadership and mentoring programs. In recognition of her work, Sadhana has received Dartmouth College's Sheila Culbert Distinguished Employee Service Award, the Australia Government's Endeavor Executive Leadership Award to adapt and implement leadership curricula for Australian Indigenous communities, and acceptance into the Fulbright Specialist Program. Over the past few years, over 25 students in the Center's leadership programs, who have also participated in other organizations throughout Dartmouth, have gone on to receive awards including the Rhodes, Truman, Fulbright, Knight Hennessey, Schwarzman, and Pickering scholarships. She is the co-author of *Teaching Leadership: Bridging Theory and Practice*. Hall earned an M.A. in history from the University of Rajasthan, India. She also completed an M.P.H. in public health from the University of North Carolina in the United States.